The Complete
Baseball Handbook

The Complete Baseball Handbook

Strategies and Techniques for Winning

SECOND EDITION

WALTER ALSTON

and Don Weiskopf

Boston London Sydney Toronto

Contents

Chapter 13   TEAM DEFENSE   359

Chapter 14   ORGANIZATION   387

Chapter 15   TRAINING AND PRACTICE PROGRAM   415

Chapter 16   CONDITIONING   487

Foreword

If in the annals of baseball history Casey Stengel will be reverently referred to as the "Ole Professor," then surely Walt Alston must be enshrined as the "Quiet Teacher"—with perhaps a degree as Doctor of Pedagogy (teacher of teachers).

The long list of those men who are so successfully coaching and managing in the major leagues is living proof of the skills learned in the schooling under the "Walt Alston's Dodger way to play baseball."

Walt Alston was a superb technician and was always able to reduce the most complicated techniques and strategies into the simplest terms, and always in a "quiet way." So subtle was his approach that the superstars as well as the rookies were eager to add to their skills—both physical and mental.

In this entire manuscript there will not be a paragraph, nor a sentence, that will not in a "quiet way" convince the reader-coach that the Alston way is truly *the* way to play the game.

I have been an intimate observer over many years of the Walt Alston superbly trained teams, and I join those who believe that he truly is one of the great managers of all time. I consider it a great honor to have the privilege of participating in the foreword of this great book, and I heartily recommend it to those high school and college coaches who enjoy teaching the great game of baseball.

Rod Dedeaux
Head Baseball Coach
University of Southern California

Preface

The second edition of *The Complete Baseball Handbook* represents a major revision of the 1972 publication which enjoyed sixteen printings. While the many positive reviews and columns have been most gratifying, perhaps the greatest source of satisfaction has been the book's widespread use as a guidebook on baseball techniques and strategies. It has been translated into several foreign languages. Coaches and managers on all levels of play have told us how valuable it has been to player development and team success.

When we started preliminary planning on the development of the new manuscript, our major focus was the training and development of a baseball team. How could we improve upon the first edition and meet more effectively the needs of coaches and their teams? We knew we had to update the instruction with new pictures and faces, ideas, and concepts relative to the fundamental skills and techniques. The chapters on team offense and team defense have been updated with the strategies and philosophies of many current managers, including Tommy Lasorda, Whitey Herzog, Ralph Houk, Sparky Anderson, Steve Boros, Jim Frey, and Dick Williams. As for the conditioning of players, we were aware that physical strength and flexibility represent one of the greatest improvements in baseball. Therefore, we developed a strong chapter on conditioning, including the Dodgers' very successful stretching and flexibility routines, preventative arm and shoulder exercises, and strength building and running programs. Then, what was needed to make the *Handbook* a more valuable instructional manual? *A more indepth approach to training and practice schedules, drills, and methodology.* Organized practice is the key to a progressive training program, so we developed a brand new chapter—Training and Practice Program. In it, we have described in detail the offseason, preseason, and during season training programs, including unprecedented coverage on indoor practice and facilities. The highlight of Chapter 15, however, has to be the "blue chip" assortment of training drills developed by many of America's most successful collegiate coaches. Their "favorite" drills, effectively presented with diagrams and procedures, are easy to read and understand.

Acknowledgments should go to the many major league players, past and present, for their excellent demonstrations of the basic techniques of baseball and their candid commentary on how they play their positions. Instruction in this new edition features pictures and how-to tips from numerous players, including Mike Schmidt, Jack Clark, Rod Carew, George Brett, Jim Rice, Pete Rose, Henry Aaron, Steve Garvey, Ron Cey, Bill Buckner, Ted Williams, Fred Lynn, Mark Belanger, Steve Sax, Maury Wills, Lou Brock, Billy Grabarkewitz, Willie Davis, Tim Raines, Rickey Henderson, Fernando Valenzuela, Jerry Reuss, Burt Hooton, Doyle Alexander, Greg Minton,

Mike Boddicker, Dave Stieb, Joe Sambito, Bob Knepper, Vida Blue, Scott Sanderson, Steve Carlton, Tom Seaver, Gary Carter, Jeff Torborg, Johnny Bench, Tom Haller, Butch Wynegar, Mike Scioscia, Bob Brenly, Wes Parker, Cecil Cooper, Keith Hernandez, Glenn Beckert, Bobby Grich, Davey Lopes, Jim Gantner, Bobby Knoop, Robin Yount, Dave Concepcion, Ozzie Smith, Jim Fregosi, Joe Morgan, Rick Burleson, Don Kessinger, Bill Russell, Brooks Robinson, Graig Nettles, Reggie Smith, Jim Northrup, Ron Fairly, Dusty Baker, Chili Davis, Jim Wohlford, Dave Bergman, Willie Wilson, Matty Alou, Jim Barr, Dan Petry, Louis Aparicio, and Fred Besana, Sr.

Many major league coaches have made significant contributions to the *Handbook*, including Johnny Pesky, Dave Bristol, Charlie Lau, Manny Mota, Dick Sisler, Harry Walker, Frankie Crosetti, Johnny Sain, Warren Spahn, Red Adams, Danny Ozark, Roger Craig, Johnny Podres, Bob Cluck, Ron Perranoski, Jim Brewer, Bob Shaw, Sandy Koufax, Don McMahon, John Vukovich, Bobby Winkles, John Van Ornum, Ray Miller, Walt Hriniak, Bobby Valentine, and Bill Mazeroski.

Likewise, numerous coaches on the college, university, and high school levels made noteworthy contributions, among them Jerry Kindall (Arizona), Ron Fraser (Miami), Jerry Cougill (Reed Cutter High, Braidwood, Ill.), Lowell Scearcy (Bramerd, Minn. High), Dave Kielitz (Central Michigan), Norm DeBriyn (Arkansas), Bill Wright (Tennessee), Tom Dedin (Illinois), Dave Alexander (Purdue), Hal Baird (East Carolina), Jack Stallings (Georgia Southern), Gary Pullins (Brigham Young), Rolan Walton (Houston), Marty Berson (Santa Monica), Don Miller (Chico State), Lee Eilbracht (Illinois), Pat Doyle (San Joaquin Delta), Bill Wilhelm (Clemson), June Raines (South Carolina), Gene McArtor (Missouri), Jack Smitheran (California-Riverside), Berdy Harr (Cal Poly), Bob Milano (California-Berkeley), Jim Bowen (Cal State-Stanislaus), Ron Polk (Mississippi State), Danny Litwhiler (Michigan State), Robert Wells (Frostburg State-Maryland), Bob Hiegert (Cal State-Northridge), Jim Bush (UCLA), Bob Bennett (Fresno State), and John Winkin (Maine). Special thanks must go to the coaches who contributed their favorite drills. I am particularly grateful to Coach Winkin whose innovative indoor program and facilities are presented in detail in Chapter 15, and Dr. Bill Harrison, optometrist, for his contribution on vision training.

To Bill Buhler, head trainer of the Dodgers; Dr. Frank Jobe, Dodgers' team physician and orthopedic surgeon, Los Angeles; Pat Screnar of the Dodgers; and Dusty Baker, Terry Forster, and Arthur Jones, Nautilus Company, for their authoritative assistance in the chapter on conditioning.

To Rod Dedeaux, University of Southern California, whose outstanding Trojan teams have won numerous NCAA titles and produced such major league standouts as Tom Seaver and Fred Lynn, for writing the foreword to this text. Rod will serve as head coach of the USA baseball team in the 1984 Los Angeles Olympics. He has contributed a great deal to college baseball, as well as having had a strong influence on the game in other countries.

To Fred Claire, vice-president, Public Relations of the Los Angeles Dodgers, for his excellent assistance in support of this publication, and Steve Brener, the Dodgers' Director of Publicity. The many other public relations directors who contributed valuable photographs and information are likewise acknowledged and commended.

To Bowie Kuhn, commissioner of baseball; Charles S. Feeney, president of the National League; L. S. McPhail, Jr., American League president; and Peter O'Malley, president of the Dodgers, for their cooperation in behalf of the book.

To Lela Alston, wife, Emmons and Lenora Alston, parents, and other members of the Alston family, all of whom have been a source of inspiration through the years.

To Sandy Koufax and Don Drysdale, for their permission to use the truly memorable pre-game warm-up scene photo. Sandy's four career no-hitters and Don's fifty-eight and two-thirds consecutive scoreless innings are two of the greatest accomplishments in baseball history.

Several companies that manufacture baseball equipment and training aids provided information and resource materials. These included the Athletic Training Equipment Company, JUGS Pitching Machine Company, and World Sporting Goods, Inc.

To Elmer Blasco and John Griffith of *Athletic Journal,* for the use of the high-speed sequence camera, and to the numerous photographers nationwide who contributed photographs. Dave Drennan did some outstanding printing work in the photo lab, as well as various game-action camera assignments.

To Mrs. Annegrete Weiskopf and daughter, Christine, for long hours of dedicated and efficient service in typing the new manuscript and handling a variety of important assignments.

Sincere thanks to Elydia Siegel and her staff at Superscript Associates, especially Janet Dooher, Pat Torelli, Lyrl C. Ahern, and Marvin Davis for their very able editorial assistance and their excellent page designs and layouts. Thanks to Valerie Ruud for her excellent copyediting assistance and to the publishing direction of John Gilman, Hiram Howard, and Jack Stone of Allyn and Bacon. Their close cooperation and support is very much appreciated by the authors. Grafacon, Inc. is to be commended for their superb technical illustrations. Jerry Kindall's review of the new manuscript proved to be most helpful in developing a textbook we sincerely believe is much superior to the 1972 edition.

Walter Alston   *Don Weiskopf*
Oxford, Ohio   Sacramento, California

1

Batting

Too many hitters are still swinging for the fences. Ball players have a natural tendency to try to hit every pitch out of the park. As a result, they swing too hard, adversely affecting timing, level swing, stride, thinking, and everything that goes toward making solid contact. I firmly believe that if hitters concentrated on making good contact, they would hit more home runs. Players will be surprised at how hard they can hit the ball using a short stroke.

A good, quick swing is the secret to good hitting. By shortening the stride and stroke of the bat, a hitter can compensate for the off-speed pitches and get better contact and better wood on the ball than he can by taking a long swing and a long, lunging stride. Unless a hitter has good bat control, he is not going to be a consistent hitter. He has to put the bat on the ball!

"The quickest way for a ball player to become a good hitter," advised Johnny Pesky, hitting coach of the Boston Red Sox, "is to concentrate more on trying to meet the ball and to hit the ball where it is pitched. Choking up and taking a shorter swing will help assure the bat control that is necessary to hit the ball to all fields."

EFFECTIVE HITTING

Major league batting coaches are in firm agreement in advocating a relaxed, smooth, rhythmic swing that stresses proper alignment of the head, perfect balance, and full arm extension. Indeed, this type of hitting swing enables a

---

Fig. 1.1 POWER HITTER Mike Schmidt of the Philadelphia Phillies made an adjustment at the plate in 1980 which made him a better hitter. No longer a dead pull hitter, Schmidt began standing off the plate and striding into the ball.

batter to hit the ball hard more consistently than does a crowd-the-plate, arms-in, tense, muscle-up, swing-from-the-heels approach.

Hitting the ball hard is more important than is hitting it to a particular field. If you hit the ball hard consistently, the base hits will take care of themselves. "When I try to pull, I have a tendency to jerk my head off the ball," said Steve Garvey, who has combined power with his ability to hit the ball to all fields. "Generally, I will go with the pitch."

The good hitter is aggressive. I like to see a batter up at the plate who will attack the ball, one who is always going into the ball. We encourage our hitters to go get the ball. They cannot let the ball get in on them too quickly. A non-aggressive hitter is one who more or less lays back and just feels for the ball. Rod Carew, seven-time American League batting champion, is always thinking, "It doesn't matter what the pitch is, I'll get my cut at it!"

While he must be aggressive, the batter should not lunge into the ball. Rather, I prefer him to take a short, casual stride into the pitch, allowing him to keep his body back. If his body moves out in front too quickly, the hitter will have a difficult time adjusting to the pitch. Consequently, he will lose power in

Fig. 1.2 AN AGGRESSIVE HITTER is able to get his bat out in front quick. A good fast swing can be a major asset to a hitter. Above, a quick bat enables Jack Clark to pull the fast ball.

his swing. He should take a stride that allows him to glide into the swing, rather than jump into it, resulting in a smooth stride.

If you can see the ball and have quick hands, you can be a good hitter.

PETE ROSE

Quickness with the hands and wrists is a most important phase of hitting. The ability to be quick with the hands, wrists, and arms will determine just how good a hitter a player is going to be. If a hitter is fast with his hands and wrists, he will be able to wait longer for the pitch. How can a hitter become quicker with his hands and wrists? To get more bat speed, he has to develop more strength. While there are many good strength exercises, I think the best way to improve arm strength is to get a bat eight or ten ounces heavier than the one the hitter uses in the game and swing it, and keep on swinging it!

The only way to become a good hitter is to swing the bat constantly, not just when taking the few swings in batting practice. It is the desire to hit and the willingness to practice that makes great hitters. While not every boy can become a great hitter, every player can improve through instruction and practice.

Perhaps the most important rules in batting are a level swing, timing, and hitting the ball where it is pitched. A level swing provides the greatest hitting arc—to hit the ball where it is pitched. Outside pitches should be hit to the opposite field, while inside pitches should be pulled. With the improved change of speeds and different pitches being thrown today, timing is probably the biggest factor in hitting. Only constant work at the plate, swinging at every type of pitch, will give a hitter timing.

A hitter should try to hit the ball where it is pitched. If it is outside, go to the opposite field, and if it is inside, pull it to your power field.

STAN MUSIAL

What is the proper swing?

The type of swing depends on the hitter himself and, of course, on where the ball is pitched. The arc of swing varies—level, slightly upward, or slightly downward. Each hitter must develop his own style to meet his physical abilities, such as power and speed. On the low ball, the batter has to come up; otherwise, he will hit the ball on the ground. On the high pitch, he has to take a slightly downward stroke at the ball.

A hitter will generally start the swing downward, but finish with a little

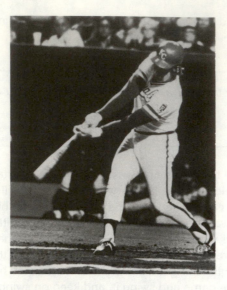

Fig. 1.3 BATTING CHAMPIONS, like George Brett, use a short, compact swing. Brett has both of his arms extended in a "perfect triangle" as he meets the ball squarely in front of the plate, just before he breaks the wrists.

uppercut. Actually, the bat starts down and then levels off through the swing. On the point of contact the swing is fairly level. The follow-through will be a slightly upward swing, especially if the hitter turns loose with the top hand and lets the bottom hand get good extension.

"The important point is to eliminate a loop," said Charlie Lau, batting coach of the Chicago White Sox. "If you keep the bat head above your hands, you will eliminate a loop. A pitcher loves to see that little loop, and can find it very easily."

An increasing number of hitting instructors are emphasizing the "slightly downward swing," the chop or slap type of swing in which the hitter shortens up and swings down slightly.

"The reason why we tell our hitters to swing down slightly," says Dick Sisler, former batting coach of the St. Louis Cardinals, "is to more or less go to the extreme to make them level off. I think that if a hitter will level off on a high pitch, he will hit the ball on a line more."

Then, there is Ted Williams, who prefers to stress "the slightly upward swing." Ted, who was one of the game's truly great hitters with the Boston Red Sox, believes that "a hitter can generate more power this way than he can swinging down on the pitch."

Most home run hitters have a slight uppercut, which is all right for a player with good power; but for the majority of hitters, I stress the level swing and have them put more weight forward to prevent uppercutting.

Spray hitters, those who hit to all fields, should use a heavier bat, choke up, and try to make contact. They will find that the ball will come off the bat more sharply than if they use a lighter bat.

Generally, I like to see our hitters stress line drives at all times. True, a batter will hit a percentage of the balls on the ground, and he will hit a percentage of fly balls. However, I feel that by concentrating on going to the line drive he is more apt to make good contact consistently.

Select a bat you can control

The weight of the bat is very important. Each player must decide for himself what type of bat is right for him. He should find one that feels good in his hands, neither too heavy nor too light. The bat has to feel comfortable to *him*.

There is no certain size bat for any particular individual. A coach should fit the bat to the individual, taking into consideration the size of his hands and his physical abilities. It should be more or less a feel. A hitter should pick up a bat, balance it, and determine whether he likes the feel of the handle, whether or not it feels good in his hands. The bat's weight should also be considered.

Many hitters have found success with the lighter and thinner bats, with the weight out on the hitting area. The idea behind using this type of bat is to swing the bat faster, thereby getting more velocity into the swing.

When the bat is too light, however, a hitter has a tendency to overswing, to swing too hard. With a heavier bat, the hitter has better control, and with more wood, he has a greater chance of hitting the ball. For the majority of hitters, a heavier bat choked up for balance is more effective than a light bat swung from the end.

Even though John Bench is a power hitter, he uses a bat considered fairly light by major league standards: thirty-five and half inches long and weighing between thirty-two and thirty-three ounces. Bench explained that, " I feel this is a perfect bat for me because I can wait until the last second to whip the bat. With the slightly heavier bat I was using before, I couldn't get any whip if I waited too long."

Assume a comfortable stance

The stances used by successful major league hitters vary. A batter should move his feet around until he finds a stance that feels good. The best stance is the most comfortable one.

As he assumes his position at the plate, the hitter should make sure he has complete coverage of the plate. He should be close enough to the plate to handle pitches on the outside corner and far enough from the inside corner to keep from being handcuffed or jammed on the fists. In general, the long ball hitter employs a wide stance, while the batter who likes to drive or punch the ball through or over the infield uses a narrow one. Some hitters vary their stance against certain pitchers. They move up in the box against breaking ball pitchers and move deeper against fast ball pitchers.

Basically, I like to start a young hitter out with both of his feet even, not closed, not open, and adjust from there. The most balanced position is one with the feet shoulder-width apart, and with the front foot turned a little toward the pitcher. The weight is distributed equally on the balls of the feet.

The head must be held fairly still. It has to move a little, but very little. It is like a good golf swing. Both eyes should be facing the pitcher and the ball. A hitter should move his eyes to watch the ball, *but never move his head.*

The hips and shoulders must be kept *level,* with the front hip and shoulder pointing at the pitcher. If a player maintains level hips and shoulders while swinging, he will very likely take a level swing, keeping his hands about chest height and above the toes of his rear foot. He should tuck the chin in close to the front shoulder to keep his head from pulling away as he swings. Some hitters believe they see the ball better when they keep their eyes level as they watch the ball.

A hitter who is a little slow with the bat should open up the stance. One who cannot handle the outside pitch, should try hitting from a closed stance and getting closer to the plate. A closed stance is effective against breaking pitches because it enables a hitter to hang in there a little better.

"Stance is really not that important," said Johnny Pesky, who compiled a life-time batting average of .307 with the Red Sox. "Various stances can be used. I advocate the closed stance because I believe that the bat stays in better position with this stance, and the bat does not move quite as far. Most of the good hitters used a closed stance—Musial, Williams, and down the line."

Whatever stance he uses, a hitter must be comfortable in the batter's box. If a hitter has a tendency to pull away from the ball, he should consider placing a little more weight on the front foot. He should keep the bat cocked back, and the front shoulder in.

Tension can be a real problem to a hitter. The solution to tension at the plate is some kind of rhythmic movement before the swing—a slight bend in the knees, shuffling of the feet, or a waggle of the hips. The movement helps the hitter relax. It is particularly important to bend the knees when hitting the curve ball. The hitter who is too stiff in the legs always has difficulty hitting breaking pitches.

The batter must keep his hips under him. If his hips and butt stick out too far, he will be on his heels, rather than the balls of the feet. He can move more quickly and maintain better control of his body if he starts in a relaxed position rather than a tense one. I do not like to see hitters bent over too much, since this position makes them stiff.

Grip

The grip of the batter should be comfortable and firm but not tense and tight. The hitter should grip the bat where he can swing it best (Fig. 1.4). He can do this by "shaking hands" with the bat and lining up the middle knuckles of both hands. Most hitters align the second and third knuckles with a flat surface of the two hands. This grip places the middle knuckle of the top hand somewhere

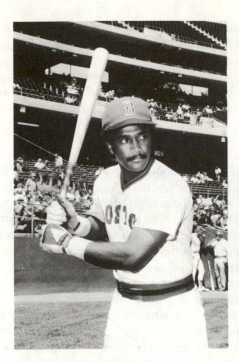

Fig. 1.4 GRIP OF THE BAT. While a long ball hitter like Jim Rice prefers holding the bat down at the end, batting champions like Matty Alou (right) find they have greater bat control choking up on the bat a few inches.

between the middle and last knuckle of the bottom hand for better wrist snap. The hands should be close together.

A loose, relaxed grip is essential for quickness and power. A tight grip has a tendency to tighten up the forearm muscles and the biceps.

While assuming a relaxed position at the plate, the hitter should have a firm grip with his bottom hand and a loose grip with his top hand.

"As far as the top hand is concerned," said Joe Torre, an outstanding hitter in the National League before becoming a manager, "the bat should not be squeezed but held loosely, in the fingers rather than in the palm, which enables the hitter to turn his wrists better at impact. This type of grip allows him to be freer and to 'pop the bat' into the ball."

Then, as he throws the bat at the ball on the swing, the batter should tighten up his grip. So, he must remember to relax until he is ready to actually swing. He keeps his grip loose, but as he starts swinging, the hands and wrists tighten, providing maximum power at the right time.

Holding the hands

The hitter should hold his bat in the "ready" position that is comfortable for him. I urge my players to hold their hands about chest height because that is where the high pitch is going to be. If the ball is above their hands, they are urged to take it. If it is below their hands, they should "jump" on it. This gives a player a better idea of the strike zone.

Most hitters hold their hands approximately letter-high, and just slightly behind their rear leg. True, hitters like Carl Yastrzemski and Fred Lynn keep their hands even higher, but they have to come down to swing.

Position in the box

Most hitters prefer to stand about even with the plate. A hitter has to be close enough to control the outside part. By touching the outside corner with his bat, the batter can tell whether he is close enough to have full coverage of the plate.

Some fellows think it is better to stand in the back of the box, giving them more time to look at the pitch. One disadvantage, however, in being in the extreme end of the box is that a breaking pitch will break even bigger back there. In other words, the ball gets the full sweep of its break toward the plate there. The farther away a hitter stands from the plate on a curve ball, the bigger break he has to take care of while covering the plate.

"Many of the major league hitters hit from the back of the box, close to the catcher," observed Wally Moses, for many years an outstanding hitter and batting coach. "I like a hitter who is more even with the plate."

"I think the hitter is better off hitting a curve ball as it is breaking in, rather than after it breaks. Therefore, the sooner he can catch it, the better off he will be, before it breaks bigger," said Johnny Sain, a great pitching coach and exponent of the breaking ball.

"Most of the young hitters have a tendency to crowd the plate," according to Ted Williams. "That, to me, is the hardest way of all to hit. If I crowd the plate, my hands and arms extend over to the inside corner of the plate, and in order for me to hit it, I have to get my bat out well in front of the plate. Because I am so close to the plate, I have to hit the ball well out in front of the plate, allowing me less time to hit the ball squarely on the meat of the bat.

"Now, in order to become a good hitter, the quicker you can be, the more time you give yourself," continued Williams. "So, in order to get more time and be fooled less, simply move away from the plate, approximately ten inches to a foot. With my hands in the same position, and with this position in the box, I don't have to worry about that inside pitch anymore, because I am not crowding the plate. All I have to do is to turn around a little bit and assume a more closed stance."

Know the strike zone

Knowledge of the strike zone is an important aspect of hitting. The more selective a hitter is in swinging at pitches, the easier it will be for him to develop into a good hitter. Once pitchers find he is going to swing at bad pitches, he will get very little else.

Fig. 1.5   THE CORRECT POSITION AND STANCE AT HOME PLATE (Cleon Jones).

A baseball, thrown with great speed and plenty of stuff on it, is tough enough to hit even when it is in the strike zone. When a hitter goes after bad pitches, out of the strike zone, he makes his job much more difficult. The strike zone is an area the width of the plate and extending from the knees to slightly under the armpits.

Watch the ball   Picking up the ball is very important to a hitter. Good hitters see the ball longer than do poor hitters. As soon as the ball is released, the batter has to pick up the spin. He should be able to tell by the way the ball is rotating whether the pitch is a fast ball or a curve.

"Pitchers tend to throw curves more overhand," explained Rod Carew. "They get on top of the ball. As a result, the ball has a great amount of overhand spin. A fast ball doesn't have that much rotation, and a slider comes in at a three-quarter angle."

A hitter should follow the ball right into the catcher's glove. He should never take his eyes off the ball, even if he doesn't swing at it.

"I try to hit the ball up the middle," said Carew. "If you look to left or right field, to where you want to hit the ball, you're cutting down on your concentration. You can't look at left or right field and at the pitcher, too. That's why I try to hit the ball to center. That way, I'm looking at the field I'm aiming for, I'm looking right at the pitcher, and I'm not swinging too early in an attempt to pull the ball."

Wait on the pitch

The good hitter is a waiter. He gets that last extra look. The better he is at watching the pitch as it comes toward him, the longer he can wait before swinging. Hitters with good wrists and hands can wait until the last split-second and then whip the bat forward with power as well as authority.

Patience is one of the most important qualities for a hitter. To hit the ball well, a hitter must wait until it gets to the plate and then rip into it. *Take a real good look at the pitch, and then hit it!*

The hitter should try to keep from watching the body motion or eccentric moves of pitchers. If he follows their pumps or motions too closely, he may be attracted to something other than the ball, such as a high leg or a jerky shoulder movement.

To be a good waiter, the hitter must have quick reflexes, quick hands and wrists, and excellent eye and muscle coordination.

THE HITTING SWING

A level, natural swing is a characteristic of all batting champions. The younger hitter, particularly, should just go for the line drive and let the home runs take care of themselves. He should always try to meet the ball solidly, and not try to overswing (Fig. 1.6).

By making good contact, a batter always has a chance for a hit. The shorter and more compact the swing, the better chance a hitter has for contact. This is the secret of hitting.

The good swing is as level as possible. Naturally, the type of swing depends on where the ball is pitched. On the low pitch the hitter does come up on his swing. He has to come up. In fact, most hitters uppercut slightly. It is perfectly natural to swing up on a low pitch. However, if he uppercuts pitches across his letters or high pitches, the hitter will have a lot of trouble. These are the pitches on which he must swing slightly down, particularly with a hard infield and if the hitter has good speed afoot. The swing is somewhat of a chopping one.

"I recommend a short, compact swing," said Pete Rose, one of baseball's greatest hitters. "I like to see a hitter go up there and swing hard and just hit the ball. I try to swing level because if I uppercut, I will hit nothing but fly balls, and I don't want to hit too many ground balls. So, I just try to take a hard, level swing."

Fig. 1.6 THE SWING OF A BATTING CHAMPION. Rod Carew has a fluid, graceful swing, with a smooth weight shift. While Rod's swing is flat, other hitters may be high. As he brings the bat forward (center), Carew begins to rotate his body. Failure to pivot results in locked hips and prevents a smooth follow-through.

The top hitters in baseball use different swings. Carew's swing, for example, is flat, while Reggie Smith's is high, but the key is that when the front foot comes down, the bat is either off or behind the back leg. The secret is to coordinate the parts of the hitting swing into perfect unison, which requires perfect timing. *Timing is the key to the hitting game.*

Quick, strong hands and his "soft" grip on the bat are two of the secrets of Rod Carew's hitting success.

Taking a rather short stride

I like the short stride because it keeps the hitter's body balanced and enables him to have split-second timing. In addition, the short stride allows him to check a swing if the pitch is bad.

The player who takes a short step controls his forward motion. He is not only properly balanced, but he is able to focus his eyes better on the ball. He can wait longer on the ball, and then he can adjust to the pitch.

"I take a short stride," said Pete Rose, "because it helps me keep my weight on my back foot. But there are hitters like Johnny Bench and Henry Aaron who prefer a longer stride. When I take a long stride, I have a tendency to start lunging, so I keep my stride to four to six inches." For many hitters, though, a four to six inch stride is not realistic. Jerry Kindall points out that, "Most good hitters stride twice that in game situations."

The purpose of the stride is to force the weight onto the rear foot and keep it there until the swing is started. The body weight must never be ahead of the swing. Motion pictures show that a batter hits the ball a fraction of a second after the stride.

We find that batters who stride longer are getting ready too quickly; this causes them to become lunge hitters. Consequently, the hitter goes out too quickly to meet the ball, and the only thing he is using to hit is his arms. Essentially, if he can stay back and wait and take a short stride, the batter will have the compact swing necessary for successful hitting.

If he finds he has to overstride and that he cannot cut his stride down, a player should try to hold his bat back until the pitcher gets the ball on the way. If he does not commit his bat with his front foot, he can take a big stride, as long as he does not start his bat with his foot.

By taking a short stride, the hitter can more or less just shift his weight from the back to the front foot. The front foot that he hits into is firm.

By striding in, a hitter will likely keep that front shoulder in and not open up too quickly. He will not make as many mistakes on the breaking ball. Schmidt credits an adjustment he made at the plate in 1980 with making him a better hitter. "I began standing off the plate and striding into the ball a little more."

The casual stride

We like a hitter to take a short, "casual stride," simply because it allows him to keep his body back. The "casual stride" is not a lunge. It is more of a lifting or shifting of the weight from both feet to a little more on the back foot. The front or striding foot is more or less free to just take the "casual stride" into the pitch.

The casual stride enables the hitter to stride forward with his front foot but not let his body go forward. The weight of the body is kept back, and the bat is back. Although he has taken the same length of stride, the player has held his body back, and his bat is back, cocked, and ready to meet the ball when it comes. He is on balance, as he is throughout the swing.

Weight shift   Weight shift is very important to hitting success. There are many ways in which hitters transfer their weight forward. A good extension of the arms will result in a good weight shift. At the point of contact, the front leg is as rigid as a board.

Batting authorities differ in their interpretation of the weight shift on the hitting swing. The high-speed sequence films of the great hitters through the years demonstrate that a baseball hitter has to hit against a firm front side, a closed front hip (Figs. 1.6 and 1.7). To obtain a controlled stride, it is essential to maintain a firm rear foot because a hitter generates his power in his push forward as he "throws the bat" at the ball.

Fig. 1.7 A CLASSIC SWING. Henry Aaron demonstrates one of the greatest batting swings in the history of baseball. Aaron's quick hands and wrists enable him to hit the ball out in front of the plate. He prefers a short stride because it keeps his body balanced and gives him split-second timing.

Many of the great hitters of baseball used a short stride because it kept their body balanced and helped them have split-second timing. The batter who takes a short step controls his forward motion. He is able to stay properly balanced.

Cocking action When the front foot comes down, the hands are back, behind and off the back leg, ready to trigger the swing forward. The back elbow is normally kept down, not up. The hitter feels comfortable at the plate. He has his bat back and his wrists cocked as he looks at the pitcher over his front shoulder. In this position, the hitter is ready to accelerate forward.

The raised back elbow has been used by a number of hitting greats, including Joe DiMaggio, Ted Williams, and, more recently, Fred Lynn and Carl Yastrzemski. The elbow-up position does add power and distance, but it can reduce consistency and good contact. Batters who hit with the back elbow up, however, are less prone to hitch than are those who hit with the back elbow down. If a hitter is slow with the bat, he generally should not raise his elbow.

Before the start of the swing, there is a little movement of the hands. The great hitters use a little "cocking" action. As the batter gets ready for the pitch, the hands move slightly up, rather than down and then up.

Keep a strong front arm

A hitter has to use his front arm correctly. The front arm more or less guides the swing, and then the top hand does a little snapping. Unfortunately, many hitters fail to use the front arm properly, one reason being that they are weak in the triceps muscle, which is responsible for "whipping the front arm out." Therefore, a hitter must build up those muscles which will give him this bat speed: the muscles in the back of the arm. The triceps muscle in the back of the arm, which throws the bat out at the ball, is the one to be built up.

Unfortunately, quite a few hitters get their top hand in too quickly and begin rolling their wrists when the ball is fairly even with them. Some batters use their top hand too much, and fail to use the front arm enough.

I like a hitter to point his front shoulder right at the pitcher. He must really push his shoulder toward the pitcher. If the batter does not drive the shoulder toward the ball, his head will move and he will lose sight of the ball.

Many hitters tend to let their front shoulder pull out just a fraction too early. This causes them to pull their body away just enough to get the ball on the end of the bat. Instead, the hitter should tuck his chin in close to his front shoulder to keep the shoulder from pulling out too early.

Rotating the hips

As well as from the wrists and arms, batting power comes from rotating the hips. According to many hitting experts, the action of the hips is more responsible for a powerful swing than is the roll of the wrists and hands (Fig. 1.8).

Getting the hips out of the way and letting the momentum and power of the body come forward into the swing is one of the most important points in hitting. The batter who hits from a closed stance and with locked hips must try to open up, in order to get his hips out of the way.

Good wrists and hands are essential because they "pop the ball" well, but on contact with the ball the hands are still fairly straight and the wrist turn-over occurs afterward, like a follow-through which provides the extra pop. So, it all comes back to the power of the hips. *A hitter has to put his hips into it!*

For good hip rotation, the rear foot must turn to face toward the pitcher.

The turn forces the front hip to open up. When the back foot turns, there is no way that a hitter can stop the front hip from opening. The hips open up to give the hitter room for his hands to come through and to bring the hands in for the tight pitch. In turning, the hitter is transferring his weight forward.

The hitter has to hit against a firm front side, a closed front hip. He actually opens up before he swings, but he should start his swing against a firm front hip. Throwing the bat then pulls the hitter in behind the ball. He pivots on the back foot, with a relaxed, bent knee. He pushes vigorously forward with his back foot.

Good hip rotation produces bat speed. Paul Waner, like his brother, a great hitter with the Pittsburgh Pirates, called it "the quick belly button." By "the quick belly button," he meant speed in the rotation of the hips. The manner in which the bat is thrown out makes the batter quick in the hips, gives him a quick pivot.

Quickness with the hands and wrists

Being quick with the hands and wrists is one of the most important phases of hitting (Fig. 1.9). "The quicker they are as the ball comes to the plate," explained Williams, "the longer you can wait to judge the pitcher, and the less you will be fooled."

Fig. 1.8 GOOD HIP ROTATION. A hitter pivots his hips to get drive and a powerful swing. The hips help turn the shoulders when swinging the bat. The pivot brings the hips and shoulders around together. The back hip is whipped around as the front hip is thrown out of the way (Ron Cey).

Once the hitter decides to pull the trigger, he must get his bat moving quickly. Everything—shoulders, hips, hands, and wrists—is brought through smoothly, unleashing his full power on the ball. The wrist snap is the final accelerator after the hips, shoulders, forearms, and hands have laid the bat on the ball.

For years, many baseball authorities were erroneously stating that the hitter breaks his wrists when the bat is across the plate. Wally Moses, in refuting this theory, said that "a hitter should hit the ball before he breaks his wrists." The head of the bat is what turns the wrists over. Again, *the ball should be met in front of the plate, just before the hitter breaks his wrists.*

Quite a few hitters, incorrectly, bring their top hand in too quickly and begin rolling their wrists when the ball is fairly even with them. Instead, a hitter should hit the ball before he breaks his wrists.

Just at impact, and slightly afterward, the hitter's wrists start breaking, and then comes the smooth follow-through. The wrists break just after contact with the ball, to give the swing that extra punch that sends the ball well on its way.

Don't try to hit the ball far—just hit the ball hard.

Full extension of the arms

The batter's hands start from the top, about shoulder high, are thrown right out in front, and then move on through. As contact with the ball is made, the

Fig. 1.9 QUICK HANDS AND WRISTS. A growing number of hitters like Bill Buckner have found success at the plate by shortening up and swinging down slightly. By shortening the stride and stroke of the bat, the hitter can get better contact and also make the necessary adjustment on off-speed pitches. A good line drive hitter, Buckner likes to hit balls up the alleys.

arms are fully extended and the eyes remain on the ball. The batter hits the ball as the front arm becomes straight.

Power hitters such as Mike Schmidt and Jack Clark like to keep their arms away from their bodies to give greater arm extension (Fig. 1.11). The hitter who holds the bat too close to the body may have difficulty getting the arms out when he swings, causing too much roll of the hands and wrists. A dominant or strong top hand can prevent a full-arm extension by taking over after contact and causing too much roll of the hands and wrists. To prevent this roll, hitting coaches such as Lau advocate releasing the top hand after driving through and making contact with the ball.

Popping the top hand is where a hitter really gets the turnover of his wrists. He should pull with his left or bottom hand, which will help him extend his arms in hitting, and then pop with the right.

Follow-through

After the hips and wrists have whipped through and hit the ball, a complete follow-through is necessary. A complete follow-through provides power to the swing and gives distance to the hits. The body follows through in the direction the ball is hit, and the bat continues under its own momentum to the rear of the body. The wrists snap and roll over. The arms swing to the rear. The hitter

Fig. 1.10 THE HITTING FOLLOW-THROUGH. Don't stop your swing. Follow through in the direction you hit the ball (Gary Carter).

Fig. 1.11   LINE DRIVE SWING. Even home run hitters like Mike Schmidt try to meet the ball solidly and not overswing. Rather than swing too hard, Mike takes a hard, level swing. He coordinates all the parts of the swing, and this requires timing. As the hitting swing starts, Schmidt's weight is shifted from the back foot and finishes on the front foot after contact. He meets the ball squarely in front of the plate.

should be in perfect balance, with the body facing the direction of the ball just hit (Fig. 1.10).

A batter should never stop or "chop off" his swing. When he completes his swing, his bat should be at the middle of his back. The rear hip follows through. The belt buckle comes around and faces left field on an inside pitch, center on a pitch down the middle, and right on an outside pitch. The weight comes forward, causing the back foot to pivot, or, for some hitters, to lift on contact with the pitch.

While some hitters have their rear foot off the ground, the lifting comes only after they have made contact with the ball. To obtain a controlled stride, it is essential to maintain a firm rear foot because a hitter generates his power in his push forward as he throws the bat at the ball.

PROPER MENTAL APPROACH

The ability to think at home plate is important. What is the pitcher throwing? What is his best pitch? What did he get me out on last time? What am I going to do? One of the best things any hitter can do when he is up at the plate is to concentrate on the pitcher and try to imagine that every pitch is coming into the strike zone and he is going to put the bat on the ball. He must have confidence in himself, *a positive feeling that he can do it!* He has to have a mental attitude that says, "I know I can do it."

Above all, a hitter has to be as relaxed as possible. He cannot react quickly enough or take a smooth swing if his muscles are tight. He should not get set too soon. He should wait until the pitcher is "ready" to pitch before he gets into his ready position.

Relaxation is essential to becoming a good hitter. Actually, concentration and relaxation go together in hitting a baseball. By concentrating on what he is doing, a player can remove tension and fear from his mind and substitute the all-important vehicles to success—a confident mind and a relaxed body.

"In hitting, the element of fear has to be eliminated," said Charlie Lau. "A hitter has to go out on his front foot and get that ball. Subconsciously, a hitter doesn't realize that he is pulling away from the ball. A lot of hitters are rocking back away from the ball, and they don't know it. Instead, he must go out on his front foot and attack that ball!"

One good way to help a hitter to overcome fear at the plate is to throw him tennis balls instead of baseballs in batting practice. He will gain confidence when he realizes he is able to move effectively away from pitches inside him, over his head, behind him, or occasionally even hitting him. Of course, wearing a helmet that provides good overall protection of the head should help in overcoming fear.

HITTING TO ALL FIELDS

The outstanding hitters of baseball are able to hit the ball to all fields. They hit the ball where it is pitched. If the ball is down the middle of the plate, they hit it up the middle. Inside pitches are pulled, and those on the outside part of the plate go to the opposite field. At all times, the good hitters are in control of the bat.

The batters who hit for average, like Rod Carew, Pete Rose, and George Brett, know how to punch the ball and push it toward left field, how to slap the ball through infield gaps, bunt for hits, and go to the opposite field. They go into the ball. That is why they are high in the averages.

What makes a good hitter is his willingness to adjust after two strikes. By spreading out his stance, he cuts down on his swing and tries to go up the middle with the pitch.

Pulling the ball

In order to pull the ball, a hitter must use strong wrist action and get out in front of the ball. The bat should meet the ball before the ball reaches him.

Hitting it out in front gives his swing maximum power and enables his eyes to judge the ball better. The front hip must be open and turned quickly to enable the hitter to get around.

Strong wrists, a quick eye, and fast hip rotation are all needed to pull the inside pitch. Although some hitters find the closed stance natural for pulling, that stance sometimes leads to hip locking.

Many hitters have pulling trouble because they commit themselves too quickly and pull away with the body. They find they can handle only one pitch, the inside fast ball.

A number of coaches, including Bobby Winkles, take a cautious view on pull hitting. "I have never been one to advocate pulling the ball if the player cannot do it consistently," explained Bobby. "In fact, I like to see my players hitting the ball all over the park—to all fields. I think a number of hitters have been ruined because they were told they must pull. It is either natural to pull, or it is not natural to pull. Some players can get in front and others cannot."

Hitting to the opposite field

Major league batting coaches are unanimous in declaring that the pitch on the outside corner can be handled best by hitting it to the opposite field. If the pitch is on the outside corner, the hitter should step toward the plate, pointing his toe toward right field (Fig. 1.12).

To me, the best way to hit the inside pitch to the opposite field is to bring the hands in across the front of the body a little sooner, so that the big end of the bat will get on the ball.

The main thing is to hit the ball squarely. If necessary, the hitter should push or punch the ball. Stepping in the direction of right field, he should keep his hands ahead of the bat and not roll his wrists. He is just slower with the bat and does not break his wrist. Contact with the ball should be made directly over the plate, not out in front. Although the batter completes a good follow-through, the weight of his body should lean toward the opposite field.

If the ball is on the outside corner, the hitter should go into the pitch. If it is on the inside part of the plate, he should rotate his hip out of the way and bring in his hands and meet the ball in front of the plate.

During batting practice, I like to see a player practice hitting to the opposite field, so that he acquires the knack of moving toward the ball.

When hitting to the opposite field, the hitter gives a pushing motion with his left side, and he does not let the right hand turn over. Otherwise, he will hit ground balls rather than line drives.

"In hitting the ball to the right side," said Torre, "I try to throw my hands out in front of the fat part of the bat, which causes the bat to contact the ball at an angle that directs it toward right field. When you drag the bat through, the only place you can hit the ball is to the opposite field."

Fig. 1.12 HITTING THE BALL TO THE OPPOSITE FIELD requires a downward inside-out type of swing. In going to the opposite field, Manny Mota keeps his hands ahead of the bat and does not roll his wrists. The batter might assume a wider stance, and rather than striding into the pitch, he might lift the left foot and plant it down as the pitch is made. He lets the hands and wrists do the work.

The hitter has to protect the plate. If the pitcher is going to pitch outside, he has to go after that ball. He can't pull away from it and try to hit it. He has to go with it and try to hit it to the opposite field.

A right handed hitter who is able to hit the ball to right field can allow a runner at third base to score on a ground ball with less than two out.

His stroke went right into the ball.

Hitting down on the ball

Many hitters tend to uppercut slightly. It is perfectly natural to swing up on a low pitch. However, if the hitter uppercuts pitches across his letters or high pitches, he will have considerable trouble. These are the pitches on which he must swing down slightly, particularly with a hard infield and if the hitter has good speed afoot. When coaches advise a hitter to come down on the pitch, generally they are referring to the letter-high pitch. By hitting down on the ball, the hitter is less likely to pop up on it.

Fig. 1.13   HITTING DOWN ON THE PITCH. On high pitches, hitters like Fred Lynn like to come down on the ball. To produce a level swing, they try to get on top of the ball by swinging down on it. The bat starts down and then levels off through the swing.

More hitting instructors are emphasizing the slightly downward swing, the chop swing in which the hitter shortens up and swings slightly down (Fig. 1.13). This type of swing will produce more line drives, rather than pop-ups into the air. To swing down on the ball, the hitter should keep his top hand on top so the wrist will not be below the front wrist at the point of contact. He should try to keep the head of the bat above the ball at all times. The reason hitters are told to swing down slightly is more or less to go to the extreme to make them level off. If a hitter levels off on a high pitch, he will hit the ball on a line.

During pepper games, hitters have the opportunity to practice hitting high pitches down. If the ball is thrown high, they can raise their arms and get the bat coming down more.

Charlie Lau method of hitting

Basically, the Lau type of hitter is one who stays off the plate, strides into the ball, attempts a level swing, and has a good weight shift. He tries to get the bat going through the strike zone in a level manner and will hit the ball where it is pitched. George Brett and Mike Schmidt both have adopted the off-the-plate, stride-into-the-ball style of hitting. By striding in, a hitter will likely keep his front shoulder in and not open up too quickly.

The three things that Lau and his hitters key on are: discipline of the head; position of the bat when the front foot hits; and weight shift. Lau strongly believes that, "If you have these three things and a little ability, you can hit!"

"The shoulder drive is very important in the hitting swing," said Lau. "You must drive your shoulder toward the pitcher. Really push it, and start pushing it out when you start your swing. The moment you fail to drive your shoulder toward the ball, your head will move and you will lose sight of the ball."

The weight shift is also very important to hitting success. There has to be a transfer of weight. "A good extension of the arms will result in a good weight shift," said Lau. "As contact is made with the ball, the arms are fully extended and the head remains on the ball. The batter hits the ball when the front arm becomes straight."

Lau is a firm believer in a one-handed swing. "A dominant top hand can give a hitter problems at the point of contact," explained Lau (Fig. 1.14). "When the top hand rolls or flops over, the bat head will rise a little, and as a result, he beats the ball down—smothering the ball, and it ends up a one-hopper somewhere."

In order to eliminate the problem, Lau suggested, "It helps to take the top hand off the bat after hitting the ball and try to get full extension right on through." Lau advocates releasing the top hand after driving through and making contact with the ball. This is why his hitters work so much on hitting

Fig. 1.14 THE LAU STYLE OF HITTING. Hitters who use the Charlie Lau style release their top hand after driving through and making contact with the ball. Willie Wilson, shown here, by taking his top hand off the bat, is able to get good extension with his bottom hand. The Lau style allows the batter to get the head of the bat out in front much quicker.

the ball to the opposite field. They take the top hand off and get good extension with the bottom hand. This allows them to get the head of the bat out there much quicker.

"To produce a level swing, the hitter has to get on top of the ball by swinging down on it," said Lau. "What actually happens is the bat starts down and then levels off through the swing, and at the point of contact the batter is swinging fairly level. The follow-through will be a slightly upward swing, especially if he turns loose with the top hand and lets the bottom hand get good extension."

Actually, I do not believe Lau and other hitting coaches would ask their hitters to take their top hand off the bat if they could get a proper follow through. As Walt Hriniak, hitting coach of the Boston Red Sox, pointed out, "The way the hitter gets the most out of his swing is with a proper follow through. And if his hands can finish high in the swing, he will get the most out of his swing. However, some hitters have such a dominant top hand that it takes over and does not allow the bat to finish high. With this type of hitter, we ask him to release his hand after he makes contact with the ball."

SWITCH-HITTING

Since the early 1960s, when Maury Wills popularized the practice of swinging from both sides of the plate, switch-hitting has been playing an increasing role in baseball. Certainly his ability to switch-hit changed Maury from a mediocre hitter to a good one. "I had my troubles with the curve ball," related Maury, "and I was often stepping into the bucket rather than into the ball. I was not getting enough leverage in my swing."

Switch-hitting is more suited to certain players. Coaches surveyed in a 1965 study indicated that switch-hitting requires a great amount of coordination, timing, and ambidexterity not found in the majority of people. The player ideally suited to switch-hitting is one with speed who is having definite trouble hitting one way, often a right-handed hitter. Players who have good running speed and are not blessed with great power make good prospects for switch-hitting, particularly if they are able to make good contact with the ball consistently.

The chief advantage is that the switch-hitter can hit breaking stuff better. He will not be fooled by the curve ball so much. Second, as a left-hander, the player is one-and-one-half steps closer to first base.

The controlled, level swing is best for the switch-hitter. He should use a short stroke to start, with a choke grip, and should try to punch the ball. The swing should be short, quick, flat, and even a slightly downward stroke.

Ideally, switch-hitting should begin early in the player's career. Pete Rose was a ten-year-old Little Leaguer when his father taught him to swing from both sides of the plate. Wes Parker and Jim Lefebvre also switched at an early age, but Wills was an exception, inasmuch as he was twenty-seven years old when Bobby Bragan suggested the change to him in Spokane, Washington. "I think the younger a player can start the better he will be," said Bragan.

When Wills was having considerable trouble at the plate early in the 1960 campaign, Pete Reiser, one of our coaches, took Maury under his wing and started him from scratch, almost like a manager would do with a nine-year-old Little Leaguer. "He selected a new bat for me," said Maury, "one I could whip around faster. He opened my batting stance and worked on fundamentals such as meeting the ball out in front of the plate, taking an even swing, and not overstriding."

"It boils down to practice, practice, and practice," said Bragan, "come out and stand on that side of the plate, and just bunt the ball. Swing easy, and see that ball coming to the plate from the other side. Hit the ball through the middle and to the opposite side of the infield. Just try to make contact and get a piece of the ball."

BREAKING A HITTING SLUMP

A hitting slump is one of the toughest things of all to shake. The player has to be encouraged. His manager or coach has to talk to him. If he has a fault, such as uppercutting, the coach should take him out and start him hitting with soft stuff. Just have him meet the ball and more or less start him over from scratch again. Try to get him into stride.

Dick Sisler

"Most home run hitters usually have a slight uppercut which is a natural uppercut. This is all right for a batter with a lot of power, but for the majority of hitters, I would stress the level swing and have them put more weight forward to prevent uppercutting.

"For some hitters, particularly spray hitters, I suggest that they take a heavier bat, choke up on it some, and just try to make contact. The ball will come off the bat sharper than with the light bat.

"My suggestion to most hitters who fall into a slump is to take some extra hitting and hit the ball to the opposite field. This will keep their head in there and it will hold them back a little longer, and they will be able to see the pitch a lot better than if they are overanxious and they go out too quickly."

Harry Walker

"Most hitting slumps come from overstriding, trying to pull the ball too much, and trying to hit the ball too hard. When this happens, they develop bad habits, and they fail to watch the ball, and the basic fundamentals begin to get away from them. Then they begin to lose confidence.

"A hitter should be encouraged to forget about swinging hard and just try to make contact. He should consider going through the middle and waiting a little longer. The secret of hitting is being able to wait and still get the bat on the ball. A coach should try to get his hitters to wait on the ball, hit the ball through the middle, and even to the opposite field."

PROBLEMS IN HITTING AND THEIR SOLUTIONS

Problem 1: *Popping up or having difficulty making contact*

Solution: Shorten up about two inches on the bat. Try to just meet the ball, even hitting down on the ball. Concentrate hard on watching the ball all the way to the bat. You might try keeping your right elbow up, away from your body.

Problem 2: *Being overpowered by the fast ball*

Solution: First, stand back as far as you can in the batter's box. By choking up on the bat a couple of inches, you will develop a quicker swing. Keep your eye on the ball and follow it all the way to the plate.

Problem 3: *Missing low and outside corner pitches*

Solution: Rather than pulling away from the outside pitch, learn to stride into the pitch. Bend your knees a little and place your weight on your rear foot. Then, instead of shying away, stride into the pitch. Of course, make sure the ball is in the strike zone. Learn the strike zone and wait for your pitch.

Problem 4: *Taking your eye off the ball*

Solution: Concentrate hard on keeping your head still and straight. Follow the ball with your eye all the way to your bat. With good arm extension and by hitting the ball out in front of the plate, you should be able to look down the barrel of the bat and see the ball make contact.

Problem 5: *Pulling away from the plate or stepping in the bucket*

Solution: Stand farther back in the batter's box and close your stance. Put your front foot closer to the plate and concentrate on going toward the pitch, rather than away from it. Tucking your chin in close to the front shoulder will help keep the shoulder from pulling out too early.

Problem 6: *Getting jammed with an inside pitch*

Solution: Very likely, you are standing too close to the plate. Move back a little and bring your arms in so that the inside pitch will not come in on your fists. By being quick with the hands and wrists, you can develop a quicker bat. Try to get around faster on the pitch and hit the ball before it gets in on you.

Problem 7: *Eliminating a herky-jerky swing*

Solution: Very likely, you are dropping your rear elbow. Try to keep your elbow up and away from the body. This will likely level off your swing and eliminate the herky-jerky swing.

Problem 8:   *Overstriding; going out too quickly*

Solution: Stay back and wait on a good ball you can hit. Hold your weight back on the rear leg. Try not to commit yourself too soon.

Problem 9:   *Trying to hit the ball too hard*

Solution: Just try to make contact. Consider waiting a little longer on the ball and going through the middle or even to the opposite field. Don't overswing with your arms, but do not let up with the hands and wrists.

Problem 10:   *Uppercutting and swinging up on the ball*

Solution: Since you are undoubtedly dropping your back shoulder, try keeping both shoulders level. Keep the head of the bat above the ball at all times, this will help make you a line drive hitter. You might try swinging down on the ball. Start with a downstroke and level off before you get into the hitting area.

Problem 11:   *Failure to hit an inside pitch*

Solution: Switching to a lighter bat should help bring your bat around quicker. Or, you might choke up on your bat a couple of inches. Your chief concern is bringing your bat around faster.

Problem 12:   *Backing away from the pitch*

Solution: Use a closed stance, with the front foot close to the front of the plate. Place your rear foot comfortably toward the back. Bend your rear knee a couple of inches, which will put more weight on the rear foot, and then stride into the pitch.

Helpful Hints in Hitting

1. Know the strike zone and swing at strikes.
2. Take a short stride. Don't lunge.
3. Don't stride too soon, but be quick with the hands and wrists.
4. Step *to* hit, not step *and* hit.
5. Hit the ball where it is pitched. *Concentrate on this.*
6. Have a positive attitude. (Every pitch is a strike, and I am going to hit it.)
7. Have confidence you can hit any pitch. ("The pitcher must come to me," not "I have to go to him.")
8. Use a level swing for a better chance of contact.
9. Try to see how well you can hit the ball, not how far.
10. Be aggressive. Start for every pitch.
11. Keep the front shoulder in.
12. Watch the ball all the way. Don't pull the head out.

2
Bunting

Bunting is *not* a lost art in the major leagues. During the post-season play-offs and World Series in recent years, the bunting game has had a significant role in the outcome of games, as managers effectively employed the bunt to their team's advantage.

The bunting game can be vital to any team's offensive strategy. An array of bunts, if used skillfully, can exert the type of pressure that can have an unsettling effect on the defense, particularly when the bunts are executed with surprise and deception. When a runner has to be advanced, the batter must be proficient in executing the sacrifice bunt.

True, the great urge to go for the long ball, emphasis on base stealing, and the running game have resulted in less bunting on the major league level. There is more speed the bases, people who can "fly," and some managers are reluctant to give up an out. Artificial playing surfaces, of course, have cut down on bunting, because many bunters bunt the ball too hard. Additionally, today's defensive alignments are more effective in defending against the bunt, especially on astroturf.

Bunting can and should be a valuable offensive weapon, even for sluggers like Gary Carter and Steve Garvey. "I believe bunting is a very important part of my game," said Carter. "Every player should be able to bunt effectively." Garvey, with an occasional bunt, has made the defense come to him. He does not allow the third baseman to play back forty-five feet and take away his base hits. The threat of the bunt tends to keep the defense honest.

To stay out of the double play, the offensive team has to use the bunt to

---

Fig. 2.1 BUNTING IS AN ART that demands considerable practice. Although Gary Carter is one of the National League's top sluggers, opposing infielders are often surprised by his ability to lay down a bunt. Here, Carter practices his bunting techniques during pre-game batting practice.

advance runners and provide the opportunity for them to score on a base hit. "I think it is important for all hitters up and down the line-up to be capable of bunting," said Steve Boros, manager of the Oakland A's. "This doesn't mean a team should bunt that much, but when it has the capability, there is always fear in the opposition's mind."

"On the high school level, especially, I would do more bunting because so often the defensive team doesn't execute," said Boros. "Young players do not handle the bunt as well. They will throw the ball away or somebody doesn't cover a position. Therefore, you can open up your offensive possibilities by bunting more."

Bunting is a lost art if you don't work on it.

JOE GARAGIOLA

FEWER GOOD BUNTERS

There are a number of reasons for the shortage of good bunters today. Perhaps the biggest one is the great urge on the part of teams to go for the long ball. The more power a team has, the less likely it will bunt. Many players, in fact, do not want to bunt. They would rather hit. As a result, they do not devote the time and practice to develop bunting skill.

Laying the ball down can be a difficult assignment, particularly if the pitcher keeps the ball high. Bunt defense has improved considerably. With the first and third basemen drawn way in, the sacrifice can be a tough play to perform. The first baseman is charging in. On our club, for instance, we had two or three set bunt defenses. Using signs, we would go from one to the other, and we did one thing on one pitch and another thing on another pitch. The bunt defense has improved to such a degree that the offense really has to have its bunting game down.

Furthermore, young ball players today just do not practice as much as people did in the past. "Years ago, a guy would go out and practice for a half-hour a couple times a week," said Jim Frey, Major League manager and coach. "Now, you are lucky if they will practice twenty minutes a season."

"Bunting is a lost art it you don't work on it," said Joe Garagiola. Well, bunting need not be the "lost art" if the coach and squad are willing to spend time and use the proper techniques in bunting. Through the years, numerous college and high school coaches have won many games on a sacrifice bunt or a suicide squeeze. Yet, these coaches did not have good bunters—they developed them by practicing the proper techniques.

Every player should not only learn how to bunt, but should devote part of

Fig. 2.2 A SUCCESSFUL BUNT is often the difference between victory or defeat in a close ball game. In addition to moving runners over by sacrificing, it is a big advantage to a team for hitters to be able to bunt for a base hit. The threat of a bunt tends to move the defense in, creates more holes, and gives the hitter a better chance of getting a base hit. Here, Derrell Thomas has just bunted the ball, and his soft hands and arms allow the bat to give.

his daily hitting practice to laying down bunts. While the sacrifice bunt has to cope with superlative defenses at the major league level, the bunt can produce huge dividends at lower levels of play. Many supposedly poised defenses have been completely demoralized by a variety of safe bunts in a row. When one considers how often bunts can get a team started—get the first man on base—it is quite easy to respect the little bunt as a major weapon.

The major reason for faulty bunting technique is poor position.

IMPORTANCE OF GOOD TECHNIQUE

The bunting game, in general, is not as good as it used to be. Perhaps the major reason for faulty bunting techniques is poor position. Many young players are so interested in reaching base safely and getting a base hit that they neglect to bunt properly. In their haste to get a good start to first base, many bunters are not squared around in time. Consequently, bunters try to bunt the ball behind the plate instead of out in front of the plate. In addition, they start for first base too quickly, before the bunt is made. If they would square around, get set, and make the ball come to the bat, they would be on their way to becoming proficient bunters.

Good bunters hold their bat fairly high, at the height of the strike zone. Pitchers are instructed to throw the ball high because the high pitch is the toughest ball to bunt. To combat this, the bunter should hold his bat at the top of the strike zone. This will enable him to go down rather than up, on any pitch in the strike zone. It is easier and quicker to bring the bat down than to raise it.

There are several theories as the actual technique of laying the ball down properly. Some coaches teach their players to hold the bat in their fingers, so that when the ball meets the bat it just hits the bat back into their hands. This technique tends to deaden the ball enough. Another theory is that the bunter has to "give" slightly with the bat when the ball makes contact. The idea is to make the ball come to the bat and "catch the ball" on the bat.

BUNTING STANCES

Basically, there are two bunting positions: the square-around and the pivot-in-tracks. For many years, bunters have squared around with the entire body, pulling the front foot back and toward the outside of the box. However, many players today do not square around to face the pitcher. Rather, they keep their feet planted and pivot in their tracks. They square only their hips and shoulders to bunt. Which style is more effective and easier to execute, is an individual thing. The position that best suits the player should be used. The idea behind a batter pivoting on the balls of the feet to bunt is to prevent the defense from knowing as long as possible he is going to bunt.

Square-around

The square-around stance (Fig. 2.3) places the bunter in a better position to handle the ball. When he squares around, the bunter has a little better coverage of the entire plate. When bunters use the pivot-in-tracks method, they some-

Fig. 2.3   SQUARE-AROUND. There are still a large number of coaches who prefer to have their bunters square around with the feet, rather than just squaring the hips and shoulder. They feel the square-around bunter has better coverage of the entire part of the plate (Mark Belanger).

times fail to get the bat out far enough in front, and it is sometimes a little hard to reach the outside of the plate.

To execute the square-around, the right-handed bunter pulls the left foot back and toward the outside of the box. The right foot is then moved forward slightly to put the shoulders of the bunter perpendicular to the pitcher. The feet of the bunter are about shoulder width apart and parallel to each other.

The inside foot is placed on the inside line of the box, as close to the plate as is legal. By flexing the legs in a squat or by leaning slightly outward, the bunter can cover the entire strike zone.

Increasingly, bunters are squaring away earlier, with the philosophy: "Who cares if I tip the play? The sacrifice is no surprise anyway." The fielders will be charging in on the grass. The batter should move into bunting position as soon as the pitcher lifts his striding foot and leg. By squaring early, the bunter may get infielders charging too much, then he can chop it past them.

Pivot-in-tracks

Many team no longer want players to square-around and face the pitcher when they sacrifice. The majority of big-league players square only their hips and shoulders and keep their feet planted to bunt (Fig. 2.4). The important point is to get the bat out in front of the plate in a position to reach even the outside pitch. Many bunters simply twist their feet at the last instant, and they find themselves off balance for the outside strikes.

The bunter remains in his tracks and on the balls of his feet. He merely pivots his feet toward the pitcher. He pivots on the heel of the front foot, so that

Fig. 2.4 PIVOT-IN-TRACKS. The majority of big-league players square only their hips and shoulders to bunt and keep their feet planted. This method helps keep the infielders from charging too quickly. The important point is to get the bat out in front of the plate in a position to reach even the outside pitch (Gary Carter).

the toe is pointing toward the pitcher, and on the ball of the back foot just enough to turn the foot a little. This turns the shoulders and hips so he is facing the pitcher.

"I prefer to keep the feet in the hitting position and just turn the upper part of the body toward the plate," said infielder Phil Garner. "This is the technique I feel most comfortable with, but a player should do what he does best, whatever it takes to get the ball down. Sometimes, form is not an essence when you are trying to get the job done."

Actually, the bat position for the pivot-in-tracks is the same as for the square-around position. The bunter can swing his hips around and square them to the pitcher without lifting his feet off the ground. By using the pivot-in-tracks method, the bunter will help keep the infielders from charging too quickly.

"Many times, instead of squaring around, I will turn the upper half of my body without stepping at all," said Mark Belanger, one of baseball's premier bunters. "What it does is not give the bunt away so quickly, which in turn enables the batter to make it more of a surprise."

BUNTING TECHNIQUE

Body position

The bunter's body should be in a slight crouch and leaning toward the plate, to make sure the plate is well covered. The trunk and knees are slightly bent and most of the body weight is placed on the front foot. Being up in the front part of the batter's box gives the bunter a better opportunity to bunt the ball fair. His knees should be slightly bent and flexible. The weight should be on the balls of the feet, slightly forward.

"A bunter has to keep his legs relaxed," said infielder Craig Reynolds, another excellent bunter. "He can't bunt stiff-legged. On a low pitch, he has to bend his knees. He can't reach and jab at the ball. He must bend down at the knees on a low pitch."

Arms and hands   The arms should be relaxed, out in front of the bunter's body. The bat should be held parallel to the ground chest-high and covering the plate, with the elbows near the body. The right hand should slide up close to the trademark as the bat is leveled off. The bat should be gripped lightly with the upper hand, keeping the fingers underneath and the thumb on top. The thumb and index finger form a "V".

"Keep the hands away from the body," advised Belanger. "If they are tied up inside and the bat is kept close to the body, the bunter has a tendency to stab at the ball. Keep the bat head above the hand. Let the ball hit the bat and kind of give with the ball. Don't stab at it or push the ball. You want to deaden the ball, so allow the ball to hit the bat."

The barrel end of the bat is extended in front of the body and points toward the pitcher. The hands and arms should give as the ball is met, as if the bat were catching the ball. Cup the bat with the top hand without curling the fingers around it. The grip on the bat should be mainly with the thumb, index finger, and middle finger. The other fingers should be tucked in and under the bat. The more firmly his hands grip the bat, the harder the batter will bunt the ball.

"A bunter should grip the bat more or less in his thumb and forefinger, with a real light touch," said Frey. "Some people say, 'You should catch the ball with the bat,' but I don't know if that is exactly correct. You should not squeeze the bat and jab at the ball. Hold the bat loosely so that when the ball hits the bat, it is not a real solid contact. A bunter should try to deaden the ball. He doesn't want to push the ball out there. The only instance where a bunter wants to push the ball is when he is pushing the ball past the pitcher on the first base side."

Caution must be taken not to wrap the index and middle fingers around the bat, which would allow the ball to hit them. The loose hand near the end of

Fig. 2.5 THE CORRECT BUNTING POSITION (Steve Sax).

Eyes on ball

Bat at top of strike zone

Slide hand up bat

Knees slightly bent

Square feet around

Or

Pivot in tracks

Don't commit yourself too soon

Catch the ball on the bat

Bat level

Move bat downward on ball

Square hips and shoulders

the bat makes it easier to angle the bat and helps produce a soft bunt. While the two-handed grip is employed by some coaches and players, I don't believe it produces bunts as soft as the three-finger grip and the loose hand near the bat knob.

Eyes   The bunter's eyes should be on the ball. From the start of the pitcher's delivery to the actual contact of the ball on the bat, the eyes should be focused on the moving ball. Only good balls, those in the strike zone, should be bunted. Successful bunting, like hitting, requires not only good eyesight, but knowledge of the strike zone.

Bat position   There are two schools of thought on the position of the bat. Many bunting instructors like to keep the bat level—parallel to the plane of the ground—at all times. Others teach their bunters to keep the bat diagonal, to keep the point of the bat in the air.

Jim Frey believes the bat should be on a diagonal to the ground, at a 45-degree angle. "The barrel of the bat should be kept above the hands," said Frey. "To keep the ball out of the air, a bunter should keep his bat on top of the strike zone and then drop the barrel of the bat on the ball down in the strike zone. The back hand has to be higher than the front hand. If the pitch is above the strike zone, he should take it."

The barrel of the bat should be above the hands, and when the bunter actually makes contact with the ball and the bat gives with it, the bat will automatically be level. Whether it starts out level or not, upon contact with the ball, the bat should be level, as shown in Figure 2.3. In the third picture, Belanger brings his bat back to deaden the ball.

Once he determines whether he is bunting toward third or first, the bunter must set the angle of his bat immediately. As the ball approaches the bunting area, he adjusts the angle of the bat. If he is going down the third base line, the barrel is pointed right at first base.

A bunter then must get the bat out in front of him. Many players end up with the bat behind them, which creates many foul balls. "If you are bunting left-handed, you would want the left hand or the back hand out in front where you can see the ball hit the bat," explained Frey. "Try to bunt the ball toward the end of the bat, which will deaden the ball."

"Getting the bat out in front of the plate is the biggest problem in bunting," emphasized Boros. "Some players are a little reluctant to get close to the plate. In order to be a good bunter, the bunter has to almost get his nose in it and get the bat out in front of the plate."

When the ball makes contact with the bat and hits the ground, it has a much better chance of staying fair if the bat is out in front of the plate," said Belanger. "Whereas if the bat is back, sometimes the ball will hit the plate and bounce foul."

Mental stance

"Staying relaxed when bunting is very important," said Billy DeMars, veteran big-league coach. "Quite often, as soon as the hitter looks down and sees that it is the bunt sign, he has a tendency to get a little nervous or upset, and this places pressure on him. He must stay relaxed, loose, and stay back on the rear leg."

Fear of the ball is a major reason for faulty bunting technique, according to Coach Dave Bristol. "Many young players are afraid of the ball," said Dave. "They want to make sure the ball doesn't hit them, and then they say, 'I will try to bunt it then.' You can't be afraid of the ball!"

When bunting, a player must first get a good pitch to bunt. Many hitters can be very patient when swinging, but when they are bunting for a base hit, they are so anxious to get a good break out of the box, that they bunt at a lot of bad balls.

TYPES OF BUNTS

There are two kinds of bunts: 1) the sacrifice bunt and 2) bunting for a base hit—the drag and the push bunts.

Sacrifice bunt

With runners on first, or first and second, the bunt is still considered good baseball by the great majority of managers and coaches, particularly with no outs. First, the runners can be advanced into scoring position, and, second, the double play threat is eliminated.

"In executing the sacrifice, the bunter has to concentrate in his mind what he wants to do before the play occurs," said Garner. "He must get himself in the bunting position soon enough, not wait until the pitch is already on the way. True, the big-leaguers are capable of waiting until the last second, just dropping the bat down."

Bunters often try to bunt the ball too perfectly down the line. They end up having the ball roll foul. If the ball is bunted properly and not too hard, and if it is halfway between the pitcher and catcher, it is a pretty sure bunt.

The key rule in executing the sacrifice bunt is for the hitter to give himself up. The purpose of the sacrifice bunt is to advance the runner at the expense of the bunter. The bunter is expendable! Making a good bunt is the main objective.

The placement of sacrifice bunts depends on which bases are occupied, the defensive positions of the opposition, and the opposition's ability to field bunts. Normally, a sacrifice bunt should not be used unless the runner or runners, when advanced, could tie the score or put the offensive team ahead.

On a straight sacrifice bunt, the batter attempts to bunt the ball only if the pitch is a strike. He must realize that he should bunt only good balls that are in the strike zone, unless, of course, the suicide squeeze play is on.

With first base occupied, a bunt down the first base line is considered good baseball. The first baseman, holding the runner on first base, will not be in a good position to field the ball, since he does not leave the base until the pitcher delivers. With second base occupied, a hard bunt down the third base line can be a good tactic. When the third baseman comes in to field the ball, he leaves third base uncovered.

Run-and-bunt play This play is a variation of the sacrifice bunt, in which the base runner attempts a steal of the next base. To protect the runner, the hitter must bunt the ball regardless of where it is pitched. A good time to execute this play is when the pitcher is behind in the count and therefore more likely to make the next pitch a strike. The best game situation is with none out and a runner on first base.

Bunting for a hit

To surprise the defense and make a safe hit, the batter might attempt to beat out a bunt. The bunt base hit is a beautiful thing to watch because it takes great skill, and plenty of action is involved. This bunt technique is used when the third baseman is playing deep. The bunter steps one stride backward with his right foot to the left of the plate, as the weight shifts to the left foot. Once the feet are set, the weight should be shifted again to the right foot. The head of the bat points toward first base.

The ball can either be pushed toward first base (right-handed bunter) or dropped down the third base line (Fig. 2.6). The batter conceals his intent until the last split-second and meets the ball on the move.

If the pitcher uses slow pitches and curves, it is easier to bunt the ball on the ground than it is if he uses fast balls. There is always danger in base hit bunts, in that once the hitter has decided to use it, he has a tendency to bunt the ball even if it is not where he wants it. He must learn to snap the bat back out of the way of bad pitches.

The left-handed batter has an advantage over a right-hander in bunting for a base hit, since he is more than a full step nearer first base. The left-handed swinger who is quick on his feet and a skillful bunter can be a real threat to the defense, particularly on a drag toward the second baseman.

Push bunt **(right-handed batter)** This offensive tactic is used when the first baseman is playing deep. The push bunt is directed toward the pitcher's left, the first base side of the infield. The batter stands at the plate, decoying a possible swing at the ball. As the pitcher cocks his arm in his delivery, the batter rotates his hips to the rear as if he wanted to take a full swing.

"I will tell the player to hide the play as long as possible," said Boros, "and not to drop the bat into the bunting area until the pitcher's arm starts to come

Fig. 2.6 BUNTING FOR A BASE HIT (right-handed hitter). This bunt technique is used when the third baseman is playing deep. The bunter steps one stride backward with his right foot to the left of the plate, as the weight shifts to the left foot. Once the feet are set, the weight should be shifted again to the right foot. The head of the bat points toward first base (Bobby Valentine).

forward. This gives the hitter time enough to get the bat out in front of the plate and yet disguise the play from the defensive player."

"I like to see a right-hand hitter drop his right foot back," said Boros. "If the pitch is inside, he can step back a little and have a little bunting room inside. If the pitch is outside, then the hitter simply leans forward and pushes the ball down between the first baseman and the pitcher."

Aiming for the hole between first and second base, the batter takes a short lead step with his front foot as the bat is pushed at an outside pitch. He must meet the ball before his right foot hits the ground. The ball is pushed or pulled by manipulating the near hand on the bat handle, sending the ball in the desired direction. This type of bunt must be hard enough to get by the pitcher. It should be used only when the first baseman is playing back.

Pushing the ball past the pitcher on the first base side can be very effective. The idea is to make the first baseman go to his right and to allow the batter to beat the pitcher to the bag. Or, if a left-handed pitcher has a tendency to fall off toward the third base side, a hitter can bunt the ball to the right side of the mound making the first baseman and second baseman field the ball. The bunter then has a good chance to beat the pitcher to the bag. In this instance, the bunter should push the ball hard.

Push bunt **(left-handed batter)**   A left-handed hitter just wants to touch the ball. He does not want to bunt the ball as hard as does the right-handed bunter. The left-handed bunter wants the ball to die about twelve to fifteen feet down the third base line. We try to tell the young left-handed bunters to bunt the ball out toward the end of the bat, where the ball will die naturally. The crucial thing with left-handed bunters is to get them to take their first step at the pitcher so they do not pull away from the pitch too soon.

Many players who try to bunt the ball down the third base line want to run to first base too quickly. "You have to wait and bunt the ball and make a good bunt, then you run," said Bristol.

Drag Bunt **(left-handed batter)**   The drag bunt is one of baseball's most exciting and potentially explosive plays. However, it is a play that requires concentration, timing, and practice. The drag bunt can be a valuable offensive weapon for a left-handed batter, usually when the first baseman plays deep. The objective is to bunt the ball to the left of the pitcher, and hard enough so that the pitcher cannot field the ball, forcing the first baseman or second baseman to do so. Success in the drag bunt comes only when the defense is not expecting the play.

Any player with outstanding speed who has little power should perfect the drag or push bunt which will keep the infield close. With the fast playing surfaces of today, the little player with speed will find it easier to be successful. But success requires practice and the great determination that Maury Wills and other smaller players have demonstrated through the years.

The batter stands at the plate, decoying a possible swing. As the pitcher cocks his arm in his delivery motion, the batter may rotate his hips to the rear as though meaning to take a full swing. Figure 2.7 shows Maury Wills stepping toward first base with his front, right foot, as he levels off the bat. This is a perfect example of how the drag bunt should be executed. He sets the angle of the bat so that the big end points halfway between third base and home plate. The bat is approximately at a right angle with the side of his body. His right hand holds the bat at the end, and his left hand is on the trademark. Maury's bat contacts the ball out in front of the plate. Notice the perfectly level bat at contact with the ball. When contact is made, his weight is on his right foot, and his left foot trails slightly, ready to cross over the right leg.

The biggest fault of players on the drag bunt is crossing over too quickly with the left foot, since most left-handed bunters run away from the ball. They try to run before they really make contact, because they are more intent on getting a good start than on bunting the ball. It is like catching a ball: the fielder has to catch it before he throws it. Likewise, in bunting, the ball has to be bunted before the play can be made.

In executing a drag bunt correctly, the bunter should step toward the ball with his right foot and meet the ball before his left foot hits the ground. Some bunters prefer to take a short step with the right foot, and then step over with the left.

"Most of the good drag bunters I have known have a slight stutter step with their back foot," said Frey. "The back foot kind of slides back six inches, then the bunter gets his bat out in front. A drag bunter will bunt and push off, running to first base all in one motion."

Fig. 2.7 DRAG BUNT (left-handed hitter). As he levels off the bat, the bunter steps toward first base with his front, right foot. The bat is approximately at a right angle with the side of his body. When contact is made, his weight is on his right foot, with his left foot trailing slightly, ready to cross over the right leg (Maury Wills).

Fake bunt

In a bunt situation, when the infield is in too far for safe bunting, the batter may want to fake a bunt and swing or slap at the ball. This is also effective when a runner is trying to steal a base. This bothers the catcher not only in receiving, but in throwing the ball as well.

In still another situation, the hitter may assume a bunting position in the hope that the first and third basemen will charge in toward the plate. If the infielders charge, the batter will move both hands up on the handle of the bat and chop down hard on the pitch. He tries to bounce the ball through or over the charging fielders.

The batter should square around to bunt or pivot in his tracks, and then fake a bunt. His hands should be together but fairly high on the bat. As the pitcher releases the ball, the hitter should rotate his hips slightly toward the catcher and take a short swing, stepping with his front foot toward the ball as he swings.

If the runner on third is stealing home, the hitter may fake a bunt and hold his ground. It will help the runner and make it harder for the catcher to tag him, especially if the hitter is right-handed.

The batter can also use the fake bunt when taking a pitch or a strike. He should make his move before the pitcher releases the ball to distract the pitcher and make it harder for him to get the ball over the plate.

Squeeze play

The purpose of the squeeze play is to bring a man home from third base. The prime objective of the bunter is to meet the ball and to get it on the ground.

Usually the squeeze is employed to tie the score, score the winning run, or provide an insurance run for the team that is ahead.

Safety and suicide plays are usually tried in the late innings with a runner on third base, one out, and the team at bat ahead, tied, or no more than one run behind.

Safety squeeze   The batter bunts the first good ball he gets—he bunts only strikes. The runner does not run for home until he sees that the ball is bunted.

The runner at third base should make his move only if the ball is bunted on the ground. As soon as the pitcher releases the ball, he is ready to run. If the ball is popped up or missed, the runner does not go. The batter should try to bunt the ball away from the pitcher. If the first baseman is back, the bunter's objective is merely to tap the ball down the first base line.

Suicide squeeze   The bunter must bunt the ball regardless of where it is thrown. He must try just to bunt the ball in fair territory and on the ground. The runner at third base knows the batter will bunt the next pitch, no matter where it is, so he starts for home the moment the ball leaves the pitcher's hand. He must make his move at the right time. The play will be in trouble if the runner is late breaking or is too early. The bunter must protect the runner from suicide by making sure to bunt the ball on the ground in fair territory.

"In a squeeze situation, a major problem is that many players try to make too careful of a bunt," said Frey. "They try to place the ball too much. In a squeeze situation, the batter has to bunt the ball out in front of the plate—get the ball down and the runner is going to score. But there are many foul balls on suicide squeeze plays, and the biggest reason is that the bunters are trying to make too good of a placement."

NEED FOR PRACTICE

The only way a ball player can become a better bunter is to practice. Dave Bristol likes to see players go out and play pepper every day and work on their bat control. Pete Rose plays pepper every day, and, often, about every fourth or fifth ball, he will just bunt the ball either to first or third base. Just the fact that he keeps doing it, the repetition, and doing it properly is what makes Pete an outstanding bunter and the great hitter he is.

As Mark Belanger pointed out: "A player can't go out there after a month of no bunting practice and expect to bunt the ball effectively. Bunting is a very difficult thing to do and requires continual practice."

Basic Tips on Bunting

1. Bunt only good balls—those in the strike zone—unless the squeeze is on.
2. Hold the bat at the top of the strike zone.
3. Bend the knees slightly, keeping the weight on the balls of the feet.
4. Have the bat level on contact with the ball.
5. Keep the bat in front of the body and in front of the plate.
6. Start high and always come down.
7. Let the hands and arms "give" as the ball is met.
8. Grip the bat lightly, with a "V" between the thumb and index finger.
9. Do not bunt down. Cast the ball outward, like a soft line drive.

3
Base Running

Speed on the base paths is such a dominant factor in baseball. It can unnerve both the pitcher and the fielders. Speed also changes defensive alignments. It forces pitchers to throw more fast balls, which gives batters better pitches to hit. The combination of quick, artificial turf and the influx of new players with sprinters' speed, has significantly changed the way baseball is played and managed.

Although speed is a great asset to a base runner, alertness and sliding ability are equally important. The outstanding base runner is not only quick with his feet, but is also expert at deciding when to and when not to steal. He is aggressive and full of hustle.

SPEED AND AGGRESSIVENESS

An aggressive offense will make the defense hurry its throws and make mistakes. I prefer my players to be the aggressive, daring type and occasionally take some chances. I feel that I can always slow them down, but it is tough to take a cautious base runner who runs scared and make him a daring ballplayer.

These fellows do not fit into the Dodger plans. We have had success with good and daring base running. There are times when we have been thrown out, but speed has been important to the Dodgers' success, possibly more important than anything else. I have never criticized anybody for being thrown out at third base or trying to steal a base within reason.

Fig. 3.1 AGGRESSIVE TACTICS BY BASE RUNNERS put the pressure on the defense. Any time a player can hustle and run fast, more pressure is placed on the defense. Ron LeFlore has the explosive speed that causes pitchers to lose their concentration.

I still believe speed will win more games than will too many slow-footed, home run hitters. If you have both, it's great, but there are not many players like Willie Mays and Mickey Mantle. Of course, the score is the big factor. When we are three or four runs behind, we do not like to take chances. However, in ordinary circumstances, when we are one run ahead or one behind and the game situation permits, I prefer my base runners to take chances (Fig. 3.2).

Aggressive base running pays off. It is more or less inborn, too. Some base runners are just timid and afraid. Others become lazy and then wonder why they are thrown out by one step.

Baseball games can be won or lost through good or poor base running. There is nothing more frustrating for a manager than seeing his team rap out a whole flock of hits, but because of poor base running failing to score the runs

Fig. 3.2 DARING, AGGRESSIVE BASE RUNNING enabled Paul Molitor to score for the Milwaukee Brewers. While more base runners are using the head-first slide, the player is more vulnerable to injuries, particularly when sliding into the catcher.

they should. Then, again, there are few aspects of baseball more exciting than a hustling ball club that knows how to run the bases. The importance of good base running is obvious—more base hits, fewer double plays, more extra base hits, and many other advantages.

While aggressive base running can win ball games, being overly aggressive to the point of foolishness can also be costly. As Tim McCarver put it, "If you are going to credit speed for stealing runs, you must also discredit speed when it consistently takes you out of innings. What may have been a big inning is not."

An aggressive offense will make the defense hurry their throws and make mistakes.

REVIVAL OF BASE STEALING

Base running had been a neglected art until Maury Wills arrived on the major league scene with the Dodgers in 1959. The long ball had dominated the game for years, and because of the lively ball managers were reluctant to place too much emphasis on the running game. Rather than employ such tactics as base stealing, hit and run, and bunting, they were inclined to wait for someone to hit the ball out of the park. Except for Luis Aparicio's 56 steals in 1959, no major leaguer stole more than 40 bases in a year throughout the 1950s. Until Wills stole 104 bases in 1962, nobody in either league had stolen 70 bases in a season since Ty Cobb stole 96 in 1915.

The fleet-footed Maury soon established himself as one of the great base runners in the game's history and, more than any other figure in baseball, helped bring about a return of the exciting running game. Maury made a science of getting as big a lead as possible. He always told me that if he could get back to the base standing up, his lead wasn't big enough.

Wills and Lou Brock of the St. Louis Cardinals were the premier base stealers in the 1960s. They restored base stealing to an art form. Brock, who broke Maury's record in 1974 with 118 steals, holds the major league record for career stolen bases with 938.

In 1972, Brock realized that getting as big a lead as possible was not necessarily the best approach to stealing second base. He realized that a little bit of momentum is worth much more than a little more distance. As a result, Brock developed a rolling start that provided even more impetus to the modern running game.

Brock made a science of base stealing, breaking down his leads into precise numbers of steps, calculating how long it takes a ball to go from the pitcher to catcher to second base—under optimum conditions, 2.9 seconds. Lou reacted to numerous keys and three-movement deliveries.

The three most important facets in being a top base stealer, according to Brock, are:

1. Acceleration from the start
2. Power-running
3. Acceleration within the slide

"I had two of three," said Lou. "I could run with power and had good acceleration."

In 1982, Rickey Henderson of the Oakland A's shattered Brock's single-season record of 188 by stealing second base on a pitch out thrown by Doc Medich of the Milwauke Brewers. On his run for the record, Henderson stole second 88 times, third 32 times, and home plate twice. He also set another record: Most times caught trying to steal, 39. Of his total "caught stealings," 13 came from pick-off plays. Brock was thrown out 33 times in his record season.

Brock believes Rickey Henderson's shortcoming is acceleration in the slide. Lou, who is not particularly fond of the head-first slide, explained that "You're vulnerable ... to spikes, knees, what-have-you. If you look at his hands, you'll see all kinds of cuts."

Although the home run is still baseball's foremost attraction, the daring, aggressive play of Wills, Brock, Henderson, and others has made major league teams more conscious of base stealing. Their success on the base paths has brought increased emphasis on base stealing and speed, providing the national pastime with added thrills and excitement (Fig. 3.3).

Speed and quickness

The Dodgers have more or less insisted that the players they sign have speed. We still consider speed to be a requisite, and it always will be in this game. The game of baseball needs speed. Although I like to have some home runs too, I still believe that speed is the dominant factor, defensively as well as offensively.

When the Dodgers bring up a young player with exceptional speed, the manager is not afraid to turn him loose in a steal situation. This is because he has been through our training camp and has been instructed about getting leads and stealing bases.

Instinct and reflexes

Good instincts and reflexes are also characteristics of top base runners—to react without giving it much thought and do the right thing automatically. In deciding to take an extra base on a hit, the coach really cannot tell a player whether or not to go. If a fellow thinks he can make it, he goes ahead and runs.

Fig. 3.3 GREAT BASE STEALERS have the ability to create "turmoil" in a game once they get on base. When they get on base, pitchers are so concerned about them stealing they make mistakes, while catchers have a tendency to rush their throws. Rickey Henderson, left, who set a major league record in 1982 by stealing 130 bases, demonstrates exceptional concentration and balance as he waits for the first indication the pitcher will throw to the plate. He keeps his eyes constantly on the pitcher. On the right, the hustle and aggressiveness of Maury Wills forced Bud Harrelson of the Mets to hurry his throw to first.

With other players, the manager or coach has to tell them, but there is just so much he can tell a base runner.

A ball player can be a good base runner and not necessarily have great speed. The main thing is quickness, speed of foot and quickness in deciding when to and when not to go—and getting a good break.

Mental approach

The proper mental approach is essential in becoming a successful base runner. When stealing a base, the player has to believe that he can make it. He must eliminate the fear of failing.

"In stealing a base, confidence, to me, is 80 percent of the battle," said Maury, "because I know I can run, have knowledge of the pitcher and know how to get a good lead. I feel I am better than the pitcher and the catcher, and I eliminate all fears of failing. I am not afraid to be picked off, and I am not afraid to be thrown out trying to steal a base. I just feel I am going to make it at all times."

Discipline is a key in base stealing. Base runners must be able to think as well as run.

"A player cannot be a good base runner and practice safety first," advised Wills; "he must take chances. He should not be careless, but he has to be daring. My success in base running can be attributed to the fact that I have eliminated the fear of failure."

Knowledge of the pitcher

The runner must know the pitcher, and the moves he is going to make. He should also know the catcher's arm. When taking a lead, the runner knows just how far he can go. He wants to keep the pitcher on the defensive at all times.

Even before they leave the dugout, players should watch the pitcher closely, studying his moves to the plate when he has men on base. As a player moves to the on-deck circle, he should continue to watch the pitcher and study the game situation.

Game situation

The base runner is controlled by the game situation. The number of outs, the score, the ability of the base runner, who is pitching and who the hitter is at the plate, and the arms of the fielders are all factors that determine whether or not he should attempt to advance.

RUNNING TO FIRST BASE

Base running begins at home plate. Batters should learn to swing so that they can recover their balance quickly in heading for first base; if the ball is hit on the ground, the concern of the batter is to cross the bag as quickly as possible.

In his prime, Mickey Mantle got down to first base in 3.9 seconds batting right-handed and 3.75 to 3.8 seconds batting left-handed. If a right-handed hitter can get to first in 4.2 seconds, you can say he has good speed. The Expos have clocked Tim Raines to first in 3.57 seconds from the right side; left-handed he has been in the 3.4s.

The most important thing is to get every player to run as hard as he can as soon as he hits the ball (Fig. 3.4). Ball players have to run only four or five times in a game, and yet when a ball player hits a one-hopper to the shortstop

Fig. 3.4 BASE RUNNING BEGINS AT HOME PLATE. No matter what side of the plate he swings from, the batter should try to take his first step with the rear foot. Observe that Billy Grabarkewitz's body has not pulled away from the plate following his swing.

or second baseman, and it looks like an easy out, many players will not give 100 percent going down to first base.

This is the first mistake the base runner makes, because anybody can kick or drop a ball; even a first baseman can drop one occasionally. To run hard from the moment he hits the ball is not asking too much of a player. In fact, that is what the fans expect, and he should do it. One of my pet peeves comes when runners do not give their very best.

The second fault of a base runner is watching the ball. Many batters keep watching the ball on a base hit. It is all right to take a quick glance at the ball to see where it is going, but once he has decided it is a base hit, the best thing to do is to go to first base as fast as possible and make his turn! Pepper Martin was one of the greatest players I have ever seen rounding first base, and he would start toward second as though he were going to make it. Then he would "slide his wheels," so to speak, and go back.

No matter what side of the plate he swings from, a batter should try to take his first step with the rear foot (Fig. 3.5). As the right-handed hitter starts his swing, his body does not pull away from the plate. His stride is directly toward first base, with his rear foot, as he drops his bat with his left hand. The left-handed hitter takes a full stride with his rear foot as he drops the bat with his right hand.

The runner should go hard for first, looking only at the bag, unless the first base coach signals and yells that it is "through" and to "take your turn." The runner tries to hit first base without a jump, stepping on the center of the base

Fig. 3.5 SPEED AND HUSTLE. Batters should learn to swing so that they can recover their balance quickly in heading for first base. In this exciting series of pictures, the speed of Willie Davis is able to turn a slow dribbler into a base hit by beating the pitcher's throw to first base. The runner should go hard for first base, looking only at the bag. He tries to hit first base without a jump.

Fig. 3.6 ROUNDING FIRST BASE. On a base hit, the batter begins circling toward first base by swerving to his right. Ideally, he should hit the inside part with his inside foot. He uses the inside corner of the base as a push-off point toward second base (Billy Grabarkewitz).

as he crosses it. This is safer than hitting the front edge of the base with the toe.

Some players, on the last step to first base, take a big, high jump. This should never be done. You lose time and while your foot is in the air, the ball will beat you. Even though a continuous run is best, there is no use in running far past first. The runner should slow down and listen for his base coach.

ROUNDING FIRST BASE

When the batter sees that his hit has gone through or over the infield, he should approach first base at full speed, turning into the bag so that one of his feet hits the inside corner (Fig. 3.6).

I do not like a player to take the big, wide turn at first base. Rather, the runner should head directly for first base and approximately fifteen feet from the bag, he should move three to five feet out into foul territory and prepare for a "tight, well-controlled turn." He should hit the inside part with his inside foot, but if he cannot we do not like him to break his stride. He should hit the base with either foot that comes in stride. As he hits the base from the inside, he should turn as sharply as he can and head for second and keep going until he either sees that he cannot make it or somebody stops him.

Ideally, the runner should keep his body leaning toward the infield and use the inside corner of the base as a push-off point toward second base. It is also easier to hit the base with the inside foot, with the right foot then crossing over. However, I do not want a runner to break stride in order to hit the base with his inside foot.

Fig. 3.7 A GOOD READY STANCE. In taking his lead, the runner at first base should be in a slight crouch with his arms hanging loosely in front of him. His weight should be evenly distributed on the balls of his feet, so he can go either way (Tony Armas).

THE LEAD OFF

The base runner has to be alert when he is at first base. First, he must look and see whether the coach has a sign for him to take. He should keep one foot on the bag when he gets his signals (Fig. 3.7). He should also check the positions of the outfielders, to see whether they are playing in. He must know the strength and accuracy of the catcher's throwing arm and what kind of a move the pitcher has. This is the type of knowledge that can make a player a more effective base runner.

The runner must determine how large a lead he can take and still get back to the base. He must know the pitcher, his habits and manners, and his ability to pick the runner off base. Studying the pitchers continuously, every day, is the thing that will help him steal bases.

Stance

The runner at first base should stand facing the pitcher, legs slightly bent, with his feet about a foot and a half apart. He should crouch a bit and let his arms hang loosely in front of him. His weight should be evenly distributed. He should be on the balls of his feet, so that he can go either way (Fig. 3.7).

Some base runners get picked off base because they are leaning toward second base. Their balance is not sufficient to make a forceful dive back to first base. *The runner must keep his eyes on the pitcher at all times.* He is waiting for the first indication that the pitcher will throw to the plate, and not to first base. He should not jump back and forth. The pitcher may catch him going the wrong way.

GETTING THE LEAD

Base runners, as a rule, are told to get a "good lead." Instead, they should become proficient with time-measured leads, such as twelve, thirteen, and fourteen foot leads at first base and eighteen feet as the starting point off second. The factor that determines the length of the lead is: "Can I beat the throw to the bag?" Runners who react quickly can afford to take longer leads.

Scouts tell me that the Expos' Raines just outruns the ball. If he gets his standard fifteen foot lead-off, Tim can steal second base in 3.3 seconds. Consider that a good pitcher takes 1.4 seconds from a stretch position to deliver the ball 60 feet, 6 inches to home plate, and a good catcher takes two seconds to receive the ball and throw it the 127 feet, 3⅜ inches to second base—a time span of 3.4 seconds, not quick enough to get a speedster like Raines.

The length of the lead depends on the game situation. If it is early in the game and our runners have not seen the pitcher's moves, we tell our players: "If you are not going to steal and you want to see what kind of move he has, make him throw over there by more or less getting a good sized lead." This should be a "one-way lead." As he takes a longer lead, the player is leaning back a little toward first. Now the pitcher will throw over there a time or two, and the runner will have an opportunity to study his different moves, particularly his shoulders.

In taking his lead, the base runner should always advance his right foot first and then his left foot, keeping both feet close to the ground (Fig. 3.8).

There are all types of pitchers who have really good moves to first base.

Fig. 3.8 GETTING A LEAD. The runner should get his lead by advancing his right foot first, followed by his left foot. Both feet should be kept close to the ground (Billy Grabarkewitz).

Yet, when they deliver the ball, the delivery is so slow that the good base runner steals on them, in spite of a good move. While a runner cannot take much of a lead, he can still steal the base when the pitcher is delivering the ball because of the slowness of the delivery.

Then, there is the other kind of pitcher who has a quick delivery but not a good move to first base. With a pitcher like this, the runner has to take a longer lead because he does not have as much time during the delivery.

Returning to first base

When the pitcher steps on the rubber, the base runner should take a lead just far enough so that he will be able to get back in time to beat any throw. Some base runners will assume such a big lead that they are forced to dive or slide back to the base. Maury felt that, unless he had to dive back into first base, he did not take a good enough lead. I think this is all right for Maury, who, of course, has base running down to the fine points. When an experienced base-runner like Wills does it, he knows how far he can go and still get back safely. The college or high school boy who tries to do this, however, may get himself picked off.

The runner returns to first base by stepping back on the base with his left foot, and his body leans away from the first baseman. For most base runners, this is the proper way of returning to the bag (Fig. 3.9).

In leading off second base, the runner can take a longer lead. He should always listen for the base coach. In taking a lead, he should always advance his right foot first and slide his left foot, keeping both feet close to the ground. He

Fig. 3.9 RETURNING TO FIRST BASE, the runner steps back onto the base with his left foot, swinging toward right field with his right foot. This elusive action enables him to lean away from the first baseman (Billy Grabarkewitz).

should make sure that a ball hit to the shortstop goes through before going to third base.

One-way lead

The base runner uses the one-way lead when trying to determine the length of lead he can take on the pitcher. He tries to make the pitcher throw to first so he can find out a little more about him.

The stance is similar to the normal stance, except that most of the body weight is on the back foot (left). Therefore, the runner is "leaning" back toward the base.

"I take an exaggerated lead toward second base," stated Maury, "and my weight is shifted to the point where I am ready to go back to first base, regardless of what move the pitcher makes. If he goes home, my first move is still back to first base, and I can still recover in time."

Occasionally, a base runner is caught leaning. Quite likely, his balance was not sufficient to make a forceful dive back to first base.

When the runner has determined how much of a lead he can take safely and is flashed the "steal" signal, then he assumes the two-way lead.

Two-way lead

With the two-way lead, the runner can go in either direction, depending on the pitcher's move. He does not take quite as long a lead as in the one-way lead. The runner must keep his weight evenly distributed on the balls of the feet and his body in a crouched position, with the knees slightly bent.

"From this position, I take as big a lead as I can," said Wills. "Sometimes I take a big enough lead so that I am forced to dive or slide back to the base when a pick-off is attempted by the pitcher."

Walking lead

In this lead, the runner walks off first base casually as the pitcher is taking his set position. Lou Brock used the walking lead very effectively. Just as the pitcher indicated his intention to throw to the plate, he would break for second base, without coming to a stop—his famous rolling start.

The walking lead enables base runners at first to get a good start or jump toward second base. Since the body is moving in that direction, experienced pitchers will make the runner come to a stop. This, of course, spoils the walking lead.

GETTING THE GOOD JUMP

A good jump is the key to stealing bases. A jump is leaving for the next base the instant the pitcher commits himself to delivering the ball to the plate. A good jump is worth two-tenths of a second. Instead of taking a seventeen-foot lead and attracting numerous throws, outstanding basestealers like Rickey Henderson and Tim Raines are more comfortable taking a fourteen or fifteen foot lead, and getting a better jump.

The expert base runner gets the jump on the pitcher by studying his moves and personal mannerisms. Some pitchers have all sorts of telltale things that they do. By watching him closely, the runner can spot the pitcher's peculiar little habits, which will give the runner the jump he needs. The runner should study how the pitcher lifts his foot and how he comes around with his arm. He should look for a hunch of the shoulders, a move of the elbow. Some pitchers drop their shoulder a little. Whatever he looks for, the base runner should remember to be subtle in his looking.

"One of the indications is when a pitcher stands with an open shoulder," claimed Wills. "When he is ready to throw toward home, his shoulder is usually on a line to the plate. If he wants to pick me off, he usually turns more toward first."

Sometimes when a pitcher goes to first base with the ball, he stands with his feet a little closer together, or maybe the other way around. Maury likes to watch the elbow and the head. Willie Mays says he watches the pitcher's head. Others study the pitcher's feet, since the feet reveal first where the pitcher will throw.

If the pitcher commits himself with a move toward the batter, he has to throw home or a *balk* is called. As soon as the runner sees the pitcher start his pitch, he can be off and running.

TAKING-OFF

The base runner should break for the base at the precise second the pitcher begins his move to the plate. Most runners prefer their first move toward second base to be a cross-over step. When they decide to go, they just pivot on the right foot and cross-over with the back foot. They should shove off for second on the left foot while pivoting on the right foot. One's weight should be forward with his legs driving hard (Fig. 3.10).

In shoving off for second, the runner should swing his left arm toward the next base in the same way a boxer throws an uppercut. This helps him cross over. The arm action pulls his body around and enables him to take a good first stride with his left foot.

"I always remember to keep my body moving," said Wills. "A runner can get away faster when he is in motion rather than standing still. I shuffle back and forth, bending my knees and trying to keep my weight on the balls of my feet. When the pitcher starts for the plate, I start for second."

Fig. 3.10 TAKING OFF FOR SECOND. After getting a good lead, Maury Wills pivots on the ball of his right foot. His first move is a cross-over step with his left foot. Keeping his weight on the balls of his feet, he lifts the heel of his right foot, which enables him to make his pivot smoothly and quickly. Observe Maury's hard shoulder and hip rotation which gets everything moving in the same direction.

Most base runners prefer their first move toward second base to be a cross-over step.

MAURY WILLS

Is it easier to steal third base than to steal second base? It is easier to steal third than second because pitchers do not watch the runners on second as much as they used to. Infielders also do not bother runners like they once did.

"The only time a player should steal third base," said Wills, "is when he is positive he can make it. This is because second base is considered scoring position. To be thrown out trying to steal third base when a player is already in scoring position is a very bad play.

"Of course, it is much better to be on third base than second base because there are nine more ways a player can score from third than from second."

Touching the bases

The base runner should never have to slow down to make a turn or to change strides in order to touch the bag with a certain foot. The beginning of the turn should be made from twenty to thirty feet in front of the bag.

Tagging up on a fly

The runner should have his left foot on third, with the right foot pointing toward home plate. His body should face the field, with the weight on his front foot.

He goes when the outfielder catches the ball. He should not depend on the third base coach to yell, "Go!" Some players prefer a position similar to a sprinter. When on third base, the runner should tag up on any ball hit in the air, even on all foul balls.

HOW TO RUN

Perhaps the fundamental least stressed and one of the most important in baseball is the art of running. While nature has endowed human beings with a basic speed, additional speed can often be obtained simply by executing the basic principles of running.

A runner should keep his head up so he can see the play. Arching his neck, he leans forward without swaying or weaving. All his motion should be straight ahead. His chin should be up and his eyes on the base to which he is running. His arms should be bent at the elbow and relaxed, and the forearm should move directly forward and backward beside the body. The faster the arms are pumped, the faster the legs will move. Taking a good stride, he should run naturally on the balls of his feet.

Most good runners swing the arm forward so that the hand swings almost as high as the shoulder, and then to the rear and to the side of the hip. The right arm should go forward with the left leg, and the left arm with the right leg.

BREAKING UP THE DOUBLE PLAY

A base runner often has the responsibility of breaking up a possible double play. When sliding into second base, the purpose is not to injure the infielder but only to unbalance him and thus prevent an accurate throw to first base. Breaking up the double play, however, is illegal now in high school and college ball. Increasing efforts have been made to prevent injury at second base. Limitations have been imposed on the types of slides, rolls, blocks, etc. into second base.

The runner on first base, of course, has to run hard to get to second base. Even then, on a fast double play, he does not always get there in time. In certain double play situations where the runner has time to get there, he should slide into the shortstop or second baseman, whoever is fielding the ball. While we do not want to hurt anybody intentionally, we want this runner to slide into the legs of the infielder and try to upset him. He should use a hard slide with the knees bent at a 45-degree angle, and try to hook the striding foot of the infielder.

If the shortstop should move far across the base and toward right field, the base runner should slide after him, rather than the bag. This is an accepted practice in baseball. Of course, the shortstop has the advantage. He knows whether he will cross the bag or stay in the inside, while the runner does not know. The only thing the runner can do is *guess* which side he will go on, and slide into him and try to knock his feet from under him.

The base runner must remember that the slide must be such that some part of the runner is within reaching distance of the bag. The runner could be charged with interference if he slides more than three feet out of the base line to hit the pivot man or if he deliberately interferes with the throw.

USE OF BASE COACHES

Whenever base runners cannot see the ball or a fielder without turning their heads very much, they should use their base coaches. They should use their own judgment as to whether or not to advance whenever they can see the ball or the fielder easily.

Runners use the first base coach for decisions on stopping at first, making the turn at first, going on to second, or hurrying back to first. They use the third base coach for stopping at second, rounding it, or going onto third, as well as directions at third base.

The third base coach gets blamed for a lot of running situations over which he really does not have control. Actually, the only time he does is when a man is on first and the ball is hit down to first base and on down the right field foul line. This is when the runner has to take a quick look at the third base coach to see whether he should go or not. About twenty to thirty feet from second base, he should cut out and at the same time glance at the third base coach, then go from there. Basically, though, the runner is on his own.

Anytime the play is right in front of the runner, such as in left field, he has a better idea then someone else as to whether he can go on to third base. As long as the play is *in front of* him, he should be on his own.

The third base coach might walk up and say: "Now that you are on third, we want you to go in on a ground ball," or, "Make the ball go through the infield," or, "Be sure to take off on a fly ball," and the like. Basically, though, the runner plays *himself* and is pretty much on his own.

Practice Tips for the Base Runner

1. Practice getting starts on all hit balls.
2. At every opportunity, practice getting leads and starts off all bases.
3. Practice your jump in leaving first using the pivot and the cross-over push step.
4. During pre-game batting practice, practice this routine after your last swing in the batting cage: run to first, take your turn, hold up, get your

lead, and break for second as the pitcher makes his pitch to the next hitter.

5. Practice taking a full swing, then follow through and try to keep from falling toward third base at the finish.

6. Practice leading off a base. Back off the bag with your rear leg behind your right. Then shuffle off to get the desired length—eight to ten feet.

Base Running Reminders

1. Where is the ball?
2. How many outs are there?
3. Look for a possible sign.
4. Do not talk to the opposing infielders.
5. Always run with your head up.
6. Touch all bases.
7. Watch the runner in front of you.
8. When in doubt, always slide.

SLIDING

A good base runner has to be able to slide, and this comes with practice. Furthermore, he must be able to slide on either his left or right side, as well as go straight in. The sooner young players learn that "it is a slide and not a leap," the sooner they will become proficient base runners.

Sliding is really controlled falling. The runner simply drops to the ground according to the slide desired, and the momentum of his run does the rest.

We stress the bent-leg slide because we feel it is the most effective slide in baseball. The bent-leg slide is the safest slide for a base runner, and the top foot is going directly to the bag as quickly as it can. When a runner executes the hook slide and reaches out with his foot and tries to catch the base with his toe, he has to go an extra distance to get to the bag.

When one considers that the bent leg also enables the runner to pop up and run, the value of this slide becomes apparent.

"The pop-up (also known as stand-up) is so much faster than other slides and you get to the base quicker," said Frankie Crosetti, former shortstop and third base coach of the New York Yankees. "Roger Maris and Mickey Mantle had it down pat. They hit the dirt close to the bag, wasted no time at all, and were up and running on a bad throw."

Because of the success Pete Rose, Rickey Henderson, and other big-leaguers have had with the head-first slide, more high school and college coaches are encouraging their players to use it. Both head-first and feet-first slides have strong and weak points. Therefore, other factors should be considered, such as:

1. Which slide will permit the player to get to his feet the quickest in the event of an overthrow?
2. Which slide will avoid the tag more effectively?
3. Which slide is least likely to cause injury?

Timing is essential for a good slide. The slide must not start too soon or too late, and the slider should keep relaxed when hitting the ground. As he goes into his slide, he should clench his hands loosely to avoid broken fingers. He must keep his head back and arms up. Once he decides to slide, he must go through with it. *He should never change his mind!*

There is a proper way to fall, of course: a controlled fall, rather than a jump, which makes the slider "strawberry" prone and subject to bruises. On the bent-leg slide, most players like to take the blow all the way from the calf of their leg up to their thigh so the fall will not be concentrated on one spot.

A player has to have confidence in his ability to slide. To overcome any fear, he should practice in a sliding pit or on soft grass.

Some of the better sliders in the major leagues are capable of watching the fielder to see which side of the base he is going to field the ball on, and they will slide accordingly. During spring training, we work on this point in the sliding pits. Somebody will toss a ball each time a runner comes in, and some of the throws will be on one side of the bag and some on the other. If the slider sees that the ball is on the left side of the bag, he will slide to the right.

On several occasions, I can remember losing important runs because a player could not slide on both sides. All he had to do was slide away from the play coming into third base, but he could not, and it cost us. *A player is just as good as the time he devotes to practice.* Only constant practice will make a player perfect in sliding.

The bent-leg slide is the safest and most effective slide in baseball.

BERNIE DeVIVEIROS

Bent-leg slide

The bent-leg slide is the safest slide in baseball and the most popular. Young players can become proficient quickly in this method of sliding. Along with the safety factor, it has the advantage of allowing the base runner to spring up quickly, ready to run if the ball goes through. Another advantage of the bent-leg is the fact that the base runner can get to the bag the quickest possible way (Fig. 3.11).

Fig. 3.11 BENT-LEG SLIDE. In addition to being the safest slide in baseball, the bent leg enables the base runner to spring up quickly, ready to run if the ball goes through (Billy Grabarkewitz).

The bent-leg slide is the most practical one because it permits a side approach when the runner must be tagged, and a front approach on force plays. In high school baseball, where erratic throwing is more common than in professional ball, the bent-leg slide can be a great asset.

We have an occasional problem when players come down with a stiff arm to lighten their fall; they sometimes get a bruised hand or a stiff elbow. The ideal way to execute the bent-leg slide is to come in with both hands in the air. If the player can learn to take the weight of the fall on the bent leg and all the way up to the thigh, he will not get a "strawberry" or a bruise through the force of the slide.

Some players like to put dirt in their hands so that, if they slide, they do so with a closed fist. When they put their hands down, they will hit on a closed fist rather than on fingers.

The most recognized authority on the bent-leg slide is Bernie DeViveiros, former major league infielder and now a scout with the Detroit Tigers. For many years, one of DeViveiros's springtime duties with the Tigers was teaching the rudiments of the bent-leg slide to every player in the system.

The base runner should be able to slide on both sides, although it is more natural for 99 out 100 players to slide on just one leg. With the bent-leg, the side he slides on is not as important as it is with the hook slide, where he is fading away from the throw one way or the other.

The following are coaching points in learning the bent-leg slide:

1. Start to slide at least nine to ten feet from the bag. *Do not slide late!*
2. Take off from either leg (whichever is most natural) and bend it under.
3. Slide only on the calf of the bent leg, which must be the bottom leg.
4. Just sit down, and nature will put the correct leg under.
5. Keep low to the ground. Do not leap or jump.

6. Throw the head back as both legs bend, thus preventing the knees from hitting the ground first.

7. Turn the instep of the bottom foot so that it is facing the direction of the slide (preventing the spikes from catching in the ground).

8. Always tag with the top leg, which is raised well off the ground and is held loosely and relaxed.

9. Keep the knee slightly bent and the heel off the ground.

10. Just ride the calf of the bottom leg at all times. Use it as a wheel.

Pop-up slide and run

Figure 3.12 shows Danny Cater executing the pop-up slide. Notice that he slides on his side and braces the bag with his right leg. Fundamentally, this is the correct side for the pop-up slide because it provides greater speed in pushing-off for the next base, particularly at third base. However, in sliding into second base, most base runners wisely prefer to fade away from the throw,

Fig. 3.12 BENT-LEG SLIDE, POP-UP. As he comes in contact with the base, the runner should brace the bent leg. The runner then rolls inward on his left knee, rising to an upright position. Aided by the speed of his slide, the runner is then ready to continue on to the next base (Danny Cater).

which moves them toward the right field side of the bag (Fig 3.12). Thus, the most effective and natural side is their right one.

As Cater slides along with speed, he lifts himself up. His left leg remains bent until his right foot contacts the base. Some base runners are able to come up to an upright position by pushing off their left hand. Most coaches, however, instruct their players to keep their hands up in the air to prevent injury.

Hook slide

The hook slide is used by a runner primarily to avoid being tagged by a fielder. It can be made to either side of the base. However, we try to stay away from the hook slide, using it only in a special situation in which the runner must evade a tag (Fig. 3.13).

Fig. 3.13 A BRILLIANT, FADE-AWAY, HOOK SLIDE enabled Derrell Thomas to evade the tag of shortstop Doug Flynn of the New York Mets. As the body falls to the right side, most of the impact is absorbed on the right hip and the right thigh.

When the base runner hook slides and reaches out with that foot and tries to catch it with his toe, he is going ninety-three feet to get to the bag, rather than straight into it.

Branch Rickey, whose long career included outstanding work with the St. Louis Cardinals, Brooklyn Dodgers, and Pittsburgh Pirates, called the hook slide the "93-feet slide," because the body of the base runner has gone ninety-three feet and he has not touched the base yet. This is the disadvantage of the hook slide.

The Dodgers discourage the use of the "93-foot slide," by teaching all players to extend both feet when attempting the hook slide.

When hook sliding to the right, the take-off is usually off the left foot. Both legs are extended straight toward the base with the toes pointed, as the body falls to the right side. The right foot is slightly raised and to the right of the base. The body is almost in a flat position as the left foot and left toes touch the right corner of the base. Most of the impact is absorbed on the right hip and the right thigh.

If the runner can keep the touching foot straight as he comes in, and then it hooks, he will be all right. The key to the hook slide is to *keep the touching foot straight until the runner hits the bag.*

As he starts to hook slide into the bag, the runner must be sure that his catching foot, that is, the one that will touch the bag, does not bend. He must keep it pretty well straight out until he makes contact with the bag. Then, the foot stays on the bag as his body hooks on by. From the safety standpoint, the runner should be sure to get the left foot up so he does not jam it into the ground.

In sliding to his left, the runner should take off on his left foot. Both feet of the runner should be turned sideways to avoid catching the spikes in the ground. Both knees should be bent, with the weight of the upper part of the body thrown left and backward.

As he slides, the left foot should be forward and away from the base, the right leg bent and dragging, and the right foot turned so that the instep faces the base. The toes of the right foot should hook the near side of the base. While sliding, the left hand should be on the ground, palm down, to absorb some of the shock.

"Do not bend the hooking knee any more than is necessary to hook the base," said Wills. "The more the knee is bent, the longer it will take the player to touch the base."

Head-first slide

The head-first slide is being used more and more by base runners, with the idea that it is the quickest approach to the base. While few studies have been made as to which is faster, head-first or feet-first, the general feeling is that the head-first slide has the edge. The thinking is that with the head-first technique, the slider does not have to move his center of gravity back, but rather moves it forward in the direction of the slide.

The head-first slide technique is not difficult to execute. Sprinting to a point ten to twelve feet from the base, the runner takes off as if diving into a pool. His arms should be fully extended, as he reaches for the base with the dominant hand. His head is slightly up as he slides along on his chest (Fig. 3.14). To protect himself from injury, the slider should keep his fingers together and glide rather than bounce.

The head-first slide may be the quickest slide, but it leaves the player open to injury. However, I don't believe the head-first slide is as dangerous as it appears to be. Most of the danger is in the exposure of the hands, which can result in spike wounds. This danger may be outweighed by the fact that the slide may be a fraction of a second faster than feet first, since the body is already leaning forward while running. Another advantage is that the eyes are always on the bag.

"The head-first slide is dangerous if you don't know what you're doing," said Frankie Crosetti. "For one thing, you are easy to tag, and the fielder can drop his knee in front of the bag and block the runner from reaching the bag. I loved to see a runner come in head-first, although not many did that in my day."

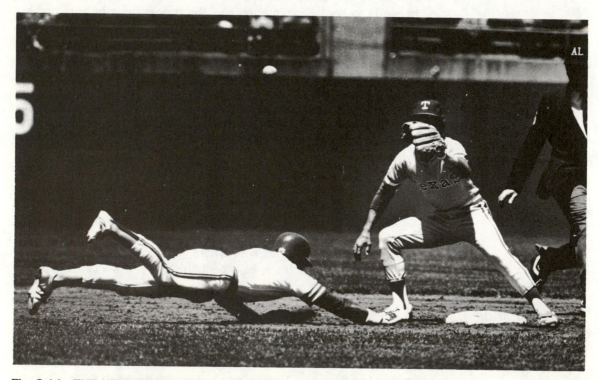

Fig. 3.14 THE HEAD-FIRST SLIDE is not a dive or leap, rather it is simply a gliding action. On the final thrust forward, the body must be low to the ground. Here Rickey Henderson, with his arms fully extended, has to dive back to second base.

"Of all the bases I stole, only one out of twenty-five I came in head-first," said Lou Brock. "The percentage is against it, and I can show you with a stopwatch. The only justification for coming in frontward is to avoid the tag. The shortstop or second baseman must tag a more narrow target."

Tips on sliding practice

A player has to have confidence in his ability to slide. To overcome any fear, he should practice in a sliding pit or on soft grass. When practicing on the grass, he should remove his spiked shoes or use tennis shoes. Sliding pads and practice pants should be used, with long nylon or khaki shorts making good pads. In the early stages, the bases should be loose.

Inexperienced sliders should start sliding at a short distance, to make sure that their legs can be bent. After the technique is mastered, the distance can be lengthened with an increase in speed. *Speed is important* in executing a good slide, but never forget: "You are just as good as the time you devote to practice."

Basic Sliding Rules

1. Once you decide to slide, go through with it. *Never change your mind!*
2. Make your slide with speed.
3. Remember, it is a slide and not a leap.
4. Learn to fall in a relaxed manner.
5. Concentrate on watching the base for the straight-in slide.
6. For hook sliding, concentrate mainly on the hands of the fielder.
7. On all force plays, employ a bent-leg slide.
8. Clench your hands loosely when sliding, to avoid broken fingers. *Stay relaxed!*
9. Any deliberate attempt on the part of a runner to spike or injure his opponent should *never* be tolerated.

4

Pitching

In pitching, the name of the game is getting the ball over the plate with good stuff on it. These are still the essentials for pitching success. The better the stuff, the less important the control, providing the base on balls is not a factor.

In looking over a young pitching prospect, major league scouts want to see that fast one move a little with good velocity. They want a boy who can throw hard because this is one thing they cannot teach a pitcher to do. With the excellent coaching of today, most pitchers with a good fast ball can be taught the other pitches. It is difficult to improve the fast ball very much unless the pitcher is doing something mechanically wrong in the delivery.

When I think of the pitching game, I think first of proper mechanics and control. Lack of control is generally the result of poor mechanics. Unless his mechanism is good, with everything working together, the pitcher will find it difficult to be "in a groove."

With the tendency for pitchers to throw additional pitches, such as the slider, screwball, and a variety of changes, I think good mechanics are even more important.

There are three physical elements to a pitch. Velocity, movement, and location—and the least important of these is velocity. Pitching is location. A pitcher may have overwhelming stuff, but if he can't put the ball where he wants to, he will not be successful. A pitcher should also learn the value of changing speeds and varying the tempo to keep hitters off balance.

How can a young pitcher master control? There is only one solution: prac-

Fig. 4.1 CY YOUNG AWARD WINNER Fernando Valenzuela has the same motion on every pitch. His delivery is the same, whether he is throwing a fast ball or his famous screwball. Perhaps Fernando's most impressive quality is his coolness when he is in trouble.

tice and more practice. Not just throwing the ball, but throwing the ball *to a target.* Control comes to different people at different times. Sandy Koufax, for example, had to work very hard to get his control, but after years of frustration Sandy finally found the key. He discovered the method that put rhythm into his delivery, but it came only by working constantly, with Coach Joe Becker at his side.

Deception is another big factor in the make-up of a successful pitcher. Along with control and a strong, live arm, many authorities believe the key to pitching is deceiving the hitter. Confusing the hitter by throwing the ball at different speeds with the same motion, hiding it until the last possible moment, and using good judgment in the selection of pitches are other factors that can increase the pitcher's effectiveness.

Along with the physical aspects of pitching, mental attitude is essential to the success of a moundsman. Like his teammates, he must have confidence in himself, a positive feeling that he can do it. He must have a mental attitude that says, "I know I can do it." He must not let a bad pitch or a lost game discourage him.

Command and poise are qualities possessed by the great pitchers in baseball. These pitchers have complete command of their actions in regard to their pitching mechanics. A pitcher has to have complete confidence that he will get them out, that he is better than the hitter. He must be in complete control.

I like to see a young pitcher concentrate on what he is trying to do. Whenever he throws the ball, he should have an idea where he wants to throw it. He has to block out everything except the job he is doing—getting the batter out. He must be alert all the time.

RHYTHM AND TIMING

Proper rhythm and timing are the basis of successful pitching. The purpose of rhythm and timing is to generate speed and momentum in the pitching arm. When a pitcher is throwing "heat," his timing is just right. On his off days, when his fast ball is just mediocre, he gives the impression of pushing or pulling the ball up to the plate.

Proper rhythm and timing can be achieved by developing good balance and body control, which enable the pitcher to transfer his weight at the proper time and create a consistent point of release. Arm speed and body momentum can be realized by getting the arm on top of the pitch—before the striding foot hits the ground.

The pitching greats of baseball, those who have stood up over a long period of time, display excellent rhythm and timing. Tom Seaver, Jim Palmer, Steve Carlton, and Jerry Reuss are modern-day hurlers who typify well coordinated pitching deliveries.

To have good rhythm and timing, a pitcher's gears have to be meshed. It is a case of meshing the arm and upper body with the striding leg and lower body. The upper and lower halves of the body should come through simulta-

Fig. 4.2 PITCHING GEM. Len Barker, hard-throwing right-hander of the Cleveland Indians, displays the form that enabled him to pitch a 3–0 perfect game, May 15, 1981, over the Toronto Blue Jays. Barker's flawless string of 27 outs was the 12th perfect game in major league history.

neously like the parts of a machine working together. The result will be action with power.

The greatest problem of most pitchers is rushing the delivery. If the body weight moves out in front too soon, a "rushing arm action" will develop, bringing about control problems and inconsistent power. Generally, when the leg stride is too quick, the pitcher has rushed his pitch, or his upper body is too slow. If the striding foot hits the ground and the throwing arm is way back, a pitcher has a pulling motion instead of action with power.

The solution is to keep the weight back during the pivot until the pitching arm gets up on top. This will set the stage for the arm and body to come through at the same time (Fig. 4.2). In simple terms, weight retention actually means, "Don't run off and leave your arm." When the striding foot lands, the throwing arm is up on top in the proper position for delivering the ball on a downward plane.

ESSENTIALS OF PITCHING

The three things we look for in young pitchers are ability to throw hard, a good live ball, and control. One has to have a good arm. Most big-league scouts use a grading system, and they look for the fellow who has an adequate major league fast ball. Control, the other top requirement, is perhaps the hardest fundamental to teach. Control means more than just throwing the ball into the strike zone. It means moving the ball around, in and out, up and down, keeping the batter constantly off balance. As he progresses in experience and skill, a pitcher will learn how to go to work on the hitter, trying to make him hit his best pitch.

Basically, I like my pitchers to keep the ball low. Most hitters like the ball up and out over the plate, which means "belt-high" and on up to the letters. However, if the pitcher can keep the ball down, he is less likely to get hurt with the exception of low ball hitters.

A winning pitcher is one who throws hard, has good control, competitive attitude, good stuff, keeps the ball down, and fields his position well.

Another requirement for successful pitching is that the pitcher have some off-speed pitches and be able to get them over. With hitting being so dependent on timing, off-speed pitches, such as a straight change or taking a little off the curve, can be highly effective. This is especially true today, when so many players are at the end of the bat. The harder they swing, the easier they sometimes are to fool with an off-speed pitch. The off-speed pitch does not strike the man out too often, but it will take some of his power and timing away.

What type of physical size do Dodger scouts look for in a pitcher? I prefer a well-built boy, with a long arm and supple muscles. Drysdale, perhaps, was the ideal size, although a pitcher does not have to be six feet three inches or six feet four inches. Drysdale had long, slender arms, the kind that do not become muscle-bound and provide the real good stuff on the ball. Tom Seaver, at six feet one inch and 205 pounds, has demonstrated not only explosive power but the strength and stamina to go all the way.

A pitcher should use a style of his own and throw naturally, providing, of course, he is not doing something fundamentally wrong. The arm angle, particularly, should be one which feels most comfortable and natural. The three-quarter overhand delivery is used most because it is the most natural delivery for the majority of pitchers (Fig. 4.3).

The thrust off the mound and quick arm movement are the prime sources of speed.

Fig. 4.3 AN EFFICIENT PITCHING DELIVERY is one that seems to flow in a smooth, full-arm swing, finishing with a powerful snap of the wrist. In the pictures above, Jerry Reuss demonstrates very efficient weight retention during the pivot, which allowed his pitching arm and body to come through at the same time. This helps to prevent a "rushing arm action." Notice that Jerry keeps his eye on the catcher's target throughout his delivery.

To be a winning pitcher, a player has to have control of the pitches he has.

SANDY KOUFAX

THE BASIC PITCHES

Through the years, Dodger pitchers have concentrated pretty much on the basic three pitches. We have had good luck, not having many fellows hurt themselves or develop sore arms.

High school pitchers, particularly, should stay with the fast ball, curve ball, and some change-of-pace, whether they take a little bit off the curve ball or throw a straight change. Quite often, a young pitcher thinks he needs another pitch, but, actually, he may not have good command of the pitches he has. He should not consider another pitch until the basic three can be delivered with control, consistency, and effectiveness.

After he progresses and can control these pitches, the young pitcher might go to a different kind of curve ball or a slider. Lately, more pitchers are turning the ball over with a good sinker—a sinking fast ball thrown from a three-quarter or sidearm delivery. The pitcher uses a sweeping arm action across the body and cuts the ball at the last moment.

If a fellow has a major league fast ball and curve ball, and a good change-up, and can control these pitches, getting them over pretty much when and where he wants to, I think he has enough to be a successful pitcher. Coming up with a couple of extra pitches is *not* the answer.

Pitchers today in the big leagues have a half-dozen different pitches in their repertoire. They throw a couple of different speeds on their curve ball, and they throw sliders. They turn the ball over on the sinker, screwball, or the change-of-pace. Pitchers who are not overpowering must rely on changing speeds and control.

The less power a pitcher possesses, the more important keeping the hitter off-stride is. However, it is possible to have too many pitches, as the refinement and control of each becomes more difficult with every new pitch added.

Seaver, of course, is the *complete* pitcher. He has low fast balls, one that rises, another that sinks. He has the ability to make his fast ball sink, sail, or tail, according to the way he holds the ball. Tom also has a good slider, a fine curve, and can change up on all of his pitches.

The Little League pitcher, particularly, should rely almost completely on the fast ball. It is the only pitch with which he can strengthen his arm with minimum risk of injury.

The slider has attained considerable prominence among present-day major league pitchers. It is a fast ball with a break and is most effective when it breaks outside and hitters go reaching for it, or when it breaks in on a left-handed hitter. However, some coaches do not advise their young pitchers to throw it, claiming it is hard on the arms of some pitchers. Those who come up with sore arms usually throw the slider with a stiff wrist. The rigid wrist transfers strain to the elbow. This is why we advocate a loose wrist for the slider. Unfortunately, some pitchers substitute the slider for their curve ball, and they cease to use the curve and do not develop it.

"I like to see pitchers change their speeds more," said Red Adams, our pitching coach. "Off-speed pitches not only get the hitter off stride, but they provide some rest for the pitcher. They also complement the other stuff. Such pitches as the knuckleball and screwball should be used only by more experienced pitchers."

I definitely believe young pitchers today are throwing too many breaking balls. Coaches on all levels have their pitchers throwing four pitches right away, and there is no question it eventually takes away velocity. Too many breaking balls can place a tremendous strain on the arm. The only way to stretch out the arm and get maximum velocity is to throw fast balls.

Grip

The pitcher should hold the ball so that it feels most comfortable and so that he gets the most life into his pitches. Ideally, the ball should be grasped in the same manner for each pitch, but this is not always possible.

We suggest that our pitchers try various grips and we let them decide which one feels the best. However, the way the seam is held is not as important as the way the ball is released.

Generally, a pitcher will grip the ball either across the seams or with the seams. If he is *with* the seams, there are two possibilities:

1. His fingers are at the narrow area where they come together.
2. He can slip on around a little further, where he can get the tip of his finger on the seams and still be with the seams.

For the pitcher with the three-quarter delivery, who does not have exceptional power, I would suggest that he grip the ball with the seams to get a little more movement out of the ball. The ball may sink for him when down, or tail in toward the hitter when up.

Many pitchers grip the ball across the seams at the widest part. The second and third fingertips are placed on the seams, while the thumb is on the seam beneath the ball. Only a slight variation of finger movement is needed to throw the curve or slider.

The thumb plays a very important role in all pitches; it can make the ball go one way or the other.

The cross-the-seams grip provides the most carry and the best control. With this grip, the power pitchers of baseball can actually make the ball take off vertically or rise. But those who are not power pitchers have greater flexibility using the with-the-seams grip. They will be able to learn a sinker or slider more effectively from this grip.

Correct spin

Successful pitching demands an understanding of correct spin on the ball. "Spin the ball easily and get the ball to spin in the direction you want it to spin," explained Johnny Sain, former outstanding pitcher and a highly successful pitching coach. "Then, apply more spin, more spin, more spin, more spin, and more spin."

Many pitchers have improved noticeably by learning how to get better spin on the ball. Additional spin not only can improve breaking pitches but can make the fast ball livelier.

The spin on Warren Spahn's fast ball was amazing—a backward rotation which helped give the pitch its hop. "In order to develop more spin on a baseball," said Sain, "a pitcher has to learn the basic idea. And from here, he spins the ball easy, applying more spin and speed until he gets the ball doing what he likes."

The pitcher should try moving his thumb a little toward his hand or farther under the ball. Some tucking of the thumb will make him "cut" the ball a little, causing a sinking movement.

In most cases, a pitcher who has trouble applying good spin grips the ball too tightly. When a pitcher grips the ball too tightly with his thumb, it seems to lock his wrist. He does not have that loose, fast wrist and finger action. Actually, it is a combination of wrist and finger action that applies the spin to the ball.

Getting better spin on the ball is one of the surest ways toward pitching improvement.

JOHNNY SAIN

A big-league fast ball is a pitch that moves, either up or down, sinking or rising—one of the two.

TOM SEAVER

Fast ball

There is no substitute for a good fast ball. Indeed, the king of all pitches is still the fast ball. A young pitcher would be wise to rely on his fast ball because of the strengthening effect on the arm. A good fast ball comes off the end of a smooth delivery, a coordinated action of the entire body, in which the strong wrist and forearm play a vital role.

To make the ball hop, a pitcher must provide backspin to the ball. He must exert strong pressure on his fingertips with his wrist, snapping down quickly as the ball leaves his hand.

The ball should be gripped as far out on the fingertips as possible. The wrist must remain relaxed in order to obtain the quick "forward" wrist snap so necessary. "When you overthrow on your fast ball, you can tense up your wrist," said Jim Palmer, one of modern baseball's most successful pitchers. The ball will lose its natural break and good snap because of the tight wrist.

There is no set way to throw the fast ball. The grip that gives the best results, of course, should be used. Generally, a two-seam grip will make the ball go down and away; four-seam grip—up and in. Many big-league pitchers throw two types of fast balls:

1. Rising fast ball (across the seams) (Fig. 4.4)   The forefinger and middle finger grip the ball across one of the wide seams, at a point where the seams of the ball are farthest apart. The thumb is underneath. The ring finger and little finger are bent and curled under the side of the ball. From this grip, the pitcher can get maximum action from the four long seams.

For a three-quarter overarm delivery, the ball is released out in front with a strong follow-through. When thrown by a right-handed pitcher, this fast ball has a tendency to ride in slightly on a right-handed hitter and away from a left-handed hitter.

When thrown completely overarm by pitchers with good velocity, the fast ball tends to rise, thus earning its title as the "riser."

2. Sinking fast ball (with the seams) (Fig. 4.4)   The "sinking" fast ball is released with an over-the-top, then outside-in, flip of the wrist. For a right-handed pitcher, this ball drives down and in on a right-handed hitter, and down and away from a left-handed swinger. In releasing the ball, the pitcher has to turn the ball over at the last moment, placing more pressure on the index finger.

This fast ball is gripped with the middle finger and forefinger curled snugly, not tightly, along the two parallel short seams.

When you overthrow on your fast ball, you can tense up your wrist.

JIM PALMER

Known as a sinker, it is a little more difficult to throw than the rising fast ball because of the over-the-top wrist flip. When a ground ball is needed, this pitch can be very effective.

The two things big-league pitching coaches look for is whether a pitcher's ball has good velocity and whether it moves. Some pitchers have good velocity but their fast ball does not move; it just comes in straight, on a line. Pitchers of

Rising fast ball (across seams)   Sinking fast ball (with the seams)

Fig. 4.4 THE FAST BALL. Most big-league pitchers throw two types of fast balls. The good fast ball must be alive. It must hop, sink, break, or sail (Red Adams).

small stature must have more body speed or momentum and extremely good rhythm in order to be fast enough.

If I don't get seven to ten ground balls a game, I would figure Tommy John (a sinkerball pitcher) isn't throwing good.

TIM FOLI

Curve ball

"The key to a good curve ball is the snap," said Roger Craig, who had a great curve when he pitched for the Dodgers. "The curve ball has to be held very loose in your hand, not tight. The elbow has to be up, and a good hard snap has to be made at the release point. The curve ball should be thrown with a little less speed than the fast ball, but with the same motion." (See Figure 4.5.)

Some pitchers have a tendency to overthrow the curve. They either release the ball too far out in front and bounce it, or they try to throw the ball too hard.

Front   Rear view

Fig. 4.5 THE CURVE BALL. Most good breaking ball pitchers hold the ball with the four seams. The ball should be held firmly, gripping tightly along a seam with the middle finger. On the left, Coach Red Adams shows how the pitcher should twist his wrist so the palm of the hand and ball will be facing his head. By raising the elbow, he will form an "L" shape with his arm. This is followed by a straight or stiff wrist snap of the ball as his elbow passes the point of his shoulder.

As a result, their front shoulder stays up and the ball is up in the hitter's eyes— it just spins.

If you don't release the curve ball out in front, you will likely hang it.

DON McMAHON

"In developing a better wrist snap, it is very important to get the hand more on top of the ball, a more downward break, and a tighter grip with the second finger," said Don McMahon. "By getting the hand in closer to the head, a pitcher can get more of a pull down and greater shoulder action." (See Figure 4.6.)

Carl Erskine, a former Dodger who possessed an outstanding curve ball, always thought of tickling his ear when he threw the curve ball. This helped him keep his wrist tucked in and provided good over-the-top spin on the ball. The more the arm is tucked in, the bigger the break. However, the fact that

Fig. 4.6 SNAPPING THE CURVE BALL. When the pitcher is ready to release the ball, he must snap his wrist as hard as he can and make the ball spin! Snapping it hard at the end, makes the ball come up to the plate and break sharply. If he doesn't snap his wrist, the ball will come up to the plate in a rolling form. The stride should be slightly shorter for a curve ball, about six inches, making for a better follow-through and spin (Scott Sanderson).

Erskine threw directly overhand should be kept in mind. Each individual should throw the curve ball from the same angle as his fast ball.

"The biggest factor with the curve is getting the ball down," says Warren Spahn, the former all time great southpaw. "The higher you let the ball go, the more chance you have of hanging it."

The curve is a pitch that should be thrown low. A high curve has a tendency to "hang," and a pitcher who keeps his curve high is simply asking for trouble. An ineffective curve often is caused by not pulling down on the ball enough or letting go of the ball too soon.

The grip is very important to a good curve ball. Most of the good breaking ball pitchers in the major leagues hold the ball with the four seams. "When they release the ball, the ball comes out and you have the four seams biting against the wind," said Craig. "This gives the ball a better bite and the good, tight spin on the ball which is hard for the hitter to pick up. If you hold the ball with the seams, only the two seams, the hitter sees more of the red seams of the ball, and it's easier to pick up. Whereas with the four seams, it is like a blur and is very difficult to pick up."

Throughout the delivery, the elbow has to stay at least parallel to the shoulder. When the elbow drops down below the shoulder, the pitcher cannot get the good power and snap.

The pitcher should wait until his arm is close to the rear of his head before going into his curve ball. The wrist must be cocked back of the head. The elbow starts forward first, and the wrist turns over and snaps downward to put a rapid spin on the ball. "Turn, turn, and PULL DOWN!" describes the wrist and hand action in providing the greatest amount of spin. It is the spin given to the ball that makes it curve.

The wrist should be completely turned over after a very quick reverse snap. The ball is released over the first and second joints of the first finger—like a ball rolling off a table. The first two fingers are close, with the thumb extended and not curled. "Let go of it in front of you," describes the type of release necessary for the curve.

The longer the pitcher can wait, the better curve he will throw. He must stay on top of the ball and put great pressure or pull on his middle finger.

The middle finger is the pressure finger, the one that controls the seam and imparts much of the spin. The moment he starts coming down is when the pitcher must really pull down hard with a sweep of the arm across the body toward the opposite knee. The hand usually comes back toward the body, whereas the hand release on the fast ball is more toward the hitter. In releasing the ball, he should let it roll over on his index finger. This is how spin is imparted for a good breaking action of the curve ball.

Perfecting the curve ball requires a great amount of practice, learning how to coordinate the speed of spin, the angle of spin, and using a natural pitching motion.

Practice to get the correct spin. The pitcher should have a catcher stand fifteen to twenty feet away from him and just spin the ball into his glove. He should vary the grip and wrist action and keep turning his wrist over until he obtains the most effective break.

Change-of-pace

Every pitcher at every level of baseball should have an off-speed pitch of some kind that he can get over the plate. A good change-up can be an extremely valuable asset to a pitcher. This is particularly true as he climbs higher in baseball. It takes courage to throw a change-up, but it is a pitch that must be learned and controlled by every pitcher. Without a good change-up, a pitcher is definitely limiting his baseball career. By perfecting the technique of his off-speed pitches, he will develop the confidence that he can use them effectively at any time (Fig. 4.7).

The change-up is particularly effective in disrupting the hitter's timing. When he is set for a fast ball, a change-up will likely cause the batter to place his weight on his front foot too soon. He will hit the ball with only an arm swing.

Typically, pitchers on the Baltimore Orioles throw as many as two dozen change-ups during a game. According to pitching coach Ray Miller, "An Orioles pitcher will start throwing them in the first inning to show the hitter he has it. He will also wind up throwing less pitches and staying fresher longer."

Fig. 4.7 THE CHANGE-UP. Many pitchers like to grip the ball back in the palm of the hand, as shown here by Red Adams. By holding the ball across the wide seams, the pitcher will be able to impart the four-seam rotation and spin, so desirable in pitching. There is greater pressure on the second row of knuckles of the first two fingers. The fingertips are raised slightly as the ball is released. These fingers straighten out.

I'm throwing well, I have good location, but the big thing is I'm getting my change-up over. That makes a world of difference.

BURT HOOTON

Off-speed pitches not only get the hitter off stride but they provide some rest for the pitcher.

RED ADAMS

In throwing the change-up, our Dodger pitchers combined three different methods. They held the ball with three fingers across the seams, used a dead rear leg, and they were instructed to stiffen and bring their wrist right down. "When I threw my change," explained Don Drysdale, "I tried to think that my wrist was going to hit the dirt. I used the four-seam rotation to make the hitter think he was getting a fast ball."

Using a stiff wrist, the pitcher pulls down on the ball. The heel of the hand should come down first. The ball is held slightly looser than on the fast ball. As the ball is released, the fingertips are raised slightly.

The palmball change (Fig. 4.8) is popular with many pitching coaches. According to Roger Craig, "The ball is placed way back in the palm of the hand,

Fig. 4.8 THE "OK" CHANGE-UP, a variation of the palmball change, is used by Doyle Alexander and many other big league pitchers. The ball is placed in the palm and "choked." Keeping three fingers on top of the ball will reduce wrist snap and take the speed off the ball. As they release the ball, some pitchers will turn the ball over just slightly, rotating the palm away from the body.

the thumb is placed on a seam, and the four fingers lay down across the ball. The pressure is placed between the thumb and the middle and ring finger where they meet the hand. The fingers just lie on the ball. If the pitcher throws it with three fingers, his little finger is placed along the side of the ball. He simply throws the ball with his palm, as if the pitcher had no fingers at all. The tight grip or pressure with the thumb and the knuckle joint will do this automatically. It will lock the wrist and kill the speed of the ball."

Pitching motion is the thing that gets the hitters out if you can just throw the ball over the plate.

WARREN SPAHN

Again, the motion on a change-up should correspond to that used on the fast ball. If he slows up his motion, the pitcher will tip off his pitch and any illusion he is trying to create will be lost.

One of the easiest ways to teach a change-up is to have the pitcher turn it over a little, like a screwball. The ball is released at the last split-second so it will come off the hand between the second and third fingers, as a screwball, but without too much wrist snap. Even though it will not break as much as the screwball, the change of speed makes this pitch effective.

Some pitchers find it effective to lengthen the stride on the change-up. Others like to drag the rear foot, using the dead rear leg method with a let-up delivery. They hold their foot on the rubber and do not allow their weight to come through. This will reduce the body motion and help keep the body low.

The change-up can be a terrific pitch, especially in tough situations. The let-up pitch is often effective on 3–2, 3–1, or 2–0 counts. After two strikes, the batters guard the plate a little more closely.

I try to tell my pitchers, "If you are going to throw an unexpected pitch, on a 2–0 or 3–1 count, it is necessary that you make that pitch a strike. You want the hitter to swing at the unexpected pitch and, therefore, it should be in the strike zone. Otherwise, the hitter will often take the pitch and we will be in worse trouble than before."

The change-of-pace is difficult for many pitchers to learn. One reason is that the pitcher tries to develop an entirely new pitching style. Instead, he should stay with the same style he uses for his other pitches. This is why the turn-over change is one of our favorites.

Throwing off-speed pitches takes practice and courage, working on them until they become natural and effective. Young pitchers must not get discouraged if they do not learn the change-up right away. It takes time to learn.

There are more grips for a change-up than any other pitch.

Move ball back into the hand, spreading three fingers on top of the ball.

Get arm up high, elbow out in front. Raise finger tips when releasing the ball.

Throw ball on downward plane, with good backspin. With a stiff wrist, pull down on ball.

Fig. 4.9 BASIC TECHNIQUE IN THROWING A CHANGE-UP (Doyle Alexander).

"Development of the straight change requires a concentrated effort," explained Adams. "I required my pitchers to throw as many as twenty-five to thirty in a row in each practice session." Practicing the off-speed pitch is like the hitter who doesn't like to practice bunting. Most pitchers have a tendency to throw more fast balls in practice than any other pitch.

Doyle Alexander, a master at changing speeds on his pitches, advised: "The best way to change speeds on the ball is to hold the ball differently, but throw the ball the same as you would your fast ball. Use the same motion!"

The change-of-pace is the most overlooked pitch in a young pitcher's repertoire.

Many big-league pitching coaches believe the secret to throwing an effective change-of-pace is getting the pitching arm up high, so the arm speed cannot be picked up by the hitter. Johnny Podres who pitched for me emphasizes the importance of good arm extension. "If a pitcher drops his elbow," says Podres, "he will have trouble getting the ball down." Don McMahon stresses getting the elbow up even with the shoulder and letting the elbow go out first and then pulling down on the ball. By reaching up high and throwing the ball on a downward plane, a pitcher can make it very difficult for hitters to pick up the arm speed. It requires a full extension of the arm and a pulling motion at the end.

Palmball

The palmball is used primarily as an off-speed pitch, but it is more effective when the pitcher has a good fast ball. Dave Guisti, an outstanding relief pitcher with the Pittsburg Pirates in the 1970s, explained that: "If I throw a palmball, with the same motion and delivery, the speed is cut down enough to throw their timing off. Essentially, that is the key to the success of the palmball."

Some major league pitchers prefer the palmball for their change-of-pace (Fig. 4.8). On the palmball, key pressure is applied by the inside joint of the thumb. The four fingers lie gently and slightly curved around the ball. The ball is stuffed into the palm of the hand. The pitcher releases the ball with a fast ball motion by letting it float out of the palm of the hand, controlled by the pressure of his thumb joint.

"I hold the ball in the palm of my hand with the pressure points being in the middle of the ring finger, and the middle of the thumb," said Guisti. "In throwing the palmball, I try to minimize the speed with the same motion and delivery. The old cliche, "pulling the window shade down," is true because you have to get the elbow out and use a stiff wrist. You simply try to cut down the speed and the spin. Cutting down on the spin sometimes will affect the pitch similar to a knuckleball and it will sink. I try not to break my wrist very much. The delivery and follow-through have to appear the same as a fast ball; otherwise, the hitters will pick it up."

Unfortunately, the palmball can be hard on the arm. Guisti started throwing the pitch while in college and according to Dave, "It did irritate my elbow to a degree. I should add that I was playing every day, and when I was not pitching, I was playing left field or third base."

Slider

The slider can be a highly effective pitch and has attained considerable prominence among present-day, major league pitchers (Fig. 4.10). Since it is usually accompanied by a hard snap of the arm, the slider must be thrown properly, so as not to hurt the arm. The stiff wrist slider will cause elbow problems.

Since it is easy to learn and control, many young pitchers in pro ball are throwing it. The curve ball takes longer to master and is more difficult to

Front view (Roger Craig)

Rear view (Red Adams)

Fig. 4.10 THE SLIDER. The secret of a good slider is to keep the spin as tight as possible. The pitcher should cut across the ball very hard with his big finger, causing the rotation of the ball to swerve laterally and make a quick hook as it approaches the plate. As demonstrated here by Roger Craig, the hand stays on top of the ball throughout the delivery and gives it a fastball snap of the wrist. In releasing the ball, twist the fingers and thumb as if opening a door knob. Pitchers who get on the side of the ball before snapping their wrist will experience problems with the muscles and nerves in the elbow area. When the fingers are more on top of the ball, the muscles of the elbow do not move as much and cause as much strain.

control. Since the slider does not break as much, the pitcher can put the ball where he wants it.

The slider is held off-center a little, with the middle and index fingers placed to the outside of the ball. If he throws a with-the-seams fast ball, the pitcher might slide 'up' the ball just a little and hold it slightly off-center. The release of the slider can be compared with the passing of a football. Using a good wrist snap through the release area, the pitcher will cut the ball and impart this tight spin. He should think of the power finger, usually the middle finger, as a knife that will slice part of the ball as it is released.

The index finger controls the release. Just before the point of release, the hand should be turned sideways, providing the football spin. Come straight down hard and let the ball come off the second finger. This will cause the ball to spin like a bullet.

The stiff-wrist slider that is taught throughout baseball is the one that will most definitely cause elbow problems. The hand, in this method, comes through the release area as if the pitcher were throwing a football. "With this hand position, the wrist cannot snap or propel the ball forward," explained Bob Cluck. "From this locked position, there is too much pressure on the elbow joint. The pitcher also has a tendency to twist his wrist at the end which places additional strain on the elbow."

To prevent arm trouble, a growing number of coaches are advocating a loose wrist for the slider. With a limber wrist, the pitcher should cut directly through the ball with his middle and index fingers, ending up with a smooth follow-through.

A slider is good when thrown to certain spots, breaking in and jamming a left-handed hitter or clipping the outside corner. It is also effective when thrown so it breaks outside to a right-handed hitter with the hitter reaching for it. But the thing that makes it especially effective is its velocity. It is a fast ball with a break, and should be kept down.

The general feeling among pitching authorities is that the young pitcher should stay away from the slider until he is physically equipped and has sufficient talent to throw it properly.

Sinker

The sinker is one of the greatest weapons of the relief pitcher, particularly those who throw sidearm. With many of the hitters today swinging for the fences, the sinker pitch has been most effective in making the batter hit the ball in the ground. With the correct motion and sinking rotation, the sinker can be a real "bread-and-butter pitch" (Fig. 4.11).

Many of the game's top relief pitchers, including Greg Minton, rely heavily on the sinker pitch. Minton developed his sinker ball when a knee injury forced him to cut down on the kick and shorten his stride. The shorter stride has caused him to hasten his arm's downward plunge, adding the type of spin necessary for a good sinker.

Fig. 4.11 THE SINKER. Greg Minton, an outstanding relief pitcher, holds his sinker pitch along the two small seams, with the two fingers close together. Rather than turn the ball over, he increases the pressure on the index finger, and a slight rotation of the wrist causes the sinking action. Prior to release, the hand and wrist turn counter-clockwise just slightly, and the arm movement across the pitcher's body gives the sinker a downward rotation.

Two popular sinker ball grips used by the Dodgers are:

1. Having the fingers close together along the two small seams of the ball.
2. Having the fingers go across the two small seams of the ball.

We also emphasize having the fingers close together and overloading the ball on the inside part, with most of the ball showing on the outside part. The left-handed pitcher releases the ball from the outside part of his hand.

Prior to release, the turn of the arm is more important than is the flip of the wrist. There is a little rotation of the wrist, not really turning the ball over as much as putting more pressure on the forefinger and getting proper rotation. The arm movement sweeping across the pitcher's body gives the sinker a downward rotation. The pitch is released off the right corner tip of the middle finger. The pitcher must stay on top of the ball until the actual point of release.

The sinker should be kept low for maximum effectiveness. Concentrate on keeping the ball from above the knees to below the knees. The thumb plays an important roll in the sinker, as it does in all pitches. The ball can be off-centered by moving the thumb up the side where the little finger is.

There are two types of sinker ball pitchers. First, there is the gifted moundsman, usually with a three-quarter to sidearm delivery, whose delivery makes possible a natural sinker. He is the hard-throwing pitcher who can get on top of the ball to the extent that he does not let it go until it is well out in front of him. He manages to cut the ball just enough in his natural motion so that it will come in and sink.

Then, there is the less gifted pitcher who has to give the ball considerable help when he is releasing it. By bringing his arm clear across the body, he cuts the ball, giving it the necessary reverse corkscrew spin to make it break downward.

The success of the sinker pitch depends on the following coaching points:

1. Hold the ball slightly off-center.
2. Execute the "drop-and-go" body movement.
3. Stay on top of the ball.
4. Release the ball off the side of the middle finger, well out in front of the body.
5. Use a sweeping arm action across the body, which cuts the ball at the last moment.

In throwing a good sinker, the pitcher must utilize a body action that drives him toward the hitter in a lower position than his fast ball and his other pitches. The "drop-and-go" movement allows him to stay on top of the ball, cutting and releasing it at the last moment, well out in front of his body.

Bending the right knee causes the body to drop down and then be pushed forward, a "drop-and-go" movement. The throwing arm is extended across the body, finishing up completely across the body. Most pitchers lengthen their stride as much as six inches more than on the fast ball.

The sinker pitch is just like a fast ball, except that the pitcher brings his arm on across his body. This gives a reverse corkscrew spin to the ball. There is a similarity between the sinker and the screwball, although the screwball is much more taxing on the arm. The sinker is thrown harder than the screwball. The screwball is about a half-speed pitch, which is thrown by actually turning the elbow and arm completely over.

Caution should be taken by the young pitcher, in throwing either of these pitches, in not trying to get too much of an inward arm turn. Too much rotation of the wrist or arm can cause injury to the elbow area.

Screwball

Thrown with an inside-out twist of the hand and wrist, the screwball breaks the opposite way from the curve (Fig. 4.12). A screwball is a reverse curve—a curve breaking away from instead of into a right-handed hitter when thrown by a left-hander. Carl Hubbell, who struck out Babe Ruth and four other future Hall of Famers, explained that "It isn't the way a screwball breaks that bothers a good hitter—it's the change of speed on the screwball compared to a fast ball." Carl got them all on screwballs after setting them up with fast balls and an occasional curve.

The screwball can be a particularly effective pitch for a left-handed pitcher, as the success of Fernando Valenzuela has proven. Yet, it is a difficult pitch to master and is considered by many pitching authorities to be hard on a young arm. Very definitely, some discretion should be shown in throwing the screwball.

Fig. 4.12   THROWING THE SCREWBALL. This pitch is normally thrown overhand, and breaks down and toward the side from which it is thrown. It has to be snapped just like the curve, but with a reverse spin. The fingers go through first, then the ball, creating the effect of a change-up (Jim Brewer).

The clockwise or inward rotation of the arm is unnatural and places undue strain on the arm. This is the prime reason why coaches and managers do not encourage this difficult pitch by young and inexperienced pitchers.

"Most pitchers don't have what it takes, anatomically, to throw a screwball," said Ron Perranoski, pitching coach of the Dodgers. "You've got to have a certain kind of delivery. It is a very difficult pitch to learn. A screwball is thrown with an elongated arc, with great arm extension—almost over your head—and Fernando does that. A pitcher also has to be real loose in all the joints. Most pitchers are not loose-jointed enough to throw it—they can't get the wrist turned over. The action of the arm and wrist as you come over the top, putting spin on the ball, is what makes it break. Valenzuela throws his screwball so effortlessly. He doesn't use the elbow at all."

A good screwball requires more of an overhand delivery, so that the pitcher is on top of the ball. The principle of the pitch is getting the ball to rotate, for a left-handed pitcher, getting the ball to rotate like a right-hand curve ball. It is spun out of the hand between the middle and ring fingers and is given its rotation by the reverse quarter-turn of the wrist and the middle finger release. The thumb is used to increase the reverse spin by being given a last-second flip as the ball is released. We emphasize turning the hand and wrist away from the body and then trying to turn the ball over to get the proper rotation.

Jim Brewer, a former relief pitcher on our club who can attribute much of his success to the screwball, explained that: "The screwball has not been hard on my arm because I extend my arm, and I am not using the elbow. From time to time, I have had a problem with my shoulder, but it has not been serious. It is just a tight muscle from throwing the screwball too much." (Fig. 4.12.)

"When a young pitcher starts to throw a screwball," continued Brewer, "they must not try to throw it too hard. They should get the feel of it and see that it is rotating properly. As they learn more about the rotation and how to throw it, they can begin to throw it hard. I would not advise them to throw more than one or two screwballs out of six pitches."

The screwball is generally gripped along the long seam providing a four-seam rotation. As the arm comes forward, the pitcher should think fast ball until the last instant, then rotate the hand and release the fingers over the top of the ball. The thumb plays a major role in imparting the clockwise rotation to the ball. Screwball pitchers often develop blisters on the top side of their thumbs because of the pressure exerted on the ball.

If the thrower has a consistent release point, the forkball is one of the easiest off-speed pitches to learn.

Split-finger fast ball (forkball)

The split-finger fast ball and the forkball are almost the same, but the reason a growing number of pitching coaches are calling this pitch a split-finger fast ball is because the "fast ball" is the key word. As the pitcher spreads his fingers apart and moves into his delivery, he should be thinking in the back of his mind, "I am throwing a fast ball."

"The way I teach this pitch is to have the pitcher throw a fast ball and gradually work the fingers down on the seams until it feels comfortable to grip the ball between the two fingers," explained Roger Craig, veteran pitching coach of the Detroit Tigers. "You simply spread the fingers apart and throw a fast ball. You get the arm speed of a fast ball, yet you have the baseball speed of a change-up. Once you practice this pitch and throw it quite a bit, the ball really starts to do tricks. Most of the time it breaks down. It's like an off-speed pitch and is very easy on the arm and easy to learn, too. It's a great pitch and gets a lot of outs!"

"Hold the ball with the seams and throw a fast ball," said Craig. "Next time, open up another half an inch and throw another fastball and gradually keep working down until the grip feels comfortable. Some pitchers who have a deep thumb hold it a third of the way down, while some a fourth of the way, but it has to work out best for each individual."

"The secret to throwing a split-finger fast ball is when you get down as far

Fig. 4.13 SPLIT-FINGER FAST BALL (FORKBALL). The arm speed on this off-speed pitch should be the same as a fast ball. A quick wrist snap by Dan Petry, right, allows the ball to come out cleanly, with no lateral movement, just vertical and downward. A forkball should not be thrown with a stiff wrist. Give the pitch a lot of wrist. Get the feeling you are throwing through the ball. The fingers are split apart as far as possible with comfort, as shown by Roger Craig, below. The ball comes out between the two fingers.

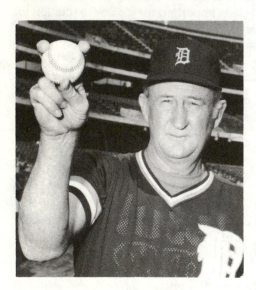

as you want to go, halfway down, or whatever, you have to think that you are throwing a fast ball. This is what deceives a hitter because the arm speed comes through like a fast ball. When I see my pitchers letting up on their motion, I tell them to think 'fast ball.' Even if the ball goes straight, you still have a great off-speed pitch."

The release point is almost identical to the fast ball. The pitcher should make sure he pulls the fingers through the ball. "You get the feeling that you are throwing through the ball," said Roger. "In releasing the ball, you have to give the pitch a lot of wrist like you are throwing a fast ball. The ball has to come out between the two fingers."

Bruce Sutter holds his thumb on the side of the baseball. He pushes in on the ball and gives it a "thumbing effect." Other pitchers may have the thumb underneath or halfway down.

As a major league pitcher, Craig never threw a forkball, but now, all but a few of his Detroit pitchers can throw it and most of them pretty effectively. Jack Morris gets 50% of his outs using this pitch. Craig explained, "It all started when I had the school with Little League pitchers in San Diego. When young pitchers have only one type of pitch, a fast ball, they want something else, and if you don't teach them something that won't hurt their arms, they'll learn something on their own and only hurt themselves. I advised some of the young pitchers to spread the fingers out in some form of forkball and throw a regular fast ball. I was amazed at what fourteen- and fifteen-year-olds could make the ball do, and I thought to myself, "Hey, if they can do it, what about major leaguers?"

After talking to many doctors and orthopedic surgeons, I am convinced that the split-finger fast ball is a very good pitch for young pitchers because there is no strain or added tension in the arm. Some pitchers who throw the forkball for the first time make the mistake of throwing it with a stiff wrist. This places considerable strain on the elbow, much the same as the "locked" wrist slider.

Knuckleball

The knuckler is the most popular of the unorthodox deliveries and has been used with great success by such modern-day hurlers as Hoyt Wilhelm, Phil and Joe Niekro. The name of the pitch, in most cases, is a misnomer because the knuckleball is actually thrown with the fingernails (Fig. 4.14).

The publicity this pitch has received is probably due to the difficulty catchers have in catching it. The knuckler probably takes the most erratic course to the plate of any type pitch. Its movement is highly unpredictable. It may sink,

Fig. 4.14 KNUCKLEBALL. The knuckler is generally thrown by digging the fingernails (not the knuckles) into the seams of the ball. The vigorous extension of the fingers causes the ball to rotate forward and drop when thrown from an overhand delivery (Hoyt Wilhelm).

swerve to either side, or jump in a crazy manner. It is not only a difficult pitch for the pitcher to control, but is easy to run on. Since this pitch is just about impossible to hide, the success of the knuckleball is due to its action rather than to the surprise element.

There are several methods used in throwing the knuckleball. The method favored by most pitchers is to dig the fingernails into the seams. On release, the fingers are extended vigorously and push the ball toward the plate. While the fingernail pitch can be thrown with one, two, or three fingers, most pitchers use the two-finger method. In this technique, the finger and wrist remain stiff. The ball rarely revolves when thrown in this manner.

The knuckleball pitch must be thrown easy. Don't throw it too hard!

The other method is to hold the ball cradled against the first joints of the fingers. The first joints of the index and middle fingers rest against the ball between the seams where they are narrowest. The thumb and fourth and fifth fingers encircle the ball and hold it tightly. As the ball leaves the throwing hand, the bent fingers are extended, giving the pitch additional speed. This method requires a good amount of wrist snap as the ball leaves the hand, plus the extension of the index and middle fingers. The result is that the ball revolves only slightly.

The floater or butterfly type of knuckleball is thrown at half-speed, with a stiff wrist. As it approaches the plate, it seems to dance, reacting to each shift in air currents.

Conversely, the fast knuckler is thrown at full speed. The fingers are extended as the ball is released and the wrist snapped, giving the ball extra velocity and sufficient downspin to make it dip sharply as it approaches the hitter, like "rolling off the table."

Certainly, the knuckleball is not recommended for pitchers in high school or lower age levels. The pitch is difficult to control and development of the pitch usually takes years.

Basic 20 of Pitching

1. Be consistent in your windup.
2. Keep the ball hidden throughout the delivery.
3. Make a good pivot, keeping the foot parallel to the rubber.
4. Retain your weight during the pivot.
5. Use your hips properly—activate them!

6. Have a well balanced leg lift—don't start the kick too soon.

7. Keep your eyes fixed on the target—*concentrate!*

8. Keep the ball in the glove longer.

9. Drive off from the rubber—get a good thrust!

10. Drop and drive right out at the hitter.

11. Open up the stride and unlock the hips—don't throw across the body.

12. Do not overstride or rush the stride.

13. Utilize good arm extension by getting the pitching arm up high and elbow out in front.

14. Have good rhythm—*put it all together!*

15. Use strong wrist and arm action.

16. Throw strikes—stay ahead of the hitter.

17. Be quick with the top part of your body—*whip the arm through!*

18. Use a comfortable and natural arm angle.

19. Create a consistent point of release.

20. Follow-through in a natural manner.

THE DELIVERY

All successful pitchers throw the ball in the way that is easiest and most effective for them. Proper form and delivery are different for each pitcher. Therefore, each pitcher should be able to work out his own natural style. I have never seen a pitcher get to the major leagues by copying somebody else's style.

A good pitching delivery is one that seems to flow in a smooth, full-arm swing, finishing with a powerful snap of the wrist. On the other hand, a half-swing, bent arm, jerky motion will likely place undue stress on the elbow and may ruin the pitching arm permanently.

A well-coordinated and rhythmic delivery will provide extra speed and power, and help the pitcher achieve better control. Rather than just the arm, every part of the body will bear the brunt of the effort.

There are four basic types of pitching delivery: overhand, three-quarter, sidearm, and underhand. Normally, most pitchers throw overhand or three-quarter style, adding an occasional sidearm pitch. It is the angle of delivery that makes the several styles different.

No matter what style is used, there are certain basic qualities which are absolutely essential. In any type of delivery, the pitcher must have balance, a proper pivot, correct stride, and a good follow-through. Practice will give him the coordination and rhythm needed for an effective pitching delivery.

Regardless of which delivery is used, every pitch must be thrown with about the same motion and released from almost the same point. If the pitcher throws his fast ball sidearm and curve ball overhand, the batter obviously will be able to detect what is being thrown.

Pitching rhythm

In pitching, everything has to work together. The throwing arm and upper body must be meshed with the striding leg and lower body. If the striding foot hits when the arm is way back, all a pitcher has is a pulling motion. In this case, generally, the leg stride is too quick or the upper body and pitching arm is too slow. The problem is that the upper half of the body trails the lower half.

The solution is to: 1) slow down the stride and 2) speed up the arm and upper body. By slowing down the stride, the pitcher give his throwing arm a chance to get through at the right time.

Proper rhythm and timing are the basis of successful pitching.

How can proper rhythm and timing be achieved? How can a pitcher generate an action of power?

1. Keep the ball in the glove a little longer. By keeping the ball in the glove longer, the pitcher holds up the thrust of the lower part of his body.
2. Do not start the leg kick too soon or employ a higher kick. Delaying the stride will prevent rushing.
3. Open up the stride and unlock the hips. Give the throwing arm and upper body the opportunity to shoot through.
4. Get the pitching arm on top and drive on through. The pitcher must get up on top before the lead foot hits.
5. Whip the arm through. The pitcher should be exceptionally quick with the top part of his body. He cannot be lazy with his arm.

Getting the sign

While standing on the mound, the pitcher should keep the ball hidden from the hitter's view. Most pitchers today have the ball in the glove just in front of their waist line. Others have a practice of hiding the pitching hand and ball behind the thigh of their pivot leg. The less the hitter sees of the ball, the better it is for the pitcher.

To take the signal from the catcher, the pitcher must stand on the rubber (Fig. 4.15). In fact, the rules require this. He is also required to deliver the ball to the batter *within twenty seconds* after he receives the signal.

The majority of pitchers place their pivot foot on the rubber and their other foot a comfortable distance behind it. The spikes of the pivot foot are over the front edge of the rubber, with the striking foot behind and just to the left.

Occasionally the pitcher might shake off several of the catcher's signals until he comes back a second time to the pitch he really wants to throw. This makes the hitter think and wonder about pitches the pitcher may not even have.

Blue   Reuss
Windup position   Men on base

Fig. 4.15 TAKING THE SIGN. Getting the signal with no runners on base, Vida Blue (left) has his pivot foot on the rubber. In placing his body weight on to his push-off foot, he takes a rocking step back on the striding foot. With runners on base, Jerry Reuss, from a set position, keeps his feet comfortably spread. His body is turned sideways to home plate, with the pivot foot resting against the front edge of the rubber.

Windup

The primary purpose of the windup is to move the body weight back in order to place power into the pitch. To transfer the body weight effectively to the push-off foot, many pitchers will take an initial step back on the striding foot. In preparing for the start of the windup, the pitcher should "gather his weight" in order to get more power into his delivery. This pattern of action resembles that of a pendulum. By reaching way back, the pitcher will have the necessary explosive charge to propel the ball toward the plate.

The main thing in starting a windup is to be consistent. As the arms swing forward and upward to a comfortable position above the head, the ball should be hidden in the glove well up into the web, so that the pitching hand is hidden by the glove. This action conceals the ball so that the batter cannot see the grip and know what is coming. When the pitcher makes his pivot, the ball remains hidden behind the glove and then his body. As a result, the batter does not see the ball until it is coming toward him. Most pitching instructors instruct their pitchers to pitch "out of their glove," as opposed to "out of their hand."

To go into this motion more effectively, the pitcher should place the front spike of his pivot foot over the edge of the rubber. By angling his foot slightly toward the side from which he will throw, he facilitates the pivot and gets his body weight behind the throw. In fact, the pitcher will be more effective by keeping his foot in front of the rubber, rather than on top of it.

Although almost all major league pitchers have eliminated the backward swing and pumping action, young pitchers may find they have better rhythm using the pumping action. The purpose of the pump is to loosen and relax the arm and shoulder muscles by bending forward and letting the arms swing backward, with the wrists flexing.

Movement of hands   Most pitchers today move their hands, the throwing hand inside the glove hand, to an area in front of or on top of the head, or to the side. When moving the ball and glove up with his hands, the pitcher should make certain they do not block his view.

Hiding the ball   The back of the glove should always face the hitter, and the ball should be up in the webbing, not in the heel of the glove. The ball and the pitching hand down to the wrist should be wrapped inside the glove.

No-pump windup

Perhaps the most significant change in pitching technique during the past two decades has been the switch from the full windup with a pumping motion to the no-pump windup that every pitcher uses today (Fig. 4.16). Until the early 1970s, both arms hung loosely down to the pitcher's sides, and the pitcher would then begin his preliminary pumping motions.

Today, the pitcher's hands are together in front of the body when he starts his delivery. As the hands come up and over his head, the right-handed pitcher steps back with the left foot. He then shifts his weight forward as he rotates into the pitch. A more compact delivery and good balance are the two chief benefits of the no-pump windup.

The start of the delivery should be as short and comfortable as possible. The important thing is to stay compact and not waste any motion. The arms should not be flailing around.

Position of the hands   The hands are held immediately in front of the waist, with the pitching hand grasping the ball inside the glove.

Fig. 4.16 NO-PUMP WINDUP. Today's pitchers use a more simplified and compact no-pump windup. Starting with both hands in front of the waist, Joe Sambito moves his hands to an area in front of or above the head. He makes certain his hands and glove do not block his view.

Fig. 4.17 FOOTWORK ON THE WIND-UP. At the start of the pivot, the toe of Bob Knepper's pivot foot is pointed out slightly toward first base. Without lifting his foot from the rubber, Knepper pivots on the ball of his left foot. By turning his pivot foot parallel to the rubber, he is able to make the body pivot to his left and back toward the plate.

Stance The pitcher starts his delivery with both feet on the rubber. As he faces the hitter, the pitcher's feet are nearly square on the rubber.

Rock-back Most pitchers take a step, either back or to the side, in order to get the momentum moving. After stepping back or to the side, the pitcher then brings the leg up. In Figure 4.17, Bob Knepper moves slightly backward to get his body rocking. "As I take a step back, a small rocking backward step, I bring my hands up to get some momentum going with my hands. When I bring my leg kick up, I want to stay fairly well compact."

Pivot

A good pivot is essential to an effective pitching delivery. If he fails to pivot correctly, very likely the pitcher will be throwing with just his arm, and he will lack the necessary balance.

As the pitcher's arms come up over his head during the windup, his weight should shift back on his rear foot. For proper balance, his pivot foot must be placed comfortably in contact with the rubber as it is turned.

The actual pivoting is executed without lifting the foot from the rubber. It is performed on the ball of the foot, and when completed, the toe points in the direction of third. This maneuver is very important, in that it makes possible the extreme body pivot to the right and back.

At the start of the pivot, the pitcher's stance should be slightly open, with the toe of his pivot foot pointed out slightly toward third base (for a right-hander).

Pivoting on the ball of his right foot, he turns his pivot foot parallel to the rubber. Keeping the ball hidden from the hitter's view, he pivots his body around and exposes his rear to the hitter. His eyes remain focused on the target.

As the pivot takes place, the pitcher brings the knee of his free foot up high across the body as the arms swing down and back. This leg action bends and pivots the body backward.

The important thing on the pivot is *proper balance*—with the weight of the body over the pivot leg, which is slightly bent at the knee. The body should *not* be leaning forward. Some pitchers have their bodies moving forward during their pivot, and actually start their kick while their pitching arm is still going down and back. The result will be the arm working all alone in the pitch.

Many young pitchers get very little kick in their delivery, because they start their body moving forward before the pivot is completed. Instead, they might take a slight pause, like Seaver, to make sure they have everything together, before they proceed. This will slow them down enough to get their balance and timing together before they throw to the plate.

Weight retention

A pitcher has to retain his weight during the pivot and wait for his arm to come through. Weight retention, on which Red Adams placed so much stress with his pitchers, means, "Don't run off and leave the arm."

If he runs off and leaves his arm, of course, the pitcher will not have time to get his arm up on top, and he will have to shorten up somehow. This could cause him to "shortarm the ball" or throw sidearm. Waiting until the hands get completely to the top lessens the chance of rushing.

Rushing is the most serious mechanical problem with which pitching instructors must deal. The term "rushing" applies to the body getting ahead of the arm. It is a problem of timing and coordination. If the pitching arm is not up, back, and extended when the stride foot is planted, the pitcher will likely rush his delivery.

To retain their weight during the pivot, pitchers should practice a slower delivery than normal while warming up. Many pitching coaches emphasize a slow, deliberate "lifting" of the free leg and a smooth, effortless stride.

Leg kick

To obtain good forward drive, the overhand pitcher should bring the knee of his free foot up high across the body as the arms swing down and back. This leg action bends and pivots the body backward, and as the pitcher strides forward with the striding foot, the entire body goes into the pitch like an uncoiling spring, providing maximum power.

Many different types of leg lifts are used by pitchers, depending on their style of delivery. The pitcher with an overhand, erect type of delivery cannot effectively turn his back to the hitter during the pivot, as it creates a horizontal type body action. However, the turning of the back to the hitter is very effective for the coiling, three-quarter or sidearm type pitcher.

A pitcher must execute a well-balanced leg kick with good body control. His weight is more on the ball of his right foot as he pivots into the backswing. He now has the balance necessary for a good thrust forward from the rubber.

As the leg lift takes place, three key points should be kept in mind:

1. The pitcher's body should be twisted back as far as possible without ruining balance.
2. His eyes should remain fixed on home plate or the target. A pitcher should look over his left shoulder as he swings back.
3. The pitching arm should drop well down behind his body and be straightened out.

At this point, the right leg should be similar to a coiled spring. Uncoiling is the movement that pushes the pitcher into the actual pitch, generating drive into the motion.

The size of the leg kick varies with the individual pitcher. However, he should not kick so high that it ruins his balance, overall coordination and control. For some pitchers, a high leg kick is a big asset because it gives them a deceptive motion and a high angle of delivery. The leg kick gives the hitter more motion at which to look and tends to bother his timing. Unquestionably, Juan Marichal's famous high kick was a prime factor in his outstanding success.

Not every pitcher, though, feels he is properly balanced with the extra-high leg kick. Each pitcher must experiment until he feels his delivery is smooth and coordinated and has the balance necessary for the push-off forward. While the deceptiveness of a high kick helps hide the ball longer from the batter, the pitcher should never sacrifice balance for deception.

Hip rotation

Proper hip action is probably the greatest single factor involved in a powerful delivery. As in batting, the hips generate a great amount of power. While a good push-off from the rubber is essential, correct use of the hips is perhaps the prerequisite for a powerful thrust from the slab.

With the weight on the pivot foot, the hips are rotated to the right. The knee of the free foot is brought up high across the body as the arms swing down and back. The pitcher's eyes are kept on the target throughout the delivery. The action of the hips is bolstered by driving the rear knee down as the hips are opened and the stride is completed.

"I like to see a pitcher use his hips as much as he can in lifting his leg," said Red Adams. "If a fellow will lift his leg and bring his knee back a little toward second base, this will throw the bottom of his foot a little bit out toward home plate. This will activate his hips, and put his hips on a slight tilt. Of course, when he comes on through, it gives him some good leg action and momentum."

"Good hip action comes from the way a pitcher raises his knee. The belt line is the key to watch for. If the belt is on a level plane during his pivot, generally his legs and hips are not activated like they could be. If they are tilted a little, the chances are he has the desired hip action."

Thrust

By bending the knee of his pivot leg, the pitcher lowers his body, thus getting a better position to drive off—*to thrust out!* This forces the pitcher to put extra effort into his pitch. When he drops and bends his knee in order to get the necessary momentum, he has to drive off the rubber (Fig. 4.18)!

A pitcher must not pitch from a lazy pivot leg. This leg should be bent in order to get balance and a good thrust forward. Pitchers who are in poor condition or just plain lazy are more apt to pitch from a stiff or dead pivot leg.

Some pitching authorities, like Bob Cluck, believe the back leg does not drive the pitcher to the plate. Bob explains that, "the 'push' is merely the violent rotation of the hips and shoulders as they open up. This momentum will pull (often explosively) the back side through and bring the rear leg forward."

Seaver is a good example of a pitcher who uses the "drop-and-drive" technique. He pitches between his hips, keeping his body weight as close under the hips as possible. He drives low and right out at the hitter. When Tom drops and drives, his right knee is dirty from hitting the ground.

As the pitcher pushes forward off his pivot foot, the entire body goes into the pitch like an uncoiling spring, providing maximum power and drive.

Fig. 4.18 POWERFUL THRUST FOR-
WARD. Bending the knee of his pivot leg,
Scott Sanderson lowers his body and
thrusts out at the hitter. In pushing hard
off the rubber, Sanderson rotates his hips
and shoulders with violent intensity, which
provides maximum power and drive.
Scott's powerful thrust forward is a combination of maximum drive off the rubber
and the violent rotation of the hips and
shoulders as they open up.

The pitcher who thrusts out too quickly with the lower part of his body can
hold up the thrust by keeping the ball in his glove longer. He might exaggerate
keeping the ball in the glove until the upper half of his body is ready for the
thrust. Otherwise, the lower part starts too soon—it gets a head start.

Young pitchers often hurry their deliveries by taking the ball out of the glove
too soon. When the glove goes, the foot goes. Therefore, the young pitcher
should delay the stride by keeping the ball in the glove a little longer.

While dropping low has been used effectively by many pitchers through
the years, it should be remembered that there is a certain advantage in throwing
from a more upright position. The flight of the ball, or trajectory, is at a greater
angle.

Stride

As the pitcher steps to throw, it is important for him to step almost straight
forward with his striding foot. This step will eliminate any possibility of throwing
across the body. The stride should be comfortable and natural (Fig. 4.20). The
stride is simply a step in the direction of home plate and is *not* a power
movement. Pitchers who use the stride as a power movement will rush their
delivery and experience the problem of overstriding.

The length of the stride depends on a pitcher's height and how it suits his
size and comfort. Most important, he should guard against overstriding, one of
the chief faults in pitching technique. Generally, if the stride is too straight, too
long, or too far crossed-over, the pitcher will have a tendency to pitch high as
well as outside.

Fig. 4.19 THE DROP AND DRIVE is the biggest power element that a pitcher has. By bending the knee of his pivot leg, Tom Seaver lowers his body and is in a position to really thrust out. Observe the manner in which Tom turns his hips, showing the hitter nothing but his number and rear end. At the top of his motion, he takes a little pause to slow himself down enough to get everything together at the top before throwing to the plate. Pushing hard off the rubber, Seaver tries to drive low and right out at the hitter. One of the key points in the stride and follow-through, according to Tom, is that the left knee of the striding leg should remain bent, thus providing the flexibility so necessary for a smooth, powerful release and follow-through.

Fig. 4.20 THE STRIDE. By stepping almost straight forward, the pitcher eliminates the possibility of throwing across the body. Above all, he must guard against overstriding. The knee of the striding leg should remain bent to avoid jarring. It should be flexible so that it will give with the pitch. In this excellent picture, the throwing arm and upper part of Dave Stieb's body is able to shoot through—to whip the ball with maximum velocity.

A pitcher can open up the stride and get his arm on top by moving his lead foot over. A straight overarm pitcher has to open up his stride more. To make sure that he does not throw against his body and that his hips are opened fully, the pitcher's stride foot should land on, or to the first base side of, an imaginary line drawn toward the plate from between the pitcher's feet. Many coaches will draw this line in the dirt with a bat.

The stride should be completed before the pitcher has reached the top point of his delivery. His left foot and leg should be planted firmly in the dirt before he starts to apply the genuine power of the pitch. In other words, he is pitching against the anchor of his left leg which braces his body.

One of the key points in the stride and follow-through is that the knee of the pitcher's striding leg should remain bent to avoid jarring. This bent knee should be flexible so that it will give with the pitch and enable the pitcher to obtain the type of follow-through necessary for speed and control.

The toe and heel should strike the ground almost simultaneously, although the ball of the foot should take most of the shock. The pitcher's toe should be pointed toward the plate. It is important that he step in the same spot for each pitch.

A pitcher must not rush the stride. He should not rush out with the bottom half of his body. The average pitcher tends to move the lower part of his body ahead too quickly. He wants to start kicking too soon. His leg stride is too quick.

To counteract a tendency to thrust out too quickly, pitchers such as Sandy Koufax, Warren Spahn, and Juan Marichal used a higher leg kick. The leg lift not only gets drive into the motion, but gives the arm movement more time to get on top of the pitch.

Arm angle

Every pitcher has an angle of delivery from which his fast ball is most effective. A change in speed and velocity can be detected by lowering or raising the arm angle even a few inches.

The arm angle for most pitchers varies from low three-quarters to high three-quarters. A high three-quarters is more desirable, since it provides a downward plane and is particularly complimentary to the curve ball.

A pitcher can lose a considerable amount of spin and action on the fast ball because of a poor angle and impairment of natural coordination. Therefore, it is important for the coach to find the best angle of delivery for each of his pitchers. The three-quarter overhand delivery is the most natural one for the majority of pitchers.

Essentially, every pitch should be thrown from the same angle, so that the pitcher will not tip his pitches. If he throws his fast ball sidearm and his curve overhand, the hitter will soon know what is coming. Occasionally, however, a pitcher might want to lower the angle of his delivery, even coming around from Port Arthur, that is, stepping toward the third-base line and cross-firing past a right-handed hitter.

"I like to have my pitchers use a natural arm action," stated Sain. "Whenever I want to see what their natural arm action is, I suggest that they catch a fly ball and then run and throw the ball. Wherever they throw from, *right there,* I would say that would be the most natural position of their arm."

Arm and wrist action

The arm action of a pitcher should be a smooth, free movement with little muscular tension. His arm should be loose and relaxed as it swings backward in the windup. He should start to cock his arm as soon as his body begins to move forward again.

A pitcher's throwing arm should be away from his body, so he can bring the ball back and throw it in one continuous motion. The arm works as a unit with the back and shoulder. When the arm starts forward, the wrist should bend back. Then the elbow comes through, followed by the forward action of the arm and wrist. The arm should be up high. The elbow should not be below the shoulder and should precede his wrist as it comes past his shoulder point.

The muscles of the pitcher's hand and wrist must be relaxed prior to the release, so that a maximum wrist snap will take place. Keeping his arm loose, the pitcher should snap it forward like a whip as he makes his throw (Fig. 4.21). The release of the ball should be off the first two fingers, with a downward snap of the wrist. A strong wrist action will impart a spin to the ball, which, accompanied by speed, causes it to hop as it is affected by air currents.

Pitching on a downward plane

A major factor in pitching success is the pitcher's ability to throw the ball on a downward plane. Many of the pitching greats of baseball utilized high arm angles, with the point of release high above the ear. The greater the angle downward, the greater the advantage to the pitcher, is a principle that pitching coach Ray Berres for years successfully employed with the Chicago White Sox. Berres was a stickler for the correct execution of the proper mechanics of pitching, particularly the arm angle and downward plane.

Pitching on a downward plane means that the ball is moving in two planes, forward and down. The hitter, generally, swings the bat parallel to the ground,

Fig. 4.21 BE QUICK WITH THE ARM AND WRIST. A pitcher cannot be lazy with his arm. He must snap the arm through quickly. A good loose wrist helps give a pitcher the necessary "pop" in his pitches. If he doesn't pop his wrist, he will not have maximum velocity. In this picture, Bob Knepper releases the ball off the first two fingers with a downward snap of the wrist. Strong wrist action imparts a spin to the ball, which, accompanied by speed, causes it to hop as it is affected by air currents.

in a single plane. When the ball is released above the ear, it follows a downward trajectory which can cause the hitter difficulty in making solid contact.

The elbow must be up, at shoulder level or above. "If a pitch is made with a dropped elbow, the pitcher's hand will be traveling almost parallel to the ground," explained Bob Shaw, former pitching star of the Chicago White Sox. "As a result, he cannot pitch on a downward plane."

While a high arm angle and overhand delivery are mechanically desirable, a pitcher should use a style of his own and throw naturally. The arm angle should be one that feels most comfortable and natural.

Throwing depends on muscle tension and the art of whipping the arm. Fast ball pitchers always have quick arms.

Release

The most effort employed in the pitching delivery comes when the pitcher is actually releasing and unloading the ball. Everything before is preparation. Proper release is essential for good control, maximum spin, and smooth follow-through. It is wrist action and the release of the ball that are most responsible for imparting good stuff on the pitch.

The arm and wrist are loose and relaxed as the ball is released with good wrist snap. The index and middle fingers pull downward on the ball to make sure that the ball will have plenty of spin.

Although the actual release point is above and in front of the head, the pitcher must think about releasing the ball well out in front of him to achieve maximum effectiveness. In other words, he must think low when releasing the ball. After coming over the top, he must release the ball with his fingers on top of the ball, imparting strong wrist action.

The pitcher tries to create a consistent point of release, just as the golfer tries to create a consistent point of contact. By throwing the ball over and over, the pitcher will be able to find the correct release point. He can tell *by feel* that he is releasing the ball correctly.

If he opens up too soon, he will release too quickly. The front arm and shoulder will be too far forward, and the throwing arm will be too far in back of the body. This type of action will result in poor control and wear and tear on the body.

Follow-through

A good follow-through is important for speed, control, and a proper fielding position. A pitching motion that stops abruptly upon release of the ball hinders the speed and control of the pitch. The pitcher's arm should snap straight across his chest to his left knee, with the pivot foot swinging around to a position almost parallel to his striding foot (Fig. 4.22). His left leg and foot must remain firmly planted, because pitching against the resistance of the right leg gives the pitch its final snap.

The pitcher's eyes should be on the target, his back bent, and his weight evenly distributed, with the knees slightly bent. His glove should be brought up in front of his body so that he is in good fielding position.

However, there are pitchers who really whip the pitch. Consequently, they often end up in poor fielding positions. Rather than change their natural delivery, it is often best to teach them to make adjustments after completing the pitch, such as getting the feet parallel and ready to move in either direction. Any move which might curtail their motion and deception should be carefully considered. A number of big-league pitching coaches believe the follow-through is overrated. They cite a number of successful pitchers who stand up straight and fail to complete the weight transfer on their pitches.

Fig. 4.22 GOOD FOLLOW-THROUGH. A full sweep of the arm and shoulder and a complete follow-through are beneficial to the pitching delivery. Here, the pitching arm of Tom Seaver snaps across his chest to the knee of his striding leg.

CONTROL

Good location of pitches is essential for pitching success. A pitcher may have overwhelming stuff, but unless he can locate his pitches, he will not be effective. I have always figured that if a pitcher puts the ball over the plate, he will give up some home runs, but a solo homer is a lot better than a three-run homer, which is what he's liable to give up if he walks people.

Young pitchers should work on developing a fast ball and location.
RONNIE KING

Throw strikes! You can't catch a walk.

The main thing in pitching is to get the ball over the plate with good stuff on it, and be able to get the breaking pitches over. Control is the big difference between a *thrower* and a *pitcher.* The pitcher rarely walks anybody and hits those corners much of the time. When he wants to keep the ball down, he can keep it down.

For good control, a pitcher must be in a groove. He must be mechanically the same. Every pitch must mean something, whether he is throwing in the bullpen, throwing batting practice, or throwing in a game itself. He must concentrate and keep his eyes continually on a target (Figs. 4.20 and 22).

The mental factor is often the chief reason for poor control. Many pitchers do not concentrate enough on what they are trying to do. Mentally, they have to feel they can get the ball into the strike zone. So, they must "think the ball over the plate."

According to many pitching authorities, low pitching is the secret of successful pitching, because if a ball is down, batters tend to hit the ball into the ground more than they do if it is up in the air. When it is on the ground, some fielder has a chance to catch it.

If a pitcher lacks the necessary control, he should not consider pitching in and out, high and low, or everything low. Instead of throwing to spots, he should aim for the middle of the plate and hope his natural stuff takes care of the corners.

Although good control involves the ability to throw strikes, there are times when the pitcher should throw a ball, like when setting up the next pitch.

More high than low pitches are hit hard.

Most pitchers prefer throwing to the glove in the middle of the body. This is the target that enables the pitcher to split the catcher. After giving the signal, therefore, the catcher should move slightly into that area, slightly inside or slightly outside and give his target. The pitcher should divide the strike zone into possibly six areas and go for an area, rather than smaller, more difficult to hit spots.

Wildness often comes from a poor stride, either over or understriding. Landing on the heel, aiming the ball, and taking the eyes off the target are all causes of poor control.

Good control takes practice—considerable practice. The pitcher must be sure his grip is correct, that his delivery is the same each time. He must not pitch across his body. "Most important, the release point should be the same," said Adams. "He shouldn't release it here one time and down there another time."

Pitchers should throw from a mound at all times. Throwing or warming-up from flat ground is one way of throwing the pitcher out of his groove or pattern.

The following points are essential for achieving good control:

1. Do not go into your windup without thinking where you are going to pitch the ball.
2. Keep your eye on the target and concentrate on the spot the catcher is giving you.
3. Make sure your catcher is always in a squatting position, and that will make you pitch low.
4. There are four pitching targets: the catcher's knees and his shoulders. Keep your eye on one of these targets during the entire motion.
5. Watch your front foot, where you place your front foot down, and make sure it always lands on the same spot.
6. Make certain you let the ball go only when your arm is in front of you. If you find that your pitches are too high, chances are you are releasing the ball too soon.
7. Be sure you follow through across your body.
8. Keep ahead of the hitter. *Make that first pitch a strike!*

PROPER MENTAL ATTITUDE

A pitcher's frame of mind is of great importance to his overall performance, particularly his control. Confidence and poise, when blended with a strong competitive spirit, can be a huge asset to any pitcher. He has to feel he has everything completely under control. He must feel deep down that he is better than the hitter. He has to think positively that "I am going to do it!" "I never pitch a game that I do not expect to win," said Seaver. "I think positively."

I liked my pitchers to be confident, even to the cocky side. Of course, it would be good if the pitcher could show some cocky confidence to the hitter but leave it at the ball park after the game.

The pitcher has to have courage to throw the ball into the strike zone and has to be confident that he has the pitches and control to retire any hitter.

Relaxation is of vital importance in acquiring a good mental attitude. Whenever there is fear in the mind of a pitcher, there is tension, and that means he is not relaxed.

Here is how a pitcher can relax:

1. Concentrate on the exact spot you are going to throw the pitch.
2. Take a deep breath before making your pitch.
3. Do not be afraid you are going to walk the hitter.
4. Do not be afraid the batter will get a hit.

A pitcher has a job to do on the mound, and if he places his complete concentration on what he is doing and how he is going to work on the hitter and get him out, there will be no room for fear in his mind.

HIDING THE BALL

Every pitcher must work hard on keeping the ball hidden as long as possible. Hiding the ball until the instant it is released gives the batter that much less time to get his eye on it.

Many pitchers throw hard, but somehow their pitches come up to the plate big as a balloon. Very likely, their shortcomings can be attributed to a lack of deception and motion. They fail to hide their pitches effectively. The batter is able to pick up the ball early and can follow it all the way.

Then, there is the successful pitcher whose motion and deceptiveness are so effective the hitter is prevented from seeing the ball until it is right on him. Consequently, the batter cannot get around in time to pull the trigger.

A pitcher's glove makes a perfect cover-up for the ball as he gets ready to make his delivery (Fig. 4.23). As a result, most pitchers use as large a glove as possible. Many pitchers change the position of their hand on the ball, and the wrist gives the pitch away as much as the fingers on the ball. Consequently, the pitcher should just lay his wrist across the heel of his glove.

Fig. 4.23 HIDING THE BALL. The pitcher must cover the ball with his glove at all times. Concealing the ball is not enough. He must hide as much of his wrist in the glove as possible. Here, Mike Boddicker lays his wrist across the heel of his glove.

How to Cover Up Pitches

1. Wear a large glove that will help cover up the pitches.
2. Hold the ball the same way for all pitches.
3. Start every pitch the same way.
4. Cover the ball with the glove at all times.
5. Keep the ball hidden behind the body during the windup.
6. Throw the knee in front of the body.
7. Keep the ball in the glove longer—until the last moment.
8. Swing the glove hand toward the hitter.

Distracting the batter

There are various ways of distracting the hitter. Many pitchers like to swing their gloved hand in front of the throwing hand as they pitch. Certainly, a flick of the glove in the batter's line of vision can prove somewhat annoying.

Kicking the leg higher in the air can provide more deception in the delivery. However, caution should be taken *not* to employ the unorthodox type used by Juan Marichal. Unfortunately, the great majority of pitchers cannot execute this difficult maneuver properly.

Tipping pitches

Many young pitchers tip off their pitches. Some type of movement gives their intentions away. Therefore, the coach should study each of his pitchers closely to determine whether or not he is tipping his pitches.

To keep from tipping his pitches, the pitcher should strive to throw every pitch in the same manner. He should hide the ball well up in the web of his glove.

The following is a list of other ways pitchers might be tipping their pitches:

1. Raising the leg higher on one type than on another.
2. Spreading the fingers on certain pitches and not on others.
3. Showing more white on certain pitches.
4. Turning the glove differently when delivering certain pitches.
5. Turning the wrist more on one pitch than another as the pitching hand raises up in the glove.
6. Changing the arm angles on different pitches.

SET POSITION

When there are runners on base, the pitcher should throw from the set position rather than from a windup position. However, he should use the same pitching procedure from the stretch as he does from a windup. He must not vary his style. Some pitchers are not as effective when working from the set position as they are when using their windup. Quite often, this is because they do not spend enough time throwing from the stretch position on the sidelines. In the set position, the pitcher keeps his feet comfortably spread, his body turned sideways to home plate, with the pivot foot resting against the front edge of the rubber.

Stretching his arms overhead, he brings his hands down to the belt. This is the set position he must come to and hold for at least one full second before throwing to the hitter. He looks at the base runner, and throws to the base, steps off the rubber, or pitches to the batter.

Most pitchers hold their hands at their belts, while some hold them with their arms straight. Others hold them up by their chest.

The rear leg should be slightly bent, with most of the weight on it, so that a strong push-off can be made. The right-hander, with a runner on first base, should rotate his shoulders slightly toward first base and turn his head down and toward first so that by moving his eyes he can see both his catcher and the runner on first.

HOLDING RUNNERS ON

Since most stolen bases result from the base runner stealing on the pitcher, it is extremely important for all pitchers to develop a good move to first base. As a rule, the more dangerous the base runner, the more often the pitcher must throw over to keep him close to the base.

"Keep the runner honest," said Spahn. "Let him know you have a deceptive move. His respect for you will keep him closer to the bag."

Quickness and accuracy, not velocity, are the essential factors in all pick-offs. The quicker a pitcher can move his feet and get his upper body into throwing position, the quicker he will be able to release the ball. The pitcher's "unloading time" is a big factor in the success of the base runner. After becoming set, the elapsed time from his first move to release the ball to the plate should be under 1.3 seconds. With concentration and effort, a pitcher can cut his unloading time, but attempts to decrease it too quickly can cause mechanical problems in his delivery.

Before pitching to the batter, many right-handed pitchers make an initial move with their shoulders, arms, body, legs, or feet, but when throwing to first base, will always lift the right heel as the starting move. As a result, the base runner will watch the right heel. He will know the pitch is going to the plate if the heel does not lift, thereby getting a good start toward second. The pitcher can remedy the situation by developing the same initial move for the throw to the batter as the one to first base.

With a runner on first base, the right-handed pitcher should use peripheral vision. He should watch the runner out of the corner of his eye. He makes his throw to first by pivoting quickly to the left on his right foot and stepping toward the base with his left foot. The throw to first should be low and to the inside of the base. Quickness is more important than the speed of the throw (Fig. 4.24).

Aggressiveness is essential in any pick-off move. The pitcher can speed up his action by hopping on his pivot foot as it is turned toward the base. A jump shift, coming down on the pivot foot first and then on the other foot, is quicker than a pivot.

The best time to throw to first is when the pitcher comes down to a set position and just as the runner starts to take his lead. This is particularly true if his first step is a cross-over, which places him in a position from which it is difficult to get back to first base quickly. Sometimes, the pitcher likes to pivot and throw when he is at the height of his upswing on the stretch. Or, he might throw when coming down or after coming to a full stop.

A pitcher must not fall into a pattern. For example, he should not look at the runner the same number of times or take the same amount of time during and after every stretch. A good base runner will spot it and will be able to get a good jump on him.

A high leg kick with runners on base can also be dangerous. Instead, the kick should be quick, or merely a flat, quick stride. Most pitchers like to employ some type of kick, since it allows them to get more hip action into their delivery.

Fig. 4.24 PICK-OFF MOVE TO FIRST BASE. In stepping back behind the rubber, the right-handed pitcher lands on the ball of his right foot, then pushes off the right foot for the throw to first base. Quickness with the upper half of the body is even more important than being quick with the feet. Rather than drop the arm as when pitching to the plate, Jim Barr moves his arm quickly above the shoulder and when the body pivots into throwing position, he makes a flip throw to first base. By stepping behind the third base end of the rubber, Barr pivots on his left foot as he pushes off toward first base.

Since he is facing first base, a southpaw pitcher is obviously in a better position to hold the runner on.

Many pitchers do not throw to first base often enough, nor do they vary their timing in throwing to the plate or to first. An effective procedure is to throw to first with medium speed to keep the runner close, and with good speed when trying to pick him off.

When holding a runner on second base, the pitcher should take a normal stance, feet parallel, with the toes pointing straight ahead. In making the throw, he uses a jump shift toward the gloved hand side, which is quicker and smoother than turning toward the throwing hand side (Fig. 4.25).

With a runner at second, the pitcher might look back toward second base, look toward the plate, look back toward second again out of the corner of his eye to keep the runner honest, then focus on the target and pitch.

All pitchers should be aware that they do not have to complete their throws

Fig. 4.25 THROWING TO SECOND BASE. When holding a runner on second base, the pitcher should take a normal stance, feet parallel, with the toes pointing straight ahead. In making the throw, he uses a jump shift toward the gloved hand side. Whirling around on his left, pivot foot, he makes a snap overhand throw as he steps directly toward the base (Bob Bolin).

to either second or third, but that they *must* in throwing to first. The rules state that, in throwing to first base, the pitcher *must* step toward the base. Once he moves any part of his body, other than his head, toward first base, the ball must be thrown to first, and he must step toward the bag along with the throw.

If the runner on first breaks before the pitch, the pitcher should back off the rubber by lifting his pivot foot and placing it behind the rubber. He is now out of the box, and cannot commit a balk. He should turn to his left and start toward the runner.

If the runner keeps on going, the throw should be made to second base. If the runner stops halfway, the pitcher should run at him and make him commit himself.

Left-hander's move to first base

Southpaw pitchers who have a deceptive move to first base have a big advantage in holding runners on base. A basic principle in developing a good move is for the pitcher not to change what he does mechanically to the plate. In throwing to first base, he should duplicate what he does to the plate, at least until the stride leg gets to its highest point. "If the left-handed pitchers can freeze the runner until this point, then the runner can't possibly gain a good jump," explained Bob Cluck. "In achieving this position with the proper deception, they must make their mechanics appear they are going home."

In throwing to first base, the left-hander must step to the left of the 45-degree angle. He should also shorten his arm arc to allow for a quicker release of the ball. Once the pitcher breaks the plane with his right foot, he cannot legally throw to first base but must go to the plate.

To prevent a base runner from getting a good jump, a pitcher must try to destroy the runner's timing. An effective tactic is to come to the set position and simply hold the ball for an extended period.

PREVENTING THE BALK

Any motion by the pitcher, such as hand or leg movement, turn of the shoulder, that is started, stopped, or in any way interrupted, is a balk. A pitcher always has the option to back off the rubber when he doesn't like what he sees. He must step back with his rear foot.

When the pitcher commits a balk, a base runner is allowed to advance to the next base. The following are ways in which the balk can be prevented:

1. The pitcher must have his foot in contact with the rubber when pitching.
2. Once the pitcher has started his motion to the plate, or to first base, he must complete the throw.
3. When throwing to first base, the pitcher must step directly toward the base.
4. The pitcher must not drop the ball in the middle of his delivery.
5. When he wants to chase down a base runner, the pitcher must step back off the rubber.
6. The pitcher must pause for one second in the stretch position before pitching the ball to the plate.
7. When he does not have the ball, the pitcher must make no false appearance to pitch.

PICK-OFF PLAY

A successful pick-off play requires perfect timing, since the throw is usually made before the shortstop actually gets to the bag. The shortstop generally teams with the pitcher because he plays behind the runner. The play is usually attempted when the run, if scored, might have a final bearing on the game. A good time to work the pick-off play is when the count is three balls and one strike, or three balls and two strikes, because the runner is frequently given the "go" sign in these situations.

Unquestionably, the pick-off play must be practiced over and over until the timing between the pitcher and infielder is synchronized perfectly, so that the throw can be made quickly and accurately.

There are several basic methods of working the pick-off play at second base.

Method 1 The pitcher gives a signal to the shortstop, such as rubbing his shirt with his pitching hand. The shortstop answers with a similar signal. The pitcher takes his pitching position, while looking toward the runner. When the pitcher turns his head toward the plate, the shortstop immediately breaks for the bag. The pitcher looks momentarily toward the batter, then turns and makes his throw.

Method 2 When the shortstop thinks the runner is off guard, he breaks for the bag. The shortstop may break for second base after retreating toward the runner's left. This retreat, in which he backs up slowly, serves as a signal to the pitcher. The runner feels the shortstop has retreated back to his original position, but actually, it keeps him about the same distance from the bag. In either case, the pitcher should watch the shortstop so that he can turn and throw as soon as the break is made for the bag.

Method 3 (The daylight play) The shortstop initiates this play by placing daylight between himself and the runner. The pitcher uses his own judgment. The time to throw is when the pitcher sees daylight between the shortstop and the runner—with the shortstop closer to the bag.

Method 4 (Count play) A signal from the shortstop starts this play. When the runner at second takes an extra long lead, he becomes "fair game" for a pick-off play. While the pitcher is looking at the runner, the shortstop flashes the signal. He breaks for the bag as the pitcher turns back to face the batter. As the pitcher turns toward the plate, he counts "ONE–TWO" and turns and throws on "THREE." The shortstop starts on the count of "TWO."

The throw should be knee-high and directly over the bag, in order for the shortstop to make a sure catch and a quick tag.

FIELDING HIS POSITION

The pitcher has the important responsibility of being the "fifth infielder." Many times, the difference between winning and losing rests on the fielding skill of the pitcher. Handling batted balls hit up the middle, fielding bunts, throwing accurately to the right base, covering, and backing up bases are just some of the key responsibilities of the pitcher. The moment the ball leaves his fingertips, the pitcher becomes the "fifth infielder."

The pitcher should follow through and be ready for the ball to be hit back at him at all times, and be well balanced, with his feet spread, ready to go either way, the glove in front of the body.

Indeed, a pitcher can help himself by fielding his position efficiently. His ability to handle batted balls and diagnose play situations can be as important to his success on the mound as the manner in which he delivers the baseball to the plate.

FIELDING A BUNT

On bunt plays, the pitcher must break for the ball as fast as he can. As he nears the ball, he should slow down a little, keeping his eyes on the ball all the time.

A right-handed pitcher should try to get in front of the ball. He should jam his right foot hard into the ground, with his body bending at the waist. Using two hands, he picks up the ball. His eyes follow the ball into his glove. Raising up to a throwing position, he turns to his left and throws.

The left-handed pitcher should face the third base line, with his right foot closer than the left to the line, and turn to his right to make the throw.

On a bunt down the first base line, the pitcher should try to get in front of the ball. If it is close to the line, he should make the throw to the inside of first base.

Good judgment by the pitcher is essential in bunts and slow rollers down the foul lines. He must decide whether to field the ball or let it roll, in the hope it will roll foul. As soon as it moves into foul territory, he slaps it with his bare or gloved hand.

If the pitcher feels the bunt is on, he should make his first pitch a fast ball just above the strike zone, hoping that it will be popped up. He should wait until the ball is bunted, and then break.

Throwing to first

When fielding a bunt, the pitcher should use two hands whenever possible. His glove acts as the shovel, with his bare hand scooping the ball into it. Both hands should come up together toward his shoulder as the pitcher plants his right foot firmly in the ground. He should pivot, look to first, take a little step and throw to the first baseman. He should have his eyes on the first baseman's chest while making an overhand throw. He should never lob the ball, and always put something on the throw.

In fielding the bunt, the pitcher should spin toward his glove hand in throwing to first, second, or third. He should make the safe play early in the game, or when in doubt where to throw.

Throwing to second

On a ball hit back to him, or when fielding a bunt, the pitcher must know who is going to cover second. With a runner on first, he should always ask the second baseman and shortstop who will cover.

The catcher directs the action on these fielding plays, and the pitcher must listen to him yell "second" or "first."

On double play balls, the ball should be thrown to the infielder covering the bag, chest-high, leading the shortstop slightly, or to the second baseman, who then makes his pivot.

The pitcher must concentrate on making his throw accurately. Therefore, he must not hurry his throw or make it while off balance.

Throwing to third

One of the toughest plays for the defense to handle is the bunt or slow hit ball down the third base line. On this big play, the defense should strive to get the lead runner going into third. However, if this is impossible, they must go for the out at first or second base.

The pitcher has the responsibility for fielding the ball hit to his third base side, with the third baseman moving back toward the base and receiving the throw.

The key to the play is the third baseman. He must make the decision the moment the ball is hit, as to whether the pitcher can field the ball. If not, he immediately yells, "I got it!" and makes the throw to first or second base.

To get the important force play at third base, the pitcher must practice moving off the mound quickly and making an accurate throw to the third baseman.

COVERING FIRST BASE

On any ball hit to his left, the pitcher should automatically break toward first base. Many games have been lost because the pitcher failed to get off the mound in time.

There are two methods of performing this play:

Method 1   On a ball hit to the first baseman's left, or straight to him, the pitcher should circle into the bag. He runs to a spot about twelve to fifteen feet in front of the base and approaches the base running parallel to the line. As he gets near the base, he should slow down slightly and bring his speed under control (Fig. 4.26).

The ball should get to the pitcher a good stride from first base. Catching the ball chest-high, the pitcher now has the opportunity to locate the bag and

Fig. 4.26   COVERING FIRST BASE. On any ball hit to his left, the pitcher should automatically break toward first base. Circling into the bag, the pitcher runs to a spot about twelve to fifteen feet in front of the base and approaches the base running parallel to the line. As he gets near the base, he should slow down slightly and bring his speed under control. In this series, the pitcher has to wait momentarily. Then, he takes a step forward with his left foot and braces with his right foot (Ron Herbel).

tag it (Fig. 4.26). He should whirl around over his left shoulder, ready to make a play on any other runner.

Method 2   On a ball hit to the right of the first baseman, or on a slow roller, the pitcher should go directly to the bag and anchor there. This also applies to the first-second-first double play with the shortstop.

On a fumble, the pitcher should stop, place one foot on the second base side of the bag and be ready to stretch or shift to either side for the throw

On slow hit balls to his first base side, if the pitcher can field the ball himself, he should yell out: "I've got it." Then, the first baseman should answer: "Take it." The first baseman will then cover the base. While this seems quite simple, it is very important.

As he approaches the area of first base, the pitcher should show the first baseman his glove, as a target to throw to.

COVERING HOME

When there is a man on third base and a passed ball or wild pitch occurs, the pitcher must be alert to cover the plate. In fact, anytime the catcher is drawn away from the home plate area, the pitcher must be ready to cover.

Coming in as fast as he can, the pitcher should drop down on his knee, facing the intended throw. He should give the runner the outside half of the plate. Straddling the inside half of the plate, he gives the runner the outside or foul line territory. He does not want to block the plate, because of the possibility of getting cut up. He tags the runner with the back of his glove facing him.

BACKING UP BASES

Every ball that goes to the outfield is a potential backup play for the pitcher, regardless of the number of runners on base. Once he has decided to which base the throw is likely to be made, the pitcher runs to a point forty to fifty feet behind that base, and in line with the player who is making the throw.

From this position on the diamond, he can easily retrieve all balls which may rebound past the intended receiver. If he is in doubt as to which base to back up, the pitcher should take a position between bases until the outfielder makes his throw. He should always be one base ahead of the lead runner.

PITCH-OUT

A pitch-out is a deliberate waste ball that the batter cannot possibly reach. The purpose of this pitch is to permit the catcher to throw to one of the bases, for runners who take long leads. Or, it might be used when an attempted steal, hit and run, or squeeze play is anticipated.

The pitcher usually throws a shoulder-high fast ball on a pitch-out sign. He tries to keep the ball high and far outside the plate. A pitch-out is released more quickly, using a snap overhand throw.

One of the cardinal rules of baseball is, "Never walk the tying or winning run intentionally." While there are situations when walking a hitter intentionally can be justified, the percentages are heavily in favor of the defense.

INTENTIONAL PASS

In giving an intentional pass, the pitcher should not lob the ball to the plate, but throw medium-speed fast balls about three feet outside and shoulder-high.

Since he cannot leave the catcher's area until the pitcher releases the ball, the catcher makes his target by holding the glove far out to the side and then takes a lateral step to receive the ball.

The primary objective of the intentional pass is to pitch to a more logical opponent, while setting up a force or possible double play. It is used *only with first base open.*

Another time the intentional pass is considered good baseball is with the winning run on third, and either none or only one of the other bases occupied.

MOVING A HITTER BACK

The inside-outside style of pitching is a regular practice of major league pitchers, particularly for hitters who crowd the plate. This means that a pitcher should learn to throw his fast ball on the inside in order to keep the hitter from covering up the outside of the plate.

Pitchers who throw too much on the outside, without an occasional inside pitch, will soon have the hitters taking picks on the seemingly "perfect pitches" that hit the low outside corner. By keeping all his pitches out over the plate, a pitcher is simply inviting the hitters to take a toehold and swing from the heels.

Pitching inside refers to the practice of throwing hard stuff in and off the plate from four to twelve inches. "We make a major effort to 'jam' the hitter, make him hit the ball near his hands," explained Cluck. "By pitching inside regularly, we make our other pitches more effective. Hitting is 'timing' and nothing destroys a hitter's timing faster than to be 'jammed'."

Larry Sherry, who was a fine relief pitcher with us early in the 1960s, had a theory on handling the batter who constantly crowded the plate. "Anyone who moves into the plate or stands close to the plate," said Larry, "you have to pitch tight. I mean you have to pitch around the neck and head inside, not to hit him, but you have to pitch tight in order to make your outside pitches effective."

Occasionally, a pitcher may come in too tight and knock down a hitter. This gives the impression that he is throwing a duster, but more than likely, his fast ball just took off. Drysdale was blamed for many pitches inside that he did not intentionally throw because his fast ball was a live one that would bear in and down. Koufax, on the other hand, seldom brushed anybody back.

A good time to brush a hitter back is with two strikes and no balls. However, a pitcher should never throw at the hitter with the intention of hitting him.

WARMING UP

A pitcher should always warm up, get good and loose and break a little sweat, before he starts to throw hard or run hard, in order not to strain or pull any muscles.

Fifteen minutes of warm-up should be enough for any starting pitcher. The opening minutes should be devoted to loosening up from both the windup and stretch positions. The last seven minutes should get the pitcher good and loose, ready to face the first hitter.

Relief pitchers sometimes have to enter a ball game with only a few minutes of warm-up.

The following are tips on warming up:

1. Always throw at a target.
2. Throw easy at first, but with your whole delivery.
3. Use straight stuff at first.
4. Start throwing breaking pitches by just twisting or spinning the ball.
5. Practice working from the set position.
6. Move the ball around—up and down, in and out.
7. Spend more time on the pitch that is not working right.
8. Make sure you are good and loose before you start throwing hard.

WORKING ON THE HITTER

The ability to work on the hitter plays an increasingly vital role as the pitcher advances upward in baseball. A pitcher can have all the stuff in the world, but without control, a variety of pitches, and the ability to set up the hitter, his live fast ball and sharp curve can be greatly reduced in effectiveness. As he progresses in baseball, a pitcher should learn how to go to work on the hitter, trying to make him hit his best pitch (Figs. 4.27 and 4.28).

The secret of good hitting is *timing,* so the batter must be kept off balance. A pitcher can disrupt the hitter's timing by throwing the ball at different speeds with the same motion. The hitter who is kept off balance never seems to get his pitch.

The key to containing good hitters is to get ahead of them and not give them anything good. Fernando Valenzuela relies on mixing up his pitches, changing speeds, and nipping the corners. He gets hitters looking for one thing, then gives them something else.

"When I don't have a good, live fastball, I use other pitches to set it up."

JACK MORRIS

A number of factors affect a pitching pattern, including the score, inning, outs, runners on base, type of hitter, and the pitcher himself. As a result, the pattern and sequence of pitches should vary from pitch to pitch.

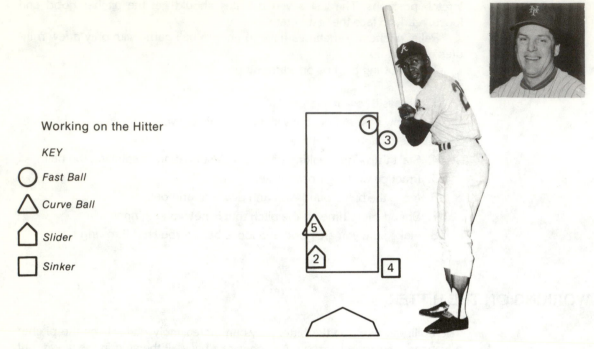

Working on the Hitter

KEY

⭕ *Fast Ball*

△ *Curve Ball*

⬠ *Slider*

☐ *Sinker*

Fig. 4.27   Tom Seaver (Mets), a right-hander, pitching to Rico Carty.

An experienced pitcher will take advantage of the weaknesses of the hitters, and his pitching pattern will be arranged accordingly. It is important that every pitch have an element of surprise.

By establishing a pattern, the pitcher can set up the hitter for his "out pitch," one which the batter is weakest at hitting. Having been set up, the hitter is made more vulnerable. Southpaw Jerry Reuss, for example, is very effective throwing his hard stuff in on the right-handed hitters. I used to tell my pitchers to crowd them with hard stuff. Those big guys like to extend their arms. Pitchers like Valenzuela and Tug McGraw, who have a specialty, work in this fashion. To be effective, they rely on their "off pitches," such as screwballs and sinker pitches. By setting him up, they make the hitter hit their best pitch.

Valenzuela has five pitches in his repertoire, and rarely does the hitter see the same pitch twice. This is because he mixes his pitches, changing speeds and moving the ball around. In addition to his famous screwball, Valenzuela can effectively throw the curve, slider, and change-up, but his fast ball sets up the rest of his pitches. If you can't back up the screwball with a fast one, the smart hitter just waits.

Even the top pitcher does not always have the good fast ball every time he pitches. This is when he has to be a *pitcher,* and not a thrower. The thrower tries to force his fast ball, even when he does not have it. Instead, he should go to his breaking stuff and begin changing speeds and hitting the corners.

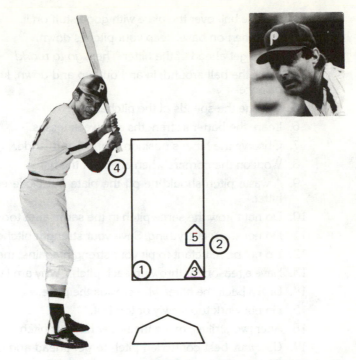

Fig. 4.28 Steve Carlton (Phillies), a left-hander, pitching to Matty Alou.

A pitcher should not try to strike everyone out. He will just tire himself out, and will press and often force his pitching. He should use his players. They will know he can get the ball over the plate, and in turn, they will come up with better plays. By conserving his energy and the number of pitches, he can call for a little more reserve energy when he gets into tough situations in the later innings.

Get ahead of the hitter

The pitcher should get his first pitch over the plate with something on it. If he can stay ahead of the hitter, a pitcher's troubles will be greatly reduced. He should try to get ahead of the batter and force him to hit his pitch. With two strikes on the hitter, a pitcher should want the hitter to go for his best pitch.

If he is ahead of the hitter, he might push him back once or twice before going for the decisive pitch. In Figure 4.28, on a one-ball-and-two-strike count, Steve Carlton's fourth pitch is high and tight, which moves the hitter back from the plate. He follows with a hard slider to the outside corner. In a crucial situation, the pitcher will either go to the hitter's weakness for a double play, or he may go to his own strength and strike him out.

The following should be observed when working on the hitter:

1. Get the ball over the plate with good stuff on it.
2. With men on base, keep your pitches down.
3. Try to get ahead of the hitter. Then, *go to work!*
4. Move the ball around, in and out, up and down, keeping the batter off balance.
5. Change the speeds of the pitches.
6. Learn the batter's strengths and weaknesses.
7. Observe the hitter's position, stance, and stride.
8. Work on the corners when ahead of the hitter.
9. A waste pitch should be off the plate but close enough to tempt the hitter.
10. Do not throw the same pitch in the same area too often.
11. Do not show everything. Save your strength pitches for key situations.
12. Do not be reluctant to pit your strength against the batter's strength.
13. Have a reason for throwing each pitch. "Why am I throwing this pitch?"
14. Brush back the hitter who crowds the plate.
15. Do not work too slowly or too fast.
16. After two strikes, make the batter hit your pitch.
17. Use your best controlled pitch to get ahead and stick to what you do best.
18. As the old adage goes, "When in doubt—curve him." This is because most ball players are fast ball hitters.
19. Let your fielders do their work.

Types of hitters

Type	Suggestion
1. Open stance hitter	Since he likes inside pitches, keep them away from him.
2. Long stride hitter	Usually a low ball hitter—pitch him high.
3. Uppercut hitter	Pitch him high and tight.
4. Crouch hitter	Since he likes low pitching, pitch him high.
5. Lunge hitter	Use a change-up or a high, tight fast ball.
6. Hitch hitter	Pitch him fast and tight, although changing-up is often effective.
7. Nervous, overanxious hitter	Take your time and make him wait.
8. Bucket hitter	Give him outside pitches, particularly curves.

9. Hitter who turns his head   Give him some curves, particularly on the outside pitch.
10. "Guess" hitter   Mix up your pitches.

RELIEF PITCHING

A good relief pitcher is one who can come in out of the bullpen, without taking too much time to get ready, and be able to throw strikes. He cannot afford to get behind the hitter. He must get ahead of him quickly.

A good bullpen has become the backbone of a major league pitching staff. It is also a big plus for high school and college teams to have a pitcher who can come in and stop the opposition late in the game. Don McMahon, pitching coach of the Cleveland Indians, pointed out: "Whether or not school teams have designated specialists, I do feel the coach should give everyone on his staff a thorough understanding of relief pitching, such as warming up effectively, training physically and mentally, and what to do when entering a tight game."

The heavy work given today's relief pitchers suggests that a pitcher is capable of pitching more often than was previously thought possible. Normally, relief pitchers who throw extremely hard and pitch two or three innings one day can come back for an inning the next day. Dave Guisti, former relief pitcher of the Pittsburg Pirates, explained: "If I went two innings, I could come back for two innings the next day, perhaps even three days in a row, and then have to take a day off. But throwing too often can take something out of you."

Fig. 4.29 THE RELIEF PITCHER. Temperament is a key factor in the success of a relief pitcher. He must be in complete control, poised, and confident. The effectiveness and sharpness of a relief pitcher increases with work (Steve Howe).

"Temperament is a key factor in the success of a relief pitcher," stated Ron Perranoski, pitching coach of the Dodgers and a former top relief pitcher. "You just cannot get excited out there. Even though one mistake can cost your team the ball game, you cannot let this bother you. You just have to feel that there will be another game tomorrow."

Baseball's most effective relievers have the ability to make the ball sink or keep it down for a possible double play. Ideally, a good relief man should have at least two pitches that he can throw for a strike anytime he wants to. If he can control his third pitch, he will make a good stopper in anybody's league.

Before a ball game

Big-league relief pitchers do their conditioning during pregame practice. They arrive on the field early and shag for the hitters, in addition to taking some cuts themselves. Generally, relief men do about eight wind sprints daily, compared to about twelve to fifteen for starting pitchers.

McMahon likes the relief pitcher's routine of pitching some before the game. "I always liked to throw three-quarters or half-speed, perhaps five or six minutes on the side, just to find out if I had my rhythm and my arm was loose. In the late innings, you might have to get up quickly and not have your full time to loosen up."

Getting ready

Relief pitching has become such a specialized phase of the game that each major league team has a short man, as well as middle and long relievers. "I know my position is going to be as the short man," said Perranoski, "from the seventh inning on. Therefore, from about the fourth inning, I prepare myself mentally, sitting in the bullpen and watching the ball game. I have to know what pitcher is on the mound and how long my manager will go with him. I must know who the hitter is, and who the next two hitters will be. I have to know how many runs we are ahead or behind."

As far as preparing himself physically to get loosened up, with Perranoski, it varies from day to day. "If I have pitched on four or five straight days," said Ron, "it may take me a little longer to get loose because of stiffness. But if I have had two or three days of rest, I can get ready sometimes after ten to twelve pitches, plus the eight on the mound. There are, of course, so many variables, such as the weather condition. If it is cold, naturally, it will take longer."

In warming up, the relief pitcher should begin his throwing with easy, slow speed pitches. He should not warm up with full velocity right away. When you have to get ready in a hurry, the easiest way to do it is to throw off-speed breaking pitches and really overexaggerate the follow-through. This seems to loosen the arm the most.

Coming in from the bullpen

The relief pitcher has to know the situation: how many men are on, the score, and who are the hitters. "Usually, if a left-handed hitter is coming up to the plate," asserted Perranoski, "I can expect they will switch to a right-handed pinch hitter.

"The first pitch is the most important pitch in a tough situation. It is not a matter of just throwing the ball over for a strike. Rather, it is a matter of hitting a particular spot."

"I want my relievers to come in and throw strikes," said Johnny McNamara, manager of the California Angels. "I also want them to get some hum on the ball."

Getting the job done

"I try to concentrate on throwing a sinking fast ball," explained Perranoski. "I have to keep the ball down because I am not an overpowering pitcher. I will throw an occasional curve, even taking some speed off of it, which makes my fast ball look a little faster.

"My greatest asset is the fact that I have commanding control of my fast ball, slider, and curve, which I feel I am able to throw in any situation. Many times, I have had to throw strikes with the winning run on third base, a 3–2 count, and the bases loaded. All in all, I think the key to relief pitching is the manner of mixing up the pitches and getting them over when you have to."

CONDITIONING OF THE PITCHER

Some pitchers have the mistaken idea that in order to get into condition, all they have to do is throw, and throw, and get their arms in shape. As a result, after five or six innings, when their legs give out, they rest under a warm shower.

Pitchers should always keep in mind that *a pitcher's legs are just as important as his arm."* The entire body must be in good physical condition in order to prevent sore arms. Whenever a pitcher does not bend the knees of his pivot foot, he is either a lazy pitcher or a poorly conditioned one. He must have spring in his legs. During the season, pitchers must follow a regular schedule in order to get the necessary throwing and running between starts.

Therefore, we want our pitchers to run a lot. Running is the most important way to exercise (Fig. 4.30). Even after the season begins, we want our pitchers to run twenty to twenty-five minutes daily when they are not scheduled to work.

Besides their daily running, most pitchers keep in condition through pepper practice, pick-ups, and shagging balls. Football pass drills, fungo drills, and fielding drills will provide needed variety.

Getting pitchers in shape for the coming season is certainly simpler when

Fig. 4.30 WIND SPRINTS. Pitchers should run twenty to twenty-five minutes daily when they are not scheduled to work. Major league pitchers, like these on the Mets' staff use the wind sprint method, running hard for sixty to seventy yards and walking back fairly briskly as they get their wind back.

they have had a good winter program. Then, some coaches feel the best way to be a pitcher is to throw the ball properly and often.

Strength development

Many pitchers can attribute their success in part to well planned weight-resistance programs during the off-season. These programs of strength development involve use of weights, apparatus, calisthenics, or isometric training. All of these items could be included in a sound program, which must be closely supervised by coaches. These programs are presented in detail in Chapter 16 on conditioning.

Stretching is the key to the entire weight training program for pitchers. Without stretching, the program could prove damaging. The pitcher must stretch after each exercise period to maintain flexibility. *Never* allow a pitcher to lift weights without stretching afterward.

In any strength-building program, it is important to continually increase the amount of resistance. The muscles being developed have to be overloaded, starting first with few repetitions, and bringing more muscle fibers into play to overcome the resistance. The result is growth in strength. However, caution should be taken to limit the weight lifted.

Calisthenics alone lack the efficiency of weights and apparatus as a strength developer. It just takes too long to overload a muscle group through calisthenics. However, they do have considerable value in maintaining body flexibility and as a warm-up activity.

Care of the arm

If he is scheduled to pitch the next day, a big league pitcher generally comes in before the previous day's game and gets a massage and stretching, which lasts about twenty minutes.

On the day of a game, a half-hour before starting his warm-up, he comes in for a massage and a light stretch. Most big-league trainers use Capsolin for this purpose because, when the body perspires, the perspiration comes through the Capsolin. Analgesic, atomic bomb, and Logangesic seem to hold the perspiration to the body. Sometimes trainers mix the Capsolin with baby oil.

On the day after a game, a pitcher will likely jog around, throw, and play a little pepper. The next day, two days before his pitching turn, he will go out and play "long toss" in the outfield. He will throw 120 or 150 feet, just to stretch out his arm, not worrying about velocity.

Ice bag technique

After the game is over, all of our pitchers use the ice bag technique made famous by Sandy Koufax and Drysdale. Today, most teams have their pitchers use immersion, soaking the arm in ice for about a half-hour (Fig. 16.17).

In the case of Drysdale, his arm was elevated and ice bags were used all the way from his wrist to his mid-back for about twenty-five minutes. Then he was given a very light stretch, which helped him with his elbow problem and got him ready about one day sooner.

A spring training running plan

A pitcher is only as good as his legs. Therefore, he must do a great deal of running.

EARLY WYNN

We start out very gradually. Since we have plenty of time to get in shape, I do not want to "kill" the guys the first few days. "The first day we might have them do ten sprints, at least 100 yards or longer," explained Adams, "and we run ten or twelve for two or three days. Generally, after the first four or five days, they start getting the stiffness out a little bit. That second or third day, when they are sore, is really tough.

"After the boys get over their stiffness, we will increase it a couple to fourteen or so, and within ten days after training began, we will be running twenty sprints. We will run twenty every day from then on—twenty good hard ones.

"When the season begins, the relievers drop back to ten or twelve," continued Red. "The starting pitchers run these with us, then after the relievers finish, they will run maybe eight or ten more on their own. Some of the fellows are doing some jogging."

Jogging, though, is better for the off-season. An athlete has to jog so much farther and longer to do the same thing he can do with his sprints.

To avoid arm trouble, my advice to the young pitcher is:

1. Build up a strong arm and body through regular throwing, running, and exercise.
2. Concentrate on the fast ball until you have built up a strong, flexible arm.
3. Forget about the breaking pitches, especially the slider, until you have matured physically.
4. Never throw hard until you are completely warmed up.
5. Do not pitch too often in competition. Make sure you have the proper amount of rest between starts.
6. Regular throwing is not only the greatest deterrent to a sore arm, but, often the best remedy for it.

PITCHING IN A ROTATION SYSTEM

Major league starting pitchers follow either a four-day or five-day pitching plan. The pitcher's arm, the schedule, and the strength of the staff are the determining factors in the rotation plan.

During the last half of the season, I think the five-day rotation is better, but early in the season, with more rain outs and more days off, a team can get by with a three or four man pitching rotation. As the season progresses, with more doubleheaders and fewer off days, it is better to go with a pitching staff of five.

To a large extent, all this depends on the individuals who make up the staff. Some pitchers work better with four days' rest. The size of the staff is a factor too. A team may have only two or three effective starting pitchers.

Seaver, for example, pitches every fifth day. If he starts on Sunday, he rests on Monday. Then he throws for about fifteen or twenty minutes on Tuesday, and rests again on Wednesday and Thursday before he pitches on Friday.

Typical pitching schedule

A typical major league pitching schedule is as follows (five-day plan):

Sunday: Pitch a nine-inning game.

Monday: Rest (do not touch a ball, but run in the outfield).

Tuesday: Loosen up (fifteen minutes of light throwing to the catcher).

Wednesday: A good workout (after loosening up, pitch batting practice).

Thursday: No throwing, but good leg work.

Friday: Pitch a nine-inning game.

CLOTHING AND EQUIPMENT

The shirt should be loose, not binding. Pitchers like the arm sleeves to be cut just below the elbow. They should be 50/50 cotton and wool or 100 percent wool in the arms. Professional pitchers have four or five of each. Most pitchers like their toe plate built into their shoe. They should always have a protective plastic cup inside the supporter.

DRILLS

Drills must be engaged in vigorously, whether they involve covering first base, fielding bunts, throwing to the bases, throwing for the double play, or backing up throws. (See Drills 15.11, 15.12, and 15.17.) A pitcher must adapt himself mentally in these drills. The biggest mistake he can make is to just go through the motions. If he performs these skills correctly in practice, very likely they will carry over and become automatic in the game. This is why he must bounce off the mound and hustle after the ball and make this play correctly in practice.

Pitchers who appear bored and handle their assignments sloppily during practice invariably are the ones who foul up in game situations—and one miscue can lose the ball game for him and his team.

Covering first base

The pitchers should line up near the mound, one behind the other, each with a ball. The coach is at home plate with a ball and fungo bat, and the catcher positions himself behind the plate.

The pitcher throws to the catcher, and the coach hits the ball toward first base. The pitcher then runs to cover first, taking the throw from the first baseman. Then the pitcher goes to the end of the line, and the process continues as the catcher gives the coach the ball he caught from the previous pitcher.

The coach can keep the pitcher from cheating by hitting an occasional grounder through the box.

Throwing to first base

This drill not only provides the pitcher valuable lessons in keeping the runner close to first base, but it serves other purposes as well. The base runner gets experience in taking a good lead, and the defense can work on their responsibilities.

The pitchers form a line behind the mound, while the base runners form a line at the first base coaching box. The pitcher tries to prevent the runner from taking too big a lead, and he may throw over to the first baseman, attempting to pick off the runner.

This drill gives the pitcher practice in making the delivery to home plate from his set position. The coach watches the pitcher closely to detect any balk motion.

Backing up bases

A good drill for backing up bases is to put the pitcher on the mound and have him go through various game conditions with runners on base. This is the same procedure used in cutoff play practice. The pitcher also covers a base that is unguarded because the catcher or an infielder has left his position.

Pick-off play

This drill gives the pitcher practice in pivoting and picking runners off second base. The pitchers form a line off to the first base side of the mound, while one of them takes his set position on the rubber. The runner assumes his lead off second base.

The second baseman and shortstop get in their playing positions and work a pick-off play with the pitcher, as described on pages 120–121.

The base runner can allow the pick-off to succeed at first, since the defensive players need practice in executing this play.

Throw-catch

The pitchers line up at the foul line in right field, facing center field. Each pitcher has his glove and a ball. A coach or reserve player stands halfway to center field.

The first pitcher runs toward the coach. When he is ten or fifteen yards away, he throws him the ball. After catching it, the coach permits the pitcher to run past and then returns the ball to the pitcher by giving him a lead throw.

Pepper

One or more players throws the ball to a hitter, who hits grounders and liners to the fielders, who are about fifteen feet away. This drill has more value when the fielders are limited to just two or three individuals

A game can be made of this fine drill, with the fielders counting how many consecutive times they can catch a ball without error.

Pick-ups

The purpose of this drill is to get the pitcher to move quickly from side to side and to pick up slow rolling balls.

The pitchers pair off about twelve feet apart, one acting as the tosser and the other as the fielder. The tosser rolls the ball first to one side and then to the other side of the pitcher.

Upon fielding the ball, it is returned to the tosser and the fielder keeps fielding the ball until he has fielded fifty of them. Then, they change places.

5
Catching

The catcher has to be the leader, a take-charge sort of person who can direct the play of his team. His performance behind the plate, in handling his pitchers, keeping the runners honest with a strong and accurate arm, setting up the hitters, and keeping the whole team inspired and alert by being aggressive and full of drive, contributes to the effectiveness of the pitcher out on the mound. Since they are all watching him, the catcher can set a good example for the defensive team.

Indeed, a team's greatest need is a skilled, clever, and spirited catcher. I do not think a team can rise to championship heights without an able and durable receiver. The confidence of not only the pitcher, but the entire defense, rests on the catcher. He must know the weakness of opposing hitters, be able to handle all types of pitches and fielding plays, and be able to throw with strength and accuracy.

THE ESSENTIALS

A strong arm can be a great asset to the catcher and his team. In fact, a player cannot hope to be a successful catcher if he does not have a strong throwing arm. He must be able to throw base runners out with consistency and keep opponents from stealing and taking extra bases.

On some occasions, the catcher may have to go out to the mound and

Fig. 5.1 THE CATCHER is the key to a strong defense, a bulwark of strength. The man behind the plate is the most vital position player on a ball team. He has the toughest job on a team, and without a good, competent receiver, a team will have difficulty winning. Here, Luis Pujols of the Houston Astros, as he awaits an incoming throw, readies himself for a close play at the plate.

give his pitcher some encouragement and suggestions. "Don't try to throw too hard," or, "Don't rush your motion" are typical of the little reminders the catcher can give the pitcher.

A receiver often has to remind his pitcher to throw to first base and be alert for a bunt play. If the ball is hit back to him, where will he throw the ball? How many outs, and what is the score? This is why the catcher has to be a good leader and a quarterback on the ball field.

A strong and accurate arm can be a tremendous asset to the catcher and his team.

Catching the low ball and throwing to the bases are two of the most important skills of a good catcher. Therefore, the receiver should practice catching the low ball as much as he can, and work diligently on his throwing. Correct footwork in shifting for the throw is essential.

Catching is a vigorous activity and demands considerable endurance. Stopping a low pitch with the body and getting a foul tip on the "meat hand" goes with the job. Perhaps this is why the catching job calls for more dedication than any other position in the game. He has to *want* to catch!

QUALIFICATIONS

A catcher has to be able to catch the ball. While this basic skill sounds elementary, the ability of the receiver to handle all types of pitched and thrown balls, bunts, and pop fouls can be a major factor in a "sound defense."

Being able to catch low throws, particularly, is of great importance in instilling the confidence of the pitcher in keeping his pitches down. Quite often, a pitcher is reluctant to throw a low curve ball with a man on third base, fearful that it might bounce in the dirt and get past the catcher. With a good receiver behind the plate, the pitcher will feel, "If I throw the breaking pitch in the dirt, I know my catcher will handle it."

Talking to and encouraging the pitcher can help make the pitcher think he can get the hitter out. Jeff Torborg had that encouragement quality. He would go out to the mound and say, "Come on, Bill, let's get this guy!" When he made a good pitch, Jeff would say, "That was a great pitch!" A catcher has to be kind of a cheerleader. His confidence actually will reflect on the pitcher. To me, this is one of the most important attributes of an outstanding receiver.

A strong, accurate throwing arm is a quality possessed by all the great catchers. The catcher who does not have a powerful arm has to make up for it in quickness. I would not trade quickness and accuracy for the fellow who just throws hard.

Fig. 5.2 A STRONG AND ACCURATE THROWING ARM. The catcher must be able to throw base runners out with consistency and keep opponents from stealing and taking extra bases (Bob Brenly).

A catcher must learn to understand each and every pitcher as a different individual. He must converse with his pitchers at all times to develop good rapport, a relationship necessary for a smooth-working battery. In a tight situation, I like to see my catcher go out to the pitcher and talk over the game situation.

Another requirement is the ability to block the plate—a rugged, rough catcher who is not afraid of a little body contact. Those runners come in there with a full force, and he has to block the plate, catch the ball and tag the runner, all at the same time. Therefore, the catcher has to be a rugged individual, with a lot of courage (Fig. 5.1).

A good receiver has to have fair size in order to take all the abuse that he will have to take. Yet, *mobility,* the ability to bounce around, fielding bunts, shifting on bad pitches, and getting foul balls, is even more important.

TYPE OF GLOVE

The single or double break glove is the dominant type used today. The "one-handed glove" has a break like a first baseman's glove. Until the mid-seventies, there were two types of gloves worn by catchers: 1) the single-break glove and 2) the non-hinged glove. The major baseball glove companies, however, are no longer manufacturing the non-hinged glove.

Single-break glove

All major league receivers use a glove with one or two breaks in it. The one-handed glove is very similar to the type used by the first baseman (Fig. 5.3). Johnny Bench, for many years the game's top receiver, explained that "with a one-handed glove, I can keep my meat hand away from or behind the glove, and I seem to have more maneuverability with a single-break mitt."

Rawlings Company has their Johnny Bench Professional models featuring a crotch-laced, high pocket web with a spiral-laced top, a single-break heel which offers an adjustable thumb and little finger loops. Wilson Company has a Professional Twin Action mitt made of premium cowhide leather, a double-break mitt with a Pro-Back design. It features the "Pro Toe" and dual-horizontal-hinge web.

The new types of single or double break gloves are very much like a first base glove. I believe the one-handed receiver behind the plate can do a fine job, unless he becomes lazy and forms bad habits about shifting on pitches.

Non-hinged glove

This traditional type of glove, until it was replaced by the single-break model, forced the receiver to become a better "two-handed catcher." A non-hinged mitt forced the catcher to catch with two hands and execute proper footwork. He had to shift to his right and left. The non-hinged glove helped the catcher learn the rhythmic footwork and obtain the proper balance necessary for accurate throwing.

One-handed catching

One-handed catching evolved primarily to protect the throwing hand from foul balls. The improved make of the catcher's glove has made one-handed receiving more convenient. Since they facilitate one-handed catching, the single or double break gloves are now highly popular among catchers.

One-handed receiving is particularly the rule today with no runners on base. Many catchers will even put their throwing hand behind them for added protection. One-handed receivers, however, catch almost every pitch near the webbing deep into the glove, and they often have difficulty getting a hold of the ball and moving it into throwing position. With runners on base, rather than use the webbing, one-handed catchers should try to catch the ball closer to the center of the pocket and the palm where control and feel is better. To reduce the pain of catching pitches in the palm, many catchers will have additional padding in the palm or wear a golf or handball glove.

Fig. 5.3 ONE-HANDED RECEIVING is the general rule today among catchers. With runners on base, the throwing hand of Butch Wynegar is cupped loosely and relaxed away from the mitt but close enough to go for the ball in the glove pocket. When no runners are on, many catchers will put their throwing hand behind them for added protection, as shown in Fig. 5.5 by Brian Downing.

With runners on base, the one-handed catcher should not position his throwing hand too far away from the mitt. Even the catcher using a hinged glove can use the two-handed technique by placing his bare hand on or near the glove for quicker exchange.

With no runners on, catcher Gary Carter rests his right hand behind his leg. With a runner on first base, however, he has his hand by the glove. "When the runner goes, I have my throwing hand there ready," explained Carter. "If the runner doesn't go, I will drop my hand out of the way."

There is no doubt in my mind that the two-handed catcher is better than the one-handed catcher. He shifts better, blocks pitches better, and throws more quickly. However, catching the ball behind the plate with two hands is certainly more dangerous in that there is a greater possibility of a broken finger on the throwing hand. This is the major reason for catching one-handed, which is not a bad reason since the loss of the catcher for several weeks can hurt a team badly.

TARGET

The catcher should give the pitcher a good target. Above all, he should give him a *full* target. After giving the signal from his crouch, he moves slowly into his ready stance, with the glove in the middle of his body. He should keep the target arm away from his body, flexed, and with encouraging gestures. He also gives his target at the spot where he wants the pitch.

To give an outside target, the catcher merely has to move about six inches farther than the normal target over the middle. When he wants to give a target on the inside, he merely has to move over six inches to his left. Many pitchers prefer this type to that of merely extending the glove into the area desired.

"If I want the ball slightly on the inside corner," said Del Crandall, one of baseball's former great catchers with the Milwaukee Braves, "I will move over prior to giving my signal. If you remain in the middle of the plate to give the signal and then move your body and glove over, you will likely tip off the hitter.

"Furthermore, if the catcher can keep his body in front of the pitch, plus his target, the pitchers seem to have better control."

HOLDING THE HAND

There are several ways that catchers hold their bare hands. Some receivers like to "cup their hand," with the fingers bent a little and the thumb touching the index finger. Another method is to close the fingers loosely, with the index finger folded over the thumb. However, the hand should not be clenched tightly.

The important point in holding the hand is that the fingers are not pointed toward the pitcher, but are curled. "I try to keep the hand loose," said Johnny Bench, "sort of a relaxed fist, like you are holding a piece of cotton, with your thumb inside your fingers to keep them from getting damaged. Should the ball hit them, you will have some cushion on your fingers so that they will give."

A catcher is asking for trouble when he holds the meat hand up to the side and away from the glove hand.

GIVING SIGNALS

There are many different methods of giving signs. Generally, our receivers use a combination of signals. They might give the location with the flaps, and then give the pitch with the fingers.

With nobody on base, most catchers use the single series; that is, one finger for the fast ball, two fingers for the curve ball, and a wiggling of the fingers for the change-of-pace. For the slow curve, two fingers are slowly flexed and extended. Some teams use a fist for a pitchout.

If there is a runner on second base, the catcher should use a sign series which is more difficult to understand, so that the runner cannot relay the pitches to the hitter. One method is to give a series of three signs, with the first, second, or third the actual sign. Another method is to add the first and third signs. If they total two, it is a fast ball; three, a curve; four, a change; five, a pitchout.

Fig. 5.4 GIVING SIGNALS. The catcher must assume a stance in which he can hide all his signals. Hanging his glove over his left knee, he gives the signs over his right leg, deep in the crotch. The left forearm rests comfortably on the thigh, with the glove blocking the view of the third base coach (Jeff Torborg).

Many big-league catchers use a hand sign to indicate whether they want the ball to be high, low, inside, or outside. These are called *location signs*. If our receivers want the ball high and inside, they give one sign for that location and then the type of pitch it is. However, the catcher should not get his glove up to the desired target too soon, so that everybody in the ball park knows where that pitch is coming.

The catcher should signal first the *type* of pitch, then give the *direction* of the pitch. Sometimes, however, catchers will signal the location first, and then the pitch.

Before the game, as well as between innings, the catcher should go over the hitters with the manager and pitchers.

Hand signals are often used for night ball and whenever the pitcher has trouble seeing them because of shadows. The catcher can "flick" his fingers out a certain number of times for the various pitches. Whatever signs are used, they should be kept relatively simple and yet not easy enough for the opposition to pick up.

Signals can also be given by the catcher when attempting to pick runners off base. Signs that can be used are wiping a hand across the chest protector, grabbing the face mask, or throwing dirt off to the side. The infielder should give an answer back that the play is on, so the ball is not thrown away. After the pick-off sign is flashed and answered, the receiver then gives a pitchout sign to the pitcher. Fielders should not leave their position unless the pitchout is given.

Switching signals

To switch a signal, a sign is given that alters the meaning of the signs in the series. This prevents the opposing team from picking up the signal pattern, particularly with a man on second. The catcher may hold the right hand on the knee with the fingers together to shift the sign from the second to the third showing of the fingers.

The pitcher should indicate to the catcher that he has observed the switch by returning a prearranged signal, possibly by touching the peak of his cap. Still further, the battery can use the switch signal to change from a curve to a fast ball.

STANCE

Catchers have two sets of stances: 1) a signal-giving stance and 2) a ready stance, the receiving position. Regardless of the type of stance, it must be comfortable, since catching is a very tiring job. The more comfortable the catcher can be, the better off he is. Since every catcher has a different physical build, what will work for him might not be best for another receiver.

Signal position

In giving signs, the catcher must assume a stance in which he can hide all his signals and prevent his opponents from stealing them (Fig. 5.4). This is *not* the same stance he catches from. He merely gives his signs from this position. Hanging his glove over his left knee, he gives the signs over his right leg, deep in the crotch. The left forearm rests on the thigh, with the mitt hand in front of and next to the left knee, with the front of the glove facing in toward the crotch.

"The right leg must go straight to the pitcher," explained Torborg, "and that blocks out all the signs from the first base coach. To block out signs from the third base coach, the glove hand, the left hand, should be held a little past the knee of the left leg. Some catchers sit a little higher than others, but they should be sitting down easily."

"When you start to give the signs," continued Jeff, "you have to keep your right arm in tight toward your body. You don't want the elbow sticking out away from the body because, if you do, your arm will move and increase the chance of giving away the signal. Therefore, you clamp it down tight."

Receiving position

After he comes out of the sign-giving stance, the catcher gets up into the ready position to receive the ball (Fig. 5.5). To be able to throw or field a bunt, he must have a stance which is not only comfortable but which he feels he can get out of quickly. Normally, the feet are more than shoulder-width apart. The toe of the right foot is about on a line with the heel of the left foot, and pointing toward first base.

"In this position, your thighs and lower part of the legs form almost a right angle," explained Torborg. "Your weight is slightly forward on the balls of your feet, however, you don't lift the heels. You are up on the toe of the right foot, and the left foot is planted a little more solidly than the right one."

The catcher should move up under the hitter, but not so close that he interferes with his swing. There are a number of advantages in staying as close to the plate as possible. Among them, he will be in a better position to throw on steals, to move out quickly on bunts, and to handle low pitches easily.

He must have a feeling of readiness, to be *ready* to go. He has to get his weight planted so that he has pretty good weight on his right foot, with a certain amount on the ball of his left foot. He is balanced, ready to move in any direction.

When he crouches down ready for the pitch, the catcher should strive for the most comfortable position he can obtain. Too low a buttocks will definitely restrict his lateral motions. Conversely, if his tail is too high, he will have difficulty looking up and getting his arms up on high pitches. Consequently, he must find the happy medium, assuming a position about knee-high. This will provide the mobility necessary in moving to his right or to his left.

Fig. 5.5 THE READY POSITION—A Good, Low Target. As he crouches down ready for the pitch, catcher Brian Downing has a low stance which is not only comfortable but enables him to move out quickly. The glove hand is relaxed and not locked. The wrist can get locked if the face of the glove is held too perpendicular (glove up) to the pitcher. Rather than see a full pocket, the pitcher should be shown more or less the top half of the glove.

The hands and arms are relaxed, and the upper arms and forearms form almost right angles. The arms and elbows should be kept outside his knees, never between them. The mitt is held in the lower area of the strike zone, moving when necessary to either corner of the plate.

In giving a target and getting ready to receive the pitch, the catcher must make sure that his hand is relaxed and not locked (Fig. 5.5). Torborg explained that, "The wrist can be locked if the face of the glove is held too perpendicular to the pitcher. A locked wrist may cause trouble turning the glove to catch a low pitch."

"If I were facing the pitcher," continued Jeff, "he wouldn't see my full pocket of the glove. He would see more or less the top half of the glove pointed toward the pitcher. From this position, the glove can be moved up or down with the quickest and smoothest results."

While the buttocks should be up, a catcher's rear end should not be too high. According to the old theory, the catcher should keep his tail up so he can move better. The first thing that happens when he puts his tail up high is that his shoulders go forward, and then it becomes a real strain to look up at his pitcher. Furthermore, on any ball that is high over his head, he will have difficulty in getting his arm up to it.

Even the one-handed receiver can speed up his release time by placing his throwing hand behind or near the glove for quicker exchange.

RECEIVING

The catcher who can come up with all types of pitches, rising fast balls as well as low curves and sinkers in the dirt, will give the pitcher much needed confidence.

The catcher's hands should be held out away from his body in a relaxed manner. He should handle pitches above the waist with the fingers pointing up (Fig. 5.8), and those below the waist with the fingers pointing down (Fig. 5.7). The belt-high pitch can be handled from either above or below. However, he has to be *relaxed with the hands!* If he keeps rigid, he will go down with the heel of his glove on low pitches.

In receiving the pitch, the catcher should give slightly with his mitt as the ball hits it, at the same time drawing the ball toward his belt buckle. If done smoothly, this will prevent borderline pitches from being moved out of the strike zone. Sloppy catching of pitches may lose a pitcher the strike he deserves.

Caution should be taken by the receiver not to block the umpire's view of the ball by excessive jumping movements or body-raising. Too much move-

Fig. 5.6 RECEIVING THE PITCH. Catching pitches with two hands gives the receiver a chance to adjust the ball in his throwing hand while bringing the arm and mitt back into throwing position. This enables him to get the throw away more quickly. The one-handed catcher has less time to get his throwing hand on the ball. Therefore, he must develop an effective method of picking the ball out of his mitt as he moves the glove and the ball back into throwing position (Bob Brenly).

ment laterally, or up and down, will often take strikes away from the pitcher. A good receiver is smooth and fluid, making as few motions as possible.

On the high pitch, the receiver must remember to get his body in position so that he can field the high ball where he is not cramped. He must get his head and shoulders up, and his tail down. Otherwise, the ball is a pretty easy pitch to miss.

"The problem is the low curve ball," stated Torborg. "First of all, it has a difficult spin on it and does not act normally. It does not bounce directly at you. It usually bounces off to the right or to the left, depending on the spin when it hits the ground."

A big shortcoming of the average receiver is not being alert on every pitch so that, when the runner goes, he is ready to throw. On too many occasions, when the base runner attempts a steal unexpectedly, the catcher is not alert and ready. *The catcher has to get into the habit of being ready to throw on every pitch.*

Catching more foul tips

Some catchers catch more foul tips than others mainly because they catch up close behind the hitter. In fact, the really good catchers catch as close as

Fig. 5.7 RECEIVING THE LOW PITCH. The catcher's hands should be held out away from his body in a relaxed manner. He must not be rigid. He handles pitches below the waist with the fingers pointing down (Jeff Torborg).

Fig. 5.8 RECEIVING THE HIGH PITCH. The fingers point up in handling pitches above the waist. The belt-high pitch can be handled from either above or below the waist. The receiver can raise or lower his body by straightening or bending his knees and hips (Jeff Torborg).

possible right behind the hitter. This way, foul tips do not have a chance to veer off that bat as quickly as they would if he were further back.

Many young catchers catch too far back, and that is why the ball always gets away from them. Of course, there is a danger zone too. A catcher can be too close. However, if he can be up there where his arms are outstretched, where he can keep them from getting in the way of the bat, he will be a good catcher.

On third strike situations, when there are foul tips off the bat, the ball that is tipped downward has a good chance of being caught. Therefore, a foul-tipped ball is more easily retained when caught with the back of the glove facing the ground.

HANDLING THE LOW PITCH

One of the most crucial plays a catcher has to perform is handling the low pitch. Many a ball game has been decided by a receiver's ability, or lack of it, in stopping the low one in the dirt. The receiver who can handle the low pitches will win the confidence of his pitchers.

For years, baseball coaches have been telling their catchers to "block anything in the dirt." As a result, the accepted practice among most catchers today on the ball in the dirt is to automatically drop their knees first (Fig. 5.9). This is particularly true in some crucial situations. With a man on third base, naturally, the defense does not want to give up a run, so the catcher is instructed to try to block the pitch any way he can. The chief concern is to block the ball and keep it in front of him.

Therefore, the catcher is taught to fall to the ground on both knees, with the glove in the middle. By getting the shin guards out of the way, he leaves the soft part of his body for the ball to hit. He keeps his body facing the ball.

Major league catchers like to catch the ball first, and then follow it up with a block. After the receiver moves his hand for the ball, his body comes in with a blocking motion.

Catching the low ball and throwing to the bases are two of the most important skills in becoming a good catcher.

 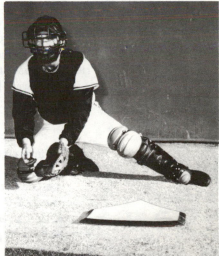

Fig. 5.9 BLOCKING THE LOW PITCH. On pitches thrown into the dirt, the catcher drops to the ground on both knees and blocks the ball with the body. By getting the shin guards out of the way, Bob Barton, left, has the soft part of his body for the ball to hit. On the ball slightly to the right, the catcher will go down on his right leg first and try to block it, as demonstrated by Dick Dietz, right. The shoulders and body are square, not on an angle.

This new approach in handling the low pitch can perhaps be attributed to the number of speed merchants on the base paths. In the past, when catchers tended to block the ball, a fast runner on first would take a base, whether the ball was blocked or not.

Now, many receivers, rather than automatically dropping to their knees, try to catch the ball cleanly, but their body is still in a blocking position should they miss.

"In my case, if the ball is slightly to my right in the dirt, I will go down on my right leg first," explained Torborg, "and try to block it. I will try to twist my body so that both of my shoulders are even and facing the ball. If I have to, I will bring down the other leg to cut off all holes."

The catcher must keep his body square to the pitcher. If the body is on an angle—say, to the right—and the ball hits him, it will still go toward the right.

"The important thing here is to keep your mask and chin right in tight to the body," said Torborg, "and looking at the ball all the way. The shoulders and body are square so that if it does hit you, generally, it will bounce out in front of you."

THROWING

For most throws, good body balance is essential for accuracy. Accuracy and quickness of the throw depends largely on how quickly the catcher can achieve proper balance of his body, along with speed at releasing the ball. The catcher should use the overhand delivery. The only exception is when he fields a bunt or a slow roller while off balance, and must throw sidearm to first or third base. He always uses the overhand throw to second base.

In throwing from the catching position, two important points should always be kept in mind:

1. Try to get the ball off the best way you can.
2. Have a good grip on the ball.

The catcher should reach into his glove for the ball with a full hand action. If he reaches in with the grip already set, he can too easily grab the ball off center. He can also turn the ball to get a "cross-seam grip." As he moves his arm back in preparation to throw, he should try using the ring and little fingers to turn the ball.

Correct grip

Gripping the ball across the seams has proven most effective for the majority of catchers. The two fingers are right on top of the ball. While it is not always possible to do this, by working at it, the catcher is able to grip the ball across the seams most of the time. Otherwise, he may throw sinkers or sliders, which are difficult for his teammates to handle.

A receiver should always be concerned with getting the ball out of his glove as quickly as possible. Rather than use the webbing, one-handed catchers should try to catch the ball closer to the center of the pocket and the palm where control and feel is better. By grabbing the ball quickly and bringing the throwing hand and glove back into good throwing position, he is able to grip the ball across the seams and get rid of it more quickly.

Throwing technique

The overhand throw is not only the most accurate way to throw but is more easily handled by the receiver. The catcher's throw is made from the shoulder, and is not a complete sweep of the arm. A receiver cannot afford to wind up. His delivery must be short and quick. A catcher who gets rid of the ball quickly and accurately generally is more effective than one who throws hard but takes too long to throw.

A catcher should perfect three types of throws:

1. The full overhand throw.
2. The snap throw.
3. The sidearm flip.

Momentum is a major factor in the catcher's ability to throw with strength and accuracy.

A quick release is what makes a good throwing catcher.

To make the overhand throw, the catcher should shift his weight to his right foot and rotate his shoulders to the right while the ball is brought back over the right shoulder with both hands. He brings his throwing hand and mitt back together, giving him a better chance to adjust the ball in his hand. He tries to get a grip across the seams in order to give the ball the necessary backspin.

Keeping his eyes constantly on his target, the catcher cocks his arm just back of the ear and completes his throw as quickly as he can. The ball is released with a vigorous wrist and arm snap while pushing off his right foot onto his left (front) foot (Fig. 5.10).

The snap throw is like the full overhand throw, except that the arm is not taken back as far. This is the short and quick type of delivery. The sidearm flip

Fig. 5.10   GARY CARTER'S THROWING DELIVERY (side view). Bringing his throwing arm straight back to a position behind the ear, Carter releases the ball with a vigorous wrist and arm snap. To gain needed momentum, he pushes off his right pivot foot as his weight moves forward onto his front foot.

is used when balls are bunted or tapped out in front of the plate, and the catcher does not have time to straighten up for the overhand throw.

In throwing to the bases, the catcher must get his body into motion and be ready when the ball hits the glove.

Shifting and throwing

The footwork of the catcher, the manner in which he shifts his body into the throw, determines his effectiveness to a great extent. By shifting his body correctly, he will have the rhythm, power and quickness to get rid of the ball in a hurry. It is essential for the catcher to get as squarely in front of the pitch as possible in catching the ball. Knowing the steal situation, he must get as close to the batter as possible and come out into his throwing position every time.

The one-handed glove has probably spoiled catchers to the point that they do not shift their feet as much as they used to. The old-time catchers did a better job of staying in front of the ball and shifting their feet. As a result, they were in better position to throw on every pitch.

Catchers are becoming reluctant to shift simply because they can reach out and backhand that ball with the one-handed glove. If they can do it, that is fine, but sometimes they get too relaxed by not shifting and some of the balls get through them. I still prefer my catchers to shift, even though they catch the ball with one hand.

On an outside pitch, by shifting and catching the ball with two hands, the catcher is in a much better position to throw the man out. By backhanding it, he has to switch the ball from there to his throwing arm and take turns getting his body into throwing position.

Crandall has an excellent theory on getting the ball away quickly. "When receiving the ball," said Del, "you do not catch the ball and then get your body in motion. If you do wait until you actually catch the ball, you are going to waste a lot of time. So, the thing to do, when you know where the ball is going and you know what you called for, get your body into motion and be ready when the ball hits the glove. Then, get it up there beside your head and throw it."

A catcher should learn to carry the ball and glove to his right ear all in one motion, adjusting the hand for the throw as it is brought up. Crandall believes, "This gets your left side in motion, and when you do turn to throw, your left side is in position; and it will bring your right side around, getting more on your throw."

"Practice going into the ball," continued Del. "It is very important not to catch the ball flat-footed. You want to be on your toes and leaning a little bit toward second base."

The jump shift is most widely used on all pitches because it creates momentum towards the target.

TYPES OF RECEIVING AND THROWING

Receiving a pitch down the middle

On a pitch over the middle of the plate, the receiver catches the ball and then steps forward with his left foot and throws. He should not move forward to catch the ball and then throw.

Receiving an inside pitch (inside alley)

"We do one of two things," said Torborg. "First, he can receive the ball and not take any steps at all, just turn and throw it. Or, he can do the same type of shuffle where he turns and throws to second base, just by having his body moving slowly through his little shuffle."

Receiving an outside pitch (outside alley)

On an outside pitch, with a right-handed hitter at the plate, the receiver will step right and slightly forward with his right foot, catch the ball, then step forward with his left foot for the throw to second base.

If a left-handed swinger is at the plate, and the pitch is also to the catcher's right, he again steps to the right with his right foot, catches the ball, then shifts all his weight back to his left foot. He then steps diagonally forward and toward home plate with his right foot, then forward with his left as he makes the throw. This shift will clear the batter.

"On the ball away to a right-handed hitter," said Torborg, "I just step over with the right foot, catching the ball at the same time, then stepping forward with my left foot for the throw."

Throwing technique

The catcher uses different types of footwork to receive the pitches and throw the ball quickly and accurately to the bases. While the styles of throwing differ, the fundamental techniques remain the same, both in terms of throwing technique and footwork. Young catchers' footwork, however, has to be more precise. While many big league receivers have the strength and size to make quick, snap throws, young catchers must execute proper footwork in order to get the necessary momentum and strength behind the throws.

Throwing to first base

If the pitch is away from a left-handed hitter, the catcher steps to the left with his left foot to take the pitch. His next step is forward with his right foot. Then he steps toward first base with his left foot. This action puts him in front of the hitter as he makes the throw.

With a right-handed hitter at bat, the catcher should step to his left if the pitch is to his left. After the catch, he shifts his weight to the right foot, then steps out with his left foot toward first base.

On a pitch over the plate, he catches the ball and merely steps forward with the left foot for the throw to first base. If the pitch is inside to a left-handed batter, the catcher may step behind the batter for his throw (Fig. 5.11). If he finds this difficult, he should step right with his right foot, make the catch, then shift his weight to his left foot, step forward with his right, then forward with his left toward first for the throw.

Fig. 5.11 THROWING TO FIRST BASE: Receiving inside pitch, left-handed batter. This is a difficult play for a catcher to perform because he has to get clear of the hitter. He can either go behind the batter or out in front of him. To go behind the left-handed hitter, Bob Brenly, here, takes a short jab step with his right foot, moving back a quarter of a step, catches the ball, brings the left foot across, and steps directly toward first base.

On an outside pitch, he moves out in front of the left-handed hitter. To do so, he steps toward the ball with his left foot, and using a jump shift, he places his right foot behind the left foot. Pushing off his pivot foot, he has the momentum to step toward first base with his left foot.

Throwing to second base

When throwing to second base on an inside pitch, many catchers take a lead step left and slightly forward with their left foot to receive the pitch. After getting their right foot behind their left, they step forward toward second base (Fig. 5.13).

Other receivers prefer to step to the left with their left foot, catch the ball, then step forward with their right foot, shifting their weight to the right foot. Then they step forward with the left foot for the throw.

If a left-handed hitter is at bat, and the pitch is to the left of the catcher, the catcher steps to the left and, if possible, slightly forward with the left foot. The right foot is then swung behind the left or a step is taken in front of the left foot, the weight shifting to the right, and the left foot strides out for the throw. This type of shift clears the batter. The shift becomes a jump shift as it increases in speed.

"Catching the ball pitched inside to a right-handed hitter can be difficult," says Torborg, "unless you reach out for the ball and cup it into you.

Fig. 5.12 THROWING TO SECOND BASE: Receiving inside pitch, left-handed batter. With a left-handed hitter at the plate, the catcher (Bob Brenly) could have difficulty seeing the runner, and he might have to make a quick throw. First, he takes a jab step directly forward with his right foot to catch the ball, then he comes back over on his left foot to clear himself to throw. The right foot comes behind the left foot, and he steps toward second base with his left foot.

Fig. 5.13 THROWING TO SECOND BASE: Receiving inside pitch, right-handed batter. The catcher (Bob Brenly) takes a short, jab step with his left foot, a quick gliding movement to create momentum toward second base. To get into position to throw, he has to shift his weight back around to his right foot. He strides directly toward second base with his left foot. Gripping the ball preferably across the seams, he throws directly overhand—over the top.

There are two ways to receive an outside pitch to a right-handed batter. A major league catcher, in receiving the ball, pivots on his right foot and steps directly toward second base. A young receiver should take a short jab step with the right foot, catch the ball, pivot, and throw to second base.

"Catchers who use the old way step over with their left foot, step behind with the right, and then move forward on the throw. Basically, that is what you still do, but you do not have time to step behind because your momentum laterally will carry you off, and you will throw with a wide open body.

"Johnny Roseboro gave me this advice on the pitch inside to a right-handed hitter: 'Catch the ball and flip your body around so that your weight is more or less on your back (right) foot, the one you push off of. You have caught the ball and you have executed the same "step-behind" footwork. However, you have kept your body down, and your shifting is similar to a crow hop. You move both your feet around, but actually, it is not a step behind because that pulls you back away from the throw to second base.' "

"While it involves the theory of stepping behind," said Jeff, "actually, it is a shuffle behind. You receive the ball and get your body into a throwing position by shifting, yet you keep your weight over your legs."

In throwing to second, the catcher should try to throw above the bag, right to the shortstop or second baseman, knee-high, instead of trying to throw exactly to the bag. By throwing above the bag, he has a leeway. The infielder might be on the bag, and then again, if the ball is a little high, he will still be able to handle it.

Throwing to third base

With a right-handed hitter, on a pitch to his left, the catcher takes his initial step to the left and then swings his right foot diagonally backward behind his left

Fig. 5.14 THROWING TO THIRD BASE: Receiving inside pitch, right-handed batter. The catcher first has to clear the batter, either going behind him or in front of him. To move behind the hitter, Brenly takes his first step to the left, and then swings his right foot behind his left foot. He then steps toward third base with his left foot for the throw, thus clearing the batter.

Fig. 5.15 THROWING TO THIRD BASE: Receiving outside pitch, right-handed batter. If the pitch is outside, Brenly goes in front of the hitter. He takes a jab step to his right, clearing the hitter, catching the ball, and stepping directly toward third base.

foot. He then steps toward third base with his left foot for the throw, thus clearing the batter and going behind him (Fig. 5.14).

If the pitch is away but not too wide, with the right-handed hitter still at the plate, the receiver steps to the right for the catch, then shifts his weight back to the left foot. He then steps diagonally in back of the left foot, shifting his weight to the right foot, and stepping out with his left foot for the throw (Fig. 5.15).

He can make this throw in front of the hitter by stepping diagonally forward with the right foot as he makes the catch. The hitter's position in the box, of course, determines the exact footwork the receiver employs. As he catches the ball, he steps either in front of or in back of the batter.

First and third steal situation

This play is used more often at the high school and college levels. A catcher should look for this play when the opponents need a run and, generally, when a weak hitter is at the plate. Defensing the double steal should be a major concern. In high school, this play is very frequent and can be devastating to the defense.

The catcher has three alternatives: he can throw to second base, throw high to the pitcher, or throw to third base. "If I see the runner moving forward or toward me as I am getting ready to throw," said Torborg, "I will immediately adjust and throw to third base."

Some catchers like to make an arm fake to second, retaining the ball, and then throw quickly to third base. However, in executing this play, they take the risk of throwing the ball into left field.

The simplest of signals should be used in the first and third situation. Most teams use word-of-mouth signals. If the catcher wants the pitcher to cut it off, he will tell him so as he goes halfway to the mound. Or, he may tell the pitcher to "let it go."

The throw to second base has the same trajectory whether or not the pitcher cuts it off, the second baseman handles it in front of the bag or the ball goes all the way down to the base. *Every player must be ready to adjust to any throwing situation.*

TAGGING THE RUNNER

A catcher must be aggressive when tagging a runner at the plate. If he has the ball, he must hang tough, especially if it is an important run or a "boom-boom" play (Fig. 5.16). After judging the flight of the ball, the catcher should move out and place his left foot in front of home plate on the third base line. His right foot is the moving one. His heels are on the plate, and his shin guards are facing the runner.

"Basically, I will use two or three ways to tag the runner," said Tom Haller, "depending, of course, on how the runner approaches the plate. Generally, he will use a hook slide, a straight-in slide, or he will try to bowl you over."

"Let the runner see part of the plate," said Haller, "preferably the outside. This way, he has more of a tendency to use his hook slide, which is to the catcher's advantage. You might come up on the line a foot or two to receive the ball and make contact there, where he has less of a chance to get to the bag. So, let him slide in and then tag him."

"Wait for the ball to come to you," advised Tom. "Do not go out after the ball and then come back. Be on balance and mobile until you get the ball, then go into action."

As he catches the ball, the catcher turns to his left and brings his left knee down to the ground. "You do not have to reach out," said Tom, "all you have to do is make contact with the runner. Make sure that the ball is in your glove, with

Fig. 5.16 TAGGING THE RUNNER. In this exciting action, catcher Dennis Little-john of the San Francisco Giants has blocked off the plate a few feet from home plate and places the tag on the Pirates' Dale Berra as he hooks for the plate. It is to the advantage of the catcher to make the runner hook to reach the plate. He doesn't want to get injured blocking the plate.

your bare hand holding the ball snugly. When you make contact, just make sure that you hold on to that ball and tag him with the back into his stomach. Do not tag the runner just with the ball. Use the glove and the ball!

"The easiest kind of runner to tag out is the one who goes into a hook slide. When he starts sliding, you do not have to worry about much of an impact because most of his weight is going away from you. All you have to do is go down on one knee and tag him, similar to the tag used by infielders at second or third base" (Fig. 5.16).

The most important thing is for the catcher to make sure he has the ball first, and he must hold it tight, particularly on the "bang-bang" play. When he does make contact, nine times out of ten, the umpire will call the runner out because the catcher has made the contact with the runner.

"The throw from right field to home can be a little more difficult," said Haller, "as well as dangerous for the catcher. Try not to get hit from the blind side. Give the runner the inside of the plate and make sure the shin guards face the runner."

The catcher should know the speed of the runner coming home, the arm of his outfielder, and the approximate distance to home plate. Normally, the catcher must have possession of the ball, or he will be called for blocking home plate. Under the heat of action, however, this is often overlooked. Obstruction, in which the catcher blocks the plate before he has the ball is very seldom called at home plate. Most catchers like to block the runner by forcing him to make an outside hook slide. They often block him a few feet from home and put the tag on him as he scrambles for the plate.

"The catcher should make the runner commit himself first, and then he counters," said Haller. "Remember, the runner has his momentum built up.

Therefore, the catcher should put his left foot right on the base line, and if he hooks, he will hook right into that shin guard."

FORCING THE RUNNER

With the bases loaded and the throw coming into the plate from an infielder, the catcher has the assignment of forcing the runner and trying for the double play at first base.

On a good throw, the catcher places his right foot on the plate. As he catches the ball, he steps forward with his left foot, and throws to first base. Throws that are received wide of the plate are caught by stepping to the side on which the ball is thrown.

"If I touch the plate with my left foot," said Haller, "then I have to take two steps before throwing. You do not have that long if you want to double that man up at first base."

"Make sure the throw is *to* you," advised Tom, "that your foot is on the plate. I try to extend myself a little bit like a first baseman, not too far out, though, because you need good balance to make your pivot and throw. Sometimes, you do not know how much time you have, but make sure you get the first out. Then, as you step toward first base, try to keep the ball inside of the runner so the first baseman can handle the ball easily."

In throwing to the first baseman on a possible double play, the receiver must be sure to get clearance from home plate. If not, he could get racked up by the runner, and his throw might end up down the right field corner.

CATCHING THE POP FLY

Most big-league catchers like to catch pop flies with their back to the infield; because of the rotation of the baseball, the ball usually comes back toward the infield. This is known as the *infield drift,* and the catcher must allow for it. The higher the foul ball, the more drift it will take, which can be as much as three to five feet. This is what makes pop foul balls hard to catch.

Experience is most important in catching high pop-ups, and it comes only after handling many pop flies during practice and games. In doing so, the catcher can build up the necessary confidence. Catching pop-ups is a matter of practice and allowing for the rotation of the ball.

"The more you catch," said Haller, "the more you know when the foul pop-up is in play, just by the sound of the ball. If a ball goes over your right shoulder, you should then turn to your right, and vice versa if the ball goes over your left shoulder."

The high pop-up hit directly over home plate is particularly difficult to catch. After judging the ball, the catcher throws his mask away and moves into the ball. His back is toward the infield. "Many catchers will go out and have the ball come back into them," said Haller. "Then, there are those who will stay there, and move out facing the infield. They know the ball will move out, and then they will overplay it somewhat, and the ball will come out in front of them."

If the pop-up is moving into the infield away from the plate, one of the infielders should handle the catch. The catcher should go after every pop-up until he is called off by either the third baseman or the first baseman, either of whom might have a better angle and a better shot at it.

The pitcher plays an important role in these situations. As soon as he realizes who should catch the ball, he yells the last name of the player, and his teammates can react accordingly.

After getting a good sight on the ball and judging its return, the catcher should be sure to throw his mask in an opposite direction (Fig. 5.17). He should avoid turning around too much.

"Most of the balls are usually away from the plate," explained Tom. "So, you do not have to worry about stepping on your mask. On those balls hit directly overhead, you should hold on to your mask for a moment and discard it to either side, depending on which way you have to move."

CATCHING THE BALL

Most catchers point their gloves upward when catching the pop-up. This technique is similar to that used by outfielders, with the hand and glove up at about eye-level, with the fingers of the glove pointed up.

"I prefer the other method," stated Haller, "with the hands close to my belt

Fig. 5.17 DISCARDING THE MASK ON A POP-UP. The catcher holds on to his mask until he has located the ball. Then he tosses it off to the side and moves under the ball. He must keep his eyes on the ball at all times (Bob Barton).

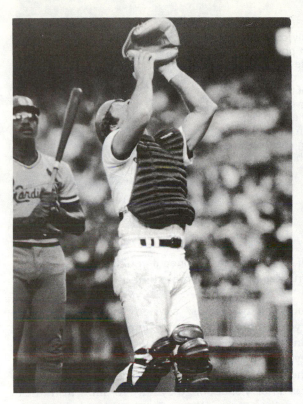

Fig. 5.18 CATCHING A POP-UP (glove up). This is the technique used by most big league catchers. The glove of the receiver is pointed upward, similar to the technique used by outfielders. The hands are positioned about eye-level (Steve Yeager).

Fig. 5.19 CATCHING THE POP FLY (glove flat). Although most catchers have their gloves pointing upward when catching the pop-up, receivers like Tom Haller, prefer keeping their hands close to their belt and opened up. The face of the glove is up and the hands are flat.

and opened up. The face of the glove is up and my hands are flat (Fig. 5.19). I just feel that if a ball hits the edge of my glove in that manner, I will have another shot at it before it hits the ground. I like to catch the ball this way. For me, it has been much easier, and I have had good success with it."

FIELDING BUNTS

In fielding bunts, the catcher must move out after the ball as quickly as possible. He has to get a good jump on the ball (Fig. 5.20).

The speed of his moves will depend, of course, on how fast the batter is

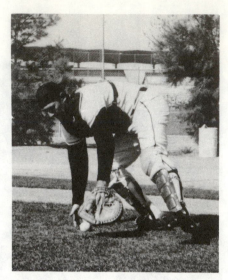

Fig. 5.19 FIELDING A BUNT. The catcher must move out quickly on bunts. He should always be ready to pounce on the ball in front of the plate. He should try to field all rolling bunts with two hands. Placing his glove out in front of the ball, he scoops the ball into his glove with the throwing hand. Although catcher Bob Barton is shown circling the ball in this series, many receivers prefer turning their back toward first base and approaching the ball directly.

running down to first base. If he is a real fast runner, it could be a desperation play. If he is only an average runner, he will have more time to get set and throw him out.

"Try to field all rolling bunts with two hands," advised Haller. "Placing your glove out in front of the ball, you want to scoop the ball into your glove with the throwing hand. Do it all in one motion and make sure you have good control of the ball. Never take your eyes off the ball!"

In throwing, some catchers like to come back over the top, while some prefer to throw sidearm. If it is a hurry situation, they have to throw from their fielding position and make a quick, sidearm throw. The bare hand should be used only if the ball has stopped rolling and it is a "do-or-die" play.

Down the third base line

There are two theories on fielding the bunt down the third base line. Most catchers prefer to turn their back to first base and approach the ball as quickly as possible, rather than take the time to circle the ball. It is generally believed to be faster for the receiver to turn his back on the play. Others like to circle the ball, since this method helps keep the play in front of them at all times.

Pivot-and-whirl method

On a rolling ball, the catcher places his left foot as close to the ball as possible, allowing him plenty of room to field it as it rolls to his right. If the ball stops rolling, he places his right foot close to the ball and makes a turn to his left on his right foot, then steps out with his left foot as he throws to first base.

The primary task is to place the glove in front of the ball to stop it. As he pivots on his right foot, he uses his glove to flip the ball into his throwing hand. As he fields the ball, his right foot is placed ahead of his left foot, thus cutting down his angle in turning around for the throw.

Circling the ball

Some catchers like to have the play in front of them at all times, circling to the left of the ball, if possible. "I prefer circling the ball because I can snap the ball to first base as fast and hard as I can in turning and pivoting around," said Haller. "While it takes another step as far as the runner is concerned, I think it is the surest way. You always have everything in front of you. If the throw is to go to second base, I do not circle as much."

Down the first base line

The catcher should move out as quickly as possible, buff the ball with his glove, take one step with his right foot, step with his left foot, and throw sidearm to the first baseman. He remains low to the ground when fielding and throwing, and by keeping the play in front of him, he should be able to make an accurate throw to the first baseman.

RUN-DOWN PLAY

On a run-down situation occurring between home and third, if he has the ball, the catcher should run the base runner as hard as he can toward third base. When the runner is about halfway down the line, he should bring his throwing arm to the area of the shoulder. As soon as the third baseman moves into the play, he should toss him the ball about chest-high, with the receiver placing the tag on the runner. One throw should be all that is necessary.

After the toss, the catcher should get out of the way to his outside and go back. The catcher and third baseman must be on the inside of the base runner, keeping the runner on one side. They should never let him bisect their view or throwing procedure. Catchers, like infielders, are advised not to make more than one fake throw.

COVERING AND BACKING UP

Whenever a ground ball is hit to the infielders with no runners on base, the catcher should move quickly down the first base line in foul territory, and back up the first baseman. Generally, he runs parallel to and about thirty-five or forty feet from the line as fast as he can.

When the first baseman goes after a short fly ball, the catcher often covers first base. He also covers third base when a bunt or slowly hit ball is fielded by the third baseman with only first base occupied.

CUTOFFS

If the throw from the outfield is accurate and if the catcher does not want the infielder to cut the ball off, he should remain silent. However, in an exciting game with plenty of noise, he will often yell, "Leave it alone," or "Let it go!" If he wants the infielder to cut the ball and make a play, he will yell, "Cut." The catcher will yell, "Relay" if the throw coming into home is to be cut off and thrown home.

WORKING WITH THE PITCHER

The catcher must call the game according to the type of pitcher with whom he is working. In sizing up a hitter, a catcher, above all, must remember his pitcher's ability, even more so than the hitter's weakness. It is particularly important to work more around the pitcher's strength if the catcher does not have a "book" on the hitter.

The type of control his pitcher has will be a big factor in what pitches the catcher will call. He does not want to get his pitcher in a hole. He should want the pitcher to work in front as much as possible. Therefore, he should try to go with pitches of which he knows the pitcher has good control.

If his fast ball is good on a particular day, he might start out with a fast ball. But he must mix up the balls, especially with some off-speed pitches. Otherwise, the hitter will learn just what to expect.

The big thing is to *get ahead of the hitter,* and work from that point. In a tough situation, the catcher should call for the strongest pitch that his pitcher has on the particular day. Just because the hitter is weak on a curve does not necessarily mean to throw him curves, UNLESS the pitcher can throw a good curve ball. If he has a poor curve, perhaps it would be best to waste that pitch, or merely "show" the curve.

Quite often, what is effective for one pitcher may not be effective for another. A letup pitch on a 3–1 count can be a good call for some pitchers and will often force the hitter to hit the ball with his timing slightly off.

On 3–1, as well as 2–0 situations, many catchers will call for an "off" pitch. This pitch, though, must be a strike, preferably low and away. The pitcher wants the hitter to hit this ball, not miss it, hoping, of course, that the batter's timing will be off.

Should the pitcher shake the catcher off now and then? If he is a young pitcher, I would prefer that he pitch basically what the catcher calls for. If he is a veteran, I want my pitcher to have the right to decide which pitch he wants to throw. He will do a better job of throwing the pitch he wants in this situation.

Studying the hitters

The pitcher and catcher must make a thorough study of the opposing hitters and freely discuss them together. They should study the hitter's stance and remember what pitch he went for and where he hit the ball in previous appearances. Batting practice is a good time to watch the opposing hitters. It does not take long to find out who the pull hitters are, those who hit straightaway, and the opposite field swingers.

However, young battery combinations are advised not to worry too much about stances and batting positions. After they get ahead of the hitter, though, they could consider his stance and his relationship to the plate.

If the batter crouches over the plate, the catcher should advise his pitcher to keep the ball high and inside. The batter who steps away from the plate should be pitched outside, while the hitter who stands up straight should be given pitches down low. Some hitters crowd the plate, because they want the tight pitch. Those who stand far from the plate invite the outside pitch.

Setting up a hitter

Setting up a hitter to make him hit the pitcher's best pitch is very important (see "Working on the Hitter," in Chapter 4). However, to a large extent, this depends on the control of the pitcher. Personally, I do not like to be beyond a 2–2 count on a hitter.

Going out to the mound

When going out to the mound, the catcher should have something definite to say to the pitcher. Some pitchers need a few harsh words to get them going. The catcher might have to make them a little angry at times. Other pitchers may need a pat on the back and a few words of encouragement.

More than likely, if a pitcher runs into control trouble, he is basically high and usually is doing one of two things wrong. First, he could be rushing, which would cause him to be high with his pitches.

"We usually look for this, and if we see it," said Haller, "we will go out and talk to him and say, 'You are rushing. Stay back and don't rush the delivery.'

"If you pinpoint one or two things wrong, very likely it will settle him down. Pitchers have a tough job. The biggest job is to concentrate for nine innings. Quite often, when a pitcher gets in trouble, he is not concentrating enough on what he wants to do."

Sometimes it is effective for the catcher to go out and talk to his pitcher just to slow him down a little. A little humor or a joke might be good at this time to help him relax.

RELATIONSHIP WITH THE UMPIRES

In their relationship with umpires, catchers generally fall into three groups:

1. The catcher who lets the umpire know that he has missed a pitch.
2. The receiver who argues on every close pitch called against his pitcher.
3. The one who does not say a word, and gives the impression that he is not in the ball game.

We like our catchers to practice more the first point listed. When a catcher is sure the umpire missed the call, he should, without turning around, let him know that he has missed his pitch. In our league, a catcher is not allowed to turn around and argue with him. If he misses another one, he has to raise hell again, but within reason, of course. The catcher has to be *sure* that he is right, though, before he makes too big an argument about it.

Crandall had this to say about his relationship with umpires: "I did not particularly like to argue with umpires, but when I thought I was right, I had my words. If a catcher feels that he is right, he has to say something because, if he does not, the umpires will feel he is not in the ball game. Then they might get a little careless. I am not saying they do not bear down all the time—they *do*, but I know as a player, if the manager did not get on me once in a while, I would get a little careless, and I think the same thing goes for umpires."

"I believe you should have a cordial relationship with umpires," said Haller. "To have their respect, you must respect them. As long as I know that he is consistent, that he is that way all the time, I do not often get disturbed. But I do not like to see a fellow changing his mind all the time. For one hitter, he will call a particular pitch a ball, and then for the next hitter, he might call the same pitch a strike. This can be very disturbing to me. Generally, though, in our league our umpires are very consistent.

"Being a habitual griper can hurt you more than it can help you," Haller believes. "You do not get many birds with salt. You get a lot more out there if you try to butter them up. If you want the respect of umpires, do not try to show them up. Then they will have a little more respect for you."

DRILLS FOR CATCHERS

One-step drill

This is an excellent drill for catchers who take too many steps and overdo their footwork. In this drill, the catcher receives the ball with his weight already on his right foot, steps with his left, and throws.

Footwork warm-up drill

This is a drill to be used just prior to infield practice, in which the catcher uses correct footwork in shifting for the throw. He and another catcher play "hard" catch from a distance of sixty-five to seventy-five feet, in which they execute the same shifting footwork they will use during the game.

Throwing drill

Practice catching low throws with full equipment on.

Rules in working on the hitter

1. Find out as soon as possible which pitch is working best.
2. Always try to get *ahead* of the batter. Get that first ball over for a strike.
3. Watch the hitter's position in the box, and call your pitches accordingly.
4. Make a thorough study of opposing hitters, and discuss them freely with the pitcher.
5. If the pitcher is wild, slow him down occasionally.
6. Call for pitches that will throw a batter off his timing or fool him.
7. Never get beaten in a tight situation on a pitch that is not the pitcher's best pitch.

Basic catching rules

1. Be the field general, and direct the play on all batted balls.
2. Keep check on the defensive positions of the infielders and outfielders.
3. Give the pitcher a good target at all times, crouching low.
4. On the intentional pass, keep one foot in the catcher's box until the pitcher releases the ball.
5. Learn the most effective pitch for every hurler you handle.
6. *Talk to your pitcher!* (He may be lonesome.)
7. Be alert for any possible steal or hit-and-run play. A pitchout may be called.
8. Back up first base with the bases unoccupied on all batted balls that might result in overthrows.
9. On throws from the outfield, call "CUT" to the cutoff man if a throw to the plate is wide, or if the runner cannot be retired.
10. If the bunt is in order, have your pitcher pitch high.
11. Study the hitter's stance, and remember what he went after, and where he hit the ball in previous appearances.
12. Make your signs simple and understandable, especially to your pitcher.

6
The First
Baseman

There is a tendency in baseball to underrate the qualifications for a first baseman. A good hitter who has a below average throwing arm or is too slow to cover much ground usually plays first base.

Some people believe anybody can play first base. Well, that is not really true; there is a lot more to first base than most people think. In fact, I believe a good fielding first baseman can *save* as many runs as the big, powerful hitter, who cannot field, will drive in. As a fielder, the good glove man can prove just as valuable to his team as the slugger whose fielding woes often lead to defeat.

Actually, the first baseman has *many* duties to perform. This is why he should possess, in addition to impressive physical attributes such as good hands, agility, and quickness afoot, the mental capability to make quick decisions. There are numerous plays at first base, such as in bunt and cutoff situations, in which he has to make split-second judgments. Playing first base may call for more varieties of talent than some of the other positions. Therefore, the first sacker should be a player who can hustle, one who wants to play and likes to play first base.

Nothing can instill greater confidence in an infielder than a first baseman who is capable of leaping high to grab the high ones and scooping low ones

Fig. 6.1 A GOOD FIELDING FIRST BASEMAN can save as many runs as the big, powerful hitter, who cannot field, will drive in. Cecil Cooper, in addition to being a Golden Glove award winner for fielding excellence, is one of the game's premier power hitters.

out of the dirt. Indeed, one of the most artistic sights in this great game is watching an agile, coordinated athlete stylishly performing his duties at first base.

The big glove used by modern first basemen has tended to change somewhat the style of play at the initial sack. First baseman gloves today are much bigger than those used by such old-time greats as George Sisler, Charley Grimm, and Bill Terry. Using the long glove with big webbing, first basemen now catch the ball in the web, rather than in the palm of their hand as they used to. This has led to more one-handed catches. Frankly, with the present style glove, there is nothing wrong with a one-handed catch at first base, particularly if the player keeps his other hand close by, ready for a possible throw.

The young player who aspires to become a topnotch first baseman must spend much practice time with the glove. Skill will not come any other way. Good examples of what I mean are Cecil Cooper, Keith Hernandez, and Steve Garvey.

The Dodgers are fortunate to have had a long string of outstanding fielding first basemen. Prior to Garvey, such greats as Dolf Camilli in the 1940s, Gil Hodges in the 1950s, and Wes Parker in the 1960s performed brilliantly at this position. Hodges, for a big man, had pretty good agility and great hands. Anything he would get his hands on, he would hold. He could make the pivot and throw to second very well for a big man of 200 pounds.

A ball player can improve *only by practice.* Sometimes it is difficult to get ball players to do this. They want to do things they do best. If they are good hitters, they want to hit all the time, thereby neglecting their fielding responsibilities.

Picking up ground balls, receiving all types of thrown balls, and catching pop-ups should be a part of every first baseman's daily chores. Steve Garvey takes twenty to twenty-five ground balls every day before a game. These are the fundamental skills which need to be developed and continually worked on to keep players sharp and effective.

Having a Garvey or Cecil Cooper play first base will help the other infielders, too. They know that if they get the ball over there within reach, their first baseman will catch it. Then, they can go ahead and hurry their throws and put something on the ball and not have to worry.

A good fielding first baseman can save as many runs as the big, powerful hitter, who cannot field, will drive in.

QUALIFICATIONS

Size is a definite asset for a first baseman, because a taller man makes a better target and has greater reach. Preferably, he should be at least six feet tall, in order to stretch and get the high throws. However, a smaller player who is quick and agile can often make up for his height disadvantage.

The ideal man for this position is tall and rangy, the Cecil Cooper type, who can reach sky-high and take any throw. In addition, he has to be agile, quick, and alert, and have a strong arm. The big, powerful slugger who is in the lineup because of his bat will not cover enough ground, nor will he be able to handle the bunted ball play. The first baseman must have a good pair of hands. He has to be able to catch the ball with sureness and dependability. This is where strong hands play a key role. He must be coordinated and agile enough to maneuver quickly and nimbly while performing his fielding responsibilities.

His legs have to be in excellent shape. Getting in position on the ball plays a vital role in fielding the ball, and the first baseman needs his legs to do this.

The ability to make quick decisions is another important quality of a good first baseman. A good example of this is when charging a bunted ball. Should he throw the ball to second base, or go to first base and play it safe? He does not have much time to make up his mind.

Defensively, the left-handed first baseman has a fielding edge over the right-handed player because he has more natural advantages, especially on the double play, when he can catch the ball and throw naturally to second base. Also, on the bunt play down the first base line, the left-hander is in a natural position to throw the ball to second base.

The first instinct of the first baseman is to get to the bag as quickly as he possibly can.

GETTING TO THE BAG

When the ball is hit on the ground to other infielders, the first instinct of the first baseman is to get to the bag as quickly as he possibly can. Ideally, he should play as deep as he can, which makes it necessary for him to run as quickly as he can to first base.

"Getting to the bag quickly is the whole secret," said Parker. "That is why speed is so important in playing first base. The faster you can go from where you are playing to the bag to receive the throw, the farther you can play away from the bag initially."

Arriving at the bag, he must find the base, get his feet in position and then turn and look for the throw.

Awaiting the throw

Standing directly in front of the bag, the first baseman is in a position to shift for all types of throws from his infielders.

Most first basemen like to straddle the bag and place both heels in contact with the bag, at the front part of the base (Fig. 6.2). This position enables them to have a feel of the bag.

However, some of our greatest fielding first basemen employ a different position when waiting for the throw. "I always put my left foot on the bag," stated Wes. "I put my toe right at the middle of the bag, not on top, but on the front edge in the middle (Fig. 6.3).

"I am standing almost in a straight-up position, with a slight bend of my knees, with my hands up. As I look for the throw, I am always anticipating a bad throw."

FOOTWORK

The footwork involved in taking thrown balls is probably the most important phase of first base play. By shifting his feet correctly, the first baseman will be able to handle the ball more smoothly and quickly, with a greater natural motion.

The shifting of the first baseman is often called a "waltz-step." If the ball is to his left, he shifts to his left and touches the bag with his right foot. If to the

Fig. 6.2 HEELS TO BAG WHILE WAITING. Most first basemen like to straddle the bag and place both heels in contact with the bag, at the front part of the base. By keeping both heels on the base, they know exactly where the bag is (Rich Reese).

Fig. 6.3 AWAITING THE THROW. Many big league first baseman, like Steve Garvey, prefer placing the same foot on the bag at all times. By doing so, they know exactly where the bag is. Here, Garvey places his left foot on the base, steps out into the diamond with the other foot, and reaches for the ball.

right, he shifts to his right and touches the base with his left foot (Figs. 6.4 and 6.5).

On a ball hit directly at the second baseman, the first baseman has to come in, turn around, and put his right foot on the bag. Then, he is facing the second baseman and can see where the throw is coming from.

"If the throw is toward the home plate side, and I am stretching out," explained Parker, "I will slide my foot right to the corner closest to home plate. If it is to the other side, then I will slide my foot to the corner closest to right field and, in this way, I can get a longer stretch."

If the ball is thrown directly to him, the first baseman places his toe against the side of the base, steps well out into the diamond with the other foot and reaches for the ball. Occasionally, he may have to leave the base to catch the

Fig. 6.4 SHIFTING TO THE RIGHT. On balls thrown to his right, the first baseman shifts to his right and touches the base with his left foot (Wes Parker).

Fig. 6.5 SHIFTING TO THE LEFT. If the ball is thrown to his left, he shifts to his left and touches the base with his left foot (Wes Parker).

ball and make a tag play on the runner coming to first. This is done with a sweeping motion.

On close plays, he has to stretch out as far as he can, so that he can get the ball as quickly as possible.

One of the faults of many young first basemen is committing themselves too soon. On a close play, they stretch out too quickly. If the ball should happen to sail a little bit, he finds that the throw is not exactly where he thought it would be. He is all stretched out, and if the ball is off to the side, he cannot reach it. So, he must not commit himself too soon. He should wait a moment, so that he can shift and stretch any way that is necessary to catch the ball.

CATCHING THE BALL

Although there is nothing wrong with the one-handed catch at first base, the first baseman should get in the habit of using two hands whenever he can (Fig. 6.6b). While the large glove has led to more one-handed catches, the majority of big-league first basemen try to use two hands whenever they can. Two hands are surer, and also enable the player to move more quickly into throwing

Fig. 6.6 TAKING A THROW FROM AN INFIELDER. Although the big leaguer uses one hand on many plays as shown here by Cecil Cooper, the young first baseman should use two hands whenever he can. As Wes Parker demonstrates below, two hands are surer than one hand. Notice that Wes has his head just behind his glove as he looks right over the top of his mitt. He follows the ball right into the glove.

position. If he does use one hand, though, he should have his other hand close by, so that he can get the ball out of the glove if another throw is necessary.

In receiving the throw, the first baseman should try to follow the flight of the ball right into the mitt. "This is a major weakness of many young first basemen who are starting to learn the position," according to Wes. "On a low throw, for instance, they will stand almost straight up and merely reach down to catch the ball. This is the worst thing they can do because as the ball approaches them, their head has to move down very quickly to follow the ball right into the glove. Many first basemen are lazy this way, and they will lose sight of the ball and drop it. So, what I do, on a low throw—or any throw, for that matter—I try to get my head just behind my glove so I am looking actually right over the top of my mitt."

The throw into the runner is possibly the toughest play for the first baseman to catch, especially coming from the third baseman who has come in to field a bunted ball or swinging bunt. There is a tendency for that ball to break in toward the base runner.

This is a tough play because it will be close. The first baseman will either have to tag the runner or keep his foot on the bag. Quite often, the runner and the ball will arrive at the same time. The good first baseman will know whether he has a chance of catching the ball standing on the bag or if he has to tag the runner. Or, he might cross over in front of the runner and tag the bag with his other foot.

In going after wild throws, the first baseman often has to make a quick decision as to whether or not he can stay on the bag and still catch the ball. If he cannot, he should move off the bag and catch it, then tag the runner.

Low throws

The fielder has to "give" with a low throw. Rather than let his hands and glove go out toward the ball, he has to pull his hands back into his body the moment the ball enters the glove (Fig. 6.7).

"The reason for this is that you are 'cushioning' the ball," explained Parker. "You are making the impact softer. So, the ball is more likely to stay in the glove

Fig. 6.7 CATCHING LOW THROW (two hands). The first baseman has to give with the low throw, as he cups the glove under the ball. With the palm of the glove facing up, he draws the glove and hand in toward the area of his belt. In cushioning the ball, he makes the impact softer (Wes Parker).

when it hits it. If you are moving out toward the ball the same time it is moving toward you, then the impact is going to be greater, and the chances of that ball bouncing out again will be greater."

The good fielding first baseman has a nice, easy "give" motion to the scooping action, a soft touch to the catch. His head is down, and his eyes follow the ball right into the glove. While a beginner might have a tendency to lift his head up, he must learn to keep it down.

The in-between hop can be a difficult play for the first baseman. A ball within two feet of him is not considered too tough because the ball does not have enough room to take a bad hop. The tough play is out in front of him, anywhere from five to ten feet, because the ball has to take almost a perfect hop for him to be able to catch it.

High throws

In catching a high throw, the first baseman must decide whether he has to jump and come back down on the bag, or stay on the bag and try to reach it (Fig. 6.8).

Fig. 6.8 LEAPING FOR THE HIGH THROW. A first baseman like Wes Parker can time his leap to catch the ball and come down on the base. When reaching for a high throw, the first baseman should use the bag to get the greatest possible height. If he doesn't have to jump, he merely rises up on his toes to make the catch.

Before he does anything, he has to know *where the bag is*. If the throw is fairly straight and high over the bag, there are two ways he can go after the ball:

1. If he has to jump for it, he can jump straight up in front of the bag and come down with his foot on the bag.
2. He can shift behind the bag into foul territory and take the throw without jumping. This is because the majority of the throws he gets are coming down. Therefore, on high throws the ball will be lower behind the bag than it will be in front of it. This is why the first baseman can stretch behind the bag and not even have to jump for it. However, to do that, the throw has to arrive in plenty of time. Otherwise, he will either collide with the runner or the throw will be too late by the time he catches it behind the bag.

FIELDING POSITION

The fielding position of the first baseman depends on a number of factors, such as the game situation, the score, the base runners, the pitcher, the hitter at the plate and—*very important*—the speed of the first baseman himself (Fig. 6.9).

The depth will depend on the hitter and the speed of the first baseman. With nobody on base, the normal fielding position for major league first basemen is approximately fifteen to twenty feet in back of the bag and about the same distance from the base line. This is the deep fielding position. However, the depth is not as great in the lower leagues. The important thing is for the fielder to get to first base in plenty of time to take the throw.

"I will change my position according to the score," says Parker. "If we are way ahead and a runner is on first, Walt will have me play behind the runner. In this case, I would play three to four feet behind him and two to three feet off the line. If the game is tight and this guy is likely to steal, I have to hold him just as close as possible."

With men on first and second, and only one out, the fielder should assume a double play type of situation. In this case, he still would be ten to fifteen feet off the first base line but only about five to eight feet behind the runner. In other words, he has to move up closer to the hitter in order to increase the speed of the double play.

With a left-handed hitter at the plate, he plays as deep as he can, but still so as to be able to get to the bag. With a man on, he either holds him on or plays close behind him. If men are on first and second, he does not have to hold his runner on, so he moves back halfway or to the deep position.

The first baseman can play deep on hitters who are not fast runners, but with the speed merchants, he has to be ready for a possible drag bunt.

Knowing his second baseman is of particular importance to the first baseman. If the second baseman does not have good range, for example, he will

Fig. 6.9 PROPER FIELDING POSITION. Knowing the hitters and where to play them is a major fielding responsibility of the first baseman. As the pitch is being made, he drops his glove down close to the ground. He must be alert and ready on every pitch (Keith Hernandez).

have to go out and get a few more balls in the hole. With a left-handed pull hitter at the plate, he has to play close to the foul line.

If he has speed, he can play a wide or deep first base. He can play further away from the bag before the ball is hit and still get there in time to make a put-out. Being able to play far off the base gives his infield better defense.

FIELDING GROUND BALLS

The first baseman should think of himself as an all-round fielder, and not just as a fellow who guards first base. He should not be afraid to get away from the bag and make an attempt to field all ground balls hit into his territory, except those hit to his right which the second baseman can play. He should try to get in front of the ball and then keep the glove low to the ground.

"I try to keep my glove low," said Parker. "When I assume my position as the pitch is being made, I actually drop my glove right down on to the ground so that it is practically on the dirt. This has become a good habit for me because it helps me stay low when the ball is being hit hard at me."

"I always work to get a big hop," said Parker, "and not the in-between hop. A first baseman can do this more than any other infielder because he has more time to make the play. He can always throw the ball to the pitcher who covers first if he cannot get there in time. But he should go to the base himself whenever possible."

When the first baseman cannot make the put-out himself after fielding a ground ball, he throws to the pitcher covering first base. On a ball hit to his right, the first baseman will often field the ball and have to make a quick throw from his fielding position.

Possibly the toughest play for the first baseman to make is the ground ball to his right. This is definitely a judgment play. Let us assume he is playing a normal position and a ball is hit hard between him and the second baseman. Now, should he go after the ball or go to first base? Many times he feels foolish if he goes to first base and the second baseman cannot get there. He will ask, "I wonder if I ran away from that ball?" This is the greater of the two evils.

It is better to go after a questionable ball between first and second than let it go through for a clean base hit. If the first baseman goes after it and cannot get to it, the pitcher is still responsible for getting over there. Also, the second baseman has a chance to make the play.

Once he commits himself, he will not have time to get back to first base; therefore, it becomes a judgment play.

HANDLING BUNTS

In fielding a bunt, the first baseman should always assume that he will make the play at second base. Otherwise, it will be too late. If a bunt is likely, he should move in quickly toward the batter as the ball is pitched (Fig. 6.10). When charging the bunt, he should be saying to himself: "Second base, get him at second base!"

When charging in on a bunted ball, the first baseman must be able to make quick decisions. Should he throw the ball to second base, or go to first base and play it safe? He does not have much time to make up his mind.

Although some people say the catcher should call this play, basically, I think the first baseman must make up his mind whether he can get the man at second or not. He knows whether a slow runner or a Tim Raines is running. He knows how hard the ball was bunted, how smoothly he fielded it, and whether he still has time to throw it to second.

"When I field the ball and intend to go to second," said Parker, "I will lead with my left foot so that my hips are open and I am not closed. This is particularly important. The first baseman must know where second base is, and then make a strong throw.

"You have to move quickly the first two or three steps, then, as you get about halfway, you start slowing down to get your balance. This will help you keep your body weight under control and be able to make a good throw to second base."

With runners on first and second and a bunt expected, the first baseman plays on the grass in front of the runner on first. The force play at third base is the prime objective.

I field bunts with my arm cocked to go to second or third. I can always turn and get the batter.

KEITH HERNANDEZ

Fig. 6.10 FIELDING A SACRIFICE BUNT. The first baseman must move quickly the first few steps, then as he approaches the ball, he should start slowing down to get his balance. Hard bunted balls are often played to second base, whereas slow bunted balls are thrown to first base, with the second basemen covering (Wes Parker).

THE UNASSISTED PUT-OUT

Since the pitcher runs to cover first base on all balls hit to the left of the mound, the first baseman, after fielding the ball, must decide immediately if an unassisted put-out is possible. If so, he should call to the pitcher or wave him away at once, saying: "I have it," or, "I'll take it."

"When you wave the pitcher off," said Parker, "do not wave him off with the glove of the hand that the ball is in. I have seen it happen, when a guy will wave and drop the ball accidentally."

If he fields the ball away from the line, he should tag the second base edge and either cross the base ahead of the runner or back away a step. If the play is close, he may use a straight-in slide.

THROWING TO SECOND

All throws by the first baseman to second base should be made quickly. It is quickness and accuracy that count. The throw should be made overhand, if possible, and high to the shortstop's face, right over the bag or to the third base side of the bag. In making this throw, good timing is essential. The play should be timed so that the ball reaches the shortstop about one-half step before he steps on the base.

A right-handed first baseman can make this throw two different ways, depending on how far from second base he fields the ball and how much time he has. Generally, a right-hander will pivot to his right side a quarter-turn of the body. If the ball is hit to his right, he has to backhand it and, at the same time, make a jump shift to the right. He uses a snap overhand throw (Figs. 6.11 and 6.12).

In executing the 3–6–3 double play, the left-handed first baseman has a definite advantage over a right-hander, since he can throw to second without pivoting and can do so by taking a normal step toward the base. As he picks up the ground ball, he is already in good position to make a quick sidearm throw.

"In making this throw, the left-hander should try to keep his hips open," advised Parker. "He cannot lock his hips. Ideally, he should field the ball with his left foot slightly ahead of his right foot. Keeping his hips open will accelerate the throw to second base."

After making his throw, the first baseman should always hustle back to the base to take the return throw. On a ball hit to his right, he might have difficulty getting back in time for the return throw. In this case, the pitcher should be at the bag to take the throw from the shortstop.

Fig. 6.11 RIGHT-HANDER'S THROW TO SECOND (pivot to outfield). On the ball hit to his left, the first baseman pivots with his back to second all the way around to his left and steps out toward second base to make the throw. He makes one continuous motion as he whirls around (Don Mincher).

Fig. 6.12   RIGHT-HANDER'S THROW TO SECOND (jump shift to right). Anytime the first baseman can get in front of the ball, he should field it off his right knee. In this series, he makes a jump shift to the right and uses a snap overhand throw (Don Mincher).

TEAMING WITH THE PITCHER

After picking up the ground ball, the first baseman should move toward the pitcher and lead him with a smooth underhand toss, about chest-high, and at least two steps from the bag. The fingers of the hand are stretched out, and the hand movement stops about chest-high (Fig. 6.13).

"Get the ball to the pitcher as soon as you can," advised Parker, "usually ten feet before the bag. This way, the pitcher does not have to worry about catching the ball and stepping on the bag, both at the same time."

"When you underhand him the ball," advised Wes, "do not hide the ball from the pitcher. Hold it out in front so that he can see the ball, and do not throw it too hard or too soft."

As he releases the ball, the first baseman does not stop running. He continues running toward him, which adds a little momentum to the throw itself, and also helps him make a straighter throw.

CUTOFFS AND RELAYS

The first baseman generally takes all the cutoffs from right and center field, even left center when he has time to get there. The only one he does not take

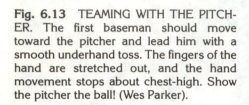

Fig. 6.13 TEAMING WITH THE PITCH-ER. The first baseman should move toward the pitcher and lead him with a smooth underhand toss. The fingers of the hand are stretched out, and the hand movement stops about chest-high. Show the pitcher the ball! (Wes Parker).

is the base hit directly to left field. In this case, we like our third baseman to take the cutoff. He should dash in and take up a position between home plate and the mound so the throw can be cut off if necessary. He should be in a position to catch the ball and throw it to second base.

"On throws from center field," said Parker, "I prefer a position about where the pitcher's foot lands after he makes his pitch. Go to a spot right in front of the mound, about four to five feet down from the rubber.

"When a throw comes in from right field, I like to be about halfway between home and first base, a little toward home. A straight-up stance is best in this fielding situation. He might hold up his glove in the air to serve as a target for the outfielder."

Watching the base runners closely is most important on these plays, so that he can anticipate making a play either at the plate or cutting the ball off and throwing to second or third base. In other words, the first baseman should try not to rely on the catcher or someone else telling him what to do. Usually, the crowds are screaming pretty loudly in these situations, and he will not be able to hear instructions anyway. So, he has to use his own visual information in order to make the play. Some coaches, however, prefer having him listen to the catcher's instructions as to letting the ball go through or cutting it off.

When he lets the ball go through, the first baseman should fake catching it in order to confuse the base runners, at least momentarily.

Many first basemen make the mistake of just standing there and letting the ball come all the way from the outfield and having to catch it on the short hop. I prefer my cutoff men to be a bit closer to home plate than necessary and move into the ball. Then, they are in a position to throw to second base or wherever the play might be.

When the ball comes that far, there is no reason for him to catch the ball on the short hop. He should have time to either maneuver in or back and catch it on a big hop or on a fly—and the ball is much easier to handle.

POP FLIES

The first baseman should call for and take any pop fly to the right side, where he will move in on the ball and make the catch. He should take all the fly balls that he can possibly reach, within reason.

Pop flies midway between first base and home plate are plays that are easier for the first baseman because the spin of the ball is bringing the ball toward him but away from the catcher. It is easier for him to catch the ball coming into it, than for the catcher to attempt it when the ball is breaking away. Besides, the first baseman's glove is better than the catcher's glove for catching pop flies.

"If the ball is anywhere near the stands," said Parker, "you should always run first of all to the retaining wall. If there is any doubt in your mind as to whether that ball will drop into the stands or into foul territory, get over to that wall! And once you get there, you can either move away from it to catch the foul ball, or stand there and make a play into the stands."

HOLDING THE RUNNER ON

Assuming a position next to the bag enables the first baseman to catch throws from the pitcher just in front of the bag, and requires only dropping the glove to the ground to complete the tag.

Most players like to have their right foot to the right side of the bag, with their left foot about on the foul line. Facing the pitcher, with his body slightly crouched, he extends his glove hand as a target about waist-high. He is now in a comfortable position, ready to handle throws to either side and tag the runner's foot in the same motion. By turning to his right, he sweeps his glove down and into the runner.

"In tagging the runner, he should just get his glove down by the bag," said Parker, "and not sweep it down and then through again (Fig. 6.15). Some runners can be pretty tricky when they return to the base."

Parker placed his foot almost six inches from the bag. By doing it this way, it was a little easier for him to turn and tag the runner, even though his foot was six inches away, rather than go right down to his foot.

Occasionally, the first baseman will play two or three steps behind the runner but close enough to hold him near the base. If he feels a bunt is likely,

Fig. 6.14 HOLDING THE RUNNER ON. Facing the pitcher, with his body slightly crouched, first baseman Mike Squires of the Chicago White Sox extends his glove hand as a target about waist-high.

he will not even stand close to the bag, but about four or five feet toward home plate. He might even take as big a lead as the runner does, and he will stand almost in a sprinter's position. This facilitates his running to home plate. In moving off the base, the first baseman may take a cross-over step with the left foot, a step with the right foot and a shuffle step into fielding position.

When a runner starts for second, he should alert the catcher by calling, "There he goes!" Garvey will call the catcher's name. If it is Steve Yeager, he just yells, "Steve!"

In receiving a throw from the catcher, the first baseman should put his left foot on the base and his right foot out toward second base. His glove is held slightly to the outside of his right shoulder as a target.

PICK-OFF PLAY

While holding the runner on base, the first baseman must be ready for a pick-off throw from the pitcher at all times. When he is playing behind the runner,

Fig. 6.15 TAGGING THE RUNNER. By turning to his right, the first baseman (Pete LaCock) sweeps his glove down and into the runner. He must quickly get his glove down by the bag. The first baseman should place his right foot on the home plate side of the bag. If the runner slides back feet first, he could be spiked if his foot is directly in front of the bag.

he gives the pitcher a sign for a throw, such as hitching his pants or adjusting his cap.

"I will give a sign," said Wes, "and he will give an answering sign. Either one of us can initiate the sign, and the other one has to confirm it. Otherwise, the sign is not on."

We worked it like this: The pitcher went into the stretch, looked back to second and saw Wes break out of the corner of his eye. He then turned and tried to throw him the ball directly over the bag.

Cooperation between the pitcher and first baseman is essential on any pick-off play. When the play is on, the first baseman must feel free to break for the bag. We do not like to see him break toward the bag and then have the pitcher make a pitch to the plate. By having signs between the pitcher and first baseman, there is no reason this play should get messed up. We do not like them to be obvious, yet the signs have to be simple enough so that both players are able to pick them up.

The Dodgers also employ a pick-off play with the catcher. It could be with a man on first, first and second, or with the bases loaded. In this type of play, the first baseman might rub his leg and the catcher might go to his shin guards.

Setting up the run-down play

If a runner is caught off first base and breaks for second, the first baseman should throw the ball to the second baseman as soon as possible, unless there is a runner on third. This will set up the defensive players for the fastest and most effective way of handling the run-down. The key to this play is to get the runner moving back to the base from which he came.

BACKING UP AND COVERING

When the bases are unoccupied, the first baseman backs up second base on all throws from the left field side or the second base side. After a single to left field, for instance, he should be ready to retrieve overthrows to second base. He also covers second base and the plate when these bases are left uncovered.

First Baseman Drills

1. Footwork drill—shifting to the left, right, and stretching forward; using the cross-over step while touching the base
2. Tagging the runner returning to the bag (throws from the pitcher and catcher), and other pick-off plays
3. Feeding the pitcher when covering first
4. Catching pop fly balls
5. Fielding bunts down the first base line and in front of the plate; working with the pitcher in fielding drag bunts and hits
6. Practicing the 3–6–3 double play
7. Handling cutoff and relay plays (working on use of the voice for the direction of the throw)
8. Mastering the run-down play (with the second baseman and shortstop)
9. Fielding ground balls (to the left and right)
10. Throwing to second base, to the plate, and making long throws to third base

11. Receiving all types of throws (low, high, wide, straight-in, and in the dirt)
12. Leaving the bag to catch wild throws and making the tag
13. Infield practice

7
The Second Baseman

When I realize that one of the keys to championship baseball is the double play, and that the second baseman is in more double plays than anybody else, I have to believe that this is a very important man.

The keystone combination must be able to make the double play *consistently* if a team is to play championship baseball. The pivot at second base on the double play is perhaps the hardest defensive skill to learn. This is why the shortstop and second baseman must practice making this play over and over, until they know all the moves each one makes at his position. The longer they work together, the better they will be.

THE ESSENTIALS

Quickness is most essential! The second base position demands quick hands, a quick throwing arm, and quick foot action. The day is coming when speed and quickness will be at more of a premium than they are right now. This is particularly true when playing on fields with synthetic turf, where the ball comes

Fig. 7.1 THE DOUBLE PLAY. The second baseman who shows no fear of oncoming spikes or body contact is a most important factor in making the double play consistently. Here, Jim Gantner, in preparing to double up the hitter at first base, concentrates on his target at first base, rather than on the approaching base runner, Wayne Nordhagen.

through with surprising quickness. The player who can start in a hurry, take a quick cross-over step, and reach his full motion on his second or third step is the type of player I want at second base.

The individual who performs at second base should practice throwing the ball from every position. He must even practice throwing with a man sliding into him. While a strong arm is vital to his success at making the double play, a quick snap throw is also important. He handles a variety of slow bouncing balls, which require a quick and accurate release to first base.

Like all players in the field, the second baseman must learn to play the hitters properly. This can be a major asset to him. The more knowledge he has of a particular hitter and the pitcher on the mound, the better he will react. He must know where the batter will likely hit the ball. Experienced infielders get a good start on a ground ball because they know what pitch is being thrown and the type of hitter at the plate—a pull, opposite field or straightaway type.

In addition to covering second base on steals, he serves as a relay or cutoff man on throws to various bases.

During batting practice, when our coaches hit ground balls in the infield, I like to see my second baseman and shortstop work on the double play. In spring training, they go through drills almost by the hour. These drills not only provide good footwork practice but they also serve as ball handling practice.

The footwork involved in the double play pivot has to be done automatically; the infielder has to hustle into the bag and then be ready to go either way, depending on where the ball is. The key to a second baseman's footwork is not to commit himself too quickly. He has as many as four or five ways of making the pivot, but he should not commit himself until he sees where the ball will be thrown to him.

QUALIFICATIONS

Quick feet, good hands, and an accurate arm with a quick release are the requisites for second basemen. The player with a strong arm and a quick release could be another Bill Mazeroski. Mazeroski was one of the best at turning the double play. The second baseman must have speed and agility to cover the bag on double plays and be able to throw from any position. He has to be able to move to his right or left for hard hit balls. He must be a good judge of fly balls, and of pop-ups behind the second and first base areas.

Along with speed, agility, and aggressiveness, he should be the type of athlete who does not get upset too easily by the runner who slides into him (Fig. 7.2). The timid infielder sometimes becomes spike-shy and has a tendency to watch the runner instead of the ball.

Since he often fulfills the role of team leader, the second baseman should be an intelligent, alert individual who can anticipate every type of play. He has to have a sound knowledge of the game in order to make the many types of decisions that have to be made during the game.

Fig. 7.2 THE SECOND BASE POSITION demands quick hands, a quick throwing arm, and quick foot action. Lou Whitaker, left, uses some quick footwork to evade a hard sliding base runner, while Manny Trillo, right, fields a ground ball to his left, takes a short, gliding shuffle-step and makes the throw to first base.

STANCE

The second baseman should assume a stance which is comfortable to him, one in which he can maintain good control of his body. He keeps his body low and more or less relaxed. Most infielders keep their feet approximately shoulder-width apart and pointing slightly outward, not straight ahead. This will make it easier for them to turn or jab-step as they start to move to their right or left. The hands are on their knees until just before the pitch, at which time they hang down loosely at the side.

As the ball is being pitched, most infielders like to move forward a step or two. They do this so they will not be caught flat-footed or on their heels in the event the ball is hit their way. The hands which were on the knees now hang loosely as they shift forward.

"I like to have my feet under me," said Mazeroski, "so I can move quickly in any direction. First, I will go into a preliminary stance, with the heel of my hands above my knees. Then, as the pitcher goes into his pitch, I drop down low so my glove hand is almost on the ground.

"On every pitch, I move or step forward," said Bill; "I will always step

Fig. 7.3 INFIELDER'S STANCE. The weight of the second baseman is distributed evenly and comfortably on both feet, which are approximately shoulder-width apart. By having his feet under him, he can move quickly in any direction. On every pitch, he steps forward with the left foot about a foot, followed by a slight shuffle with his right (Bill Mazeroski).

forward with the left foot about a foot, followed by a slight shuffle with my right. I time this movement with the anticipation of the batter hitting the pitched ball."

The glove and bare hand should hang relaxed, close to the ground (Fig. 7.3). Both knees are bent, and the fielder is on the balls of his feet, *not on his toes*. He keeps his arms close to his body in the event he has to move laterally. He will be able to move faster because his arms are close to the body.

By being comfortable and staying low to the ground, he can get a quicker start in any direction. As he goes for the ball, he gradually rises up into a running position.

BASIC FIELDING POSITIONS

With no one on base, the second baseman should play as deep as he can, his position being determined by such factors as his arm and the speed of the hitter. The condition of the playing field should also be a factor. Other points to consider are where the batter usually hits the ball and how his pitcher is working on the hitter. Normally, he plays approximately thirty feet from second base and twenty-five feet behind the line.

With a runner on first base and less than two outs, he will move to his double play depth. This will bring him in four or five steps toward home and move him toward second base by one or two steps. This fielding position should put him about twenty or twenty-five feet from the base and approximately twenty feet behind the line. Of course, these figures will vary according to his speed and quickness and the hitter at the plate. It will be to his advantage to play as far from the base as he can and still be able to get there in time to make a play.

Carry your glove low. It is easier to come up on the ball than it is to go down.

The left-handed pull hitter should be played three or more feet back and a few steps closer to first. With a right-handed pull hitter at the plate, he will likely move in and position himself as much as fifteen feet closer to second.

With a runner on second or runners on first and second, he is responsible for keeping the runner close to second. Generally, he will be at double play depth, particularly if the bunt is not expected. By breaking for the base occasionally or making fakes toward the base, he can help keep the runner close to the bag.

Percentagewise, the second baseman generally will find it to his advantage to play closer to the base. First, he can go to his left more easily than to his right, and, second, more base hits go up the middle than through the hole.

FIELDING A GROUND BALL

Perhaps the key points in fielding a ground ball are to watch the ball, keep more or less relaxed, and stay low on the ball. The ball is fielded with the hands out in front, loose and relaxed. Most infielders like their hands to "give with the ball." They have to use soft hands to catch the ball properly (Fig. 7.4).

As the player fields the ball, his tail is down and his knees are bent. He is in front of the ball. *His head must stay on the ball.* He must not lift his head. Recall that, in hitting the ball, if the batter pulls his head away from the plate, he will not hit the ball with consistency. The same rule applies to fielding. If he takes his head off the ball, he will have less chance of catching it.

Generally, an infielder should move in on all ground balls except the hard shots that do not require coming in. The reason a good infielder rarely gets a bad hop is that he makes every hop a good one by the way he plays it.

An infielder must remember to play the ball, and *not* have it play him. "Naturally, it is easier to catch a big hop than it is for a short hop," said Bobby Richardson, former star second baseman of the New York Yankees. "So, as soon as the ball is hit off the bat, if you can kind of take a couple steps in and play the ball where you will get a big hop, it is easier. Now, a short hop is also

Fig. 7.4   FIELDING A GROUND BALL. The infielder should field the ball with two hands out in front of him, and with a continuous motion, he "gives" with the ball and brings both hands back into a throwing position. He has his legs apart, his knees are bent, and he steps toward the base (Bobby Grich).

easy to catch. The one bad ball that seems hard to catch is the in-between hop that you sometimes cannot avoid."

More often, it is better for the second baseman to charge the ball then to lay back or back up.

Richardson then went into the "secret" of getting rid of the ball quickly. "First, it should be said that an infielder should make sure he has the ball before he tries to throw it. You cannot throw the ball if you do not catch it! Now, in getting rid of the ball quickly, you catch the ground ball with two hands out in front of you, and with a continuous fluidlike motion, you 'give' with the ball, bringing both hands back into a throwing position. As your hands go back, your right hand has a chance to grab onto the ball securely and you find yourself ready to throw. You save time by having the catching maneuver continue right into your throw, but again, *make sure you catch the ball first!*"

"The main thing in fielding a ground ball," according to Pee Wee Reese, for many years a great shortstop with the Dodgers, "is to watch the ball and stay low on the ball, because it is much easier to bring your hands up than it is to take your whole body down."

Pee Wee also suggests this: "Charge the ball—always keep coming in on the ball. If you are weak on going to your right or on balls being hit directly at you, practice at it. Practice the things you do not do well!" As one of his managers, I know Pee Wee practiced what he preaches.

More often, it is better to charge a ball than to lay back or back up. An infielder can usually get the big hop by taking a couple of steps in. If he backs up, he will likely field the ball between hops. This often lets the ball play him.

One of the worst habits that infielders develop is trying to be too sure. They will wait for the ball to come to them, wanting to be really sure, and they find themselves letting the ball play them. For the great majority of ground balls, they should charge the ball, unless it is a real "hot shot" which doesn't give them time to do anything.

By charging the ball, they will have more time to recover a fumbled ground ball. They will have time to pick it up and still throw the man out at first.

"Watch the hops and try to get it on the big hop," advised Glenn Beckert. "If the ball is not too hard, I like to round off slightly so I can field, step, and throw to first base.

"Never give up on a ground ball. If you fumble a ground ball, go after it as quickly as you can. There may still be a chance to make the play. However, do not make a useless throw."

Basically, we keep yelling at our men to "Stay in front of the ball," "Stay low," "Charge the ball," "Go toward the ball," "Go after it" and "Be aggressive."

In fielding ground balls, the fielder has to relax his hands and arms. They cannot be stiff. The hands and arms have to be relaxed and fluid so the fielder can move them quickly if the ball should take a tricky bounce.

Many young infielders do not bend their knees properly, and instead of getting in front of the ball, they catch the ball at the side. Another problem is not getting into position to field and throw the ball in one motion.

One of the hardest plays for a second baseman to make is the ball hit hard directly at him.

Hard hit ground balls

Strange as it may seem, one of the hardest plays for a second baseman to make is the ball hit hard directly at him. This play can be difficult because he does not have a chance to gauge the hop of the ball. He cannot see the hops as well as he can on balls hit to his side. He just has to try to get in front of it, knock it down, and throw the man out. Actually, it is often hard for an infielder not to charge the ball coming directly at him. The main thing is to try not to let the ball play him.

On hard smashes, the infielder may drop to one knee or go into a squatting position with his heels together. He might even have to use his body to help block the ball. Usually, he will have time to pick it up and beat the runner with his throw.

FIELDING SLOW ROLLERS

A slow roller can be most difficult, since the ball must be fielded on the run and thrown while the second baseman is off balance. For many youngsters, this is one of the most difficult of all infield plays to execute. The throw must be started from where the ball is fielded. Coming in fast, the fielder scoops the ball (Fig. 7.5) and makes a sidearm throw across his body while straightening up on his right foot. He keeps his eyes on the ball until it is safely in his glove. This fielding play occurs on drag or push bunts, or with slow hit grounders.

In making this play, it is best to field the ball with the left foot forward. Field it with two hands, then take a step with the right foot to make the throw.

The infielder races in with his body bent at the waist. He moves with his feet apart so that he has good balance. After picking up the ball, he has to throw it sidearm, across the body. He cannot waste time straightening up, because that split-second might cause his throw to be late. "Getting the jump" on the ball is essential. He must charge in and go right after the ball.

For the most part, I do not advocate picking up a ground ball barehanded. Naturally, in a "do-or-die" situation, an infielder has time only to come in and grab the ball with one hand and throw it across his body. If at all possible, he should go down with both hands to make the play. To make plays barehanded, he will need good, relaxed hands as well as excellent playing facilities. The

Fig. 7.5 FIELDING THE SLOW ROLLER. The second baseman must field the slow grounder on the run. The throw is started from where the ball is fielded. Coming in fast, he scoops the ball up and makes a sidearm throw across his body while straightening up on his right foot. Fielding the ball with two hands, he takes a step with the right foot to make the throw (Glenn Beckert).

barehanded play has its place in professional ball, but even there, it can be overdone.

If the ball should stop or almost stop rolling, however, the barehanded pickup can be effective. With a scooping motion of his hand, the player fields the ball about even with the toe of the left foot and in line with the right foot.

Perhaps the most basic skill in fielding the slow roller is to get to the ball as quickly as possible and still have the body under control to field it. The infielder who fails to get to the ball quickly will likely have to rush his fielding and throwing execution. The stronger the throwing arm, the deeper the second baseman can play.

GOING FAR TO THE RIGHT

The most difficult play for most second baseman to make is the ground ball hit to their right side, behind second (Fig. 7.6). In fielding the ball, the player

Fig. 7.6 GOING TO THE RIGHT. The ground ball hit to his right side is a play the second baseman must be able to make consistently. It requires ability and daily practice. Moving quickly to his right, he must keep his eye on the ball, backhand it, and come to a full stop. Then, bracing on his right foot, he has to turn and make an overhand throw (Bobby Grich).

has to move away from first base. There is no question that this play takes a great deal of practice and ability.

In making this play, he should turn on his right foot and take a cross-over step with the left foot. He pushes off with the left foot and takes a step with his right foot. Then, he crosses over and digs after the ball. If he can, he should try to get in front of the ball. However, if he cannot, he has to make a gloved, backhand stab at the ball and come to a full stop. His weight is braced on his right foot as he turns and makes his throw. The body should follow through in the direction of first base as he completes his overhand throw.

It is important to keep the glove face "square" with the ball. Failure to do this will result in balls hitting the face of the glove and bouncing off to the side. Bringing the left elbow in close to the body will help correct this situation. If he has to backhand the ball, he should try to keep his right foot forward as he fields it so he can move quickly into throwing position.

Some second basemen try to round the bag and go deep behind the base, where they cannot make the play anyway. They get to the ball, but they cannot make the play. Consequently, we encourage our fielders to go straight across and take the short route. Then, if they get to the ball, they still have a chance to throw the man out.

GOING TO THE LEFT

On a ball hit into the hole, the second baseman must move quickly to his left. Since he is driving quickly toward the first base line, his throwing motion can be difficult. In fielding the ball on his left side, he has to pivot his body around so that he can make the throw to the first baseman (Fig. 7.7). This is similar to a right-handed first baseman throwing to second. If he is able to handle it, he should be sure to call for it so the first baseman does not have to make an unnecessary attempt and can go immediately to the bag for the throw.

"If the ball is to my left," said Beckert, "I like to stay as low as possible and dig with my arms as I cross-step my right leg over the left. Actually, I do not lift my foot. I merely turn the left foot, just so the spikes barely clear the ground. Then, I take a cross-over step with my right foot as I break to my left for the ball, making sure to stay low."

In approaching the ball, the second baseman makes a quick one-two step directly behind the ball. He takes a step with his right foot, and then brings his left foot down. This places the heel of his left foot in line with the right toe.

He takes a short, quick step with his right foot while turning his body to the right as he brings the ball and his glove up into throwing position. Since he does not always have time to get set in front of the ball, he should try to field it with his left foot forward.

Fig. 7.7 GOING TO THE LEFT. Moving quickly to his left, the second baseman follows the path of the ball right into his glove. By bending his knees and waist, he is able to stay low on the ball and field it with his left foot forward. Turning his body to the right, he brings the ball and his glove up into throwing position (Davey Lopes).

Like all fielders, the second baseman should catch the ball with both hands whenever possible.

CATCHING THE BALL

"Watch the ball into your glove" is a phrase worth repeating over and over when catching the ball. A fielder should always keep his eyes on the ball.

The ball should be caught with both hands whenever possible. This places the throwing hand on the ball as it hits into the glove. Too many young players make the mistake of catching the ball with one hand and then having to reach into the glove with their bare hand to make the throw. Catching the ball with two hands is not only surer, but the fielder can move more quickly into throwing position.

In addition, he should be in the correct position to throw the ball as soon as possible. This can be done by moving as the ball approaches. In this way, he can catch it on the throwing arm side of the body. The fielder who reaches out or across his body and catches one-handed wastes valuable time, which may cost his team the ball game.

Keeping the hands relaxed is most important in handling a ball. Do not jab at the ball. The fielder should "give" with the catch, and, as he catches the ball, he goes into his throwing motion.

"Quickness of the hands can be improved with practice," said Mazeroski. "By practicing constantly, an infielder will soon be able to get the ball out of his glove quickly and smoothly. As the ball is caught, the hands should give a little, and as he gives with the catch, he takes the ball from the glove."

THROWING

The second baseman's throw is more of a snap throw than are the throws of other infielders and outfielders. This is because he almost always has to get rid of the ball from the position in which he fields the ball. Quite often, he will not have time to straighten up.

Although several methods of throwing may be used, the overhand throw has more carry and is more accurate. However, if he has to hurry, he should come up only part way and throw with more of a sidearm motion. On a long throw, he will plant the right foot so that he can get a full throwing motion and greater force.

Above all, the fielder must not hurry the throw. After straightening up for the throw, he steps toward the base with the left foot and completes his throw.

Grip

An infielder holds the ball with his fingers well spread across the seams where they are widest, and his thumb underneath. This helps prevent the ball from sailing or sliding and it will generally go in a straight line. The pressure is on the tips of the fingers.

As the ball is being taken out of the glove, the player can quickly twist it around to the proper grip. Sometimes, though, he has to grab and throw the ball regardless of how the ball is gripped.

Throwing technique

Most infielders who throw well have a good forearm and wrist snap which gives the ball good carry (Fig. 7.8). They keep their throwing arm away from the body and throw the ball in one continuous motion. The elbow not only comes back first, but it leads the forward drive as well.

Keeping the arm loose, the fielder snaps it forward like a whip as he makes the throw. He uses a powerful wrist action with the wrist rolling over just as the ball is released off the ends of the first two fingers. He should follow through with his body to get the proper power behind the throw.

To obtain a good push-off, the fielder must turn his body to the right. He does this by turning his pivot foot to the right so he can push off the entire inside edge of the foot. Many players fail to turn their pivot foot properly. As a result, they find themselves throwing off the toes or balls of the foot. They lack the strong push-off necessary to make a strong throw.

Fig. 7.8 OVERHAND THROW. On the long throw from behind the base, the second baseman must plant his right foot so he can get a full throwing motion and greater push-off on his pivot foot. Bobby Grich holds the ball with his fingers well spread across the widest seams. Concentrating on his target at first base, he executes a smooth follow through in the direction of the throw.

A fielder should not ease up on his throwing. This usually happens when he has excessive time. He must keep everything in rhythm. When he fields the ball, he should execute his footwork, grip the ball across the seams, and throw it in a fluid motion.

By achieving full arm extension, a player will throw the ball harder and farther. The "short-armer" is the player who has a bad arm arc and does not achieve full extension.

When warming up, infielders should throw at each other's face or chest. Remember to *always throw at a target.*

Taking too many steps before throwing the ball can be a dangerous habit for all fielders. Too many steps are unnecessary, and should be discouraged by the coach. As he throws the ball, an infielder need take only one step in transferring his weight from the rear foot to the front foot. Those who have a tendency to take too many steps should practice the "one-step-and-throw" drill while warming up.

MAKING THE DOUBLE PLAY

The good infielder is always looking for the double play. In fact, he wants to make it. In a tight situation, a good double play combination actually wants the ball to be hit to them, rather than to someone else.

The secret of a successful double play is getting to the bag early, so that the pivot man is waiting, rather than running across the base. Most young infielders are usually too far from the base when trying to make the double play. Invariably, they end up sprinting for the base, providing a difficult, moving target. Then they try to catch and throw the ball off-balance.

A veteran infielder gets to the bag as early as possible. He must strive for perfect control of his weight so he can step inside or outside the base line. He should be able to execute either of these options because he knows the runner will attempt to slide into him to prevent a double play. With his weight balanced evenly on both feet, he makes the necessary adjustments and completes his pivot and throw to first base.

We want the second baseman to get there as fast as he can. His footwork will be governed by the throw and by the way the runner comes into the base.

Proper position

In covering for the double play, it is important that the shortstop and second baseman move a few steps in and over closer to second base. To execute a good pivot, the infielder must reach the bag and be on balance before the ball arrives. Since this is difficult to do from a regular fielding depth, the second baseman must shorten up or cheat toward the bag in a double play situation.

Some teams, however, have their keystone combination cheat by shortening up on the play, rather than moving close to the bag. In double play situations or steals, they will cheat toward home plate. This will bring them closer to the bag.

First, it must be decided who will cover second base. Use the voice to let each other know who is going to cover. The closed mouth says, "Me," which means, "I will take the bag." The open mouth, "You," is the signal for the other infielder to cover.

On a normal double play, the man who is not fielding the ball covers the bag. However, when the first or third baseman fields the ball, then the man who is playing nearest the bag covers.

Getting to the bag

In making a double play, the first thing a second baseman should think about is getting to the bag as quickly as possible (Fig. 7.9). Then, as he approaches the base, he should shorten up his stride a little so that he is capable of adjusting himself to the particular situation. He will go either to the left or the right side of the bag, across the bag, or possibly touch the bag and back up.

Fig. 7.9 GET TO THE BAG QUICKLY. The pivot man should move to the base as soon as the ball is hit. He receives the ball chest-high (Bobby Knoop).

Actually, he has as many as four or five ways to maneuver at second base, but he must not commit himself too quickly—not until he sees where the ball is going to be thrown. If he comes in and decides the ball is going to be on the inside, he commits himself to touching the bag with his right foot. Now if the ball happens to end up somewhere else, he will find himself in a difficult position. Therefore, as he nears the bag, he should slow down by means of short, choppy steps, to get on balance and be ready to shift in either direction for the throw.

The second baseman should try to round off a little as he approaches the bag. When he gets within three or four steps of the bag, he should round off. This will make it easier for the third baseman and the shortstop in the hole to throw to him. By rounding off slightly, he can get more momentum on the throw, providing, of course, he receives the ball over the bag or slightly in front.

A difficult double play situation is when the runner gets to the bag at the same times the ball does, such as on the hit and run. The pivot man has to use some really quick footwork on this play.

SECOND BASEMAN'S PIVOTS

There are at least five ways in which the second baseman can make the pivot. As in the case of the shortstop, one way of pivoting is not sufficient. The footwork he uses depends on where the throw is caught and how much time he has.

Once he sees where the ball is, the pivot man should not find it too hard to use the proper pivot. The pivot man may hit the bag with his left foot, drive back off it, and throw to first. Or, he can go on across the bag, drag his foot across the bag, and make his pivot on the other side of the bag.

Any number of ways can be used, but many players will find that one method is easier than the others. The young infielder should learn several methods, so he will know eventually which one is his best. However, if he always goes the same way each time, the base runner will know which way to come into the base.

There are no set rules in making the pivot. Each fielder should make the pivot the best way suited to his physical ability. While Bill Mazeroski could back off and make his throw from behind the bag, other pivot men whose throwing arms are not as strong as Bill's should consider other pivots.

The pivot man should strive for perfect control of his weight so he can step inside or outside the base line. He wants to be in position to use all of his options because he knows the runner will attempt to slide into him to prevent a double play.

"Always anticipate a bad throw," said Bobby Knoop. "I always expect a bad throw, not a good one. This way you are on guard, ready to move quickly for the errant throw."

Taking out the pivot man in a double play is not only a legitimate play in baseball, as long as the runner does not go outside the base path to accomplish it, but it is something every smart base runner tries to do.

In the big leagues, teams play each other numerous times during the season and if an infielder can make the double play in only one position, the base runners will soon realize this and will start after him. Therefore, the pivot man must know how to pivot several different ways, and must be able to pivot on either foot.

While most second basemen will touch the bag with either foot, Mazeroski prefers to use only his left foot. "On all pivots, I always touch the bag with my left foot," said Bill. "Generally, I will use the push-back pivot, since I have found this to be the best method of keeping away from the runner. After hitting the outside of the base with my left foot, I will push back on the right, and step toward first base on the left foot for the throw."

The footwork used in executing the mound side and backing-off pivots carries the second baseman away from the path of the slider. A prime objective of the pivot is to *move away from the path of the slider.* Unless he avoids contact with the slider, the double play throw is not likely to be successful.

Again, the key to the whole thing is where the ball is thrown. This will determine what type of pivot to use. Therefore, he should know two or three types.

The straddle and drag with the right toe

One of the easiest and surest ways to make the pivot is to ease into and straddle the bag, then drag the foot over the bag (Fig. 7.10). The second baseman takes

Fig. 7.10 STRADDLE AND DRAG. The second baseman must get to the bag quickly and straddle it. If the throw is accurate, he steps out toward first base with his left foot and drags his right toe over the bag (Bobby Knoop).

the throw and makes a fast flip to first. Pivot men of the New York Yankees, from Willie Randolph back to the days of Bobby Richardson, Tony Lazzeri, and Joe Gordon, have been executing the straddling technique.

"On the straddle and drag," said Richardson, "it is particularly important for the pivot man getting to the bag quickly. If the throw is accurate, he steps out toward first base with his left foot and drags his right toe against the left field side of second base as he makes the throw to first.

"If the shortstop's throw is to the pitcher's side of the bag," said Bobby, "he hops to the left toward the mound. If the throw is to the left field side of the bag, he should drag his foot over the bag and throw from behind it."

As soon as a ground ball is hit to the third baseman or the shortstop, the idea is to get to the bag quickly, straddle it, and then be in a position to go either to his left or right. If the throw is to his left, he takes one step with his right foot, placing his right foot on top of the bag, turns, and throws all with the same motion. Naturally, he jumps from his left foot as he avoids the runner.

However, if the throw is to his right, he can hook onto the bag with his left foot to provide a little more momentum to bring him back, and get a little something extra on his throw to first.

Is it difficult to get to the bag in time to straddle it properly? In answering this question, Richardson said: "The only time I had trouble getting to the bag is on a ball that is hit sharply at either the shortstop or the third baseman. On this play, though, I did not have to get to the bag quickly because it would possibly be an easy one."

"I tried to get to the bag a fraction of a second before the ball," stated Mazeroski, "so that I could use the bag for leverage and push off it to get more zip and accuracy on my throw to first base. The throw must be quick, with the body moving toward first base for speed and accuracy.

"When you arrive too late," explained Bill, "you give the thrower a moving target at which to shoot. You will either miss the ball, be undressed by the runner or make a poor throw yourself."

Although the straddle technique is the surest way, the chief drawbacks are the vulnerability of the second baseman to being jarred by the runner and the lack of force on the throw to first.

Mound side of second

The second baseman steps on the base with his left foot and into the infield with his right to throw. A favorite of many infielders, this pivot is used when the runner is close to the base and on the outfield side of the base line.

As shown in Figure 7.11, Knoop receives the throw chest-high as he steps on the base with his left foot. After catching the ball, his right foot comes down two feet past the bag in on the infield. He braces on his right foot and steps toward first base, making an overhand throw to first.

"The throw will determine where he will go," said Knoop. "Usually, the shortstop feeds the ball to the second baseman only on the inside part of the bag so that his momentum coming across will enable him to complete the play. However, if the throw is to the outfield side of second base, he cannot come on across because he will be fielding the ball across his body and off-balance."

Backing off

This pivot is effective when the runner is close and on the infield side of the base line. During his career, Mazeroski used this pivot almost exclusively in making the double play. This was his favorite pivot. "By throwing from behind the base, I was able to keep away from the sliding runner," asserted Mazeroski. "I might add that my arm was strong enough to do it this way. Someone else, though, might not have a strong enough arm to throw from behind the base."

The second baseman steps on the base with his left foot, and as he is catching the ball, he pushes back off the base, landing on his right foot. He steps toward first base with his left foot to complete the throw (Fig. 7.12). By pushing his weight back onto his right foot, he can get rid of the ball more

Fig. 7.11 MOUND SIDE OF SECOND BASE. The second baseman steps on the base with his left foot and into the infield with his right to throw. He pushes off his right foot and steps toward first base, making an overhand throw (Bobby Knoop).

quickly and get something on it. He should bring the left side of his body back vigorously toward right field.

"If the throw was to the left field side of the bag," said Mazeroski, "I would hop to my right, dragging my left foot over the bag, and then I made my throw from behind the base."

Stepping with right foot and throwing

A simple pivot to make is to step on the base with the right foot. The fielder plants his foot right on the bag and accepts the throw at the same time. He then steps toward first with the left foot for the throw (Fig. 7.13).

This seems to be one of the quickest and most popular pivots used by the second baseman. He can get rid of the ball immediately after catching it chest-high.

When Roy Hartsfield was on our coaching staff he reminded us: "On this

Fig. 7.12 BACKING OFF. The second baseman steps on the base with his left foot, then pushes back toward right field as he throws. He steps toward first base with his left foot to complete the throw. This pivot is effective when the runner is close (Bobby Knoop).

Fig. 7.13 STEPPING WITH RIGHT AND THROWING. A simple pivot, the second baseman merely steps on the base with the right foot. He then steps toward first with the left foot for the throw (Glenn Beckert).

pivot, he should jump in the air and relax a little and get his spikes loose because he never knows exactly where that runner is going to be."

Straddle and kick with the left foot

If the throw is to the left field side of the base, the second baseman hops to his right, dragging his left foot over the bag, and throws to first from behind the base. After stepping away from the base runner, he braces on his right foot and steps out with his left foot for the throw.

Right foot leap and flip

This is one of the fastest ways to make the double play, but a difficult one to perfect. The second baseman jockeys into second base and straddles the bag with his right foot, just touching it. Upon taking the throw, he makes a fast fliplike relay to first. As he throws, he lifts his left foot or leaps into the air off his right foot to avoid the sliding base runner.

The left foot leap and throw is another way to make the double play pivot. When he has to take the throw a few steps before arriving at the bag, he will hit the bag with his left foot and throw as he comes across the bag, leaping and throwing at the same time to get accuracy and power on the ball.

SECOND BASEMAN'S THROWS

The success of a double play usually depends on the manner in which the ball is fed to the pivot man. Therefore, the throw must be executed accurately and as quickly as the situation calls for. Speed and control is, of course, vital in handling the ball.

The second baseman uses as many as three types of throws to the short-stop: the underhand toss, the sidearm throw, and the backhand flip. Whatever the type, all his tosses should be made letter-high for easy handling. He should throw in front of the shortstop so that, if possible, the shortstop receives the ball one step away from the bag. We call this "leading" the shortstop with the ball. Generally, the second baseman throws to the outside corner of the bag.

Sidearm throws are used by the second baseman more than by any other player on the field. The sidearm delivery enables him to get rid of the ball more quickly. Very few second basemen throw really overhand because they cannot always position their body to get something on it that way. Quite often, they have to move quickly to the side, reach down low for the ball, and, without straightening up, make an accurate throw to the shortstop. A little snap with the wrist and forearm helps to get something on the ball and get rid of it quickly. The farther he is away from the bag, the more speed he can put on the ball; the closer he is to the shortstop, the softer the toss.

If the runner stops to delay the tag, the second baseman should not chase him. Instead, the throw to first should be made to retire the batter, then the play is made on the runner. If the latter runs out of the base line to avoid the tag, he should not be chased—*he is automatically out.*

Underhand toss

If he is close to the bag, the second baseman should field the ball with both hands and use a simple underhand lay-up, similar to a bowler's throw (Fig. 7.14). We want our pivot men to keep the ball chest-high and to throw it firmly, not just a "lollipop" toss.

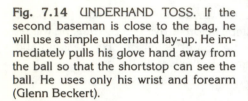

Fig. 7.14 UNDERHAND TOSS. If the second baseman is close to the bag, he will use a simple underhand lay-up. He immediately pulls his glove hand away from the ball so that the shortstop can see the ball. He uses only his wrist and forearm (Glenn Beckert).

"As soon as I start my throw," explained Beckert, "I pull my glove hand away from the ball so that the shortstop can see it. Then, using only my forearm and wrist, I toss the ball underhand to him. I flip my wrist in an upward motion, the palm of my hand facing the shortstop upon release of the ball. A little farther out, I use a long lay-up, or else half-turn and throw sidearm."

Sidearm throw

Beyond twelve feet or so, the second baseman has to turn and throw, a quick sidearm throw across his body. It is a short arm throw and requires a great deal of wrist action to get speed behind it (Fig. 7.15).

"Whenever possible, be in a position to throw when you field the ball," suggested Beckert. "Practice picking up fast grounders and getting rid of them in a hurry, yet accurately, from any position. Farther from second, you will turn the same way, but you will cock your arm and put more shoulder into it."

From a medium distance, the second baseman pivots to his right on the balls of both feet, so that his toes are pointing toward the base. Then, he makes a short sidearm snap from a squat position.

On a ball hit slightly to his left where he still can get in front of the ball, he should field the ball with his left foot ahead. This makes a pivot to the right easier. He will pivot to the right on his right foot and step toward the bag with his left foot to make the throw. It is just a twist of the body and a snap throw with the wrist and forearm. This has proven to be quicker. As this play is speeded up, it will become a jump-shift. The right foot should come down first, as the left foot steps out in the direction of the throw.

Fig. 7.15 SIDEARM THROW. Beyond twelve feet or so, the second baseman has to turn and throw, a quick sidearm throw across his body. He pivots to the right on his right foot and steps toward the bag with his left foot. It is a snap throw with the wrist and the forearm (Glenn Beckert).

Some infielders like to make a jump pivot or a little hop in the air. They turn their body around so that they are in a position to throw and be able to put something on the ball. Generally, they will release the ball from a low body position with a forearm snap. Or, the player will pivot to his right on his left foot and bring the right foot in back of the left. Then he steps out with his left foot to complete the throw.

If he moves far to his left and back and is unable to get in front of the ball, he pivots to the left, and, turning his back to second base, makes a halfturn of the body to throw. He usually catches the ball with the weight on his left foot and makes a little hop in the air to turn his body. When he comes down, he is in a position to throw.

Backhand flip

This type of throw is executed similarly to the way a basketball player passes to a teammate on his right. Big league infielders like Knoop and Beckert can backhand the ball accurately from twelve feet away (Fig. 7.16). They find they can get rid of the ball more quickly and throw it faster than they can by laying it up.

The backhand flip, however, requires a certain amount of skill. By executing it with a stiff wrist, the fielder can be more accurate. In addition, it is essential that the shortstop see the ball and be able to follow it.

In the Dodger organization, we never shovel with the glove because it is very difficult to control the ball this way. The ball can roll off the glove at different angles.

Fig. 7.16   BACKHAND FLIP. Similar to a basketball type pass, the second baseman can backhand the ball accurately from twelve feet away. The fielder is more accurate when executing the flip with a stiff wrist. Let the shortstop see the ball all the way (Bobby Knoop).

On a ball fielded directly behind second base, some big-league second basemen will occasionally backhand it from the gloved hand to the shortstop. "Do not make a practice of doing this unless you absolutely have to," advised Knoop. "Throwing from the glove can never be as accurate as throwing with your free hand."

While an infielder must be constantly reminded to get rid of the ball, he must know when hurrying the play will result in more damage than good.

RELAYS AND CUTOFFS

Relays and cutoffs are team plays which require a great deal of practice to be executed properly. Failure of the second baseman to carry out his part of these plays will result in a serious breakdown of team defense which could mean the ball game. The most important thing to remember, in taking a relay, is to be sure that he catches the ball on the glove side, the side on which he is going to pivot (Fig. 7.17).

On a base hit to right center field, for example, the second baseman will go out to take the relay throw. Raising his hands in the air, he should yell, "Here!" In order to catch the ball on his throwing side, he should take the throw with his body turned toward the left. He steps forward with his right side in the direction of the throw. This maneuver turns his body slightly toward the infield, to his left, enabling him to make his throws more quickly. Failure to turn his body more into throwing position will merely use up valuable time.

Most teams use a double cutoff. They will send out the shortstop or the

Fig. 7.17   TAKING THE RELAY THROW. The relay man on a throw from the outfield should run approximately forty to fifty feet out on the outfield grass. To save valuable time, the second baseman should catch the ball on his throwing side. Taking the throw with his body turned toward the infield, he steps forward with his right side in the direction of the throw (Joe Morgan).

second baseman. They will put either one behind the other, in case there is a bad throw. The outfielder has to hit the first man who comes out for the throw. It must be a good throw, quick, and on a line.

Use of the voice is important in this defensive situation. The shortstop is the backup man, about thirty feet or so behind. He should tell the relay man where the ball should be thrown. He should call out: "Home!" "Second base!" or "No play!" depending on where the play should be made.

On routine ground balls to right field, we instruct our second baseman to go directly to the bag, and the shortstop to back him up. We feel this is better than going out for just a short relay. The proper maneuver depends entirely on where the ball is hit, though.

TAGGING THE RUNNER

All infielders must remember that the runner actually *tags himself out*. After breaking for the bag, the fielder should straddle it with both feet. He catches the throw from the catcher with two hands whenever possible, but the tag is made with the gloved hand only. He tags the runner by sweeping the ball across the line of his slide, snapping the ball down and in front of the base. By keeping the ball between the runner and the base, he will cause the runner to tag himself.

If he has to wait, an infielder should not plant his glove because the runner

Fig. 7.18 TAGGING THE RUNNER. Straddling the bag with both feet, second baseman Davey Lopes makes the tag with his glove hand only. Keeping the ball between the runner and the base causes the runner to tag himself.

has a better chance of kicking the ball from the glove. He holds the glove cocked to one side and times his sweep. When the base runner slides, he snaps it down and across his foot (Fig. 7.18).

FIELDING FLY BALLS

Beside handling fly balls hit in his general direction, the second baseman must have the range to move behind second base and into the outfield, and even behind first base into foul territory. These fielding responsibilities call for speed and quickness, in addition to the ability to judge high, twisting pop flies that can be difficult to handle. This is particularly true when he has to cope with a glaring, bright sun or adverse wind conditions.

The second baseman and the shortstop are the logical fielders of most short fly balls in the outfield territory. If the fly should move out near enough for an outfielder to grab, they should back off, since the outfielder coming in has the better play on the ball. But they should keep going until the outfielder calls for the ball. Furthermore, the outfielder is in a better position to throw. On pop flies behind first base, the second baseman has a better angle than the first baseman because he is often coming in on the ball. If the sun tends to bother him, he should use his gloved hand to shade his eyes. On sunny days, an infielder should consider painting black charcoal on the skin below his eyes to lessen sun glare.

If a pop fly is hit over his head to his left, his first step is backward with his left foot. On a pop-up to his right, he steps back first with his right foot. It is important to keep after the ball unless another player calls for it or the catch cannot be made (Fig. 7.19).

In chasing fly balls, the fielder should run on the balls of his feet. Running

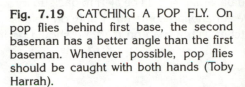

Fig. 7.19 CATCHING A POP FLY. On pop flies behind first base, the second baseman has a better angle than the first baseman. Whenever possible, pop flies should be caught with both hands (Toby Harrah).

on the heels tends to make the ball appear to jump with every step. Therefore, he will see the ball more clearly and follow it better if he does not run on his heels. He makes the catch with his hands just below eye-level and in front of his right shoulder. The fingers of his glove point upward.

Good communication

Outfield flies can be difficult to handle unless the infielders and outfielders work together and communicate with each other. It is essential that the fielder who has the best play on the ball call for it. If he can catch the ball, he should simply wave his arms, while yelling, "I have it!" If the outfielder calls for the ball, the infielder will step out of the way and yell, "Take it!" An infielder should always be listening for the outfielder calling, "I have it!" or "Take it!"

COVERING AND BACKING UP

The second baseman should cover second base on all ground balls and most fly balls that are hit to the left field side of second base. He also covers the bag on attempted steals with a right-handed hitter at the plate. With a right-hander at the plate, he should be prepared to drive a runner on second base back to the bag.

On a single to right field with no one on, he should move quickly to the base, face the right fielder and take the throw-in. The shortstop will back him up.

On a single to left field in which the shortstop will go to the bag, the second baseman must back him up on the play. On a base hit to center field, generally, the player closest to second base will handle the throw-in.

On a bunt situation, he should move closer to first base and be ready to cover first and make the put-out. He should run straight to the bag as quickly as he can and place his left foot on the bag to receive the throw.

The second baseman should be alert to back up throws to first and second bases unless he is handling some other duty on defense. On throws from the catcher and pitcher with a man on third, he should be in the proper backup position.

THE INFIELDER'S MENTAL ATTITUDE

When he is on the playing field, the infielder has to concentrate on his fielding. *He cannot let his mind wander.* He must be alert and thinking all the time he is on the field.

"You have to watch the hitter," added Mazeroski, "and see where the pitch is—whether he is going to pull it or not. We have to see how he swings."

The good infielder is one who is hoping that, when his team needs one or two more outs in a tough situation, the ball will be hit to him.

A ball player must have confidence in himself, a positive feeling that he can do it! He has to have a mental attitude which says, "I know I can do it."

The young player so badly wants to be sure not to make a mistake. As a result, he is a little too cautious. Being cautious, he is reluctant to charge the ball. With more experience and practice, he will become more positive and aggressive. The moment he sees the ball hit, he will know what he has to do. If he must charge the ball, his instinctive reflexes, developed by habit, will direct him to move in for it.

When an infielder makes an error, he should not let it get him down. *It is just one of those things.* Even the greatest players in the game will make an occasional error. Nobody is expected to catch them all—so a ball player who commits an error has to forget it. He must make sure he grabs the next one.

Practice Tips for the Second Baseman

1. Practice constantly with the shortstop—playing catch, throwing to each other, and working together on double play drills.
2. Spend fifteen minutes a day picking up ground balls.
3. Get daily practice on pop flies hit in all directions.
4. Practice going to your left, pivoting around, and throwing to first base.
5. Practice the slow roller, coming in, picking a ball up, and throwing while still bent down.

6. Practice going far to your right behind second and making the long throw to first.

7. In warming your arm up, keep moving back until you are throwing from the same distance as that from your deepest area behind second base.

8. Every day, when your legs are loose, work at stopping and starting quickly.

9. Squeeze a hard rubber ball several minutes each day to develop your throwing arm and wrist.

10. Do a lot of running to strengthen your legs.

8
The Shortstop

The shortstop, even more than the second baseman, is the key man in the infield. More balls are hit to his side because there are more right-handed hitters. Actually, it takes a more specialized ball player to play short, for the simple reason that he must have a great arm. He has a longer throw to make and has less time to handle the ball. Most balls hit to the shortstop have to be handled cleanly.

The real test of a shortstop comes when he has to go into the hole toward third base and backhand the ball. Then, we can see how good an arm he has. Quick release of the ball overcomes some of the need for a strong throwing arm.

Indeed, the shortstop must have a strong throwing arm and be quick on his feet in plays of all kinds. He must be able to make the double play consistently. In addition to going deep into the hole, he must possess the ability to charge slowly hit balls, and also to go far to his left behind the bag to get the runner going to first base.

The shortstop should have the strongest arm in the infield and be able to range far to his left and right. Good lateral movement to the ball can be achieved by a better ready position, more efficient cross-over step, proper angles to the ball, and good glove position.

Fig. 8.1 OUTSTANDING ON DEFENSE. Diving stops, slippery-smooth double plays, and a rifle arm are trademarks that put Ozzie Smith of the St. Louis Cardinals in a class by himself.

THE ESSENTIALS

Quickness, plus speed and a strong, accurate arm, are the prime requisites of a good shortstop. He has to cover a lot of ground. The Rick Burleson type, at 5 feet 10 inches and 165 pounds, or Dave Concepcion at 6 feet 1 inch and 180 pounds, are both ideal types for covering ground (Fig. 8.2). Maury Wills, who played for me, had all the essentials to play shortstop. In addition to having a strong arm, Maury's speed afoot was a tremendous asset. A leader on and off the field, Maury gained a vast knowledge of the game. Certainly, he was the captain of our infield.

Playing the hitters is essential to the play of a good shortstop. All major league shortstops keep a mental "book" on every hitter in the league.

Fig. 8.2 FOR ALL-AROUND ABILITY AND RANGE, Dave Concepcion is one of baseball's top shortstops. Here, he shows exceptional footwork and agility in taking a high throw from the catcher.

QUALIFICATIONS

A shortstop should have a strong throwing arm and be quick on his feet. He must have exceptional speed in covering and fielding ground balls to either side of him. From a variety of positions and areas in the infield, he must be able to throw accurately with either a sidearm or an overhand movement.

The athlete who plays shortstop is often the team leader, the "take charge" type of player, and the one to keep his teammates on their toes. Therefore, he must be a resourceful player with sound baseball sense and a talent for anticipating plays—something which Pee Wee Reese excelled in for many years.

The history of baseball shows that few teams have risen to championship heights without a smooth-working, dependable double play combination. Certainly, the success of any baseball team lies in its strength down the middle (Fig. 8.3).

A shortstop not only has considerable ground to cover, but because of the long throws he has to make, it is essential that he field the ball cleanly. Contrary

Fig. 8.3 GET TWO! The shortstop must always think of the double play. Whenever there is a man on base, it should be the first thing on his mind. This is the play that has to be made consistently if a team is to play championship baseball. Above, Robin Yount has moved swiftly across the bag, dragging it with his right foot, and is preparing to double-up the hitter at first base.

to the shorter throws of the second baseman, the shortstop cannot afford to fumble. He must often throw without straightening up; although, when time permits, he should raise up and get his normal movement into the throw.

The good shortstops have the ability to charge the ball aggressively but still be in control when fielding the ball and making an accurate throw. This can only be achieved through practice and close supervision. Carrying the body low during lateral movement will allow the glove to stay close to the ground. Many ground balls scoot through because the infielder did not carry his glove low enough.

GLOVE

Most major league infielders like a "flat glove," one with minimum padding. A deep glove only gives the ball a chance to get buried. When the fielder takes the ball deep in the pocket, it seems to get lost in there.

STANCE

As he takes his position before the pitch, the shortstop should stand with his feet comfortably spread shoulder-width apart. His eyes are on the pitcher. Both feet should face out just a little, not straight ahead. This will make it easier to turn or jab as he starts to go right or left. The knees and hips are bent slightly, and his back is straight. His hands are placed on the knees, with the upper part of his body resting comfortably on them.

As the pitcher goes into his delivery, the shortstop takes his hands off his knees and lets them hang loosely between his legs. He shifts his weight a little forward to the balls of the feet, while still keeping his heels on the ground. An infielder can get a jump on the ball by watching the pitcher's hand as the ball is thrown. Follow the ball to the hitter and keep your eyes on it when the ball comes off the bat.

As the pitcher throws to the plate, the infielder will step or hop forward with the left foot, about a foot, and a slight shuffle with his right. This process is timed with the anticipation of the batter hitting the pitched ball.

In moving laterally to his left or right, I recommend that a player use a cross-step. Many players have a habit of lifting their right foot high in the air and stepping with it before crossing over with their left foot. Instead, they should keep eveything low.

The important thing is to take *short, quick steps* when starting for the ball. The shortstop may jab to the right and then cross with the left.

"If the ball is hit to my left," said former Chicago Cub favorite Don Kessinger, "I will keep as low as possible, dig with my arms as I cross-step my right over the left. If the ball is to my right, I will push off my left foot, jab-step with my right foot, cross-step, and dig after the ball."

Fig. 8.4 STANCE (the "ready" position). Alfredo Griffin has his feet comfortably spread, slightly more than shoulder-width apart, as the pitcher moves into his delivery. After taking the "ready" position, he moves into a "set" position as the pitcher delivers to the plate. His hands and arms are loose and down low, as he shifts his weight a little forward to the balls of his feet.

PLAYING THE HITTERS

The basic fielding positions of the shortstop depend largely on his own strengths and weaknesses and the type of batter at the plate. Generally, he will play about thirty feet from second and about twenty to twenty-five feet behind the line. He can play deeper for slow runners.

With a right-handed pull hitter, he should play more toward third base. Likewise, with a left-handed swinger, he should move over toward second four or five steps. He should move in a couple of steps for the fast runners.

With a runner on first base, the shortstop moves into his double play depth, perhaps three to five steps toward the plate. Although he should play as far away from the bag as he can, he must get to the base in time to complete the play.

When runners are on first and second bases with no one out, and the bunt situation is in order, he should move in directly in back of the base runners but should not leave his fielding position too vulnerable. His big responsibility is to keep the runner close to second base, to prevent him from getting too long a lead.

Playing the ball in the hole is probably the most difficult play for the shortstop. This is why a strong arm is such a great asset at this position. If he lacks the outstanding arm, then he must play in closer to compensate for it. With men on first and third attempting a double steal, he must move quickly from his normal position after the ball has passed the plate, and go to a spot approximately one step in front of second base. There, he must watch for an attempt by the runner on third base to score. If the runner breaks for the plate, the shortstop should charge in fast to cut off the catcher's throw and return the ball to him.

If the runner on third decides not to go, the shortstop, in his position one step in front of the base, should wait for the catcher's throw and pivot around to make the tag at second base.

Using another method to defense the double steal, the shortstop runs quickly to a spot about halfway between the pitcher's mound and second base. There, he watches for an attempt by the runner on third base to score. If the runner decides to go, the shortstop will catch the ball thrown by the catcher and return it to the plate.

If the runner does not make a break, he will be in position to let the throw from the catcher go through to the second baseman, who is covering the base.

The score and the inning of the game influence whether the shortstop should try to cut the runner off at the plate or try to get the runner atttempting to steal second base. By all means, if the run is the winning or tying run, the play should be made *to the plate.*

FIELDING GROUND BALLS

The main thing in fielding a ground ball is to watch the ball and stay low on it. The infielder's glove should be close to the ground. It is much easier for him to bring his hands up than it is to take his whole body down. He must get in front of the ball quickly, plant his right foot, and make the throw. His eyes follow the ball into his glove (Fig. 8.5).

Ground balls, like fly balls, should be fielded with both hands if at all possible. Using the glove hand and throwing hand together is not only surer but enables the fielder to move into his throwing motion more quickly. He will have much better control of the ball and will make fewer errors. As the ball approaches, he has his glove close to the ground and his bare hand next to the glove. He keeps the glove facing the ball.

"Charge the ball," advised Pee Wee Reese. "Always keep coming in on the ball. Most often, it is better to charge a ball than to lay back or back up. If an infielder backs up, he will likely field the ball in between hops. This often lets the ball play him." However, on hard hit balls directly at him, the infielder has to be less aggressive.

Since the shortstop seldom has time to straighten up to throw, he must make throws from the position in which he fields the ball. Often he must charge balls hit directly at him and play them as quickly as possible. He has to throw across his body in order to get rid of the ball quickly enough. By fielding it quickly, he has more time to throw the ball.

A slow-bounding flip ball hit just past the pitcher calls for a quick off-balance underhand flip throw. A play deep in the hole near third base requires a long, more powerful throw. By moving in or charging the ball, the infielder will

Fig. 8.5 FIELDING A GROUND BALL. The shortstop should get in front of the ball whenever possible and handle it with two hands. After moving quickly to his right, he slides his right foot in the dirt and fields the ball at the same time. Putting on the brakes, he places his weight on his right foot. He then pushes off his right foot and makes the long overhand throw (Rick Burleson).

get the hop that he needs by either speeding up his forward motion or by slowing it down. If the ball is not hit hard, some infielders like to round off slightly so they can field, step, and throw to first base.

To cover the most ground quickly, the infielder's first step should be a cross-over step. Keeping his body low, he gets to the line of the ball quickly. After fielding the ball, he plants his right foot and makes the throw.

Coming in for a slow roller

A slow roller is always tougher to field than a hard hit grounder because the fielder must run in faster and throw it to a base while on the move. If he waits for a slow grounder to reach him, a fast runner will take advantage of the time loss and reach base safely. The fielder must charge the ball at full speed, catching and throwing it without straightening up (Fig. 8.6).

On this play, the underhand throw has to be strong and accurate, and the fielder has to get rid of the ball as quickly as possible. He must make this play with two hands if he possibly can.

If he has to approach the ball from the side, the shortstop should field it with the gloved hand only and in front of the left foot. The glove should be used as a scoop, with the ball rolling into it.

The barehanded grab and running throw should be used only as a last resort, in a "do-or-die" situation. The difficulty of the barehanded pickup is increased greatly on a poorly maintained field filled with rough spots. Even on

Fig. 8.6 COMING IN FOR A SLOW ROLLER. The slow roller must be fielded on the run. The fielder must charge the ball at full speed, catching and throwing the ball without straightening up. Fielding the ball with his left foot forward, he then takes a step with the right foot to make the throw (Jim Fregosi).

big-league diamonds, the barehanded grab requires considerable skill and finesse.

If the ball has stopped rolling, the infielder should charge it from the left side and field it with the bare hand only, and about even with the toe of the left foot. With a scooping motion of the bare hand, he picks the ball up and makes the throw.

GOING TO HIS RIGHT

The toughest play for the shortstop is on the ball hit to his right (Fig. 8.5). Since he has to move far to his right, he has to go for the ball very quickly. Then, he has to plant his right foot, sliding in the dirt and fielding the ball at the same time. Since he is a great distance from first base, he has to get control of his body very quickly and really get something on the ball. The braced leg gives a firm support as the fielder steps out with his left foot in the direction of the throw. This is a very tough play.

In the Dodger organization, we teach our shortstops to get in front of the ball whenever possible. We want them to backhand it only when necessary. We want them to get in front of the ball and handle it with two hands. Just as he gloves the ball, the shortstop has to put on the brakes, placing his weight on his right foot. He then pushes off his right foot and makes the long overhand throw. With the right foot sliding the last few inches as he gets the ball, he has to grip it and get the necessary body control to deliver the ball to first base.

Fig. 8.7 GOING FAR TO THE RIGHT. On the ball that he cannot get to with both hands, the shortstop has to backhand it with his glove hand. After fielding the ball, he stops his momentum by bracing on his right foot. The braced leg provides a firm support as he steps out with his left foot in the direction of the throw. This play is perhaps the shortstop's toughest play (Chris Speier).

However, on the ball that he cannot quite get to with both hands, the shortstop has to backhand it with his glove hand. For most infielders, this is more difficult than getting in front of the ball and fielding it with two hands (Fig. 8.7). First, he backhands the ball and then plunges his right foot into the dirt to make the play.

The real test of a shortstop comes when he has to go into the hole toward third base and backhand the ball.

A good cross-over step with quick movement to the ball and good body balance are the essentials in making the backhand play. As the fielder extends his glove for the ball, the knees must be bent. In making the backhand play, the left foot is forward, followed by a bracing step with the right foot. He must see the ball into the glove.

GOING TO HIS LEFT

This is the play toward or behind second base in which the shortstop does not always have time to get in front of the ball. If not, he should try to field the ball with his left foot forward. Then, he takes a short, quick step with his right foot while turning his body to the right. At the same time, he brings the ball and the glove up toward the throwing position.

On a hard hit ground ball, the big-league shortstop will start by turning rather than pivoting, on his left foot. The foot is not lifted, merely turned so that the spikes barely clear the ground. Then, he takes a cross-over step with his right foot as he breaks to his left for the ball. He wants to stay low to the ground as he makes his move for the ball.

As he catches the ball, he should step forward and in front of the left foot with his right foot to check his momentum. He then steps forward with his left foot in the direction of the throw.

MAKING THE DOUBLE PLAY

The success of any keystone combination rests upon a vital question: Can they make the double play? This is the question asked of every shortstop and second baseman because the double play is believed to be the key to championship baseball. Therefore, these two infielders must be able to make the double play consistently.

Fundamentally, the double play pivot is not a difficult maneuver to learn. Although some infielders have trouble executing it properly, their difficulty usually results from poor execution before the pivot, not the fundamentals of the pivot itself. Actually, the pivot is easier for the shortstop because he comes into the bag moving toward first base, while the second baseman is almost always moving away from first (Fig. 8.8).

For maximum efficiency, the shortstop and second baseman should know all the moves each one makes at his position. This was true of the Kessinger-Beckert combination, and likewise with the Kubek-Richardson combination of

Fig. 8.8 THE DOUBLE PLAY is the most intricate and difficult maneuver in the infield, but surely the most rewarding. Above, Rick Burleson has moved swiftly across second base to the right side and is about to double-up the hitter.

a few years back. These players spent all their major league careers together. They knew each other like a book, i.e., their running speed, the type of ball each one threw, their mannerisms, and their mutual reactions to various situations.

"As far as cooperating," explained former Pirate infielder Bill Mazeroski, "we have signs back and forth which signify who is covering with a man on first base. As a general rule, the shortstop covers on left-handed hitters and the second baseman on right-handed hitters. There are exceptions, of course, like for the hitter who goes a lot to the opposite field. On a steal, we try to watch the signs from the catcher if it is a curve ball or fast ball. On a ball hit back to the pitcher, we want to know who will receive it from the pitcher."

Like any other play, young infielders should learn to make the double play in a fundamental manner. Before they try to be fancy, they should master the basic maneuvers. *There is no substitute for executing baseball skills in the fundamental way.*

Getting to the base

To execute a good pivot, the infielder must be able to get to the bag and be on balance before the ball arrives (Fig. 8.9). However, for most infielders, this is difficult to do from a regular fielding depth. Consequently, in double play situations, the shortstop and second baseman must shorten up, or "cheat," toward the bag.

"Of course, your speed will determine how much you can shorten up," said Fregosi, "but I find I can reach the base in plenty of time by moving three or four steps closer to it."

Fig. 8.9 GET TO THE BAG QUICKLY. The shortstop must move swiftly and be on balance before the ball arrives. He likes the ball over the base and about chesthigh (Don Kessinger).

As soon as the ball is hit, the infielder who is responsible for covering the bag should break for second base at full speed and try to get there as quickly as possible. The shortstop will often sprint toward the bag and slow up as he nears it. When he sees the throw coming, he will increase his speed again and hit the bag at a fairly good speed.

Generally, the big-league shortstop likes to run hard until he is four or five feet from the bag, then jockeys in, bouncing from one foot to the other like a boxer. His knees are bent so he can move to either side for the throw.

"As I get near the bag, I like to slow down by using short, choppy steps to get on balance," explained Fregosi. "I want to bring my body under control. I want to see where the throw is. Then, I am ready to shift in either direction for the throw. "I like to have the ball over the base and about chest-high," said Fregosi. "I want the ball thrown pretty hard, firm, and accurate."

SHORTSTOP'S PIVOT

The shortstop has no standard pivot because a good double play man pivots a number of different ways. Otherwise, the base runner will know where to slide to upset the shortstop's throw and break up the double play.

Much of the time, on perhaps 98 percent of the plays, the shortstop uses one of two basic ways of making the double play pivot; moving to the right field side, dragging with the right foot as he glides across the base; to the infield side, touching with his left, stepping with the right and throwing.

On the other plays, his footwork is the result of his reactions to the various situations, i.e., the type of throw, the speed of the base runners, and his position when the ball is released to him.

The majority of the time, the shortstop is going into the play and his momentum is carrying him toward first base. Generally, he will drag his right foot across the back corner of the bag and get into position to make his throw. Actually, instead of moving directly toward the base, he angles off between first base and the outfield, thus avoiding the runner.

For the shortstop to come across the bag in this manner, the throw must be just right. If the throw is to the pitcher's side of second base, he will go to the "infield side," touching the base with the left foot and stepping with the right and throwing to first base. Or, he can hop to his right, brush the bag with his left foot, and throw to first from inside the base line.

A simple but effective pivot is for the shortstop to step on the base with his left foot and throw. He receives the throw in front of the bag. One of the fastest ways is to straddle the bag, take the throw, and make a fast fliplike relay to first base. Another way is for the shortstop to come in, hit the bag with the left foot, and then back off toward left field as he throws to first base.

Occasionally, when he is close enough to the bag, the shortstop will handle the force play himself, rather than risk the possibility of the second baseman dropping his short toss. One step from the bag, he will take a stride with his left foot and make his throw as his foot makes contact with the base.

When throwing to first base, most shortstops use a three-quarter natural throwing delivery. *Under no circumstances should they throw around the runner.* It is the job of the base runner to get out of the way or hit the dirt early.

Across base to the right side, dragging with the right foot

Easing across the bag, dragging with the right foot is considered the most popular pivot among major league shortstops. This maneuver is most effective when the shortstop has very little time and quick action is needed to get away from the approaching slider.

"I like to receive the throw from the second baseman a step in front of the bag," explained Fregosi. As shown in Figure 8.10, the ball arrives as Fregosi straddles the base. "As I catch the ball, I place my left foot down a foot past and to the right field side of the bag. Dragging my right foot through, I kick the corner of the bag. As I drag the right foot over the base, I place it behind my left foot and I hop in the air, placing my weight on the right foot.

"Meanwhile, I am moving the ball into throwing position," continued Jim, "and I step toward first base with my left foot and make a three-quarter delivery

Fig. 8.10 ACROSS BASE TO RIGHT FIELD SIDE. This pivot is effective when the shortstop has very little time and quick action is needed to get away from the oncoming slider. He drags the corner of the base with his right foot as he glides across the bag (Jim Fregosi).

throw to first base." Fregosi finds himself past second by several feet, making his throw outside the base line.

If the runner is too close for the shortstop to make the throw on this step, a short hop or shuffle-step is made to the left. This footwork carries the shortstop farther out of the runner's path. He makes his throw to first as his right foot lands, thus stepping toward first base on his left.

Touch with left foot, step into infield with right

If the runner is outside the line, the shortstop should make the double play by going to the inside of the base. He can touch the bag with his left foot, then step into the infield with his right and make his throw to first base. The left foot is the one which makes contact with the base, either with a drag or a step (Fig. 8.11).

"Catch the ball one step in front of the bag," said Kessinger. "Then step forward with your left foot, placing it immediately in front of the base. As you hop into the infield on your right foot, you drag the left foot over the bag."

By making his hop toward first base, the shortstop transfers his weight to the right foot. Then, pushing off on the right foot, he steps toward first base with his left foot.

Actually, the shortstop is in a better position to make a good three-quarter delivery throw when he goes to the right. By dragging with his left foot, he can be more sure of the force play, while the step method can carry him farther away from the bag and out of the path of the runner.

Fig. 8.11 INSIDE PIVOT: LEFT FOOT AND THROW. When the throw is on the inside of second base, the shortstop touches the bag with his left foot, steps into the infield with his right, and makes his throw to first base (Don Kessinger).

Touch with left foot and throw

This pivot is used when the shortstop has more time. He can straddle the base and make his throw in front of the slider. He receives the ball chest-high, one step in front of the base, with his weight on his right foot. As he brings the ball into throwing position, he lifts his left foot and places it on the right field side of the base. Pushing off the right foot, which is behind the base, the weight of his body moves up onto his front foot, which remains rested on the bag.

"If the runner is close to you," said Kessinger, "make your step with the left foot away from him."

A similar maneuver is to step on the middle of the base with the right foot; then, as he takes a normal stride with the left foot, he completes his throw to first base.

The drag method can also be used with this type of pivot, and is one of the surest ways to make the double play. The shortstop takes the throw while straddling the base, and with his right foot forward, he drags his left foot across the top of the base as he throws to first base.

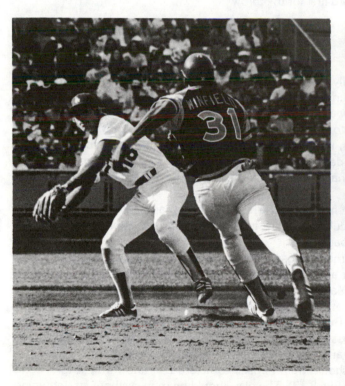

Fig. 8.12   PROTECTING HIMSELF FROM THE BASE RUNNER. Rather than be a stationary target, some shortstops, after completing their throws, jump into the air to avoid the runner. Others will side step to the left or right, depending on the path of the base runner. Here, Bill Russell gets off his throw to first base just before the hard sliding Dave Winfield arrives.

Right foot flip and leap

Although this is a quick maneuver in making the double play, it is one of the most difficult to learn. The shortstop hits the base with his right foot and makes a flat, flip throw to first. He then jumps in the air to avoid the runner.

Young infielders might find it difficult getting much power behind the flip throw and, until skill is achieved, they might toss a few in the first base dugout.

Backing off

On a close play, the shortstop comes in and hits the base with his left foot. Then, he steps back with his right foot and braces it for the pivot and throw to first. The step toward first base should be away from the runner.

One disadvantage to this pivot is that it places the shortstop farther away from his target at first base and, unless he has a strong arm, he might lack the carry to throw out some of the fast runners. Using a variation of this maneuver, the shortstop will hit the bag with his left foot and back off toward left field before stepping toward first for the throw.

SHORTSTOP'S THROWS

The shortstop actually has four types of throws he can make when feeding the ball to the pivot man. A successful double play depends as much on the accuracy of his throw as on the pivot man's throw to first.

A young shortstop should learn how to throw overhand, sidearm, and underhand. However, in throwing to the second baseman, I recommend just the sidearm and underhand throws. Then, as he gains more experience, he might find the backhand toss or flip quite effective in getting the ball to the pivot man.

Because of the nature of the second baseman's pivots, the throw by the shortstop is difficult to execute. It has to be just right, approximately chest-high, directly at the bag.

If a second baseman is close to the base, he will use a simple underhanded lay-up. A little farther away, he has to use a long underhand toss, or a half-turn and sidearm throw. Many big-league infielders like to use a backhand flip from twelve feet away, because they can get rid of it more quickly and throw it faster than by laying it up. Beyond twelve feet or so, they usually turn and throw with a quick arm flip across their body. Far from second, they will turn the same way but, in cocking their arm, they will put more shoulder into it.

The shortstop should train himself to field a ball and throw it to second base in one motion (Fig. 8.13). The play should be made without straightening up, and the glove should be pulled away from the ball in order for the second baseman to get a good view. Practice will develop the timing and teamwork so necessary for perfection.

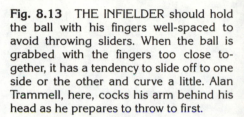

Fig. 8.13 THE INFIELDER should hold the ball with his fingers well-spaced to avoid throwing sliders. When the ball is grabbed with the fingers too close to-gether, it has a tendency to slide off to one side or the other and curve a little. Alan Trammell, here, cocks his arm behind his head as he prepares to throw to first.

"I always throw at the bag," said Fregosi, "because a moving target will be at different spots on different plays. I expect the second baseman to be at the bag when the ball arrives. I figure, the better throw I make to him, the better throw he will make to first."

A fielder should never ease up on his throwing. He must keep everything in rhythm and make his delivery as smooth as possible, finishing with a good snap of the wrist.

If he can remember to execute his footwork correctly, grip the ball across the seams, and throw the ball in a fluid motion, he will seldom make throwing errors.

Grip

The ball should be held the same way for every throw. It is gripped with the index and middle fingers on top, the fingers spread about one-half to three-quarters of an inch. The thumb is directly under the index finger. The infielder should make sure there is a space between the ball and the "V" formed by the thumb and index finger, to get good wrist snap as the ball is released (Fig. 8.14). *He does not grip the ball too tightly.* A tight grip will often prevent good wrist snap.

Sidearm throw

On a ground ball hit to his right, the shortstop should stop squarely in front of the ball by bracing his right leg and sliding the inside of his right foot in the dirt.

Fig. 8.14 BASIC THROWING TECHNIQUE. Most fielders who throw well have a good forearm and wrist snap which gives the ball carry. Don Kessinger, here, keeps his throwing arm away from his body and throws the ball in one continuous motion. The elbow not only comes back first, but it leads the forward drive as well. Keeping the arm loose, Kessinger snaps it forward in a whiplike manner as he makes the throw. He uses a powerful wrist action with the wrist rolling over just as the ball is released off the ends of the first two fingers. Observe the good follow-through which gets the proper power behind the throw.

"Begin the sidearm throw immediately after you field the ball," explained Fregosi. "Then, step with the left foot in the direction of the throw. Do not be deceptive. Show him the ball all the way."

As shown in Figure 8.15, Fregosi brings his glove and the ball up into a throwing position. He grips the ball as he brings the glove up. When he uses only arm action, sometimes he has to throw from a squat position.

Many times the sidearm throw is made without the shortstop taking a step with his left foot, but merely throwing from the position in which he received the ball. This enables him to get the ball away quickly.

If the ball is hit sharply, the shortstop may have time to straighten up a little and take a step with his left foot.

Underhand toss

When close to the pivot, the shortstop should lay the ball up clean and simple. It is a simple, stiff-wristed, underhand toss. Staying low to the ground, his legs bent sharply, he comes up with the ball from a fielding position (Fig. 8.16). This throw has little arch, because it goes in a straight line to the second baseman's chest.

"Give him the hand," said Fregosi, "and then let it follow through after the

Fig. 8.15   SIDEARM THROW. The shortstop begins his throw from a fielding position. He brings the glove and ball up together into a throwing position. He takes the ball out of his glove and throws sidearm across his body. Keeping the arm loose, he snaps the ball forward like a whip, stepping with his left foot in the direction of the throw (Jim Fregosi).

Fig. 8.16   UNDERHAND TOSS. The lay-up is used when the shortstop is close to the pivot man. He makes the throw clean and simple, a stiff-wristed, underhand toss. He does not let his arm follow through any higher than waist-high (Jim Fregosi).

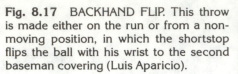

Fig. 8.17   BACKHAND FLIP. This throw is made either on the run or from a non-moving position, in which the shortstop flips the ball with his wrist to the second baseman covering (Luis Aparicio).

ball. It is a simple, stiff-wrist, underhand toss chest-high. Do not let the arm follow through any higher than waist-high."

Backhand flip

When fielding the ball far to the left and behind second base, many big-league shortstops such as Luis Aparicio use a backhand flip (Fig. 8.17). The throw should be aimed toward the third base side of the base. It is made either on the run or from a non-moving position, in which the shortstop flips the ball with his wrist to the second baseman covering.

Throwing on the run

On high bounding balls over the pitcher's head, the shortstop has to move in quickly and throw on the run. After grabbing the ball, he straightens up and throws off his right leg. With a good snap of the wrist, he employs a quick arm flip across his body.

GIVING SIGNS

The shortstop usually gives the sign to the second baseman as to who will cover second on a possible steal. This is done by hiding his face from the opponents with the glove, and giving the "open" and "closed" mouth signs.

The open mouth means the second baseman will cover, while a closed mouth indicates that the shortstop will cover. These two infielders must get in the habit of glancing at each other after every sign given by the catcher. Generally, the shortstop covers the bag on left-handed hitters and the second baseman on right-handed swingers. They can also cross their letters or their belts, which will indicate, "You take it, or, "I take it."

TAGGING THE RUNNER

Stationary tag

There are two basic ways in which an infielder can tag a sliding runner. Perhaps the safest way to tag the runner is the stationary tag. Straddling the base, the infielder places his glove on the ground in front of the bag and lets the runner slide into it. Closing the thumb over the glove, he lets the runner slide into the back of the glove (Fig. 8.18). As a result, there is less chance of the ball being kicked out.

Fig. 8.18 TAKING THE CATCHER'S THROW. The shortstop must get to the bag as quickly as possible to get set up properly for the throw. To do so, he must "cheat" closer to the base on steal situations. In making the tag, Bill Russell has the back of the bag hooked under his left foot so he can be under better control. As the ball is caught, both knees are quickly bent to get the glove down close to the ground. The glove is placed in front of the base with the back of the glove making contact with the runner. *The ball is never exposed to a sliding runner.* As the runner makes contact with the glove, the infielder pulls his glove out and away in a sweeping motion.

Sweep tag

The second-method is the sweep tag. Standing with one foot on each side of the base, the infielder sweeps the ball across the line of his slide. In receiving the throw, he sweeps the ball in an arc, down across the front of the bag and up again. If he has to wait, he should not place his glove in the runner's path with the ball exposed; this is a good way to have it kicked out. Instead, he should hold it cocked to one side and time his sweep. When the base runner slides, he snaps the glove down and across his foot.

CATCHING POP FLIES

The shortstop, like the second baseman, must work hard on fly balls hit back of the infield. He must learn to keep going back without calling for the ball until the outfielder calls him off the play. The outfielder should take every ball that he can take because it is much easier for him to catch it than for the shortstop going back. If a throw has to be made following the catch, the outfielders moving in will have the better play. All pop flies hit directly behind the first and third baseman are the responsibilities of the second baseman and the shortstop.

Whenever possible, fly balls should be caught with both hands, thumbs together, and fingers pointing up. The infielder uses his glove to shade the sun on pop flies. In calling for the ball, he yells "I have it!" and uses one hand to wave his teammate away.

If the ball is hit over his head, the shortstop should turn his head and run as hard as he can back after it. This procedure will enable him to position himself under the ball, rather than timing the ball.

CUTOFFS AND RELAYS

On extra-base hits to left and center fields, the shortstop serves as the relay man. He moves quickly out to a position where he will be in line with the throw from the outfielder and the base to which the throw is to go. He should be close enough to the outfielder so that the relay can be caught on the fly.

When he takes a relay from the outfield, he should listen for instructions from the second baseman or third baseman on where to make the throw.

COVERING AND BACKING UP

The shortstop covers second base on all bunt plays and all ground balls, and on most fly balls hit to the right field side of second base. He is partly responsible for keeping the runner on second close to the base. In addition, there are some situations when the shortstop should cover third base. With a runner on second and a base hit to left, the third baseman is usually the cutoff man to the plate and the shortstop covers third.

The shortstop should back up second base when the second baseman covers the base on throws from the catcher or pitcher, and on throws made by outfielders. He also backs up third base on throws from the catcher.

PICK-OFF PLAYS

We have found pick-off plays to be very helpful. The number of runners picked off is not the prime objective of this play. Rather, it is trying to keep runners close, so if there is a base hit, we have enough time to throw them out. The fact that the Dodgers have a reputation for good pick-off plays is often enough to keep the runner close to his base.

The shortstop and second baseman play a very important role in setting up the pick-off play and giving signs to the pitcher. After all, the pitcher can be concentrating so much on the hitter that he sometimes forgets there is a possible pick-off play which can get him out of a tough jam.

The pick-off with the pitcher is usually a signal play, worked in either of two ways: on a "count," or by the "daylight" method. Maury used the "daylight" play on occasion, plus the "count" or flash systems. Four methods of the pick-off play are presented in detail in Chapter 4, on "Pitching."

Practice Tips for Shortstops

1. Practice constantly with the second baseman, playing catch, throwing to each other from all angles, and executing double play drills.
2. Spend fifteen to twenty minutes daily on picking up grounders.
3. Practice fielding the slow roller over and over. Come in and charge the ball.
4. Concentrate particularly on coming in, picking the ball up and throwing while still bent down.
5. Get plenty of practice going to your right, using both techniques, i.e., getting in front of the ball and using two hands, and employing the one-handed backhand method.
6. Get plenty of practice on pop flies hit in all directions.
7. Practice the play behind second base, moving quickly to your left and throwing to first base.
8. Do a lot of running to strengthen your legs.

9

The Third Baseman

Third base is called the "hot corner" because there is never a dull moment around the bag. The third baseman often has to react automatically, both mentally and physically. He has to be able to field slow rolling bunts, block hard hit balls, and make long, accurate throws.

A third baseman must have a strong, accurate arm, sure hands, and quick reactions. Of course, the ideal man at third is the fellow who has the agility *plus* speed—the fellow who can come in on bunted balls and make the one-handed throw like Brooks Robinson, who played so brilliantly for the Baltimore Orioles. The two toughest plays at third base, charging a bunt or slow roller and catching the hard shot, depend largely on the quickness of the fielder's hands and feet. With more fields using artificial turf, balls are coming faster and faster. It takes quickness and courage on the part of the third basemen to defend against those hard hitters.

More and more hitters in baseball today are using their speed and agility to get on base by using drag or push bunts. Therefore, a third baseman has to be alert at all times. He has to move around and vary his position, anticipating every possible play.

Brooks and present-day third basemen such as Ron Cey and Mike Schmidt

Fig. 9.1 QUICKNESS, quick hands and quick feet, is the major attribute of a good third baseman. Here, Ron Cey hops forward onto his right foot, enabling him to get more time to grip the ball. By transferring the weight to his rear leg, he can push off with greater power.

Fig. 9.2 A SURE PAIR OF HANDS and the ability to handle the ball with speed are valuable assets of the third baseman. Art Howe, here, has just made the force-out at third and is preparing his throw to first base for a double play.

know how to play the hitters. They know the fellows who might bunt on them and those who cannot, the hitters who pull the ball, go up the middle, or to the opposite field. They know when to guard the line and when not to.

With a runner on third, the third baseman must stay alert to receive pick-off throws from the catcher. Occasionally, he will have to run out to catch high pop flies that sail into short left field, or he may have to move into foul territory to grab pop fouls.

During the past two decades, the Dodgers have had some truly fine glove-men at third base, such as Billy Cox, Don Hoak, Jackie Robinson, Junior Gilliam, and Ron Cey. Cox was one of the very best, having a good glove and a strong arm. He could catch bad hops, good hops, and everything else. Cey has also been a standout with his quick hands and feet, in addition to having a strong and accurate throwing arm.

"Quickness is so essential at third base," said John Vukovich, coach of the Chicago Cubs. "Any lost movement will hinder your range. Every good third baseman is on his toes, ready to move when the ball reaches the hitting zone."

QUALIFICATIONS

In playing third base, quickness is more essential than great speed afoot. Since balls are hit so sharply at third, the first two steps of the third baseman have to be quick. They either "do or they don't" down there. Quick hands are another great asset (Fig. 9.2), and can make up for mediocre running speed.

The third baseman must have a good arm to make the long throw to first with plenty of speed and carry on the ball (Fig. 9.3). This is why, in addition to the bunt threat, he must play in closer than other infielders in order to field the ball as soon as possible and get it across the diamond ahead of the runner. Playing that close when a powerful pull hitter smashes a drive his way certainly can make things hot for him. Since his fielding position often brings him close to the hitter, hard hit ground balls cannot always be fielded cleanly.

Consequently, an aggressive athlete is needed at third base who is willing to dive after balls and stay in front of hard hit balls. In addition to having courage, he should have the agility to retrieve them in time to throw out the hitter. Every manager likes a fielder who will knock a hard hit ball down with his chest like Pepper Martin used to do, then pick it up and throw the runner out. Pepper could dive sideways and knock a ball down and then get up quickly and throw the man out.

One of the mistakes made most often by third basemen is the assumption

Fig. 9.3 A QUICK AND ACCURATE RE-LEASE is perhaps more important to the third baseman than having a strong arm. George Brett, above, snaps the ball forward in a whiplike manner as he makes his throw to first base.

that a hard ground ball between third and shortstop is not their ball. Everything they can reach cleanly on either side is their ball.

It takes a tough competitor to play third base in the manner it should be played. Hard work and considerable practice will improve every player's game. He must have someone hit him ground balls of all types, directly at him, to his left and right, hard shots, along with medium and slow rollers.

GLOVE

A player's glove can be his best friend. A good glove, well taken care of and broken in, can improve his fielding a great deal. Most big-league third basemen prefer a long one, an outfielder's glove.

Generally, infielders take most of the padding out of their gloves. They feel they can grab the ball more securely this way and have more feel and touch when catching it.

An aggressive athlete is needed at third base who is willing to dive after balls and stay in front of hard hit balls.

STANCE

A third baseman should use a semi-crouch stance, with his legs spread shoulder-width apart. He keeps his knees bent slightly because sudden adjustments, forward or backward, left or right, can best be made from this crouch.

An infielder should be a little bit on the move when the ball approaches the plate. It is a lot easier to control the body from a moving position than it is from a dead, standstill position. Just a little movement in toward the hitter is always good. He must not be caught flat-footed or on his heels if the ball is hit his way.

All good fielders say that the glove should be low because it is easier to come up with the glove than it is to go down. By starting low with the glove, they can keep their tail a little low, which is good. The weight is evenly distributed. The legs are spread in a comfortable position so that they are ready to go in any direction.

"I like a stance that feels comfortable to me," explained Brooks Robinson, regarded by many as the greatest fielding third baseman in baseball history. "After taking my preliminary or ready position, I will move a half step forward as the pitcher releases the ball. On every pitch, I move that half step forward when the ball is sent to the plate. I will take my hands off my legs and get into a set position. My arms are loose, and I am low and ready on every pitch."

I want our infielders to get down low enough so their back is straight or

Fig. 9.4 THE THIRD BASEMAN has been described as a steel trap, always poised, waiting to spring in any of several directions. Moving into a set position, Graig Nettles places his body in motion so he can jump in any direction the moment the bat meets the ball.

parallel to the ground. The left foot is slightly ahead of the right foot. As demonstrated by Graig Nettles of the Yankees in Fig. 9.4, both feet should face out just a little, *not* straight ahead. This will make it easier to turn or jab as he starts to go right or left.

The third baseman must be ready at all times, and have his mind made up as to what he is going to do with the ball before it gets to him. He must expect every ball to be hit to him. If he does, he will be ready.

PLAYING THE HITTERS

The fielding position of the third baseman depends on a number of factors. Of course, he must consider the type of hitter at the plate, whether he is a pull hitter or a late swinger. Does he often bunt for a base hit? What kind of running speed does he have? These are the questions the third baseman must ask himself throughout the game.

There are three basic positions, or depths, which the third baseman assumes: normal to deep position, halfway, and "in."

Normal to deep position

The normal to deep position is approximately four or five steps from the line. The depth is anywhere from a spot even with the bag to about two or three yards beyond the base. With a pull hitter at the plate, he plays closer to the line. If the batter hits straightaway, he can play further over from the foul line. His position, however, will depend on the ball-and-strike count on the hitter, as well as the score and inning of the game.

Halfway (double play depth) position

In the halfway position the fielders play squarely on the base line, and not behind the bases. A batted ball will take less time to reach them. Thus, the execution of the double play can be made more quickly.

"In" position

To play "in," the third baseman moves in close to the front edge of the grass, with the idea of trying to stop a runner from scoring from third on a grounder. In a sacrifice situation, the third baseman will want to be positioned in on the grass.

"I have to know the hitters," said Brooks, "and that actually governs my position. However, it should be kept in mind that more balls go by a third baseman on his left than on his right."

This is why a third baseman has to think ahead on every play. What will he do with the ball when he gets it? Hesitating for even a split-second can make the runner safe at a base or allow him to score a run. So, he must think over each play before it happens.

"Although some second basemen and shortstops shift positions as much as twenty or thirty feet for certain batters," explained Robinson, "I rarely shift more than a yard to either side of my normal position. I move back on pull hitters and forward when I expect a bunt. Of course, when my shortstop plays close to second base for a left-handed pull hitter, I will move over toward the hole."

With a bunt in order and a runner on first base, the third baseman will move in on the grass a step or two as the pitcher delivers the ball.

With men on first and second, the third baseman has a real judgment play on a bunt, considered by many to be the toughest play at his position. He has to decide whether to charge the ball or go back to the bag. I like the third baseman to be three or four feet in front of the bag, but he should not commit himself until the ball is actually bunted. We will discuss how he should handle this bunt situation later in the chapter.

FIELDING A GROUND BALL

An infielder must get as low as he can when fielding ground balls. Certainly, it is easier to go up for a high hop than to go down for a grass cutter. Therefore, he must keep his glove low (Fig. 9.5).

When fielding, the third baseman must keep his eyes on the ball, not the

Fig. 9.5 FIELDING THE LOW GROUND BALL. By staying low, the third baseman will be able to maintain good body balance and will stay with the hops and bounces much better. By using both hands in bringing the ball into throwing position, he can get the proper grip on the ball (Sal Bando).

runner. He should follow the ball right into the glove. "Have the glove open as soon as possible, facing the oncoming ball," asserted Robinson. "Do not wait until the last second."

The ball should always be fielded with both hands. By using both hands in bringing the ball into throwing position, the fielder can get the proper grip on the ball. The weight should come back on the right leg, which braces and pushes the body forward in a position to make a hard, accurate throw. Some fielders often take a hop step while throwing.

In going after a ground ball, most infielders jab step and then cross step. They try to stay as low as possible in going short distances after ground balls. By staying low, they can judge the hops or bounce of the ball better.

Generally, the fielder will have more success if he moves in toward the ball than if he lays back or backs up. If he backs up, he will likely have to field the ball between hops and the ball will often play him.

On balls hit to his left, the third baseman often finds it necessary to cut in front of the shortstop and field the ball with his glove hand. This is particularly true of slow hit balls which the shortstop finds difficult to field and throw out the runner at first.

Since he has many opportunities to start a double play, the third baseman must always be thinking in terms of "two" with runners on base and less than two outs.

Hard hit ball directly at fielder

The ball hit directly at the third baseman is one of his toughest plays. "I try to stay as low to the ground as possible," said Robinson. "I feel I can judge the hops or bounce of the ball better."

If the ball is hit right at him, he has to keep his body right in front of it so that if the ball hits his glove or any part of his body, it will drop down in front of him. Then, he has a chance to pick it up and throw the batter out. Quite often, the ball is hit so hard the third baseman does not have a chance to field it cleanly.

"If it must hit you," explained Brooks, "let it hit you, but do *not* let it get by you! Knock it down and go after it quickly. Then pick it up and throw the man out."

"Third base is an instinctive, reflex position," said Mike Schmidt. "You have to learn to cradle the ball, to have a limp body so the ball doesn't bounce too far when it hits you."

On hard hit balls to his right along the foul line, he has to pivot on his right

Fig. 9.6 FIELDING THE HIGH BOUNCE. This excellent series of Don Money demonstrates the effectiveness of a fundamentally sound two-hand pick-up and a quick throwing delivery. On the ball hit directly at him, the third baseman should stay as low to the ground as possible. In doing so, he will be able to judge the hops or bounce of the ball better. In fielding the ball above his waist with two hands, Don Money has the fingers of his glove pointing up. Observe how intently Money keeps his eyes on the target, the first baseman. Fielding the ball with both hands, he brings the ball quickly into throwing position. A jab step is followed by a cross step. Money hops forward on his right foot, pushes off it, and steps forward on his left as he throws.

foot before grabbing the ball. On hard hit balls to his left, he pivots on his left foot and crosses over to the spot where he can field the ball.

Going to the right

The drive down the line, the two-hopper, is perhaps the most difficult play for third basemen. Yet, a good fielder can turn a double down the left field line into an out.

The third baseman handles the play to his right, pretty much like the shortstop's play to his right. He usually has a little more time, though, than the fielder has at short. This is a play that requires good reflexes and the infielder's ability to keep his eyes on the ball. He steps to his right, reaches out, and backhands the ball. He then braces on his right leg and makes the throw across the diamond (Fig. 9.7).

Using the cross-over step with his left foot, he moves quickly to his right. On this type of play, most third basemen will veer back at a 45-degree angle when they pivot, in order to be in a better position for the throw. When he gets in front of the ball, he braces with his right leg and gets low to the ground. If he does not have to reach out and backhand the ball, he should pick it up with two hands, in front of the right leg. He throws off his planted rear foot with an overhand motion for the long throw.

Fig. 9.7 GOING TO THE RIGHT. Using the cross-over step with his left foot, he moves quickly to his right. If he can get in front of the ball, he picks it up with two hands, in front of the right leg. He throws off his planted right foot with an overhand motion for the long throw (Brooks Robinson).

Going to the left

We tell our third basemen to take any ball to their left they can reach because this usually is an easier play for them than for the shortstop. A third baseman has a shorter throw to first base and is going with the throw. However, if the grounder is hit fairly hard and cannot be reached in a balanced position, the third baseman should let it go through to the shortstop.

The fielder starts his move to the left by using the cross-over step. He must not raise his pivot foot too high. As he moves over and in front of the ball, he should be low to the ground, grabbing the ball with both hands if he can. He must be sure to keep the open face of the glove toward the ball. Since his momentum is still going to the left, he places his right foot behind the left and steps off the right foot in the direction of first base. He makes a sidearm to three-quarter delivery to first base (Fig. 9.8).

Once in a while there is a play in which the third baseman will attempt to field the ball and just get the top of his glove in it and not come up with it. However, I still feel a coach has to tell his third baseman to go ahead and get everything he can. If he does boot one or two of these plays a year, it is still better than staying back on balls which the shortstop will not have adequate time to field.

To be aggressive, a third baseman must try to get everything to his left. However, the shortstop might yell the third baseman off if he feels he is in better position to field and throw the ball. This does not happen very often, though,

Fig. 9.8 GOING TO THE LEFT. The third baseman should take any ball to his left he can reach. He starts his move by using the cross-over step. After fielding the ball, he places his right foot behind the left and steps off the right foot in the direction of first base (Ron Cey).

because a third baseman will usually be in a better throwing position than the shortstop.

The slow roller

Most big-league third basemen rate the slow roller down the line as the toughest play at their position. This is the unexpected slow hit ball which comes as a result of a bunt or a topped ball. Hours of practice must be spent in order to learn the play properly. Those who cannot make this play will be in for a lot of bunting.

The speed of the ball and the closeness of the play determine whether the third baseman uses his glove or his bare hand to scoop up the ball. Although the one-hand technique is an exciting and picturesque play to watch, most bunts and slow hit balls should be fielded with two hands because there is less likelihood that the ball will be fumbled.

Young third basemen should employ the two-hand technique whenever possible, and resort to the one-hander only in "do-or-die" situations when the split-second speed of the one-hand pickup is demanded.

To make plays barehanded, an infielder needs good, relaxed hands as well as excellent fielding facilities. The bare handed play has its place but it can be overdone.

Two-hand pickup   Coming in quickly, the third baseman fields the slow roller with both hands. In Figure 9.9, Robinson is shown fielding the ball with his right foot forward. As he comes down with his left, he moves the ball up into throwing position and makes the throw while straightening up on his right foot. The arm swings up and across his chest for a sidearm throw to first base.

Fig. 9.9 SLOW ROLLER: TWO-HAND PICKUP. Coming in quickly, the third baseman fields the ball with both hands. In this series, Brooks Robinson is shown fielding the ball with his right foot forward. As he comes down with his left, he moves the ball up into throwing position, maintaining a fairly wide stance as he fields the ball. This gives him the necessary balance in throwing off his right foot and making a hard, accurate throw. The arm swings up and across his chest for a sidearm-to-overhand flip to first base.

When he is able to field the ball with his left foot forward, he merely takes one step onto his right foot and makes his throw off the right foot. This footwork is particularly effective when he has to hurry his throw.

If he wants to field the ball with just his gloved hand, he should pick up the ball off his left foot. Then he makes the throw while straightening up on his right foot. A good follow-through is essential.

One-hand pickup   The third baseman races in as quickly as possible. His eyes are squarely on the ball. He places his left or right foot down close to the ball (whichever comes naturally). In Figure 9.10, this happens to be his left foot. As this foot comes down, Robinson's bare hand comes in contact with the ball. His leg bends in order to get his body low to the ground. Notice that Brooks's hand is open and acts like a cup, letting the ball roll into it. Moving his right foot forward, he goes into throwing position by pushing off his right leg to make the throw to first.

"The slow hit ball should be fielded on the run," says Robinson, "and in front of or just outside the right foot. I like to have the ball roll into the palm of my bare hand while I have my left foot forward. I will then make the throw as I step onto my right foot.

"If you field the ball with your left foot forward, you can throw right away," explained Robinson, "but it's awkward to bend down with your right foot forward. I always used a little stutter step to get the left foot in front."

"Always field a bunt with your glove," said Robinson, "unless it is coming to a stop or has stopped. That is the only time you should use your bare hand."

Fig. 9.10 SLOW ROLLER: ONE-HAND PICKUP. Third baseman Brooks Robinson races in with his eyes on the ball. As his left foot comes down, his bare hand comes in contact with the ball. His left leg bends in order to get his body low to the ground. Moving his right foot forward, Robinson goes into throwing position by pushing off his right leg. Although he comes over the top with an overhand flip on the run, he often whips the ball sidearm across his body.

THROWING

The third baseman should throw overhand to first base whenever possible. An overhand throw is generally faster and more accurate than other types of throws. It carries better and is also easier to handle. Sidearm throws have a tendency to sail away and down. However, the sidearm and snap underhand throws are used in making the double play at second base and when moving in quickly to field a slow roller. When the fielder has to go into the hole toward second base to field the ball, sometimes he has to throw across his body to make the play. When he has plenty of time, though, the third baseman should throw from a three-quarter to directly overhand delivery.

One of the biggest mistakes of young players is to just "lollipop" the ball over to first base. Thinking they have a lot of time, they want to be very careful with the ball, so they let go with a mediocre half throw, instead of turning the ball loose. This is the ball they are more likely to throw away than the one with something on it.

"When fielding a grounder, practice bringing yourself into position immediately to throw overhand," asserted Robinson. "When you can do this without wasting any time, you will be a better third baseman."

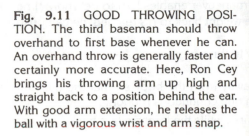
Fig. 9.11 GOOD THROWING POSITION. The third baseman should throw overhand to first base whenever he can. An overhand throw is generally faster and certainly more accurate. Here, Ron Cey brings his throwing arm up high and straight back to a position behind the ear. With good arm extension, he releases the ball with a vigorous wrist and arm snap.

The third baseman has five different ways of throwing:

1. Overhand (on balls hit directly to him, to the right or to deep third)
2. Sidearm (in making the double play and when fielding bunts)
3. Underhand (in fielding bunts)
4. Fielding ball with bare hand, jumping, and throwing off right foot
5. On the ball hit slowly to his left; underhand, sidearm, or overhand, depending on the position in which the ball is fielded

Grip

Most big-league third basemen favor gripping the ball across the seams for proper rotation, carry, and accuracy. The first two fingers are on top, the thumb underneath, with the third finger along the side of the ball. The first two fingers are slightly spread across the seams, with the pressure on the balls of the fingertips. In figure 9.11, Ron Cey demonstrates an effective throwing grip for a third baseman.

Throwing technique

As stated before, I recommend that the third baseman throw overhand to first base whenever he can. It might often be easier to use a sidearm motion, but an overhand throw is generally faster and certainly more accurate.

When throwing to first base, the fielder usually has time to crow-hop before making the throw. He hops forward on his right foot, pushes off it, and steps forward on his left as he throws. This maneuver enables him to get more time to grip the ball, and by transferring the weight back to his rear leg, he can push off with greater power.

The following key principles apply to throwing:

1. The throwing arm should be away from the body so that the ball can be brought back and thrown in one continuous motion.
2. The elbow should come back first, while the forearm lays back from the elbow.
3. Bring the arm, wrist, and right hand forward, with the elbow leading.
4. Keep your arm loose and snap it forward like a whip as the throw is made.
5. Use powerful wrist action with the wrist rolling over just as the ball is released off the ends of the first two fingers.
6. Execute a good follow-through with the body to get the proper power behind the throw.

Fig. 9.12 THROWING TO SECOND BASE. In making the double play, the third baseman must give the pivot man the ball quickly, about letter-high over the bag. As he picks up the ground ball, he braces on his right foot and uses a sidearm delivery across the front of the body. Generally, the fielder takes a short jab step toward second base (Brooks Robinson).

Throwing to second base

In making the double play, the third baseman must give the pivot man the ball quickly, about letter-high over the base. If possible, he should lead the second baseman to the bag by throwing a step in front of him on the first base side of second base. A young infielder should concentrate on throwing directly to the bag. As he picks up the ground ball, he braces on his right foot and uses a sidearm delivery across the front of the body. His elbow should move back and then quickly forward as the wrist snaps the ball toward the target (Fig. 9.12).

Generally, the third baseman takes a short step toward second base, sometimes just a jab step. If the ball is to his right, he fields the ball, steps, and throws to second base. If the ball is directly to him or to his left, he steps with his right foot toward second base, either in front of or behind his left foot, depending upon the angle at which he receives the ball. Then, he steps with his left striding foot and completes his throw. This enables him to put something into his throw. Those with strong arms often can throw without stepping, but this is not recommended for the young player or the fielder with an average throwing arm.

MAKING THE DOUBLE PLAY

With the bases loaded, the third baseman has several ways to make the double play. If he is near enough to his base when he fields the ball, he should step on third, and then relay the ball to second or first. This route is the easiest. But if there are none out, and the situation warrants it, he should try to make the first out at the plate, by throwing to the catcher. With one out, he can choose to ignore the man going home and start the double play by throwing to second, which is the shorter throw.

With a man on first, or men on first and second, he should always go for the double play starting at second base.

THE BUNT SITUATION

With a runner at first and the sacrifice on, the third baseman comes in a couple of steps on the grass; then, as the hitter squares around, he charges in a little more. When the batter drops his bat, he starts toward the plate for a bunt.

Most offensive teams in this situation will make the first baseman field the ball because they know the third baseman is right up there close. If they bunt the ball down to the third baseman, he may force the man out at second base, or even make a double play.

So, most big-league managers say, "Make the first baseman field the ball." Therefore, with a man on first, the third baseman does not have as many good chances to field the bunt.

In a bunt situation with men on first and second, it becomes a judgment play for the third baseman. He must decide whether to move in to field the ball or return to the bag and let the pitcher handle it. Ideally, of course, he would like the pitcher to play the ball so that a force play can be made at third base. I like him to be three or four feet in front of the bag. The important point is for him *not to commit himself too soon.* He must stay there until the ball is bunted. He must be ready to come in or go back to the bag.

"The third baseman must know his pitcher," said Brooks, "that is, how much ground he can cover. I like to angle my stance so I can see the runner on second as well as the batter. I will take a step or two in as the ball is bunted and decide who can make the play. If the pitcher can field the ball, I will cover third base by placing my right foot against the base.

"If it is a hard bunt, I will yell the pitcher off and field the ball and make my throw to first base," continued Brooks. "If it is the pitcher's ball, I will keep my mouth shut and cover third base. The catcher will then control the pitcher and yell at him whether to throw to 'third' or 'first.' "

We do about three different things in a bunt situation. The old fashioned way is for the pitcher to make the pitch and break toward the third base foul line. The third baseman has to stand there and wait to see if the ball is bunted hard enough to get by the pitcher. If the pitcher cannot get it, he must charge the ball and make the play to first base. Of course, this is exactly what the offense *wants* the third baseman to do: field the ball.

However, from the defensive standpoint, the pitcher has to get over there in time to field the ball. Then, the third baseman has to go back to third base and make the force play at third.

In this same bunt situation, we may signal for a different type of execution, for example, if there is a slow runner on first base and the pitcher is at bat. We have our third baseman ignore the runner and just charge in for the ball. We are gambling that the third baseman will get the ball.

We tell our pitcher to cover the pitching area. The first baseman covers the area in front of him, and the third baseman is going to charge in. Then, if the ball is bunted toward third, the third baseman may have time to go to second for the double play.

The third possibility has the shortstop covering third base. With the third baseman charging in, the shortstop will move over to third for the force play.

This is one reason why the bunt defense is so tough today, why it is more difficult to get a man over than it used to be. Many clubs have the shortstop go to third in a bunt situation, and the third baseman goes ahead and charges in.

OTHER PLAYS AT THIRD

Tagging the runner

On throws from the right side of the diamond, most third basemen like to straddle the bag, facing second base, with their feet on either side of the base, an inch or two behind the front edge. Many like to bring the glove down in front of the base and then look for the runner's foot, tagging it with the back of the glove (Fig. 9.13).

In taking throws from the catcher, the fielder should also straddle the bag. His left foot is placed on the left field line but he turns his body a quarter-turn to the right so he can face the catcher's throw. Bringing the glove down quickly

Fig. 9.13 TAGGING THE RUNNER. Bringing his glove down quickly in front of the base, the third baseman looks for the runner's foot, then tags it with the back of his glove. Never place the glove in the runner's path with the ball exposed in the glove. This is a good way to have it kicked out (Art Howe).

in front of the bag, he looks for the runner's foot. Some infielders like to tag the runner with both hands, providing they can catch the ball with both hands.

Cutoffs

On base hits to left field, the third baseman acts as the cutoff man for the throw to the plate. The cutoff position on the play is in direct line from the left fielder to the catcher, approximately forty-five feet from the plate, between the mound and the third base foul line. It depends, of course, on where the ball is hit. He listens to the catcher for directions whether to cut off the ball and throw to a particular base or home or let it go.

We prefer the cutoff position to be a little deep, so that the fielder can move toward the ball in order to make any necessary adjustments. The ball definitely should be caught on the fly or on the big hop. There is nothing more disgusting than to see a throw come in all the way from the outfield and have the cutoff man just stand there as the ball travels 200 feet and hits on a short hop. By taking one step forward or backward, he could make an easy catch.

So, we prefer him to start closer to the plate so he can go into the ball. Then, when he cuts the ball off, he is in a better position to throw to second base or elsewhere.

While the third baseman takes the cutoff throw, the shortstop covers third base.

On throws to third from the outfield, the third baseman should assist the cutoff man (shortstop). If the throw is wide, or if there is no play, he calls, "Cut!" If he thinks the runner can be caught, he does not call.

Covering and backing up

The third baseman covers third base in almost all play situations. On a hard hit ball to left field with a runner on second, he acts as the cutoff man for the throw to the plate.

On throws from right field, the third baseman backs up second base unless he has a possible play at third. He also backs up the pitcher on throws from the first baseman.

When both the shortstop and second baseman go for a fly ball with no one on base, it is the third baseman's job to cover second. In this case, the catcher moves down to cover third.

Catching pop flies

I want my third baseman to take any questionable ball between third and home plate. He should call for any ball he can reach. This is because he is coming in and has a better angle than the catcher does in going out. He should always call for the ball in a loud, clear voice.

On fly balls back of the infield, he should keep going back without calling for the ball until the outfielder calls him off the play. All pop flies hit directly behind the first and third basemen should be the responsibility of the second baseman and the shortstop.

On a foul fly close to the grandstand fence, he should follow the same technique as explained for the first baseman. He should move to the fence as quickly as possible. Then, after locating the ball, he can move back to the spot where it will come down.

Run-down plays

On run-down plays between third and home, the third baseman should get the ball to the catcher in plenty of time to keep the man from scoring. Then, it is the catcher's job to drive the runner back toward third base.

The run-down, however, is the most frequently messed up play in baseball. The fewer throws made the better should be the guiding principle. The catcher should run the base runner as hard as he can toward third. As soon as the third baseman moves into the play, the catcher tosses him the ball about chest-high, and he places the tag on the runner. Actually, only one throw should be necessary.

The catcher and third baseman must be on the *inside* of the base runner, keeping the runner on one side. They should *never* let him bisect their view or throwing procedure. Additional instruction on run-down situations is given in Chapter 13, Team Defense.

Pick-off plays at third

With a runner on third, the third baseman and the catcher should have a signal when a pick-off play is in order. There is usually a pitchout on this play. The third baseman must wait until the catcher receives the ball before he breaks for the bag.

Practice Tips

1. Spend 15 minutes daily picking up ground balls.
2. Practice continually at fielding the slow roller properly, using two hands whenever possible.
3. During your daily ground ball session, field many balls going both to your left and to your right.
4. Do not make any long throws until your arm is completely loose and warmed-up.
5. Devote considerable time to perfecting throws of all kinds. This work will not only strengthen your arm, but give you the necessary accuracy.
6. Have your coach hit plenty of hard ground balls directly at you. *This is one of your toughest plays.*
7. Have your coach hit pop flies regularly to you.

10 The Outfielder

The outstanding outfielder is a great asset to his team, just like the slugger at the plate and the star pitcher on the mound. The jump he gets on the ball, his speed, the manner in which he plays grounders, and the intelligent throws he makes back to the infield prevent the opponents from scoring runs. A bobble, a slow return, or an inaccurate throw are all enough to give the hitter an extra base, and the difference between a runner on first and a runner on second can mean the ball game.

THE ESSENTIALS

To be a good outfielder, a player should have speed and the ability to get a good jump on the ball. I like a fellow who can judge the ball, an aggressive individual who wants to get to the ball as soon as possible. I do not care for a loafer. Some players have the knack of estimating where the ball is going the instant it leaves the bat. As soon as that ball is hit, they are off and running.

The outfielder with an average arm who can field and throw the ball quickly and accurately will make just as many assists as the fellow who has a great arm

Fig. 10.1 LEAPING HIGH AGAINST THE FENCE. An all-out attempt by center fielder Chili Davis made it possible for him to prevent a home run. A fleet-footed "fly-chaser" in center field is a major requisite for a championship team.

but has to take a couple more steps to get rid of the ball. This latter individual always catches the ball on the wrong side and, consequently, takes longer to throw it. Actually, it is a simple thing to catch the ball on one's throwing side and have his body in position to throw.

Not having the body in position to throw can be largely attributed to catching the ball with one hand. The big glove with the web pocket is largely responsible for the one-handed problem we have today. As a result, the fielder's body is not in position to throw quickly. I really get peeved when I see outfielders always catching the ball one-handed and having to take extra time in getting it to their throwing side.

College and major league coaches are unanimous in declaring that the two-hand method is best except for those occasions when one hand is the only approach. In the outfield, the fielder should catch every fly ball with two hands, unless it becomes necessary to catch it with one hand. Using two hands will enable the outfielder to have his throwing hand on the ball just as soon as he catches it.

An outfielder has to have a little bit of "infield" in him. There are times when the winning run is on second base in the late innings and a ground ball goes through the middle. He must come in and charge that ball, pick it up, and throw it as an infielder would. He must get rid of it quickly.

Getting the jump on the ball is mostly a matter of habit, and an outfielder will master it only if he practices constantly. The more a player plays the outfield, the better he will be able to judge every fly ball.

A good outfielder must continually be alert and on his toes, especially with men on base. He must always be thinking ahead, and should know what he will do if the ball is hit to him. Indeed, ball games are often won or lost on the judgment of the outfielder on a throw to the right base, or to the wrong base.

An outfielder should be a good hitter with adequate power, plus throwing and fielding ability. If he can swing the bat and has a strong enough arm, constant practice on fly balls and grounders should make him a respectable fielder.

Check every pennant-winning team, and you will find a deer-footed "fly-chaser" in center field.

BOBBY BRAGAN

Great fly-chasers

Down through the years, major league baseball has seen many truly outstanding fielders, but the matchless Joe DiMaggio was perhaps the finest of all. His speed and grace in fading back at the crack of the bat for a long drive enabled him to make outfielding look simple. He was a model of grace and skill as he

Fig. 10.2 HITTING THE RELAY MAN is crucial to a tight defense—the glue in the defense. Here, Reggie Smith, for years one of baseball's premier right fielders, fields a long drive off the fence and hits the relay man with an accurate throw, quick and on a line.

roamed center field. He had everything—anticipation, speed, great hands, throwing power, and accuracy.

There have been numerous fielding standouts of the Dodgers who have won the admiration and respect of fans in Los Angeles and back in Brooklyn. For judging the ball, Ron Fairly would have to be recognized, while for speed, I have to say Willie Davis.

Carl Furillo and Reggie Smith, unquestionably, had the strongest throwing arms (Fig. 10.2). They not only charged balls well, but could go back quickly for fly balls near the fence. Carl played the right field wall as it should be played, and got rid of the ball as quickly as anyone I have seen.

QUALIFICATIONS

The prime requisites for a competent outfielder are good fielding, a strong arm, and powerful hitting. From there on, the qualifications of the three positions are judged on the basis of the duties to be performed.

Generally, if he has three outfielders, the coach would put the fielder with the weakest arm in left field. The strongest arm would go to right field because the throw to third base is longer. The center fielder would very likely be the best outfielder of the trio. This is the guy who covers the most ground and is more or less the captain of the outfield. He takes all the fly balls that he can reach. However, I think that center field is possibly the easiest field to play because balls hit to center field do not have the slice or hook on them that they do to left field. Any ball hit by a right-handed batter down the line is likely to have a hook on it, and it will go toward the line. The left-handed hitter who swings late on the ball will also cause the ball to slice toward the left field foul line.

Speed can be the great equalizer. Even if they misjudge the ball slightly, fly-chasers like Dusty Baker and Cesar Cedeno can make up for it with their exceptional speed. Speed can overcome some of the mistakes of judgment.

Left field

The left fielder needs reasonable speed and a good arm, and he must have the ability to judge curving line drives. Because the left fielder has the most difficult plays to make on balls hit to his right, the right-handed thrower has the advantage, since he is in a better position to make the throws after fielding the ball.

Center field

The center fielder should be the top outfielder because he has the most territory to cover. Exceptional running speed is the key to greatness in a center fielder. He must cover the maximum ground to his right and left, and in order to do this successfully, he must be a quick starter in any direction.

The center fielder must have a strong throwing arm. He should be a roamer, always alert, and ready to race back for the long drives and to dash in for the short ones.

Right field

The player with the best arm should be placed in right field for double protection. He must guard against the scoring play from third to home, and against the all-important man on first going to third on a single.

The art of hitting behind the runner, when successful, enables a runner on first to reach third base on a single. This factor emphasizes the need for the strongest possible arm in right field to protect against this extra base.

STANCE

The outfielder should use a comfortable stance, one that enables him to go in either direction with the quickest possible speed (Fig. 10.3). Using a semi-crouch, he positions his right foot slightly back, with his hands on or in front of

Fig. 10.3   STANCE. The outfielder should use a comfortable stance. He uses a semi-crouch, with his hands on, or in front of, the knees. He is set, but not tense, and always alert. As the pitch is made, the fielder rocks forward on his toes and is ready to cross over in either direction with the quickest possible speed (Paul Blair).

the knees. His toes are pointed slightly out to move laterally as quickly as possible.

"An outfielder should use a stance that he prefers and which gives him confidence," said Pete Reiser, former great Dodger outfielder and for years a successful coach. "Through confidence, he will relax, which is so necessary in obtaining quick starts. I like a stance which has one shoulder nearer the batter than the other. Generally speaking, a right-handed thrower will have his left shoulder pointing more to the batter, and vice versa with left-handed outfielders."

As the pitch is made, the fielder rocks forward on his toes, ready to move in any direction. It is just a matter of shifting the weight off the heels and relaxing. He is ready to cross over either way.

Glove

The majority of big-league outfielders recommend a long-fingered glove with considerable webbing and a deep pocket. While infielders must catch the ball and throw it quickly, outfielders are not required to do this. They prefer a deeper-pocketed glove in order to make any necessary one-handed catches.

PLAYING THE HITTERS

Every good outfielder I have known was good not only because of his abilities, but because he knew where to play each batter. Three major factors determine how the outfielder will play a hitter:

1. the batter
2. the pitcher
3. the game situation

The outfielder has to know who is on base at all times, and must try to remember the speed of the base runners.

Usually the outfield shifts as a unit, so there are no gaping holes between them. If there is a right-handed hitter at the plate, the left and center fielders move over toward the left and deeper than their normal straightaway positions. The right fielder moves toward center field and a little closer to the plate.

The outfielder should study every batter to learn his hitting habits. To do so, he watches his opponents in batting practice, analyzing each batter, i.e., long ball hitters, off-speed hitters, pull hitters, late or straightaway hitters. Since his pitcher and catcher also will know the batter's habits, they will throw to him accordingly.

During the game, various factors will determine how the outfielder shifts his position. When the double or triple would hurt his team, he should play deeper. He must gamble at times and play shallow when the winning run is on second base, in order to throw out the base runner at the plate.

The type of hitter, plus the score of the game are probably the biggest factors in determining the position of the fielders. An outfielder needs to shift according to the count on the hitter. If it is two and nothing, or three and one, he plays deeper and more around to pull. If there are two strikes on the hitter, he does not play quite so deep.

CALLING FOR THE BALL

Outfielders should help each other by calling in a loud and clear voice for all fly balls. As soon as he is absolutely sure he can catch the ball, the fielder must call for the ball, "I've got it!," "I've got it!" and keep on calling. He should call more than once because the other fielder may be yelling at the same time. He should be answered in a loud clear voice, "Take it!," "Take it!" They must talk back and forth. Whenever I hear two fielders communicating with each other, I know that there is not going to be a collision. So, remember to repeat calls, and to answer them.

Calling for the ball too soon is sometimes dangerous in the outfield. There are so many balls hit between the outfield and the infield that if a fielder calls for the ball before he is absolutely sure, it can lead to trouble, particularly in wind-blown Candlestick Park. When an outfielder calls for the ball and the other fielder answers, "Take it.," the responsibility is with the one who made the call; and even if the wind takes hold of the ball, he has to stay with it and make the catch.

On long drives near the fences, the outfielders should tell each other how much room there is near the fences and where to make the throw. One may call out: "Lots of room, you take it," if a ball can still be caught.

In calling for the ball, a center fielder, for example, may use his right hand to motion his left fielder away from the area. The same practice should prevail when an infielder and an outfielder are both involved in a play. In this case, the outfielder runs the infielder off the play whenever he can. It is usually an easier catch for him, since he is coming into the infield and the play is in front of him.

CATCHING THE BALL

An outfielder should catch every fly ball with two hands, unless it becomes necessary to catch it with one hand. Using two hands enables the outfielder to have his throwing hand on the ball just as soon as he catches it. This is particularly true on ground balls, when he has to charge the ball and make a quick throw.

I have observed that the best place to catch a routine fly ball is above eye-level (Fig. 10.5). If he can, the fielder should catch the ball facing it, in a stride position. The glove should be up in front of his face and on his throwing side. Youngsters should not try to make fancy catches—the simpler, the better.

We often think of the belt, or sometimes the chest, being the dividing line. On any balls above the belt, the fingers are up, while on balls below the belt, the fingers are down. While Willie Mays's basket catch has been effective for him, I would not recommend this technique for the majority of players.

Good outfielders learn to catch balls both ways. Usually, when a fielder comes in hard for a fly ball or line drive, he catches the ball with fingers down; when going back or handling a big drive, he catches the ball with fingers up. Handling balls between these two areas is a matter of preference and confidence.

The outfielder should learn to run immediately to the spot where he thinks the ball will go, and wait for it. Some fielders like to thrill the fans by drifting on the ball, making their catches on the run. Joe DiMaggio had a style that all fielders should try to emulate. He made them all look easy.

The outfielder should run on his toes, since running on the heels makes the ball "dance." By running on his toes, he will make a smooth approach to the ball and eliminate the dancing ball.

The fielder should be relaxed when he makes the catch. The arms should be extended, thumbs together, and his hands loose. He should not try to "box" the ball.

As the ball starts to settle into the glove, there should be a slight give of the outfielder's hands and wrists. This softens the impact of the ball when it hits the glove.

Fielding: one hand or two?

In recent years, the big glove, in addition to other factors, has resulted in a significant increase in one-handed fielding. Initially, this practice was not looked upon with alarm by many coaches since large, deep-pocketed gloves proved convenient and effective in catching the ball. However, too often today, a one-handed fielding effort is a liability resulting in the hitter beating the throw or the base runner taking an extra base. In a sport in which speed and split seconds of time often determine success or failure, fielders are wasting critical time when they catch the ball with one hand and attempt to get their throws away quickly. They are in poor fielding and throwing position as they attempt to grab the ball with one hand.

There are a number of major league outfielders who have a tendency to use only one hand in fielding. Reggie Smith, for years one of baseball's premier right fielders, does not feel this is a good example for young players to see, even with no runners on base. "Personally, I try to be as consistent as possible," said Reggie, "and do the same things at all times, whether runners are on base or not. I have seen players catch the ball with one hand with men on base and have to make a throw. They are very slow in getting the ball into throwing position. I could mention some big-league outfielders who have a bad habit of always catching the ball with one hand and that's why people run on them."

Every ball should be caught with two hands whenever possible. Jack Stall-

Fig. 10.4 ONE HANDED FIELDING, used excessively, has proven a problem for many outfielders. At all levels of play, fielders are experiencing difficulty getting the ball out of their big gloves and are too slow moving into throwing position. Above, Dusty Baker, grabs the ball with one hand, but there are no runners on base. Even on these plays, however, an outfielder could be practicing his footwork and developing the habit of getting into proper throwing position.

ings, veteran coach at Georgia Southern College explained: "The two-handed method does two things: gets the body weight and center of gravity closer to the ball, thus providing better body balance and body control, and makes it easier and faster to get the ball out of the glove and into the throwing hand (Fig. 10.5). If a player catches *every* ball that he can with both hands, then when he has to make a catch and throw, he will do it easily and properly because he is accustomed to it. If you catch five balls in a row with one hand, and then must make a throw on the sixth catch, it will not be natural. So, catch all possible plays with both hands!"

"If you catch the ball with both hands up, you can get into the glove quicker," said Smith (Fig. 10.6). "If I put one hand up and have to bring the glove down to my throwing hand, that is time! It is time that has to be made up, and many outfielders have a tendency to rush their throws and not get as much behind them or be as accurate."

Fig. 10.5 FIELDING THE BALL WITH TWO HANDS. When a quick and strong throw is required, the outfielder should move into a good throwing position, catch the ball with both hands and get his throw away quickly. Using two hands enables the fielder to have his throwing hand on the ball just as soon as he catches it. Above, Jim Wohlford is coming into the ball to catch it. In a stride position, he has his glove up in front of his face and on his throwing side. After catching the ball, he hops forward on his right pivot foot, pushes off it, and steps forward on his left as he throws. By transferring the weight to his rear leg, he is able to push off with greater power. The throwing arm is away from the body so that he can bring the ball back and throw it in one continuous motion. Holding the ball across the seams, an overhand delivery provides important backspin for carry and accuracy.

Fig. 10.6   CATCHING A HIGH FLY BALL. An outfielder should try to be facing the ball, in a stride position, and catch a routine fly ball above eye-level. His fingers are up for any balls above the belt (Jim Northrup).

Coming in for a low fly ball

Most major league center fielders rate low line drives the toughest balls to handle. These balls tend to sink rapidly. Some veer away from the fielder. It is not only a difficult play but also a dangerous one because if the fielder does not get the ball, it will go through him and allow the hitter to get an extra base or two.

The best way to play the low liner is to wait an instant before moving. Then the fielder will have a better idea whether to go back or forward. If it is a sinking low liner in front of him, he has two alternatives: hold up and catch the ball on a long hop or continue in for a possible shoestring catch. If he charges and goes for it, he should try to lower his body as he comes in to get his eyes as much in line with the ball as possible. If the fielder decides not to try for it, he should shorten his steps and try to get his feet together and his body under complete control. He gets his glove quickly down in front of the ball, the fingers pointing down (Fig. 10.7). His prime concern is keeping the ball in front of him, and if he has to, he can block the ball with his body.

The low liner that is particularly troublesome is the one that the fielder has

Fig. 10.7 CATCHING A LOW FLY BALL. In catching the ball below the belt, the fingers of the outfielder should be pointed down. The dependable fly-chaser uses two hands whenever he can. As he follows the ball into his glove, there should be a slight "give" of his hands and wrists (Jose Cardenal).

to go to his right and move in on to make a low catch, reaching across his body. If the fielder, for instance, is a right-handed thrower, and the glove hand is on his left side, he must go to his right and in, at full speed, and catch the low drive as he reaches across his body. This play often becomes a shoestring catch, that is, indeed, a tough play.

The diving, one-handed catches by Dusty Baker in left field have given Dodger fans many thrills and excitement (Fig. 10.8). To what does Dusty attribute his success? "As I dive and grab for the ball," said Dusty, "I make sure the elbow of my glove hand is fully extended to prevent the ball from being jarred loose when I hit the ground. To help cushion the impact, I will slide on either my chest or legs, as I keep my eye on the ball. Sometimes I will use my throwing hand to help cushion my fall."

Generally, an outfielder does not attempt a shoestring catch unless the winning run would cross the plate on a base hit in the late innings of a game. He should be very careful in attempting this type of catch. Mickey Stanley, who made countless game-saving catches during his outstanding career with the Detroit Tigers, said: "To make a diving catch, stay relaxed, double up, and roll as you hit the ground. Tuck your chin and one shoulder in and roll over. By doing this, you can usually come right up on your feet and be in position to make a throw."

Going to the left or right

The cross-over step is recommended whenever an outfielder has to move laterally. It should be kept in mind that all balls going to left and right field have a tendency to break toward the foul lines. For instance, a right-handed hitter

Fig. 10.8 SPECTACULAR DIVING CATCH. Great fielding plays like this one have characterized the play of left fielder Dusty Baker. Here, Baker makes a diving grab of a low line drive. He dove for the ball with his body fully stretched out, landing on his stomach.

will often get out in front of the ball and give it a counterclockwise spin, and the ball will hook around toward the left field foul line.

If the outfielder has to go to his right, he brings his left leg over his right and shoves off with his right foot. This enables him to cover a much greater distance on his first step than if he were to lift his right foot and push off his left (Fig. 10.9).

The fielder will get quicker starts to either side by using the cross-over step. A good push-off in the direction in which he is going is most important (Fig. 10.10). He should try to run quickly to the spot where he feels the ball will come down.

By using a little wider stance, an outfielder can get a quicker start sideways. To his right, he merely pivots on his right foot, cross steps and goes after the ball, and vice versa to his left.

Going back for a fly ball

To be a good outfielder, a player must be able to go back for a fly ball. Then he can afford to play shallower. In going deep for a fly ball, an outfielder will find his job easier if he runs to the spot where he thinks the ball will come down and wait for it. In moving back, he should make one or two quick glances over his shoulder to check on the ball's flight. By playing it this way, he will be in the proper position for the catch.

Can an outfielder go back as fast as he can forward? I do not think he can, but he certainly can improve his ability to go back through practice. The only

Fig. 10.9 GOING TO THE RIGHT. Whenever an outfielder moves laterally, he
should use the cross-over step. He breaks
for the ball by pivoting on the foot nearest
the ball and crosses over with the other
foot. In going to his right, he brings his left
leg over his right and shoves off with his
right foot (Bill Russell).

Fig. 10.10 GOING TO THE LEFT. A good push-off in the direction he is going is
essential in getting the proper jump on the ball. In moving laterally, the outfielder
uses his natural running motion (Billl Russell).

way an outfielder can go back as fast as he can forward is when he turns his back on the ball and takes his eye off it.

While the veteran fielder can turn his back on the ball and run to the spot, the younger player should keep his eye on the ball as long as possible. With practice, he will learn to turn his back completely on the ball and run to the spot where he thinks it will fall, making one or two quick glances over his shoulder to check on the ball's flight.

We asked Willie Mays whether his famous over-the-shoulder catch was really a tough one. He answered: "I don't think so. I thought it was when I first started doing it, but I practiced it during spring training and I don't find it too hard because actually it is just a football catch."

Theory of shallow outfield play

According to this theory, the outfielder should play as close to the infield as his fielding ability will permit. The great outfielder plays closer to the infield than the poor one, because he is able to go back better for a fly ball.

During their brilliant playing careers, Tris Speaker and Terry Moore played the shallowest center field in the game because they were masters at racing back. Dwayne Murphy and Rickey Henderson are two of the best at this among fly-chasers today.

Terry Moore, who gave St. Louis fans plenty of thrills when he was with the Cardinals, explained the theory this way: "If you are a center fielder, it is an advantage if you can play close and go back on a ball because the majority of the hits are hit in front of you. You have that short line drive which you can come up with, and you have the ground ball. The man is on first, and he is trying to go to third. You are in close, that ground ball is going through there

Fig. 10.11   GOING DEEP FOR A FLY BALL. The outfielder pivots on both feet in the direction he is going and takes his first step with the foot nearest the ball (Bill Russell).

and you can charge it. You can be closer to the infielder, you can be closer to your target and it is the big advantage of playing shallow. Of course, there is a certain time in the ball game when you have to move back to protect a one or two run lead."

While Terry's theory is still a sound one, I do believe outfield play is much deeper now than when he played over twenty-five years ago. I have to feel the ball is livelier, and with artificial turf, ground balls seem to "shoot through" the infield with greater speed. Therefore, outfielders have to play deeper in order to cut off ground balls up the alleys, plus the long drives off the bats of some of today's hefty sluggers.

Playing the fly near the fence

As soon as the ball is hit, I like to see an outfielder turn and run as fast as he can to the fence. He should really *hustle* to that fence! Then he is ready, even if he has to come back five feet and catch it. That is so much better than backing up into the fence, when he is back-pedaling the last four or five steps and is not sure when he will hit the fence. (Fig. 10.12).

What often happens is that the fielder catches the ball one or two feet in front of the fence and then backs into the fence, and the collision knocks the ball out of his hands.

Fig. 10.12 PLAYING THE BALL NEAR THE FENCE. The outfielder turns and runs as fast as he can to the fence. Then he is ready, even if he has to come back five feet and catch it. When the fielder runs from grass to the cinders of a warning track, he will know he is nearing the fence. Above, Jim Northrup goes directly to the fence and places his hand on it for possible leverage.

Many parks today have a "warning track" made of cinders or skinned dirt, so that when the outfielder runs from grass to cinders, he will know he is nearing the fence. If the ball is the line drive type, the fielder has to judge the distance by the warning track.

The outfielder should know how the ball will rebound from fences or walls. If a fly ball cannot be caught and hits the wall, he runs three or four steps toward the playing field and then turns around and faces the fence, ready for the rebound.

The fielder should *never* try to rush in and smother a ball that is coming off the wall. Instead, he should play back a few feet and let it show him in which direction it is going before he tries to pick it up. After he scoops up the ball, he whirls in the direction of the glove hand to make the throw.

Playing the sun field

The majority of ball fields are layed out with the sun facing the right and center fielders, but occasionally the left fielder has to cope with the sun.

Catching balls hit into the sun can be very troublesome, especially for the individual who neglects to work on this important phase of outfield play. Flip-down sunglasses which reduce glare from the sun can be very beneficial to an outfielder. However, it takes practice to get used to them.

Whether or not sunglasses are used, the glove should be used to shield the eyes. If the sun is low, the fielder should hold his glove on the sun as the pitch is made. He then sights the ball, either above or below the glove, and makes the catch.

The most widely used sunglasses have an adjustable band which fits around the back of the head. The glasses are kept in the "up" position until they are to be used. When the outfielder wants to snap the glasses down to look into the sun, he merely taps the peak of his cap. This action forces the glasses down.

"I play the sun slightly to the side," said Mays. "This may make it a little more difficult because you may be overplaying a certain hitter. Even with sunglasses, I cannot play or field a ball going directly into the sun. If at all possible, I like to play the sun by sighting the ball from an angle, that is, getting a side view of it."

During spring training, we have our outfielders go out in the sun field and practice using their sunglasses and flipping them down. After practicing with them, it becomes a habit; then, when a fly ball comes out to them, they automatically knock their glasses down.

Getting the jump on the ball is mostly a matter of habit, and you will only get it if you practice constantly.

DOM DI MAGGIO

Getting the jump on a fly ball

The outfielder who gets the fastest start catches the most balls. In order to do this, he must be alert and ready to move in any direction as the ball leaves the bat. Getting a jump on the ball is mostly a matter of habit, and he will master it only if he practices constantly. The good jump has to come through experience. The great outfielders have that sense of where the ball is going.

Concentrating on the hitter is perhaps the key to getting a good jump on the ball (Fig 10.11). In order to be ready to go, the fielder must get up on his toes so that the instant the ball is hit, he makes his move. Even though he is as far as 350 feet away from the plate, he should be able to tell the type of pitch as it travels toward the plate.

"When the ball is pitched," said Bill Virdon, a former great center fielder and now manager of the Montreal Expos, "the outfielder should be in a semi-crouch, with his knees bent, and the weight on the balls of his feet. He must be ready on every pitch."

"As soon as the pitcher starts his windup," continued Virdon, "he should take his eyes off him and place them on the hitter. In order to get the direction the hitter is hitting the ball, he has to watch him all the way to see the general direction in which he is swinging the bat and the direction in which he might hit the ball."

Dom DiMaggio, a truly great fly-chaser when he played for the Boston Red Sox, cites six basic rules in getting a better jump on the ball:

1. Find a comfortable position.
2. Be in position on every pitch.
3. Know the batters, and play them accordingly.
4. Do not listen—look!
5. Follow every pitch to the plate.
6. Be able to tell the type of pitch.

"A player has to be alive and be in the game," asserted Mays. "He must know his pitcher and the hitter at the plate. By watching the ball, he sees how it comes off the bat. During practice and in a game, he cannot stand around in the outfield just daydreaming. He must be ready all the time, physically and mentally, and stay in the game."

One of the toughest balls to get a good jump on is the line drive directly at the outfielder. For awhile, he does not know whether the ball is the sinker type that will drop in front of him or the one that is hit extremely well with a little backspin and that keeps on rising as it goes. The worst thing that can happen is for the fielder to charge the ball and have it go over his head.

The difficult aspect of the ball hit directly at the fielder is that he has no side view of it. It is like an individual watching a train coming at him. He cannot see how fast the train is going if he is standing on the tracks, but if he gets off the side, he can tell. A fly ball presents practically the same problem. The fielder cannot tell immediately how hard the ball is hit.

Backing up

Outfielders have a key responsibility in backing up thrown balls to the bases and balls hit to the infielders and other outfielders. If possible, they run to a point behind and in line with the fielder and the player who is hitting or throwing the ball.

The left fielder backs up second on all plays from the right side. He backs up third on all bunts, pick-offs, and run-downs. He should back up third when a bunted ball is played to first base for a possible return throw to third. The center fielder backs up second on all bunts and plays at that bag. The right fielder backs up first on all bunts, pick-off plays, and throws made there. He backs up second on all throws from the left side. On run-downs between first and second, he should move in quickly and back up first base.

FIELDING GROUND BALLS

The outfielder fields ground balls in much the same manner as an infielder. Unfortunately, however, very few outfielders spend enough practice time picking up grounders. As a rule, I doubt if they devote enough practice to charging grounders, in which they have to field the ball and throw it quickly and accurately. This is something that has to become a *habit*. There is no question that the majority of errors by outfielders occur on ground balls.

When Reggie Smith came up to the Red Sox, Coach Johnny Pesky hit him a minimum of 150 ground balls a day. "At the time," said Reggie, "it seemed like a lot of work, but it really paid off. I was able to experience all kinds of hops coming at me. Having good hands is a result of being able to recognize the type of ground ball and what might happen to a ball coming to me because I have seen it before. This is anticipation. Being in the proper position to field balls is also important. It is a matter of repetition, and repetition breeds confidence."

When no quick throw is necessary, he may field the ball with his heels together, or he may drop to one knee to block the ball (Fig. 10.13). If the fielder is trying to throw out an advancing runner, he has to charge the ball and either play it with both hands or scoop it up with his glove hand and then throw (Fig. 10.14 and 15).

Never lag behind on a ground ball—charge, get set and make the throw.

DOM DI MAGGIO

Fig. 10.13 BLOCKING A HARD GROUND BALL. The outfielder tries to play all ground balls in front of his body. Here, Jim Northrup drops to one knee to block the ball. Using two hands, his eyes follow the ball into his glove.

Fig. 10.14 FIELDING A GROUND BALL. An outfielder must never lag behind on ground balls. He must charge the ball, pick it up, and make an overhand throw. Fielding the ball with two hands enables the fielder to move into throwing position faster than if he went down with just his glove hand (Bill Russell).

Fig. 10.15 FIELDING A GROUNDER WITH ONE HAND. When they have to pick up a grounder quickly in an attempt to throw out a runner, some outfielders, like Ron Fairly, feel they can make the play more quickly by using a glove-hand pickup. Young players, however, will find that fielding the ball with both hands is not only safer but probably just as fast.

The fielder should approach and field ground balls to his left or right in a semicircle, fielding them in front, at the maximum height of the bounce. By bending his knees, he is able to stay low and follow the ball all the way into his glove. His weight is transferred to the right foot with a hop. Outfielders, as well as infielders, should remember to *play the ball and not let the ball play them.*

"Never lag behind on ground balls," advised Stanley. "Even before the play begins, you should know where the throw is to be made. Charge in, then get set and make your throw. When I played sandlot ball, I was an infielder, and I often was puzzled why outfielders would wait for grounders to come to them. I thought if they would charge a ball the way we do in the infield, they would be twice as good."

If he fumbles the ball or it gets by him, the outfielder must hustle after it, *keeping in mind that the runner is running.*

HITTING THE CUT-OFF MAN

One of the biggest faults among outfielders is that they often overthrow the cut-off man, which eliminates all possible cut-off plays. By throwing the ball over the head of the cut-off man, he will not get the man at home and the offense will have a man in scoring position again. This is a bad situation.

On an extra base hit, an outfielder has to retrieve the ball and then hit the cut-off man coming out from the infield. What are Reggie's thoughts and where and how will he throw the ball? Smith said: "First, I have pretty much determined before hand, 'what if?' I know what the situation is. How many out? How many men are on base? Where will I throw the ball? It becomes a natural reaction, or reacting out of instinct. If I have to go to my left, I want to turn away from the plate and come around with good arm and body motion with one big whip. I must know where the cut-off man will be, and I try to give him a nice throw about chest high."

THROWING THE BALL

One of baseball's most thrilling plays occurs when an outfielder makes a perfect toss into a base or home plate and nips the runner who is sliding in. Base runners soon learn to respect the fielders who have the real "shotguns" in the outfield.

The main factors in throwing from the outfield are accuracy, a strong arm, and ability to get rid of the ball as soon as possible. This does not mean, however, that the fielder should rush his delivery and try to get too much on the ball. By hurrying his throw too much, he is very likely to miss the cut-off man, the worst thing that can happen.

The overhand delivery, in which the ball is held across the seams, is recommended for all outfielders because of the carry and accuracy it provides. In addition to good backspin, the ball does not veer sideways when thrown overhand.

"You can tell if a throw has good rotation if it takes a good skip when it goes into the catcher," said Danny Ozark, who had an excellent view from his third base coaching box.

In addition, the low throw has a better chance of being accurate, and will not lose as much momentum as the one with a high arc on it. I believe the use of artificial turf will encourage more outfielders to make low throws.

Throwing technique

An outfielder should try to get into throwing position while fielding the ball. Just before the ball comes down, he moves into it with his body in proper position to throw. Therefore, the ball should be caught as his left foot comes down on the ground (Fig. 10.16).

On a routine fly ball, I like him to stay back of the ball two or three steps, so that he is coming *into* the ball to catch it. As he catches the ball, the weight is shifted to the pivot foot (the right foot, if he is right-handed). The striding foot points in the direction of the throw and the body moves forward against the braced front leg.

The throwing arm is away from the body so that he can bring the ball back and throw it in one continuous motion. The elbow comes back first, and the

Fig. 10.16 BASIC THROWING TECHNIQUE. After catching the ball, the fielder shifts his weight to the pivot or push-off foot. The throwing arm is away from the body so that he can bring the ball back and through in one continuous overhand motion. Pushing off the back foot, the fielder's entire body follows through to get the necessary power behind the throw. He throws on a line to hit the relay man coming out for the throw (Bill Russell).

forearm lays back from the elbow. Then, as the elbow leads the way, the arm, wrist, and right hand are brought forward. His throwing arm is whipped through in a free and easy follow-through, coming straight forward and then down across his body. In fact, his entire body follows through to get the necessary power behind the throw.

"After catching the ball, you have to feel for the ball and get it across the seams," said Smith. "I have a little drill that I work on, that is, getting the ball out of the glove and feeling for the seams. I am turning the ball as I move into throwing position. The across-the-seams grip provides a more direct and straighter trajectory on the ball, especially from the outfield."

Throwing to the bases

Another common error of outfielders is to throw to the wrong base. This seldom happens if he keeps his mind on the ball game, and knows *where* he is going to throw the ball when he gets it. He must make his throws to the base *ahead of the runner,* never behind him.

"Throw overhand and low on the line to the relay or cut-off man, chest-high," asserted Jim Northrup, veteran outfielder of the Detroit Tigers. "Throws to a base that take a hop will usually be low enough for good tagging position."

TRAINING

The outfielder, like any other player, must take good care of his throwing arm. During spring training, his arm should be worked into shape with as much care as that taken by a pitcher.

Then, during the season, his arm must be given enough work to keep it fit. It is a standard practice in major league baseball for the outfielders to throw between innings and during delays in the game.

Frankly, I do not like my outfielders to throw batting practice. It is too short a throw, and I think it will do your outfield throw-in more harm than good.

How did Reggie Smith develop a strong throwing arm? Reggie explained that "My long fingers helped me to develop a backward rotation on the ball, similar to a golf ball being hit, which helped develop better lift and cause the ball to rise somewhat. As for the body motion, having the full weight behind the throw was something I learned at a very early age. My older brothers made sure I stayed on top of the ball, and I used to throw a lot. Throwing properly and throwing as much as I did helped me develop the arm."

Practice Tips

1. Work out in the infield to learn how to handle ground balls.
2. Practice going after fly balls that are hit over your head.
3. Drill continuously in judging fly balls, especially line drives.
4. When engaged in a long fly-shagging drill, have a halfway man handle your throws. Use him as your cut-off target.
5. Practice catching fly balls in the sun. Get used to your glasses.
6. Do not spend all of your time fielding fungos. During batting practice, practice fielding balls hit directly off the bat of the hitter.
7. Do not spend all your time on fly balls. Get plenty of practice at picking up ground balls and hops of all kinds.

11
Psychology of Coaching

Handling twenty-five different players on a baseball squad is not a simple matter. Each one has his own personality and character traits which must be handled individually. Keeping in mind the strengths and weaknesses of his players, the coach has to utilize various approaches and techniques to bring out the most effective performance of his team.

Some athletes have to be patted on the back, while others have to be coaxed or even needled. Then, there are the problem athletes with their negative forms of behavior that must be skillfully dealt with if there is to be the team unity so necessary to win.

This is why the coach must be continually alert to notice the personal characteristics that distinguish the problem athlete from the good competitor. A better psychological insight into the personality makeup of the player can be extremely valuable in motivating the athlete toward maximum effort.

I believe the average manager today is more diplomatic in his handling of players than the average manager thirty years ago, and this is good. Many old-time managers were tough, hard-nosed characters whose word was law, and

Fig. 11.1 The ability to motivate athletes into performing well is a major quality of a successful coach or manager. Challenging an athlete to do something can be a very effective method of motivation. Accepting the challenge is a real character builder. Above, Walter Alston, early in his managerial career with the Dodgers, talks to one of his young players during a spring training workout.

everyone did it his way or not at all. Today, most managers spend more time with the individual player to help him in every way possible.

"If you're honest with the players and they respect your knowledge of the game, you'll be alright."

WHITEY HERZOG

ROLE OF THE COACH

The coach, or manager, has to be able to recognize talent when he sees it on the ball field. He has to be able to find mistakes and "see the faults of a player." The coach must first recognize the fault, and secondly, he must try and correct it in a way that is acceptable and will get across to the players.

The successful manager has the ability to develop a team, to motivate and get the most from the players. In making his moves, the good manager makes the right substitution, inserting a pinch hitter, reliever, or defensive specialist at the most opportune time. He employs appropriate tactics, such as the sacrifice, steal, intentional walk, and the like.

In handling his players, consistency is extremely important for a coach. Players should always know where he stands and what to expect of him.

The league standing does not necessarily indicate how good or how bad a coach really is. If he has gotten 100 percent from his men, maneuvering them skillfully, using the proper defenses, and changing pitchers when he should, he can feel he has done a most satisfactory job.

First impression

The first impression that a coach makes on his squad is important. *Organization* is the key to the whole thing. When practice is first called, the coach must be ready. There is nothing more damaging to a team than for a coach to have his first workout, and not know where to go and what to do.

The first meeting with his team should be fairly brief. He should give them a general idea of what he expects them to do, and what they can expect of him. He may talk about some of his theories and ideas of how they can develop a winning ball club.

Generally, the coach or manager should spend more time with his planning for the first three or four practices. The rest will follow as he goes along. He will know what he needs to work on and what requires less work. But the first three or four practices are the important ones.

Ball players are a lot like kids in a school class. When a new teacher comes into his class, the first three or four days, they are pretty well-behaved because

Fig. 11.2 Most coaches and managers know how the game should be played, but their chief problem is communication; the ability to relate to the player, to instruct, and to show him in a manner that he understands. Here, manager Alston gives some hitting tips to one of his players.

they do not know what to expect. But after the fourth or fifth day, they start testing him out and try to find out what they can get away with.

If they can get away with something on the fourth day, the students try a little more on the fifth day, and the first thing he knows, they are completely out of hand. And if he waits two weeks, the teacher has let it go much too far. Now, he cannot straighten out the situation. If the teacher can jump on somebody about the fourth day severely, very likely he will go through the entire year without much trouble.

I believe ball players operate the same way. They want to test the coach to see how far they can go. After all, they are only grown boys, and the sooner the coach can achieve discipline, the better off he is.

Coaches' dress

Anytime he has his club working out, the coach should be in uniform. Then he is better prepared for work, and will command better respect. Off the field, he should be clean and presentable, not necessarily a fancy dresser. Both on and off the field, the coach should set an example for his squad.

POSITIVE MOTIVATION

A coach should try to emphasize a positive rather than a negative approach. The key is largely positive thinking. The more positive the coach is, the more the athlete wants to achieve. While positive motivation can take many forms, essentially it involves such elements as successful skill execution, encouragement, confidence, and praise (Fig. 11.2).

Successful execution can be a very effective form of positive motivation. An athlete has to learn to get the feel of a good throw or a well hit ball. The feeling often produces satisfaction and pleasure, which, in turn, serve as strong reinforcers. Usually, the least confident players need the positive reinforcement of good execution the most.

Praise is perhaps the most common form of positive motivation. It is most important to the least confident athletes. Unfortunately, the best athletes, who need such motivation the least, get most of the headlines. The most obvious example of negative thinking, punishment, will not produce the motivational rewards that positive thinking can.

METHODS OF MOTIVATION

There are various methods and techniques to motivate athletes to greater performances and achievement. Each athlete should be given challenging goals to strive for, a feeling of achievement, and an atmosphere of self-respect and friendly relations. Athletes must be emotionally inspired if they are to perform to the best of their ability.

Improvement

During the season, a coach should expect and get gradual improvement from most of his athletes. Not everyone can or will be great, but everyone should improve. Improvement—reaching goals—is the greatest motivating factor in athletics. Achievement makes paying the price worth it.

Pride

The coach at all times should emphasize pride—pride in how an athlete should look and feel, his attitudes, and the like. Everything should be done in a quality way: "Be proud of whatever you do. Have pride in your school, team, and yourself."

Coaches should consider every method of promoting pride and morale. The easiest way to develop pride, of course, is to win. Nothing succeeds like success. However, success does not come overnight. It may take time to build or develop a winning team.

Organization and careful preparation

Practices must be planned in advance to stimulate the players with the desire, as well as the tools, to improve. "Practices must be organized which will create that desire," said Jerry Kindall, former big-league infielder and now coach at the University of Arizona. "A daily practice plan should be posted in the locker room and on the field. Players will respond if they know what is in store for them that day.

Keeping records

Players need to know that the coach is basing his evaluation of them on objective standards as much as possible. "If a player is cut or benched, he deserves to see an objective, a relative measurement of his performance—a reason, not merely the coach's hunch," said Jerry.

Trust

To be effectively motivated, players must trust their coach. "In a way," said Kindall, "the coach takes on a father role for most of his players, and young men and women long to see truth, honesty, fairness, and compassion. These qualities lead to an unshakeable trust between player and coach."

Setting goals

All athletes should have a goal, and it should be stimulating and challenging. However, the player should make his goals realistic in terms of his ability and experience. If the goal is too high, and he cannot make it, then it is really useless for him to have that goal. The coach should constantly be striving to give his athletes the incentive to keep improving.

Display board

Athletes are only human in that they love to see their names in print. In addition to the recognition they receive in newspapers, radio, and television, an attractive display board can be an excellent motivator.

Other techniques

The following techniques for psychological motivation can be effective:

1. Challenge the athletes.
2. Change routine—have fun.
3. Dedicate games to a special cause.
4. Point for an opponent.
5. Develop the art of needling.

6. Deflate the star.
7. Conduct competitive practices.
8. Place slogans on walls of locker room.

Instilling confidence

Instilling in his players a positive approach to the game is an important responsibility of the coach. This is true more with young players than with the veterans, who know they will have hot streaks and slumps. The young player who is just trying out for the team needs more of this than anyone else.

Sometimes it is difficult to encourage a player who is going 0 for 10 or 1 for 19. Here is the problem—the fellow who is in a slump. The coach keeps telling a player that he can *do* it, yet he continues to fail. This is when he is susceptible to a few instructions, such as, "Try this," "Try that," or "We think that you can do it."

This individual should be brought out to practice a little earlier to hit as many balls as he can. The coach should show interest in him. Then the coach must hope and pray that, the next game, he will break loose. The only way to really build confidence is through *practice, practice, and more practice.* It does not come any other way.

When Maury Wills first came up, he was having trouble with the bat. He had just started switch-hitting, and it was quite a task for him. Maury is such an emotional fellow, and his pride is so great, that this was continually "eating away at him."

One day, following a game, Maury came up to me in the shower room and said: "Why don't you send me back to Spokane, Skip? I'm not helping the club!" He actually felt that he was not helping the club with his bat.

However, I had seen things in his makeup and in his aggressive spirit and his overwhelming desire that led me to believe that he would eventually be a pretty good ball player. The only thing I said to him was: "Maury, if you have as much confidence in yourself as I have in you, everything is going to be all right." That is about all I said to Maury, and I kept him in the lineup.

While teaching in the Ohio school system, I learned how to make suggestions tactfully enough so that they would be kindly received.

The confidence I showed in Wills at that time gave him the needed confidence in himself, and he began to pick up. Actually, the only thing we did was to open up his stance slighty. He still could hit the ball to all fields, but he just opened up more or less to get his knee out of the way so that he could get the bat through. I do not know whether it was the confidence that we gave him or the opening up of his stance, but he started to hit and, of course, anyone close to baseball knows the rest of the Maury Wills story.

Patience

Not only should the coach be patient but he should insist that the player also be patient. Quite often, when he tells a player to change his stance or his swing a little bit, it is bound to feel awkward to him in the first few attempts.

"If we have to tell a player fifty times that he should do it a certain way," said Bobby Winkles, now Director of Player Development for the Chicago White Sox, "then we tell him fifty times. We do not tell him ten times, and then say: 'Well, he cannot get it. Why mess with him?' If a player needs that much, the coach must tell him fifty times. Keep reminding him!"

Encouragement

Words of encouragement can be more helpful to a ballplayer than finding fault with him. I definitely believe a player can be encouraged to greater performance. I am sure that the compliment I gave Willie Crawford one night for his all-out hustle did him more good than criticizing him for the times he failed to hustle.

When a player makes a great play or executes a particular play correctly, the best tonic is for the coach to let him know that he, as a coach, saw this. If a player gets a man from second to third by sacrificing, or hitting the ball to the opposite field, I think the coach must let this individual know that he appreciates his effort or his sacrifice of his own hitting ability. Maybe he would have gotten

Fig. 11.3 Ball players can be encouraged to greater performance. A highly motivating coach or manager can stimulate athletes to a point where they perform to maximum efficiency. Above, manager Tommy Lasorda has gone to the mound not only to discuss the game situation but give a boost to the spirit and confidence of his pitcher, southpaw Jerry Reuss.

a base hit if the coach had let him hit away, but he has done the thing that his coach wanted him to do.

Therefore, the coach must let him know that he saw this and, in anybody's book, it is a big plus. This is not only a coach's way of showing his appreciation but at the same time an encouragement for the ball player to do it again.

Suggestive power

The coach will often find it effective to make suggestions such as: "Try this and see how it works out." He has to start out with suggestions as to how the player might improve or how the coach thinks he will improve. He must get the idea across that *this is the better way.*

The coach cannot just walk out and say: "Look, you have to do it this way." More or less, he has to sell the player on the idea that this might help him and then work on it. The coach must get him to practice enough so that it becomes natural for him. At first, however, he should not make too many suggestions, certainly not during the game, when the hitter has to concentrate and not have to worry where his little finger or toe is.

How should the coach handle the player who does not want to take suggestions? First, it depends on what kind of an athlete he is and what his problem is. If he does everything well and hits the ball well, we do not try to change him too much. If he is successful doing something his way, I would be reluctant to try to change him. The best time to try to help him is when he gets in a little slump. This is the time to make suggestions, such as: "Why don't you try *this* way?"

A coach can go only so far in trying to get the best out of a ballplayer. If he will not take his advice, there is not a lot he can do with the player. He should try and talk to him about it, but if he will not listen, the coach simply has to let him fail or make it on his own. If he fails, more than likely the player will start to listen.

Suggestive power sometimes involves forcing a fellow to do something that he does not really believe in. Possibly, he has tried it twice, and inwardly he feels it does not work. More than likely, he will disregard the coaching point saying: "This will not help me." However, the coach could suggest that, rather than try it in a game, he might achieve better results if he tried it during practice. "Try it and see how it feels to you," he could say.

Teach them to think for themselves

Too often, we, as coaches and managers, do not realize that once those kids go on the field, we cannot do a thing. We can only sit in the dugout and watch them. If we have not taught them correctly, it is out of our hands once they take the field. So, what we have to do is prepare them to mentally think for themselves in the various situations which may occur during a game.

Some coaches have as many as forty automatics. Well, I do not think anyone should have more than three or four automatics in coaching baseball. If his coach makes everything automatic for his players, a kid never thinks for himself. If a nonautomatic situation ever comes up, he will not know what he should do. Therefore, the coach or manager should not "over-coach." Instead, he must require his players to think for themselves and concentrate on teaching them the fundamentals of the game.

Demand hustle

The first thing a coach must do is to demand hustle from his players. Ball players are not asked to run too often. Maybe four or five times, they will run from home to first. Therefore, the coach should insist that they always hustle.

"The only thing I expect my players to do is to show up on time, give me 100 percent of what they have, hustle, and not make mental mistakes," explained manager Dick Williams of the San Diego Padres. "I want them to know their fundamentals, and I let them know that mental mistakes chew on me. I tell them: 'You want me to chew on you, you make 'em.' "

On the other hand, when a player does hustle and gives a little extra effort, the coach should compliment him the same as he would if he rapped out a base hit or a home run.

I remember an evening one season when Willie Crawford hustled as much as he possibly could. He made a great catch in the outfield, when he almost ran into the left field fence. He hustled on the ball that he hit and dove into second base. He ran hard on every play that he had. He backed up everything. I complimented Willie on it. I did not have too many things to compliment anyone on that night, but I made sure Crawford knew that I saw him hustling.

I expect my players to give me 100 percent for that day, not make mental errors, and know the fundamentals.

DICK WILLIAMS

The harder you play the more fun baseball is because that's when you accomplish the most.

PETE ROSE

Now, this does more good than raising heck a time or two in previous games when he did not hustle. Following the game when talking to a writer, who obviously did not have much to write about, I pointed this out by saying:

"Here is a guy who sits on the bench for two weeks and does not complain or moan, and when he got into this game, he did not hold any grudge. He went out and hustled his fanny in an effort to stay in the lineup. This is the type of spirit that we need on this club."

If I see a player not hustling, generally I will wait until the following day to talk to him. Quite often, I will pull him aside and talk to him privately. Willie Davis is one player who hustled most of the time, but one day, for some reason or other, he took it easy going down to first base, and it cost us an important run. So, when Willie came back to the dugout, I said to him: "Come here, Three-dog! Willie, you hustle for me 99 times out of 100, but what happened this time?"

The first thing I wanted to tell him was that he had hustled in the past, then to find out what happened this time. This is much better than saying: "What's the matter, Willie? Why didn't you run it out?" In other words, I wanted to pat him on the back for being a hustler and then kick him in the fanny for the time he did not hustle.

This is better psychology than just taking the negative side, which makes him feel that "Every time I do something wrong, you are on me." When a player takes a defensive attitude, you have to tell him: "Look, we are on you, we are finding fault with you, but this is our business, to find fault with you." In fact, I want my coaches to tell him, "You did this wrong."

When a coach is always finding fault with a player, he has to tell this fellow: "Don't worry. When we find fault with you, we are interested in you and want you to improve. You should start worrying when we ignore you, when we do not say anything to you. So, don't take it the wrong way."

Let them know who is boss

The players have to know who is boss. In my case, I might be a little more lenient than most managers, and this may be a fault. I am not saying that this is the right way. But when I do have a meeting and I want to raise heck, I want it to *mean* something. I like to think that they all know when I have had enough. They know how far they can go.

As a manager and coach, I do not want too tight a rein, with everybody either afraid to move or afraid of me. This is where respect comes in. They know, too, that I will go just so far, and when that happens, I have had enough.

In severe cases, the coach may take the uniform away and say: "Look, if you do not want to do it this way, then just leave your uniform in the locker." Of course, with professional players, the pocketbook is where it hurts the most, more than anywhere else. However, this should be a last resort.

Early in my big-league managing career, Don Newcombe told my pitching coach that he would not pitch batting practice. Of course, Don and I are great friends today and we joke about it every once in a while. He possibly respects me more for treating him as I did, although at the time, he was ready to kill me.

Newcombe had just been discharged from the service, and he was having a little trouble. He was not winning, so I told Coach Becker to have Don throw batting practice. Well, he told Joe he was not a batting practice pitcher, that he would not do it.

So, I called Newcombe in and told him: "Take your uniform off, and when you are ready to throw for batting practice, you can put it back on. I don't care how long it takes." The next day, his uniform was not in his locker, and he came to me and said he was ready to go again.

If I had let him get by with his refusal to pitch batting practice, the next time he might have refused to do something else, and I would be in trouble. A coach has to have a stopper somewhere. Today, Don respects me more because I did get a little rough with him at that time, rather than let him get away with it.

Enthusiasm

The coach has to be alive along with his players. He has to show enthusiasm. There are some hitters who can hardly wait to get to the plate. Then, there are other players who just mope along, almost dragging the bat up to the plate. I wonder whether or not they really want to hit. Well, the coach gives out the same impressions to his own club.

The energetic, enthusiastic ball player will accomplish more with his spare time and come nearer to his capacity than the lazy nonchalant athlete who mopes around, taking his practice halfheartedly. This type of player is not likely to improve too much. He has one thing in his favor, however. It is difficult to get him excited. In a key situation, he may be more relaxed than the fiery individual. Still, I would always take the energetic fellow who really wants to go out after them.

Concentration

By concentrating on the task at hand, the coach can often override his emotions. At least, the experienced coach is able to do this.

I remember only too well the final game of the 1955 World Series, when the Dodgers had their first chance to win the World Championship. Southpaw Johnny Podres beat the Yankees 2–0 in a very tight game. At the time, I was surprised, as the game progressed, at the extent of my concentration. Going over in my mind were such questions as: "How is Podres pitching now? Where do we move the outfield on this hitter? Whom do I have in the bullpen? What will they do in the next situation?" When the game ended, it was almost like another game, with a little something extra, and about an hour after the game, I felt a great letdown.

If a manager or coach is concentrating and thinking about what he should do, the emotional aspects of the game are more or less secondary. An hour or so after the game, though, he will likely feel that he has been run over by a truck.

Imagination

One of the enjoyable aspects of managing or coaching is doing something a little better than the other fellow and having it pay off.

The imaginative, creative type of coach is constantly on the lookout for new ideas, ideas that can be revised and improved upon to fit his own situation. He fills his mind with new information obtained from coaching clinics, the books and magazines he reads, and the many games he sees.

Sense of humor

Having a sense of humor and being able to joke with the players on occasion can be a very important quality. Even ball players can often be criticized in a joking sort of way. I have had ball players whom I could kid, ride, or needle a little bit, in a joking manner. I have also had a couple of fellows who did not exactly know if I was kidding them or if I was serious.

With certain individuals, this is a good procedure, because they know they are getting the needle—and that *I* know they did not hustle on a particular play, or did not do something right. Yet, I am giving it to them in a joking, kidding, or needling sort of way.

Certainly, an occasional laugh or funny moment can break the tension, particularly before an important contest. "I tell my kids a few jokes and funny stories before we play an important game," said Winkles. "Baseball is not a game where you want your kids all tensed up. Baseball is a loose game. You may want football or basketball players tensed up but baseball is a game of looseness. You have to be loosy-goosy when you are playing this game."

Show them how

If the coach can show a boy by demonstrating how to do it, this is better than talking. In my case, I did not have that advantage. I had to get respect through years of managing and handling men.

In cases when I could not demonstrate, I would try to get a great hitter or base runner to demonstrate for me. I was never a great base runner so I have had Maury Wills instruct on the fine points of base running. So, I think it is good to pick out a player who can do something well and who has the ability to instruct, and let him demonstrate for you.

Actually, many of the great coaches were not great athletes. A good example is Paul Brown, one of football's truly great mentors. I believe that one reason why these coaches have been so successful is that, more than likely, they made a little more effort in learning and studying the fundamentals than the star who had all the natural ability who just went out and performed.

Composure under stress

Every coach, during his career, will experience situations of emotional stress and despair in which he must try to hold his composure in a dignified manner. We were in the final play of the play-offs in 1962, and we had a fairly good lead going into the ninth inning. Then the Giants broke loose to beat us. Possibly, this was my most trying moment in regard to holding composure.

The season was over for us, and there was nothing we could do. We tried to take this crushing defeat the best we could, and take it like men. Every coach must realize that this is going to happen to him, and be prepared if and when it happens. Then, he will know how to handle the situation and do his best to go through with it.

Relationship with umpires

In dealing with the officials, the manager or coach must be respectful to them, yet show them that he knows when they have made a mistake. I like to restrain myself from going out there and arguing on every close play. There will be close plays, some of which will go against us and some for us.

When a manager does go out, however, he should have a legitimate gripe. However, he should make it as short as he can and then get out of there. Some umpires will take a bit more than others, without abusing their personalities.

Every ball club expects its manager to fight for its team. Therefore, he should argue for his team as much as he can, within reason.

TEAM MORALE

Morale and team unity are extremely important to the success of any ball team, particularly with a club such as the Dodgers, where we have no big stars. In a way, we are lucky because everyone feels he is part of this club. I think the fellows on the bench feel the same way because, when somebody gets in a little slump, we put the other fellow in.

The more a coach can make the twenty-fifth ballplayer on his club feel that he is a part of the team—that he is playing an important role in the team effort—the better off he will be.

Following a great catch by Manny Mota, for instance, Wes Parker came up to him and complimented him for his all-out effort. It is good to have one ballplayer complimenting another on his fine play. As I sit on the bench, I like to see our fellows patting each other on the back, saying, "Nice going!" This is important to the success of a team.

The coach can promote morale and team unity by talking about it and praising the guys who show this type of spirit. I like the fellow who hustles when he is not hitting, or the player who does the little things for the good of the ball club.

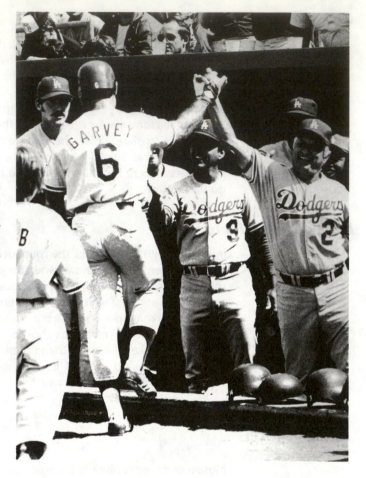

Fig. 11.4 The thrill of victory or an individual achievement should be shared with members of the team and the coaching staff. Team unity and morale are extremely important to the success of any ball team. Here, Steve Garvey is congratulated by his teammates and his manager, Tommy Lasorda, right.

The skipper can bring this out during squad meetings by saying: "This guy may be in a slump, but at least, he is showing me something by hustling." I will also mention in the meeting the fellows on the bench who have not played for a week but who are making more noise than anybody else.

Loyalty works both ways

On a major league squad, the manager likes to have his entire squad loyal to him, and he has to be loyal to them, too. Team loyalty is just as important on the lower levels of play. *It is essential to a winning baseball team.*

All my life, I have tried very hard not to criticize any ball player publicly. I will on occasion make excuses for him by saying: "This is possibly the only thing that could have happened," or, "He was playing it this way." Sometimes, you have to dig pretty deeply to find an excuse. But I much prefer to give an excuse publicly than to say: "Well, he made a mistake. He was a bonehead player," or something like that. The coach has to protect his players this way.

The player who continually criticizes the coach with his teammates is looking for his individual glories. He is more interested in having a good year than he is in worrying about the team. Of course, this will happen occasionally, but the more the coach can keep it down the better off he is. We try to discourage arguments and hard feelings between team members. Our prime objective is to develop a feeling of pride and respect for each other.

Our prime objective is to develop a feeling of pride and respect for each other.

TEAM EFFORT

To play winning baseball, a strong team effort is required. An individual cannot do it by himself. I am referring to the little things in baseball, such as advancing or protecting a runner. These are the things that will win ball games. Every player must work together as a team and try to say, "We can do it!"

In his early meetings, the coach should preach constantly that "THIS is a team effort." He should tell his squad that he will recognize the individual who can advance the man from second to third, or sacrifice himself and do the little things that are good for the club. He will tell them that he expects everyone to hustle and give 100 percent effort whenever he is on the playing field.

These are the qualities I look for in each of my players. Even though he may not hit as much as somebody else, he will do these "little things" for the good of the team. If he is sitting on the bench, he will be pulling for the *team,* not the individual.

HANDLING MEN

The manager or coach should live the life that he expects his players to lead. He should treat them as he would like to be treated if he were a player. Above all, he must treat them as *men;* he should joke and work with them and be as close to them as he can, without being "buddy-buddy." The manager is more or less the "lonely guy." He cannot afford to get "buddy-buddy" with his players. True, he wants to be respectful to them but must treat them all alike.

I do not feel that a manager can show partiality, such as going to the movies with one or two of his players or playing pool or golf with them. The worst thing that can happen is to have little cliques here and there, in which the manager associates with some players and not others.

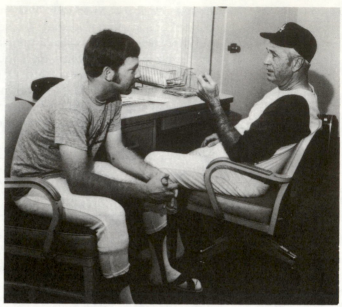

Fig. 11.5 Talking over a problem is more effectively handled behind a closed door than in front of the entire squad. When a player comes to him with a problem, the manager or coach can be helpful sometimes by just listening to his troubles.

A manager or coach must have the ability to deal with diverse personalities, knowing when to be stern and when to be gentle.

Criticize a player privately

Generally, if I want to talk to a player about his performance, I will talk to him individually, rather than in front of the entire squad (Fig. 11.5). Of course, there are certain times when it will be necessary to criticize a player in front of everybody for the good of the team, but mostly this sort of thing should be private.

Do not use two sets of rules

No coach should make a set of rules for one player and another set for twenty-five other players. *He cannot show favoritism to anyone.* All personnel have to abide by the same rules. Sometimes, when a coach is critical of his team, he should criticize the star rather then the rookie who has made two or three mistakes.

The star should not receive preferential treatment from the coach. Sometimes, the coach has to find fault with the star in order to justify getting on other players who possess less talent.

If he handles his players fairly, I believe every coach can get respect out of the players on the bench. One point he has to get across to his entire squad is that, "It has to be a *team* effort even if there is a lot of individual talent."

When a player comes to him with a personal problem, the coach can be helpful sometimes by just listening to his troubles. However, as a rule, a coach should not interfere with a player's private life too much.

Know each individual

In order to impart the right instruction to his players, the coach must know the individual. The first time he tries to correct some players, they will take it as finding fault with them, rather than as constructive criticism. That is, use *constructive* criticism, rather than merely finding fault. Some athletes are very touchy. The coach has to be sure that the athlete realizes he is trying to help him, and not simply finding fault with him.

Keep the door open

Private interviews with the players are better than any other method. Players prefer to come into the coach's office and discuss their individual problems privately.

Players who are not playing, naturally, have more problems than those who are in the starting lineup. This is to be expected. A player sitting on the bench would not be a very good athlete if he did not feel he should be playing. He feels that he is better than the fellow playing, and this is the attitude the coach wants.

The problem is: "Why isn't he playing?" Well, the only thing the coach can tell this fellow is that he has no grudge against him. He likes him personally as well as anybody else on the club. However, in his own estimation, the other player has the edge. He might say: "You wouldn't want me to play you just because I liked you a little better than the other fellow."

Pep up a ball club

Personally, I prefer to have too few pep meetings than too many. Of course, in football, when a team plays only once a week, most coaches give some type of inspirational message.

On occasion, I believe it is necessary to pep up a ball club, but a coach should not try to do it too often. We have a lot of meetings, at which time we go over the hitters to determine how we want to throw to them. But as far as trying to pep up a club, there are simply too many games to do it very often. The first thing a coach knows, his pep talks are bouncing off their backs "like water off a duck."

In basketball and football, when a team plays only one game a week, the coach can start two or three days in advance and mentally build up his club. In baseball, though, a coach cannot handle his team in the same manner.

The players know whom they are playing, anyway. When we play the Giants, for instance, it is rather silly to have a pep talk because our players are already keyed up and ready to beat that team. In the World Series, the same thing holds true. It is not usually necessary for a manager to key up his club. In fact, he might be doing more harm than good.

Baseball is a game in which a team of players has to bear down and be aggressive, but at the same time, keep as relaxed and loose as possible. Surely, a coach does not want his pep talk to put his players into a nervous state. More than anything else, he has to *relax them.*

Getting the players themselves to instill spirit into the team is even more important than the manager saying such things as, "Let's go out and get them!" Spirited messages mean more coming from the players themselves.

Keep cool under pressure

I have always felt that the attitude of the coach in regard to the game will brush off and carry over to his players. If he is a nervous individual, jumping up and down at every little thing, his players may become jumpy, too.

A player has to be *relaxed,* whether it be hitting the baseball, fielding, or throwing. Of course, we would like everybody keyed up, hustling and bearing down at all times, but at the same time, under pressure, the athlete has to be relaxed.

If he wants his players to show a "desire to win" and a "never-give-up" spirit, the coach has to get this in his own mind. Then, it has a good chance of carrying over into the players themselves.

It would be silly for me to say that I do not feel the emotions and excitement of a ball game. To me, the best way of all to lessen the emotional aspects is to concentrate on the game situation. What can you do in this situation, or what is the best route to take? What might they do if I change pitchers? Whom will they counteract with? Will this guy hit and run? What do we do now?

Concentration and relaxation go together, whether it is throwing strikes or fielding ground balls.

Help the over-stimulated player

Every athlete should be a little excited and keyed up prior to a ball game, but when this brings on excessive feelings of tension and anxiety, his performance can be affected. Any way the coach can divert this player's attention away from the game to something else is usually effective. A little recreation is often helpful. Before a game, some of our fellows like to play cards, such as hearts. This helps to take their minds off the upcoming game, and sometimes this is good. However, we do not tolerate any gambling in the clubhouse.

Encourage the squad wit

It is good to have a ball player on the club who can be an outlet, the funny guy to provide a few laughs now and then. A squad clown can be particularly helpful when the work begins to become tiresome.

Jim Brewer was one of the quiet, easygoing funny guys. He said funny things at just the right time and made everybody laugh. Len Gabrielson was pretty much the same way. He was a witty character, although he did not play too much. Nobody thought of Gil Hodges as a funny guy, but the dry wit that he possessed was very pleasing to a ball club.

Of course, if a team does not have a wit, the manager or coach himself has to provide a little humor. Sometimes, just taking the pressure off can be very beneficial.

Baseball players are probably more agitators and needlers on the field than many other professional athletes. To a certain extent, this is good, unless it reaches a point where the fellows are sore at each other. But a little agitating and needling is all right.

Be impartial

The coach has to be fair to everybody and treat them all as much alike as he possibly can. There are always going to be some fellows on the team whom he personally likes better than others, but this is something he cannot show.

The better he knows his players personally, the better he will be able to get the best out of them. There will be some he will have to pat on the back, while others, he will have to kick a little.

When a coach shows favoritism or lets one player get away with little extra things here and there, he not only spoils this fellow but gains the resentment of the entire team. The first thing he knows, he is in trouble, because just one player can cause resentment. It would not be so bad if it involved only this one individual, but it could involve the whole team. One bad apple can make the whole barrel bad!

On occasion, suggestions from the players are good for a team. Sometimes, after a player has given me a suggestion, I will say: "You have told *me* what is wrong, now I am going to tell *you* what is wrong."

Or, I might ask for their suggestions by saying: "We are doing this too much. Does anybody else have any suggestions how we can do better?"

If there is a team problem, it is often good to get it out into the open so the entire team can discuss the situation. It helps to get them all talking. If a team has a leader, this is often the man who stands up and talks for the welfare of the team.

Admit your mistakes

Every coach will make mistakes occasionally. I think it does the players good sometimes, when things go wrong, if he says: "Well, I blew this one myself" or

"I made this mistake." Anyone hates to admit that he is wrong, but sometimes it is necessary for him to say to his team that, "I made an error in judgment."

Use a personal approach when cutting the squad

The toughest part of the manager's life is cutting a player. Usually, the young kids are the ones who are so energetic and so willing to listen. They probably work harder than some of the veterans. Yet, there comes a time when there is room for only twenty-five men on the ball club, and the manager has to send out this kid who has worked so hard through spring training. The boy did everything he was asked to do, and then the manager has to tell him, "We are going to send you back."

Now, the manager should be honest with him and explain to him by saying, "Look, you are just not ready." He should not make the player believe something that he does not believe himself. He has to be as honest as he possibly can, and tell the player: "We want you to go back, and this is the reason we want you to go back. Here is a plan or schedule we would like you to work on."

In addition to tacking the names of the squad on the board, I want to talk to each and every one of the individuals I had to cut off. By following this procedure, I think the coach will have a better relationship with these players later on. Who knows, some of my starters may get hurt, and I might want to recall some of the boys I dropped.

The more personal attention a coach can give his players he cut off, the better. I am sure they will respect a coach more if he has at least enough time to talk to them.

DISCIPLINE

For various reasons, some athletes need to be guided a little more than others in order to get the best out of them. I do feel, however, that a coach or manager would be better off to try to get his players to *want* to do things for the good of their own future in baseball, or for the welfare of the team.

I would much rather have them do the right things on their own than to try to be a detective and always be checking everybody. When he is the detective, the coach may catch two or three players, but there might be four or five others doing the same thing. Sure, he may find two or three, but what will happen is that they will become sore because the others were not caught. This can become a continuous thing, with the players playing "cat and mouse" with the coach. The coach might check them in one night; then, the next night, they will go out again after he has left.

A coach will be better off to get his players to do these things for the good of the team, rather than to make such rules as the exact minute or hour they have to be in at night. He should not have to tell them to do *this* and not do *that*.

If he has a "bad actor" on the club, there is no way that he can correct the situation by fines. He may fine him a time or two, but this will not likely change him. He will still cheat and do things the coach does not want him to do. It is much better if the coach can get the player to act on his own. If he cannot, then he will be better off with somebody else anyway.

A player has to learn that he cannot run the show. No coach should ever let a player run him. Somebody has to be boss, and the sooner the player knows that, the better off he is.

The coach should want to get a player started off on the right foot. He is like the kid growing up. The sooner he is disciplined, the better. Once he gets out of hand, it will be very tough to win him back.

Again, the best approach is to get him to do as much as he possibly can on his own. Then, if he does not do it, the manager can resort to fines and the coach can sit him on the bench or ask for his uniform. This alternative, though, should come only as the last resort.

"You should put your arm around them once in a while," continued Bobby Winkles. "They like to have the feeling of an arm around them. They may not be getting that at home. They want and need a little affection. Heck, they are *kids*. Even my guys in college are that way."

In disciplining a ball club, everybody should be treated alike. True, everyone is a different individual, and when he talks to his players, the coach does not talk to everyone the same way. However, as far as rules are concerned, each and every player must abide by the *same* set of rules.

Meeting a problem head-on

Whenever a problem arises, the coach must meet it head-on. He cannot back up. The players try to test him by trying little things, but once he has made a decision, he should not back down one iota. Take a fine; if he decides to fine a player, he must go ahead and take the money and not give it back.

On occasion, though, I have given a fine back, near the end of the season, if the offense did not happen again. I might say: "Well, if it does not happen again, you will get it back. You'd better prove to me that you want to do what is right, or the money stays where it is."

When a coach has to resort to disciplinary action, or when upset over the conduct of a player, it might be advisable to wait until the next day. Of course, the particular situation will often dictate how he handles the troublemaker. It might have been a tough ball game, everybody is disgusted and the player himself had a bad day. If they get together at that time, with the coach sore, he will likely say more than what he should say. The player, being upset, is liable to sass him more than he should.

By the next day, both the coach and player have cooled off, and now they can sit down and talk rationally about the problem and come to a better agreement. There are times when the coach has to handle the situation right at that moment, but 99 percent of the time, he should wait until the next day.

Missing practices

When a player misses too many practices, the first thing I do is start looking for somebody else in his place. Very likely, he has not enough desire to play the game to improve to the point where he will be a winning ball player. This is often the player who has all the ability, and the coach does not want to lose him, so he coaxes him along. However, when the season is over, the coach may be better off to get a player who is not quite so good but who does not miss practice. The dependable player probably has more desire to improve, and by the end of the season, may be a better ball player than the one who has to be continually coaxed.

If a coach has to keep coaxing his players to do something, it does not help too much. The more he coaxes them, the more of it they expect and the more independent they are going to be. The sooner he lets them know that the world will go on without them—that there will still be the game of baseball, whether they play or not—the better off it will be for everyone concerned.

Late for practice

As for the player who keeps coming in late for practice, I would recommend that the coach put him on the bench and leave him there. Or, he might take his uniform away for a day or so, and see if he is interested enough to come back with the knowledge that he will get to practice when everyone else gets there.

Here, we are sometimes concerned with the star performer who knows he is good and wants to have a few extra privileges. Frankly, I do not think you can have very good team morale when you have special privileges for certain players. As a team, everybody is supposed to have the same privileges. *This* is the ball player I do not particularly admire.

Missing curfew

Laying down curfew rules for college and high school athletes is a little different from big-league rules, because they play mostly day games. Here, again, I would rather employ the honor system and not be the detective. I do not believe in checking in closets and under beds and knocking on people's doors at night, except as a last resort.

I would prefer them to want to keep in shape and do good for themselves and the team. Then, if they are not willing to sacrifice here and there and stay in condition, they are not the ball players I need on my club. They should realize that, in order to be pennant-winning ball players, they must be in top condition.

According to Winkles, parents should be encouraged to help the baseball coach with curfew at the high school level. "If you set down a curfew, a parent should make sure that the kid is home," said Bobby. "I would put an obligation on the parent to call me if the kid is not in at a particular time."

The problem of "senioritis"

Some athletic teams experience the situation in which the senior feels he has the club "made." As a result, he does not put out quite so hard. He is late for practice a time or two, and it is evident he does not have the old desire and zeal for the game. As to how a coach can handle this situation, I feel there is nothing better than for a junior or sophomore to take his place a time or two to get him back in line.

Post-championship complacency

Some ball clubs, after winning a championship, have a tendency to become complacent. In high school and college, it depends on how easy the championship was won and the individual players themselves. In professional ball, very seldom do the players become complacent. Playing against pros, they know how tough they are.

Actually, though, the word "complacent" is sometimes overrated. Very few players become complacent, at least among the good athletes. *As soon as an athlete is satisfied with his performance, that is when he stops improving.*

Handling a player's temper tantrum

Several years back, I sent up a pinch-hitter for a light-hitting third baseman, who then showed his indignation by staging a temper tantrum in the dugout in front of the entire team.

There are, of course, two sides to this type of situation. From the player's standpoint, he *should* want to hit in a tight situation and feel that he can drive in the run. However, when he outwardly shows his disgust at the decision by the manager or coach to take him out, this becomes a situation no manager can tolerate. He is indicating in a way that *he* wants the glory, and he is not the team man that the manager wants. After a brief confrontation with the player to settle him down, it might be good to call a meeting of the entire team to prevent a similar situation.

The proper attitude for a hitter who is replaced is to come back and offer some encouragement to the player who takes his place. Only by this type of team spirit can a ball club win the extra games. *It has to be a team unit.*

Dropping a player from the squad

Dropping a boy from the squad for training rule violations should be the last resort in disciplinary action. Sometimes, the coach will drop the player permanently, while at other times, he may suspend him for a week or ten days and hope he has cured the individual.

When a coach has to deal that severely with disciplinary problems, he has a player who does not really want to excel enough to be worth the trouble.

Unfortunately, this may be the individual who has the natural ability. If he wanted to play badly enough, he could be outstanding.

PROPER MENTAL ATTITUDE

Mental attitude plays a tremendous role in the success of a baseball player. An athlete can have great natural ability but will never reach his potential unless he can develop a proper mental attitude. The ball player with the right frame of mind will make his natural ability work.

If a team *thinks* it can win, it will have a much better chance to win. This is the attitude we try to instill in our players. To achieve our objective, we use as much encouragement and suggestive power as we can.

Positive thinking on the part of the player is so important. To be a good hitter, he must feel he can hit, and to be a successful base runner, he has to have the confidence that he can steal a base. There is no other way.

When he takes the field, a ball player's thoughts should be strictly *baseball*. He can groove his mind and body to perform a skill only by concentration. He must be alert and thinking *every minute*.

When a pitcher is in a jam, rather than getting excited, we want him looking for a way to get out of it—such as using a pick-off play. We try to get our players to think out there, and think positive. This is why we drill on pick-off plays and all the other fundamental plays. Then, they repeat them over and over again until they become conditioned to the various moves and actions.

Relaxation is essential in acquiring skill and perfection. Actually, concentration and relaxation go together, whether it be throwing strikes or fielding ground balls. By concentrating on what he is doing, an athlete can remove tension and fear from his mind, and replace them with a confident mind and relaxed body.

Six Qualities of a Good Athlete

There are six basic qualities in a good athlete. They are:

1. Willingness to take coaching and study baseball
2. A spirit of competition in practice and in games
3. An intense desire to win, and to accept nothing less than victory
4. Willingness to practice hard at all times
5. Willingness to make sacrifices for the team
6. A desire to improve himself on and off the field.

The real competitor

Every coach would like to have the athlete who has the ability to concentrate when he must bear down a little extra hard. He is the competitor who will punish himself when he has to give that 100 percent. He is willing to put in a lot of work, not only on his strong points but on his weaknesses as well. Very few athletes have been able to get to the top without punishing themselves to a certain extent.

If he wants to excel, an athlete has to do the extra things that the average fellow will not do. It is easy to hustle when a player is hitting .300 or so. The player I look for is the fellow who is willing and able to kick himself and put forth with more hustle when things go bad. *This* is the test of a winning ball player—not when he is a front-runner. When a player is not hitting, he should hustle even more.

Tough in the clutch

There are certain ball players who seem to be better hitters in the clutch. The more intense the situation, the better they are. Others just seem to be born losers. I believe this all gets back to the mental aspect of believing that they can win and wanting to win, and putting forth that 110 percent of effort.

The other fellow is more or less defeated before he goes up to bat, and thinks: "This is a tough situation, and the pitcher will likely get me out," and he usually does.

Those who have the ability to hit in the clutch actually want the bat when a game is on the line, "These are situations that stimulate you," said Steve Garvey. "I consider it a challenge to face a good pitcher in a pressure situation. I enjoy the competition."

"I don't believe I could ever think of hitting a baseball as pressure," said Pete Rose. "Hitting is the best thing I can do in life. It's not pressure . . . it's fun!"

Every manager or coach wants the winning type of ball player. He wants the athlete who is at his best when the chips are down, or the fellow who does not tighten-up in a tight situation.

Quite often, the chief difference between the winner and the also-ran is the willingness of the winner to punish himself. We like the player who can put forth that little extra and still be relaxed during the crucial moments of the ball game. Sometimes I believe the game is as much mental as it is physical.

Courage

One of the great qualities of an outstanding athlete is being able to give his very best when he is in a slump or has lost some tough games. Instead of giving up and saying: "Well, they are too good for us," a ball club has this "bulldog" in the lineup who will not quit. This is the type of player a manager or coach is looking for. He is the fellow who will pull the team out of its slump.

Having the capability to come from behind is a tremendous attribute in an athlete. These are the players the coach needs when he is in trouble.

In addition to the coaches and manager, certain team leaders can play key roles in getting their team to bounce back. They can do it on the bench by saying: "We will get this guy, just keep pecking away at him." The first thing they know, they are back in the game. Now, if they can get a break or two, they have a chance.

Whether they won the games or not, the important thing is that they did not quit when the score was nine to one. They went ahead and got four or five more runs, which indicated they did not quit.

Pride

The great athletes have a tremendous desire to excel, the urge to be the best. They take pride in their play. They hurt when they lose. Too many athletes are satisfied with fair or good performances, when they could do better with more effort.

An athlete should always be striving for perfection. He must never be content with mediocrity. When a coach has players who take real pride in being champions, his team will always be tough to beat!

Competition

A good baseball player welcomes competition. Most people do not compete enough—they give up too easily. They never press on. If a player is to play to his true potential, he must be willing to put out just a little more. This willingness to put out a little more than the opponents often makes the difference.

"Rather than talking about winning to the kids, I emphasize competing," said George "Sparky" Anderson. "I just hate to see all the pressure on players when their coaches talk so much about winning. I prefer to tell my players to go out and compete and give the best they have got—total effort."

Every manager or coach wants the winning type of ballplayer. He wants the athlete who is at his best when the chips are down, or the fellow who does not tighten up in a tight situation. A good clutch player is one who can put forth that little extra and still be relaxed during the crucial moments of a ball game.

Profanity

Cussing, the use of profane words, has no place on an athletic field, and the coach must not permit abusive language of any type. Actually, swearing is a sign of weakness, an admission that the individual cannot control his emotions, and shows the lack of vocabulary necessary for expressing himself in a socially acceptable manner.

Fig. 11.6 An occasional laugh or funny moment prior to an important game can be good for a ball team in breaking the tension. Here, manager Whitey Herzog, loosens things up with a little humor with catcher Jamie Quirk of the Cardinals. Along with humor, a little agitating and needling can be good for a ball club. It keeps everybody alive and on their toes.

Self-discipline

If he wants to win and play his best, a baseball player must discipline his life—he must lay off smoking, drinking, overeating, or anything that keeps him from doing his best.

To be mentally tough, an athlete must show a tremendous amount of self-discipline. He must *never* break the discipline of his mind. There have been athletes with great physical qualities, but who could not control their tempers.

Intelligence

Baseball today requires a considerable amount of intelligence—game smart-ness, the ability to learn offensive and defensive plays well, and then apply that knowledge to the proper situation.

Therefore, a player must study hard, not only on the field but in the school classrooms as well. He must keep up his grades, and remember that his primary interest is education and baseball is secondary. Besides, a college scholarship or a lucrative professional contract might be at stake. Players who let down in their studies are usually the ones who let down in a game.

A hard worker

Occasionally, a manager or coach will come in contact with a player with just ordinary ability who literally "works his tail off." I can remember Bobby Lillis, who finally made it to the big leagues after a lengthy stint in the minor leagues. Here is a fellow who did everything as hard as he could. He worked and hustled all the time. He worked on everything that he possibly could work on. He lived cleanly and obeyed all training rules. Although he was never able to be an outstanding ball player, he has demonstrated outstanding leadership qualities as a coach and manager of the Houston Astros.

The most disgusting thing is to observe a player with a lot of natural ability who is not willing to work hard enough and is not willing to apply himself to the job. As a result, the coach ends up with another good athlete with just mediocre ability who continues to get into trouble. Sometimes, he would be better off without this player.

The superstitious athlete

As long as there are athletic events, I imagine there will always be some silly little superstitions. Frankly, I do not see any harm in this, unless it gets out of hand.

We all agree that acts of superstition do not help anyone, but as long as a player wants to engage in them and believes they help him, we let him go ahead and "do his thing." If nothing else, he will display a positive approach. For instance, if a player feels he has made so many base hits wearing a certain sweatshirt, he usually will wear it out before changing to another one.

How to take a defeat

A ball player should feel the same way the manager does after a loss. *He should hate to lose!* It is not good for anybody to take a loss lightly. However, when he loses and he feels he has done the very best he can, he should not let it carry over into tomorrow's game. The other club has just outplayed his team. In other words, a ball player should forget about the defeat and start fresh. When he plays again, he should be even more determined to correct his mistakes and concentrate on winning this next one.

This does not mean that there should be any joking and laughter in the locker room following a defeat. This sometimes occurs in amateur ball, when an individual or two mistakenly take a defeat too lightly. In pro ball, we do not run into this very often. If we do, the coach should just go up to the players and ask, "What was the score of the ball game?" This can cut them down a little bit. Each situation, of course, demands a different approach.

After managing the Dodgers for twenty-three years, did defeat come any easier? No, it was always the same—you *always* hate to lose. In some respects, though, it was tougher to lose with a good team than it was with a bad one. If a manager or coach has a poor team, he cannot expect to win as much.

Perhaps the worst thing for a losing manager to do is try to secondguess himself. He will say, "I should have bunted here rather than going for the hit and run." This is the kind of thing that hurts. Or, perhaps somebody has made a mental mistake and has cost him the ball game. These losses hurt more than those in which the other club outhits or outpitches his team.

These situations are bound to occur, but as long as he has done the very best that he possibly can and his team has played as well as it possibly can, fretting and stewing will not help the situation one bit. Even though these moments can be severe, they should not carry on into the night and into the following day or week.

12
Team
Offense

The best teams in baseball during the last two decades have had power and speed. One complements the other. Many teams today have moved in the direction of speed. As Oakland A's manager Steve Boros remarked, "Home run hitters go into slumps, but legs never do." You can do so much more when you have players who can run."

"A manager has to choose between power and speed," said George "Sparky" Anderson, "and he has to go for speed. Pitching today has become so special that the team at bat doesn't dare consider the big inning. He has to score piecemeal with his legs. He must go for the players who steal and who take the extra base on a hit."

Tommy Lasorda doesn't place as much premium on speed as Anderson does. "There is no way you'll get me to knock good base running," explained Lasorda, "but if I had to choose between power or speed, I would take power. If a batter beats out a hit and steals second, you've got no assurance he is going to score. But when a man hits one out of the park, you've got a guaranteed run."

Lasorda was asked: "But how often can a man hit one out of the park?"

Fig. 12.1 AN AGGRESSIVE ATTACK, the best offense in baseball, exerts continual pressure on the defense. This has been the trademark of some of the most successful major league teams in history, including our championship Dodger clubs. They have combined power at the plate with speed and aggressiveness on the bases.

Tommy replied: "And how often are base runners thrown out? The record books don't tell you how many rabbits are cut down trying to stretch a single into a double."

As Harry Dalton explains the debate, "Clubs go through strange cycles. For a while, they get heated up on speed, than they shift back to power. There is no formula that can be applied to producing a winning team. That's because the amount of talent available is limited. The manager has to go for the best players. Sometimes they have power, sometimes they have speed. Swiftness afoot characterizes the top teams in baseball today."

An aggressive attack, capable of exerting continual pressure on the defense, is the best offense in baseball.

TYPES OF OFFENSE

The type of offense used depends entirely on the type of club the manager or coach has, whether it is a power or a speed club. The type of pitching that he has is another determining factor. If I have a real fine pitching staff, for example, four or five outstanding pitchers the likes of Sandy Koufax and Don Drysdale, then I know the opponent is not going to score too many runs.

If I have a club that lacks good power, I am more inclined to sacrifice or play for one run earlier in the game than I would if I had a weaker pitching staff. Therefore, the offense is more or less determined not only by the type of hitters but also by whom the coach has pitching for him.

The manager or coach often tries to estimate how many runs his opponent is going to get. If someone like Koufax is pitching, I will say: "OK, let's bunt in the first inning, or steal the base, try to get one run, and hope that we can hold it."

Now, it there is somebody else pitching, and we are playing a team that scores a lot of runs, I might say: "Well, they are going to score three or four runs, so we have to go for a bigger inning." Therefore, I would play my offense differently.

A team that lacks the home run hitters should have players who are able to bunt, drag, and push, and have all sorts of ways to bring the infield in. With the infield in, the offense has a better chance to hit the ball past the infielders for a base hit.

The home run is a great weapon. I wish we had a few more. But if the manager does not have this type of hitter, he has to go the other way. In fact, good pitching generally can handle good home run hitters because they are free-swingers. They either hit the ball out of the park, or they hit into a double play, or strike out. With the infield back, they are not as much of a threat as is the hitter who slaps the ball around and can bunt, drag, and run.

Hitting away is not the only way to score runs. Bunting, the steal, hit-and-run, run-and-hit, and the squeeze play can all advance runners to scoring position or score them. In a close game, when one run can mean victory, the advancement of a base runner can be a significant factor in the outcome.

The ability to move runners along is a requisite for a winning ball team. With a runner on second and nobody out, the hitter has to get him to third. If he can't hit behind the runner, he has to bunt him over. With a runner on third base and less than two outs, the batter must get him home. To be a winner, a team must do this very well.

Emphasis on power and speed

Major league clubs today, are emphasizing power and speed. "If a team has power and good hitters, it will hit away," explained Steve Boros. "If a team has speed, it will run with them—either steal or hit-and-run. Unless we get late in the ball game, we really don't utilize the bunt that much. In the American League with the designated hitters, teams are going more and more to either the running or the hitting game in a bunt situation. Many coaches and managers today refuse to give that out, and they prefer moving the runners around some other way."

AN AGGRESSIVE OFFENSE

Basically, the more aggressive a team can be, the more successful it will be (Fig. 12.2). This starts with the hitter himself. The hitter has to be aggressive and believe that every pitch is going to be a strike. He should start after every pitch and be able to hold back if the pitch is a ball.

Then, he must run hard from the moment he hits the ball until he rounds first base or second and is stopped by the play. His own judgment may force him to stop, or the coach may hold him up.

As soon as he is on first base, the base runner immediately has to "think positive" that he might be able to steal second. When he gets the sign, he must be ready with his lead and break quickly with the proper cross-over step. If the hitter gets a hit behind him, he should not be satisfied in stopping at second; but should go to third or as far as he can go within reason. *He must be aggressive all the way.*

An aggressive offense has many advantages over the team that plays conservative, safe baseball.

The offense must exert continual pressure on the defense, and in doing so, they force mistakes. When a top base stealing threat such as Rickey Henderson

Fig. 12.2 HIT-AND-RUN. Baseball teams, increasingly, are emphasizing a smart, fast-running offense, built around the hit-and-run, the steal, the bunt, and the squeeze play. Here, Andre Dawson (#3 hitter) and Tim Raines (lead-off man) of the Montreal Expos team up together on a hit-and-run play.

gets on first base, he can exert considerable pressure on the pitcher. The pitcher will say to himself: "I've got to throw over there three or four times. I've got to rush my delivery." He becomes so concerned about the man on first stealing second that he gets behind the hitter. In addition, this concern takes a little concentration away from the pitcher, which is very helpful.

When the base runner gets on first base, the outfielders are thinking: "With this man on first, the chances are that he will be going to third. If the ball is hit to me, I have really got to charge this ground ball and hurry up my throw." And so, this type of aggressiveness and pressure rushes the defense into misplays and errors.

An aggressive hitter goes after the ball. He really wants to go after it, and, if it is in the strike zone, he will swing at it. If it is not in the strike zone, it is like seeing the red light on the street. Everything is green and his foot is on the gas until he sees the red light. Then he has to stop. With practice, this becomes a reflex action, but the most important attributes of an aggressive hitter is that he starts after every pitch and really wants to hit it. This is the attitude a hitter should have.

Pressure on the defense

An effective running game, sparked by well-executed bunts, the steal, and hit-and-run, and highlighted occasionally by the exciting squeeze play, can place considerable pressure on the defense. The drag bunt, clever and daring base running, and skillful sliding are methods and techniques that develop the fast-moving situations that cause mechanical and mental errors by the defense.

Indeed, an aggressive offense has many advantages over the team which plays conservative, safe baseball. The threat of a steal will often cause pitchers to lose their concentration on the hitter, while the threat of a bunt will bring in the infield, decreasing their fielding coverage. Thus, the element of threats can be effective in keeping the defense off-balance and unsettled.

There is nothing nicer to see than a player getting a base hit and rounding the base at full speed. When he decides to stop, he almost slides his wheels and goes back. If he rounds the base properly and the outfielder just juggles the ball, he may keep going right into second base. These are the things that can get that one or two extra runs a team needs to win.

True, there are times when the runner is thrown out. It looks bad in these instances but, percentagewise over the season, this aggressive style of play pays off. Certainly, the coach finds it easier to slow his runners down and make them a little more cautious than to make them more aggressive.

An early lead

One of the pleasant aspects of baseball is that, if a team can get out in front early in the game, the coach can do so many things. He can hit-and-run, steal, or sacrifice if he is a run or two in front. But as soon as he gets behind three or four runs, he cannot do so many things. He can neither take wild chances nor can he keep the pressure on the defense. So, he has to sit around and wait until his team collects three or four hits in a row.

IMPORTANCE OF SPEED

Speed is as extremely valuable offensively, as it is defensively. To win today, a baseball team has to run the bases, take good leads, and go from first to third. The player with speed has a greater advantage in beating out the infield hit. He will go from first to third on 90 percent of the base hits, more so than the slow-footed fellow who has to stop at second. The runner at second base with good speed is difficult to throw out at home plate.

Some of baseball's best teams have achieved success largely on exceptional speed. The Dodgers have played, and still play, for one run, using the hit-and-run, the steal, and the bunting game. The runner at second may steal third and score on an infield ground ball. Actually, a team may go this route the entire game and be able to pick up three or four runs from these tactics.

However, it has to be a team that has speed, can bunt, and is able to move the ball around, such as with the hit-and-run play and hitting to the opposite field.

Whitey Herzog, who was largely responsible for developing the 1969 Mets, the Kansas City Royals, and the St. Louis Cardinals, has never placed emphasis on power. He is always looking for speed. "I don't mind having some power hitters who can play defense," explained Whitey. "You got to have a little bit of both, but I figure I must have four or five guys who can run and play their position good."

"With a speed team like the Cardinals," said Herzog, "if we're down two runs going into the eighth, we still may try to steal. That way if we get the steal, we would score on a single and stay out of a double play. Every time you steal a base, you generally only need one hit to score a run," said Herzog. "If you don't steal, you need two hits. I think it's easier to steal a base than it is to get two hits."

Team lineups today are sprinkled with swift runners who can steal and take the extra base on a hit. Speed can unnerve both the pitcher and the fielders. Speed also changes defensive alignments. By forcing pitchers to throw more fast balls, it gives batters better pitches to hit.

Aggressive attitude

Building an aggressive attitude, offensively and defensively, should be the prime concern of the coach or manager. An aggressive offense is particularly demoralizing to a high school team. Quite frequently, the team that scores first breaks the opponent's spirit.

A high school team cannot rely consistently on the hitting prowess of their top hitters in a scoring situation. Instead, the coach must develop techniques and plays, such as the steal, to compensate for his team's uncertain hitting and to support scoring potential.

The aggressive, positive type of coach who takes the initiative and employs the elements of surprise and deception in his offense can achieve considerable advantage.

BATTING ORDER

The forming of a batting order is not as simple as it seems. The manager or coach must arrange his batting order according to the players he has available. He should try to balance his lineup so that the attack is as strong as possible from the lead-off man through the ninth hitter.

The lead-of man should have a good "on base" average; he should be a fairly good hitter, although not necessarily a long ball hitter. He is the type of hitter who has a good eye and does not swing at bad balls. Possessing good speed, he should have two or three ways to get on base.

The lead-off man must get on base. The 1982 world champions St. Louis

Cardinals had a very revealing statistic. When their lead-off man walked, he scored 42 percent of the time. Any manager will settle for almost half a run for every time he gets the lead-off man on.

The number two man should have the bat control to hit-and-run and go behind the runner. He must be a man who can lay the ball down if the sacrifice is needed. He should be able to pull the ball if he has to, or go the other way when the occasion calls for it. Some managers feel there is an advantage in having a left-handed swinger in the number two spot. If he is a left-handed hitter, he can hit the ball through the hole. The right-handed swinger should be encouraged to go to right field.

The number three and four men, of course, are the power hitters. If these players have equal ability, I would prefer my left-handed batter to hit third, feeling that, if either of my first two men got on base, he would have the hole at first base to hit through. Ideally, the number three man should be a left-handed hitter who can pull the ball and have the power to drive in a few runs.

Generally, the number three man is faster than the number four hitter. I like to have my speed up in front. The number four hitter would be the RBI man

Fig. 12.3 A GOOD LEAD-OFF HITTER is able to get on base often. Pete Rose is one of the greatest lead-off batters the game has ever seen. Possessing good bat control, he consistently makes contact with the ball, and, going with the pitch, he can drive the ball to all fields.

who has the most power. He should be the hitter who occasionally can hit one out of the park. There is not a great deal of difference between the four and five hitters. The number six man is the next power hitter, although not as good as the three, four, or five men.

The seventh, eighth, and ninth positions are filled with the three weakest hitters playing. As a rule, the pitcher will bat in the ninth position, but the catcher is not always necessarily the eighth man in the lineup. In high school, and sometimes in college play, the pitcher may be one of the better hitters on the team.

OFFENSIVE TACTICS

Hit-and-run

The hit-and-run is one of the greatest plays in baseball, but it requires a hitter with good bat control to hit the ball through the hole. He should be told to hit the ball on the ground. If he cannot get a piece of the ball, the runner will likely be thrown out by the catcher. This is because, on the hit-and-run, the base runner does not get the daring lead that he would if he were stealing.

When the hit-and-run is on, the manager will say: "I need a run, so I am going to sacrifice a little of my hitter's power in order to get the runner to second or third base."

There have been some fine right-handed hitters who could go to the opposite field and had the bat control to go to the spot the fielder was leaving. If the coach does not have this type of hitter at the plate, he should tell the batter to just be sure to get a piece of the ball and hit it on the ground. If he hits it in the air, everything is lost.

While the runner at first can be bunted over, the right type of hitter can accomplish more by hitting the ball into right field, thereby ending up with men on first and third. Besides, defenses against the bunt have become so formidable that many big-league managers are employing the hit-and-run more than they did in the past.

The purpose of the hit-and-run play is to advance the runner an extra base and to protect him from the double play. It is often used in the middle or late stages of the game. It is a good play when the pitcher is behind the batter, especially on the three-and-one pitch. With a runner on first base, the right-handed hitter will often try to hit the ball behind the runner, thinking the second baseman will cover. The batter must swing at the ball wherever it is pitched, even if he has to throw the bat at it.

"Executing the hit-and-run takes a certain knack on the part of the hitter," said Bobby Hofman. "You must work on it. You have to wait until the ball gets to the plate. Bill Rigney taught me just to keep my right elbow into my side so I cannot get the bat out in front of my body. You lead with your hands. The hands are out in front and you just try to hit the ball to right field."

If the catcher guesses and calls for a pitchout, the offense, of course, is in trouble. If a wild pitcher is on the mound, a manager is a little reluctant to put the hit-and-run on.

Run-and-hit

Instead of hitting behind the runner, the hitter simply tries to hit the ball, which for young, inexperienced players, is an easier skill to execute. The run-and-hit can cause many problems for the defense, such as breaking up a double play with a slow runner at first.

A good time to call for a run-and-hit is when the pitcher is behind in the count (2 and 0, 3 and 1, or 3 and 2), because he must come in with the pitch. The runner should be on the move, and the hitter is instructed to go for the ball if it is in the strike zone. The run-and-hit is used more with a fast runner on base. If the pitch is out of the strike zone, the runner has a chance to steal a base.

The hitter should know that the runner is going, and if it is in the strike zone, "I am going to be cutting." The worst thing that can happen on a run-and-hit is for the runner to go and then have the hitter take the pitch right down the middle.

Hitting behind the runner

When the situation is right, some managers prefer hitting behind the runner rather than employing the bunt or a hit-and-run play. This offensive tactic is usually attempted when only first base is occupied and there are less than two out.

In an effort to advance the runner on first to second base, the hitter tries to hit the ball on the ground between the first and second baseman. The runner will break for second. Many times, there is a lot of space in there to hit the ball behind the runner. The batter should attempt just to meet the ball. Right-handed hitters find it effective to go after an outside pitch.

With a man on second base, the manager will usually try to advance him to third base. With the bunt play proving not as successful as it used to be, many teams will have the batter go to the opposite field. The batter should try to hit the ball on the ground.

Hit the ball to the opposite field

The batter who has the short, quick stroke and quick wrists is the fellow who is likely to have the bat control necessary to hit the ball consistently to the opposite field. Whether this is hand-and-eye coordination or what, some hitters have it and some do not.

The double play is a great morale booster for the defensive team. That is why I want my players to find a way to hit the ball to the opposite field. By doing so, the batter is hitting *away* from the double play, and, more important, we have runners on first and third with only one out.

Getting a run with an out

One of baseball's unsung heroes is the hitter who is capable of getting a run with an out. With a man on first or second base, he can hit the ball consistently to right field, moving the runner around.

When that one run is so important, the hitter should actually sacrifice himself in order to score the run. All he has to do is hit the ball on the ground.

Therefore, a hitter should know how to make himself be put out. He must be able to ground the ball to the second baseman, especially when the infield is not in. He has to concentrate all the time to "Get the run! Get the run!"

If the first man doubles, the next man should ground the ball to second base, moving the runner to third.

If a left-handed hitter comes up with a man on first base, he should not even dare to think of hitting the ball to left field. For two reasons, he has to think about driving the ball through that hole. If he singles to right field, we are on first and third. If he singles to left field, we are on first and second, and still in jeopardy. But, if we have a man on third base, then *they* are in jeopardy because, now, we can get a run with an out.

Run-and-bunt play

This play is a variation of the sacrifice bunt, in which the base runner attempts a steal of the next base. To protect the runner, the hitter must bunt the ball regardless of where it is pitched.

On occasion, the run-and-bunt play is used more or less as a surprise tactic. With the bunt in order, the first baseman charges in, and as he moves in quickly, it is difficult for him to know whether or not the runner has left. Under ordinary circumstances, he will make the force play at second, but the man at first is already running and often beats the throw. This play can be dangerous, however. If the hitter pops the ball up, misses it completely, or it is a bad pitch, the runner might get thrown out.

We feel it is a good play, though. I am disappointed that we have failed to employ this play often enough. To combat the defense that teams are putting up against the bunt today, I believe it is a play that should be used more and more.

The skilled bunter and speedy runner at first can put the run-and-bunt play on with amazing results. The bunter bunts the ball to third and makes the third baseman field the ball. The runner just keeps on going, and if the third baseman is not alert, or the catcher is slow in covering third, he has an occasional chance to go to third base with one out. This was Pepper Martin's favorite play—but the bunter has to make the *third baseman* field the ball.

A good time to execute this play is when the pitcher is behind in the count, and therefore more likely to make the next pitch a strike. The best game situation is with none out and a runner on first base.

SQUEEZE PLAY

The safety and suicide squeeze plays are usually tried in the late innings with a runner on third base, one out, and the team at bat ahead, tied, or no more than one run behind.

Suicide squeeze

I like the suicide better than the safety squeeze. If a team is going to squeeze, they should go ahead and squeeze. One of the dangers of the suicide squeeze is that, if the runner leaves too soon or gives the play away in any way, the first thing the pitcher will do is knock the hitter down. The hitter, or course, does not have a chance to bunt the ball, and the runner will very likely be tagged out at the plate.

Instead, the runner should wait until the pitcher's front foot hits the dirt, or until his arm starts coming through. Then, he cannot change the direction of his pitch. Now, it is up to the hitter to bunt the ball on the ground. It does not have to be a good bunt, merely on the ground, not too hard, but toward the pitcher.

Fig. 12.4 A QUICK START is essential on a suicide squeeze, but the runner does not break for home until the pitcher starts his stride toward the plate (or until the front foot touches the ground). The runner at third base (Jeff Cox) has to be leaning in the direction of the plate with a walking lead, taking a step or two up the line, and having his weight going forward. As soon as the pitcher's throwing arm and hand are by his head, he will change gears and go into a run.

Many bunters, in this situation, try to lay down a perfect bunt. But the ball rolls foul and it defeats their purpose. If the runner starts at the proper time, all that is necessary is for the ball to be bunted on the ground in fair territory.

To make sure nobody fouls up on his play, a "hold" sign is often given to the hitter, to be sure he gets it. He might answer by picking up dirt and tossing it, pulling his belt, or using any simple signal .

Safety squeeze

The runner at third base should make his move *only* if the ball is bunted on the ground. If the ball is popped up or missed, the runner does not go.

A speedy runner should be on third when the safety squeeze is employed, because the runner must not start too soon. He waits to see where the ball is bunted, and then takes off.

Fig. 12.5 A VARIED ARRAY OF BUNTS, if used skillfully, can exert the type of pressure that has an unsettling effect on the defense. Here, Jim Wohlford practices bunting for a base hit. He pushes the bunt just hard enough between the pitcher and the first baseman to prevent the pitcher from fielding the ball.

The ball is not bunted unless the pitch is a good one. The runner will try to score only if he thinks he can make it. A quick start is essential for the runner on third base.

As I said earlier, I do not like the safety squeeze as well as the suicide. It involves "negative" thinking: "I am not *sure,* but I will give it a try." The first thing the manager knows, his runner is bluffed back to third, or is thrown out. If he is going to squeeze, he should go ahead: "You either do it or you don't!"

BUNTING

The bunting game is still an important part of a team's offensive strategy. Normally, the bunt is not used in the early innings of a game. In these innings, most teams play for a big inning and do not sacrifice an out. Of course, a bunt has more chance of working when the play is unexpected.

In addition to being an effective weapon to move runners around, the bunt can be a surprise tactic to cross up the defense. Players today are getting better each day at faking the bunt and then swinging the bat. This tends to keep the third baseman and the first baseman back just a little, and it helps.

The ideal time for a squeeze play is with one out. If a manager has a good base runner on third and a pitcher is at the plate, he might try to squeeze him in. If he lets the pitcher hit, he will more than likely strike out or hit a double play. So, he has the pitcher lay one down.

Or, if the winning or tying run is on first base, the coach might want to get his runner down to second base and, in addition, score the man from third. So, he tries to bunt him over. He will tell his pitcher to bunt the ball down the third base line, with the idea of getting this runner to second base. As the third baseman comes in to field the ball, the runner at third should follow him in just a step or two behind him. If he throws to first base, a fast runner might have a good chance to score. Actually, this is not a squeeze play. The offense is just trying to get the man to second and not hit into a double play.

Sacrifice bunt

The key rule in executing the sacrifice bunt is for the hitter to *give himself up.* On the straight sacrifice bunt, the batter attempts to bunt the ball only if the pitch is a strike.

Late in a ball game, with the score tied or the team one run behind, the manager probably wants to move over his runner on first base. He tells his hitter to bunt the ball down the first base line, because the first baseman has to hold the man on. Besides, the third baseman very likely would be right on top of the bunter.

To have the best chance at all to get the man over, the bunter has to bunt the ball down the first base line. Of course, first basemen today often cheat a little and start running in before the pitcher releases the ball, so unless the base runner can take an extra step or two to counteract this, he could be in trouble.

Bunt for a hit

Since the sacrifice style of bunting would alert the infielders, a hitter should not square around toward the pitcher until the very last instant. The drag bunt and push bunt are both attempts at a base hit.

In bunting for a base hit, the hitter must know where the first baseman and third baseman are playing—if they are playing deep or shallow, and whether they are expecting the play. Some pitchers fall off the mound, so, if a right-hander falls off toward first, the bunt should be directed toward third base. If a left-hander keeps falling off to the left, the drag bunt could be aimed at the first baseman, in hopes that the bunter can beat the pitcher to first base.

A "hard bunt" or "slap bunt," is when the hitter squares around to bunt, but, instead, just slaps the ball. This is a pretty good challenge against the charging bunt defenses being used now.

BASE RUNNING

Base running is controlled by the game situation. The number of outs, the score, the ability of the base runner, and the fielder's arm are factors that determine whether or not the runner attempts to advance. The batter and base runner must be alert to react quickly to passed balls, overthrows, and errors.

Some pitchers have a good move to first base but a slow delivery. In this case, the runner cannot take as big a lead but he can still steal because he steals on the delivery. Other pitchers have a quicker delivery but a poor move to first base. Here, the runner should try to take a bigger lead because, when he throws to the plate, there won't be as much time.

A pitcher who varies his tactics can be tough to steal on. He may quick-pitch occasionally. Next, he will come to a set and then wait a long time before his pitch. On the next pitch, he will come in quickly.

Home to first

Base running begins at home plate. The ability to start quickly and get into running stride often spells the difference between a "safe" and an "out" call. No matter which side of the plate he swings from, the hitter should try to take his first step with the rear foot. He must go hard for first, looking only at the bag, unless the coach signals or calls that the ball is through and for him to take his turn.

There is nothing more disgusting than to see the batter hit the ball to the outfield or infield, and then watch the ball, and not put out full effort in going to first base. The infielder fumbles the ball, picks it up, and throws the hitter out by half a step. Whereas, if he had run the moment he hit the ball to first base, he would have been safe by a full step.

A fast, intelligent base runner can place tremendous pressure on a pitcher.

There is no excuse for a player not to run to first base. The only exception would be a pitcher at bat, on a hot day, in the seventh or eighth inning, after a tough inning of pitching. I would excuse him sometimes, *but no one else.*

The steal

If a team can use the steal successfully, they can eliminate the sacrifice. By stealing the base, the coach is much better off because, now, he does not have to sacrifice to *get* him there.

The steal is not only a great asset to the offensive club, but it also rattles the pitcher and the fielders. The pitcher is so worried about the runner that he gets behind the hitter or makes a bad pitch. The second baseman or shortstop often has to "cheat" a little toward second base, so as to be there for the throw. Consequently, there is a wider gap to hit through.

The manager or coach, of course, has to decide whether to steal or not to steal. My "steal" sign simply tells the runner: "We want you to steal if you can get your lead." However, it does not necessarily mean he has to go on that pitch. If the manager gives a "steal" sign, and insists that his runner must go on that particular pitch, on that pitch the pitcher may quick-pitch him. Therefore, we do not want a base runner to steal unless he can get a good jump.

The good base runner has to be aware of the pitchout. Usually, if a pitchout is executed properly, even runners as fast as Maury Wills and Willie Davis have trouble stealing the base, unless the pitcher's delivery is particularly slow. The count has to be right. Quite often, Maury would guess for a curve ball because it is better to steal on an off-speed pitch than on a fast ball.

An aggressive stolen-base philosophy has proven successful for many teams, particularly at the high school and college levels. A young pitcher may not have a good move to first or a quick delivery to the plate. In addition, a young catcher may not have a quick and accurate throwing arm.

The single steal   The single steal is usually tried when a team is ahead, tied or no more than one run behind. When the "steal" sign is put on with a 3-and-1 or 3-and-2 count on the batter, the runner should be instructed to go on that pitch, although the hitter does not have to swing at the pitch. However, on any other count, the runner should steal only if he gets a good jump on the pitcher.

Basically, a team should not run when more than two runs behind, but, when an outstanding runner is on base early in the game, the coach might say: "Well, I am going to go ahead and gamble. If I get this man on second base, maybe I can pick up the one run."

The "steal" sign might be given the runner when he is on second, or even third, but the runner goes only if he gets a good jump. A good jump is the key to successful base running. A jump is leaving for the next base the instant the pitcher commits himself to delivering the ball to the plate. It is worth as much as two-tenths of a second. Instead of taking a seventeen-foot lead and attracting numerous throws, a top base-stealer may feel more comfortable with a fourteen- or fifteen-foot lead, enabling him to get a better jump.

Double steal   There are various types of double steals with runners on first and third. Some coaches start with the straight single steal from first base, while others use the break before the pitch, delayed, or long-lead types. Here again, it depends on the pitcher.

If successful, this play can result in one run scored and a runner on second base. For example, the runner on first breaks for second on the pitch, and if the throw goes through to the base, he pulls up short and becomes involved in a run-down situation. The man on third, meanwhile, waits until the thrown ball is over the pitcher's head before making his break for the plate.

Actually, the Dodgers do not use this type of double steal, in which we send a man from first and try to score the runner from third base. It often works at the high school level, but the major league defenses are too good for that. What happens, is that the catcher "looks" the runner back to third and then throws on to second base. If the runner starts too soon at third, he will be caught in a run-down play.

In executing the double steal, the runner at first should start toward second with a straight steal. Now, as soon as the catcher releases his throw to second base, the runner at third base has to have as good a lead as he can and then take off quickly.

Sometimes, the defense might try to trick the runners by throwing directly back to the pitcher, and the offense would likely be in trouble. However, it is a gamble play, so the runner at third base will say to himself: "I will get as good a lead as I can. I will stand still, and wait until I see that the catcher has actually thrown the ball to second base."

There are times when the catcher fakes a throw to second, and the runner at third is caught in a trap between third and home. Again, I believe the double steal can be defensed against quite well.

Delayed steal   The player with good speed who selects an opportunity to run should have a good chance of pulling off a delayed steal. The base runner should exploit any carelessness by the keystone combination, the pitcher or the catcher. The delayed steal is often tried with two outs, when the catcher has been lobbing the ball back to the pitcher, and the second baseman and short-

Fig. 12.6 THE STEAL OF HOME PLATE is an exciting play but a real gamble. It can be used as a surprise weapon, particularly to rattle or demoralize the opposition. An exceptionally fast and gifted base runner like Rickey Henderson will get an occasional "green light" but usually against a pitcher taking a long full wind-up. Generally, it should not be attempted with a left-handed batter at the plate or with two strikes on the hitter. Here, Henderson slides across the plate after Tony Armas has stepped back out of the batter's box. Rather than give the catcher a clear shot at the runner, a right-handed batter may "cooperate" by remaining in the box. By merely spreading his legs, he can let the runner go right between them.

stop are playing deep. Or, it is sometimes tried when the second baseman has a habit of looking down after the pitch is past the hitter.

The runner should break for second base the moment the catcher starts his throw to the pitcher. The pitcher has to catch the ball, pivot, and throw, while the infielder who covers must come in from his deep position to make the play.

One type of delayed double steal might be used against a rookie pitcher, especially a left-hander. As he comes down and gets set, the man on first base should start to run. I do not want him simply to jog, because, if he starts jogging, it will look too much like a trap. I want him to break as though he were actually going to steal.

Although the pitcher knows there is a man on third base, if he is not concentrating at that particular moment, his first impulse is to back off, and he will likely throw to second base. The runner on third base knows this play is on, too, so he is creeping off; then, as soon as the pitcher backs off, he starts to go. Many times, if the pitcher makes only a motion toward second, the runner on third has a good chance to score before the pitcher can recover and throw to home.

The delayed steal should work particularly well at the college and high school levels. I do not think it should be used against a veteran pitcher, though, because he will step off the rubber and look to third before he commits himself to second base.

The natural impulse of many pitchers is to follow the runner. "There goes that runner!" Because he wants to do something about it, he steps off the slab and starts his motion to second or throws to get the runner in a run-down. Before the defense knows it, it is too late to stop the runner going home. If the pitcher does not step off, he will very likely balk.

In fact, we have worked the delayed double steal a half dozen times in the major leagues, and it has proven to be a daring, tricky play that works. We have been caught only two or three times. However, a manager has to know how to pick his spots and situations.

SIGNALS

The secret language of baseball is signals, and no team gets very far without them. If a team is to win, a simple but effective system of communications must be set up. Flashing his signals from the bench or from the coaching lines, the manager or head coach can coordinate individual efforts into team action.

Signs, in the case of young players, can be quite simple and few in number, while signs with older and more experienced players can cover more situations and plays. Whatever the system, each member of the squad should know the signs perfectly.

Too many signs on a team can be worse than none at all. A baseball player may have enough trouble keeping his mind on the game situation, without having to worry about a long, complicated series of signals. As Yogi Berra once said, "How can you *hit* and *think* at the same time?" Yogi, of course, was exaggerating the situation, but it is true that a player must concentrate on the task at hand, whether it be hitting or fielding.

Signals that take too much mental effort to comprehend should not be used. They should be simple. Unquestionably, the effectiveness of signals depends upon their execution. A simple set of signs, combined with an indicator or key, plus some decoy motions for camouflage, can be most difficult for the opposition to intercept (Fig. 12.7). Any natural movement of the cap, hands, or arms, mixed in with other natural actions, will do the trick.

Actually, the causes of missed signals are quite simple. The player did not look at the coach, he did not look at the right time or the manager did not give the signal properly. There is no excuse for a player not to know the signs, even if they are somewhat complicated. He has all his free time to learn the signals.

After the signals are used awhile, there should be no missed signs. That is the trouble with the "flash" sign. If the manager gives a "flash" sign and the player does not happen to be looking at the right time, he does have an excuse. However, the first time the hitter turns around and looks at the coach, the coach should give a "yes" or "no." "Yes—I'm going to give you a sign," or, "No—I won't."

For instance, if the coach rubs down below the belt, it means, "No, there is not a sign." If he rubs anything above the belt, the player has to be alert, because a sign will be given. As soon as the coach hits the key with one hand, he will give the sign with the other hand.

A simpler set of signs should be given a high school player—more holding signs, such as hands on the knees or belt, keeping them there a little longer. The coach should either face him, walk toward him, or walk away from him. It is more important to have the players sure that they get the sign, rather than be too concerned about the opposing club stealing them.

Coaches should be pretty good actors. They have to make some kind of movement or signal-giving motion on practically every pitch. They should do a lot of faking constantly, so that, when they *do* give a sign, it is not obvious.

Practice

The manager or coach should not be satisfied just to go over the signs with his team and let it go at that. Sufficient practice time should be devoted to executing them until they are well understood. They should be used in all intrasquad games, with the coaches performing their duties on the base lines under typical game conditions.

Major league players have a chance to practice their signs all through spring training. The signs are basically the same as those used the previous year, but there might be a change in the key or in the "yes" and "no" part of it.

In a meeting, we go through them quite thoroughly. Then, we have a coach stand up and give the men a sign. I pick out somebody and ask, "What sign is *that?*" We go through them until we have them down quite well.

TYPES OF SIGNALS

The most common types of signals given by a coach or manager are: flash signals, holding signals, block signals, combination signals, pump signals, and word signals.

Flash signals

Flashing signs is a common method used to make them harder to detect. Actually, they are just what the name implies. They are *flashed* to the players through a particular act. While they are fine for the more experienced player, they are not recommended for players in the youth leagues.

The value of "flash" signals is that they can be given quickly. By mixing them in with other movements, the coach can camouflage his signals. However, the player may miss the signals, since the coach has to give them quickly. He can give the "flash" sign in one quick motion. He may touch his face for a "bunt," flick a hand across his uniform chest for the "take," or touch his leg for a "hit-and-run." However, without the indicator, they would be meaningless. Suppose the indicator sign is touching the belt buckle; the next signal is *it,* the sign that counts. If it is the "steal," he will rub the left thigh with his left hand.

After flashing the actual sign, he will continue signaling in order to avoid detection. The batter can do his part by continuing to look at the coach briefly after receiving his orders.

Holding signals

"Holding" signals are those which are held for several seconds, and are ideal for younger players. The clenched fist, the bent elbow, or the hands on the knees are all examples of the "holding" type of signal. If the coach took off his cap for a few moments, he would be giving a "holding" sign.

The third base coach might assume a natural, relaxed position with his hands on the knees, which could be his "bunt" sign of the day. However, he had better give decoys before and after. He can make the hands-on-knees sign even more difficult to intercept by instructing his players to ignore the sign unless his thumbs are widely extended from the fingers.

The "holding" sign is the simplest for the player to get because it is held long enough for the message to sink in. A player can look more than once if he is in doubt about the signal.

The disadvantage of such a signal is that the sign is held for so long that the opposition may catch on to it. If the coach feels he is being closely watched by the opposition, he may have the player next to him send the signals to the players.

Block signals

Signals that use different parts of the coach's body, or divide his body into blocks or sections, are called "block" signals. The coach can go from the head down to his shirt or arm. He can go clockwise, dividing his body into four parts. Or, he can go up and down.

The bunt could be touching the face; hit-and-run, the letters of the shirt;

the steal, the belt, etc. Or, the coach could give the hitting signs on one side of his body, and the running signs on the other side.

Touching the cap, head, or face could be used for the first three hitters in the lineup, rubbing the shirt could be used for the next three hitters, while rubbing the pants could affect the last three.

The signal is sometimes determined by the number of rubs. For instance, the take sign could be one rub, and the bunt, two rubs. If he rubs his shirt once or twice while the first three batters are up, this would mean nothing, since the shirt signals apply only to the fourth, fifth, and sixth hitters.

Regardless of the age level or the experience of the players, block signals are good to use. This system does have a disadvantage, in that occasionally the coach has trouble remembering the numerical position of the players in the lineup.

Combination signals

A combination sign is two or more motions tied together to represent a single sign (Fig. 12.8). Quite often, one of these motions or acts is the key sign. The key signal, for example, is covering the belt buckle with the hand. This by itself means nothing. The "steal," which is touching the cap, also means nothing by

a. The key (touching #24 with left hand).

b. Both hands to letters (indicates he will use second signal after key).

c. Going to sleeve (first signal after key).

d. Back to letters for hit-and-run signal (second sign after key).

Fig. 12.7 MANAGER'S KEY METHOD TO SIGNAL COACH. The key to start the signals is #24, using the hit and run as an example. The first sign touched after touching the key is the signal, unless otherwise indicated by using both hands to touch the same spot. Then it will be the second signal after the key is touched. Using the key method, a set of signals can be as follows: Take (touching the cap); Bunt (touching the opposite leg); Hit-and-run (touching the letters) and Steal (touching the opposite sleeve). (Walter Alston)

a. Indicates second signal after key will be used.

b. Going to key #24 (tells coach to start taking signs now).

c. Going to leg for first signal after key.

d. Completing steal signal by touching opposite sleeve.

Fig. 12.8 GIVING THE STEAL SIGNAL. In picture a, the manager moves both hands to his cap, to indicate that the second signal after the key will be the steal sign. After giving the key and his first signal, he flashes the "real" steal sign (as shown in picture d). (Walter Alston)

itself. However, when the cap is touched and the belt buckle is covered, the "steal" is on.

The coach could have a set of signs starting with the cap, face, shirt, and pants, which can be one, two, three, and four. He will tell his players: "I am going to give you a certain number of rubs, and anytime I hit one of those spots, it counts."

Combination signals can also be used for the hit-and-run, bunt, and squeeze play. Although a different sign is used for each, the same key sign can be used.

Rub-off signals

A "rub-off" signal is a last-instant order used by the manager to cancel previous signs. Every team should have a "rub-off" sign which, when flashed, takes everything off. As an example, I have given the "hit-and-run" signal. However, I might reconsider because I feel a pitchout could be coming up. Changing my mind, I give a "rub-off" signal, which takes the play off.

Removing the cap is commonly used as a "rub-off" signal, since it is easy for the players to catch.

Word signals

Although word signals have some merit, they have a disadvantage in that the noise of the crowd will sometimes prevent the third base coach from hearing them distinctly. Word signals can be associated with the action desired. They are sometimes used for the base runner on third when the squeeze is on.

GIVING SIGNALS

Baseball signals are taken either directly from the head coach or from the manager on the bench, or relayed to the coach on the coaching lines. While high school rules prohibit the head coach from going on the base lines, one college coach is now allowed to coach on the line. Most major league managers prefer to stay in the dugout, while their lieutenants handle the duties on the coaching lines.

Whatever arrangement is used, the system should not be awkward to the hitter at the plate. With the head coach in the dugout on the third base side, the right-handed hitters will have to turn around constantly to look for the signs, unless they are relayed to a coach on the base lines.

If the team at bat is occupying the dugout on the first base side of the diamond, and the head coach is on the bench, right-handed hitters might take their signals directly from him. The hitter can take an occasional glance at the coach as he approaches the batter's box or as he steps into the box.

Left-handed batters can take their signs from the coach in the third base coaching box. The head coach should give this coach the signal in plenty of time so he can relay it on to the hitter. When the team occupies the third base dugout, left-handed batters get their signals directly from this coach, and right-handed batters from the first base coach.

Indicator system

Major league teams place considerable emphasis on the indicator system, using combination signs. In simpler terms, a specific key sign determines whether the signal is off or on. A coach may give any signal he wishes, but it does not mean a thing unless he has given an indicator sign first (Fig. 12.8).

I like the indicator because we can do a lot of faking. If I do not give the indicator, nothing happens. If I give the indicator, the first thing I touch is usually the sign I want to give.

Let us assume the indicator is a clap of the hands. The coach can touch any part of his body but he is not giving a signal. However, if he claps his hands and then adjusts the peak of his cap, the sign (the "take") is on.

The position of the coach in the coach's box may also be used as an indicator. If the coach is standing at the far end of the box, the signs are off, but if he is standing at the end nearest the hitter, the signs are on. This procedure can also be used in reverse, of course.

RECEIVING SIGNALS

The correct execution of signals demands that the player look at the coach or manager at the right time. The proper times for the batter to look for the signals are when he is approaching the plate before entering the batter's box, and just after each pitch thrown to him while he is at bat.

After he receives the signal, the batter should continue looking at the coach so the coach can decoy the opposing team with additional motions and gestures. The hitter can take the signals either in the box or out of it. However, base runners should take the signals while standing on the base.

Pee Wee Reese probably was the best player I have seen at receiving signals. After I gave him a sign, he would just keep looking and looking. The first couple of times, I was not sure whether he got the sign or not, but in his own way, he was decoying to keep the other club from knowing the sign was given. All good sign-takers react the same way, in a nonchalant manner, and go ahead and execute it.

If the batter is doubtful about a sign, he should ask the umpire for time, step out of the batter's box and take another look. I would rather have my hitter sure that he has not missed the sign. He can act as though he is tying his shoelaces. Then he can take another look at his coach, who can either give the sign again or give him the "rub-off."

On the squeeze play, which is a surprise tactic, the coach might take the play off if he thinks the hitter has tipped off the play.

To prevent the other team from stealing the signals, we have added a "release" sign. If I give a player a signal, I tell him it will be the first or second sign after the key, but he must keep looking until I release him. This is what we call a *release sign.* The batter will also know that he has not missed anything. Besides, it prevents a player from looking away as soon as he gets the signal.

SIGNALS FOR THE BATTER

The signals that are given to the batter are: 1) the "take," 2) "hit," 3) "hit-and-run," 4) "run-and-hit," 5) "sacrifice bunt," and 6) "squeeze bunt" (suicide or safety).

When explaining signs to the players, the coach should tell them: "You are always hitting, unless I give you a sign to do something else. The sign I give you stays on until I take it off or give you a different sign."

The "take"

The "take" sign is one of the most used signals in baseball. When the hitter looks down at the third base coach and we give the "take" sign, the batter must not swing at the next pitch. The team may be several runs behind, and the coach wants the hitter to wait out the pitcher in hopes of getting a walk.

Managers, however, should not put on the take so often they make the players feel "he is taking the bat out of my hands." The "take" is used mainly to control the ball and strike on the count of three balls and one strike, two balls and no strikes, three and nothing, or the first pitch following a base on balls.

To signal the batter to "take," the manager might touch the peak of the cap, which means the batter should keep right on taking pitches until the manager rubs the sign off or gives another sign.

"Hit" sign

We like to have definite "hit" signs. Normally, when the manager wants his hitter to hit a 3-and-0 pitch, it is already understood that, "Anytime I don't give you a 'take' sign, you are hitting." Too often, however, the hitter will look around, and if his manager does not give him a "take," he may in his own mind wonder, "Well, I wonder if he gave me the 'take,' and I didn't see it."

Consequently, in certain situations, I will give the hitter a definite "hit" sign. He is in a much better frame of mind when I give him a definite "hit" sign, than if he worries about whether he missed the "take" sign.

"Hit-and-run"

The "hit-and-run" is employed to protect the base runner. The batter swings or throws his bat at the ball, regardless of where the pitch is thrown. The coach might place his hand on his nose, and it is important for him to know that both the hitter and runner have the sign. The runner might answer by putting either hand to his belt buckle. The hitter can answer by putting either hand to his face. On this play, the hitter must try to protect the runner and endeavor to hit the ball on the ground.

"Run-and-hit"

When the count is 3-and-1 or 2-and-0, the "run-and-hit" sign goes to both the runner and the hitter, which actually means that, "I want the runner to go on this pitch, regardless, and the hitter should swing at the pitch if it is in the strike zone."

"Bunt-and-run"

On this play, the batter must protect the runner who is breaking for second with the pitch. He must bunt at the pitch, whether it is a strike or not. Putting the right hand on the left wrist could be the sign for the "bunt-and-run."

Like the "hit-and-run," the runner should answer the sign by placing either hand to his left buckle. The hitter can answer by putting either hand to his face.

"Sacrifice"

The "sacrifice bunt" is given to the batter when the coach wants to advance a runner or runners. In the sacrifice, the hitter should bunt only if the pitch is a strike. The runner on first base does not break for second until he is sure the ball is bunted on the ground.

Actually, I have about six ways to give the "bunt" sign. When I am sitting on the bench, I often cross one leg over the other. Anytime I take my left hand and place it on my right leg, the "bunt" sign is on. Lately, I have gone to the open hand. The third base coach will then relay these signs to the hitter.

"Squeeze bunt"

There are two types of squeeze bunts: the suicide and the safety squeeze. The success of the squeeze play, of course, depends upon the bunting ability of the batter.

1. Suicide Squeeze This play requires the greatest precaution to make certain nobody fouls up. As a result, a "holding" sign is often used to be sure the batter gets it. In turn, the batter can use a set "flash" reply, like picking up dirt and tossing it.

a. Indicator (sign to follow)   b. Bunt sign

Fig. 12.9 SIGNALS FROM THIRD BASE COACH. After receiving a signal from the manager on the bench, the base line coach has the responsibility of relaying it to the hitter and base runners (Danny Ozark).

When the third base coach feels the hitter has the sign, he gives a signal to the runner on third base, a word message such as, "Be alive," or a remark giving the runner's first name.

The runner can acknowledge the signal by touching a part of his uniform.

2. *Safety squeeze* On this play, the batter should bunt only if the pitch is a strike. Actually, the same sign for the sacrifice can be used for the safety squeeze because the batter bunts only if the pitch is a strike.

Typical Set of Signals from the Base Coach

Indicator (sign to follow)—Right hand to belt buckle
Take—Right hand rubs letters of shirt
Hit and run—Right hand rubbing right thigh
Take-off—Rub down on right arm
Steal—Rubbing left hand on left thigh
Bunt—Moving right hand to cap
Release (hitter may look away and hit)—Rubbing down on left arm

---

SIGNALS FOR THE BASE RUNNER

The signals that are given to the base runner are: 1) the "steal," 2) "double steal," 3) "delayed steal," and 4) "suit yourself." These signals are given directly to the base runner.

The "steal"

The "steal" is a holding or combination sign which is relayed to the runner on first base by the third base coach. The "single steal" sign could be pulling up the belt or placing the left hand on the right elbow.

On any count, the runner should go *only* if he gets a good jump on the pitcher. If the runner does not go down on this pitch and his coach does not rub the sign off, the "steal" sign is still on.

"Double steal"

There are various types of double steals with runners on first and third. Many coaches start with the straight single steal from first, while others use the break before the pitch, the delayed, and the long-lead types.

The signal for the "double steal" might be placing the left hand on the right wrist, or clasping both hands. To signal the runner on third base, the straight "double steal" sign should be given, followed by another sign to tell him the type he wants to use. Many teams employ an entirely different sign for each type of double steal.

If the pitch is fouled off by the hitter, the sign stays on unless the coach rubs it off. If the coach does not want the runner on third base to try to score, he will put on the "single steal" sign.

"Delayed steal"

Only a fast runner should attempt the delayed steal. A signal such as touching the neck could be used, and the runner will break for second base the moment the catcher starts his throw to the pitcher.

"Suit yourself"

On this sign, the base runner has the prerogative of stealing any time he can get a good jump on the pitcher.

STEALING SIGNALS

Some coaches and managers often tip-off their signals. They never seem to acquire the knack of giving them properly. Perhaps they are not good enough actors, which really is what topnotch signal callers are: good actors. Many coaches have the habit of being too deliberate when they give a sign. Although their decoying tactics are nonchalant, when they flash the actual signal, they overemphasize it. Consequently, they give most of their signals away.

Primarily, the "hit-and-run" and "steal" signals are the ones to look for. They can help a team, especially a hit and run. If we can pitchout on a hit-and-run play, we have a good chance to throw a man out.

Opposing managers and coaches, along with keen infielders and catchers, are always watching for tip-offs of this type. In picking up signals of the opposing team, a coach and player on the bench might combine to decode the play. One man will sit there and watch the coach to observe what he is doing, or what he touched, while the other man will watch the hitter. He will say, "He's looking, he's looking, he looked away!" Quite often, the last thing the coach did before he looked away might be the signal. This goes on for a couple of innings, and before long, they will come up with the signal.

After receiving a signal, many players will immediately stop looking at the coach. This often enables the defensive team to steal the signal. When a weak-hitting pitcher comes to bat with a teammate on first base and fewer than two out, the "bunt" sign can often be picked up.

I like to believe our signs are pretty foolproof; at least, I hope so. In addition to having many sets of signs, we have signs that are easily switched from a fast ball to a curve ball, and vice versa. We can switch them by just a little extra rub here and there. Basically, the signs remain the same but, once in a while, I will add a "switch" sign which reverses the set. Now, they are getting fast balls instead of curve balls.

Stealing signals from the catcher is a calculated risk that a lot of hitters are willing to take. Most hitters will take signs if they are 75–85 percent sure they are correct. Most of them are stolen from second base, with the runner watching the catcher giving the signals. If he happens to recognize a set of these signals, he may start immediately relaying signals to the hitter.

DUTIES OF BASE COACHES

Essentially, their primary duties are giving signals and assisting base runners. Therefore, they must be constantly alert and be the type of individuals who can remain calm and make the right decisions even when the action gets hectic.

First base coach

The coach at first base gives encouragement to the hitter, and once the ball is hit, he helps the batter-runner any way he can. If there is an error on the throw, the coach will instruct the runner to go to second or stop. If the ball is hit to the outfield, he will move to the front of the box and point toward second and yell, "Make your turn!" or, "Go for two!" He might wave his arm in a circle in addition to yelling for the runner to go to second. If he is sure the runner cannot advance, he should yell, "Hold up!"

The coach should tell the base runner how many outs there are and remind him to be alert for signs. He might cup his hands around his mouth so his voice is better directed at the runner. He can advise him whether this is the tying or winning run, especially if the team is two or three runs down in the eighth or ninth inning. If he is the first man on, he might say, "Your run doesn't mean anything—do not take any chances!"

If the first baseman is playing behind the runner, the coach has to face the first baseman and let his runner know when to get back. He should warn the runner to be careful if the pitcher has a good move. If a fly ball is deep but will likely be caught, the coach should tell the runner to tag up, or if it is shallow, to go halfway. A constant chatter helps the runner become more familiar with his voice. The coach say things such as, "All right, all right," "Get back," or "Look out."

Third base coach

The coach at third base takes over the guiding of a base runner after he passes first base, particularly when the ball is behind the runner. Actually, the only guidance from the coach is on the ball hit down the right field line. If the ball is hit in front of him, we want the runner himself to make the decision.

When the ball is hit down the right field line, the ball is behind the runner, and we do not like one of our runners to turn around and look at that ball while running. Rather, he should look over to the third base coach to see whether he should come to third or stay at second. Some coaches instruct the base runner to look at the coach when he is about twenty feet from second base.

If he wants the runner to round third base, the coach should move down the line toward home plate fifteen feet or more. If he wants to stop him at third, the coach has to be in front of the runner where the runner can see him. He can motion by signs: "Stay," "Hold up," or "Stay on the base."

If the runner is coming from second base and it is a question of whether or not he can score, the coach should go down the line where the runner can definitely see him. In this situation, we instruct our runner, "You run until the coach stops you." Now, we would not have the coach down the line if we did not want him to round the bag. Therefore, it is necessary for the runner to keep running until he is stopped. This give the coach a little more time to make up his mind whether this man can score or not. As he rounds third base, the runner can see the coach and hear him say either "Get back!" or "Come on!" Most of this coaching is done by waving the hand or by arm motion, rather than by mouth.

When a runner is on third base, the coach should give him the same type of information as that given the runner at first base, such as outs, game situation, and the location of the ball. He should be reminded how the infield is playing, or to tag up on all fly balls. The coach might tell the runner to go home only if the ball goes through the infield, or to try and score on an infield ground ball.

OFFENSIVE DRILLS

No time should be lost while practicing drills. Anytime a team runs any type of drill, the coach must insist that no time be wasted. He must line his players up and get them going quickly. Unless the coach keeps his drill nice and snappy, sure enough, the players will die on him. So, do not give them any time to rest. *Keep them moving!*

Game situation drill (Fig. 12.10)

A base runner is placed at first base, with nobody out, and the batter is told to hit the ball anywhere he pleases. We instruct our pitcher not to throw the ball hard. Rather, it should be nice and easy so the batter will hit the ball somewhere. We encourage him to practice going to the opposite field and hitting behind the runner. When three outs are made, we clear the bases and bring the runner back to first base and start again. We never start without a runner on base.

We never permit an outfielder to lob the ball back in. He must throw it hard every time he fields the ball. We want him to fire the ball and hit the relay man.

Most base runners do not take the extra base the majority of the time when they could. The best way to teach a boy to take the extra base and not get caught is to have him make up his mind when he rounds his base. On a single to right field, with a runner on first and the throw going to third base, the runner must look for the ball immediately as the relay goes into the cutoff man. The only time he goes on to second base is when he knows the ball is going to be over the head of the cutoff man. Therefore, he must look at the height of the ball when it comes in.

We do this drill for about thirty minutes, since there are so many different situations involved in it. Then, we change and put the other players in the field, and the regulars come in and get some good base running experience.

When we do this drill, we make sure we have coaches at third and first base, so that it presents a regular game situation.

Base running drill (Fig. 12.11)

Lining up at home plate, the players run down to first and practice rounding the base. We want them to tag the inside of the bag, making their pivot properly, and continuing to second base. The runners should practice proper running form.

We will then have our players line up at first base to practice their leads and breaks. After taking a lead of about twelve feet from the bag, he breaks for second base on a signal from the coach. The first step should be a cross-over step.

The coach will call out the normal lead, the steal lead, the one-way lead, the regular steal, the delayed steal, and the hit-and-run. The runner will make the proper start as the pitcher delivers the ball to an imaginary hitter.

In another routine, a coach will hit a ground ball to the outfield to be

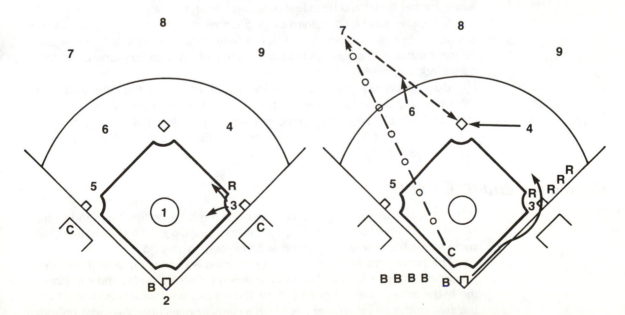

Fig. 12.10 GAME SITUATION DRILL   **Fig. 12.11** BASE RUNNING DRILL

handled by an outfielder. We have the batter-runner round first base and see how far he can go toward second and still get back before the relay. A player can find out by experience how far he can go. These types of setups are all excellent gamelike drills, very similar to the various game situations.

Double steal drill (Fig. 12.12)

The infielders and the battery combination take their positions, with runners on first and third. This drill not only provides offensive work but the coach can establish his defensive set-up at the same time. The drill begins when the pitcher starts his delivery. The runner on first starts for second in a straight steal attempt, and the man on third waits until he is fairly sure the catcher is throwing through, then he breaks for the plate.

This drill can be performed in two parts:

1. The catcher makes all his throws to second base so that runners learn the technique of the play.
2. The catcher tries to outmaneuver the runners. The runner at first base should purposely get caught in a run-down occasionally.

Squeeze play drill (Fig. 12.13)

With the coach observing the action, the batter and base runner at third execute the squeeze play. The runner practices his timing on when to leave, while the batter turns around and bunts the ball. A line of runners is at third base, while another line could be at first or second base, or both.

Getting a good lead at third base, the runner breaks for the plate as the pitcher is about to release the ball. It is advisable to work this drill with signals so that the batter and runners learn to execute this play under game conditions as realistic as possible.

During our base-running drills, instead of squeezing the runner in from third, we will instruct him to score on a ground ball. We have him wait at third base and, when a ball is hit on the ground, he practices his walking lead and timing on a ground ball. If the ball is hit on a fly to the outfield, he has to go back and tag up.

Hit-and-run drill (Fig. 12.14)

While we are taking batting practice, we place a runner on first base and a half-dozen hitters take turns executing the hit-and-run. On the first pitch, the hitter must hit the ball where it is pitched and the runner must go.

The pitcher receives good practice holding a runner on, and the runner practices taking his lead and moving to second base on the hit-and-run play. If the batter misses the ball or fouls it off, the runner stays at second base. Now, the same hitter takes the next pitch with a runner on second base, with nobody out, and tries to move the runner to third.

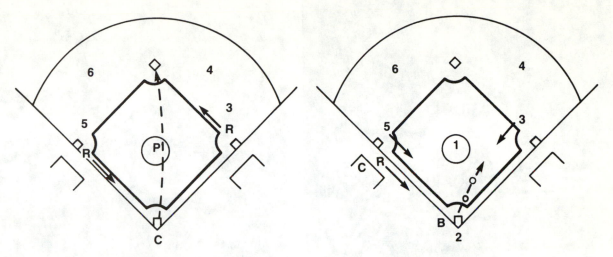

Fig. 12.12   DOUBLE STEAL DRILL   Fig. 12.13   SQUEEZE PLAY DRILL

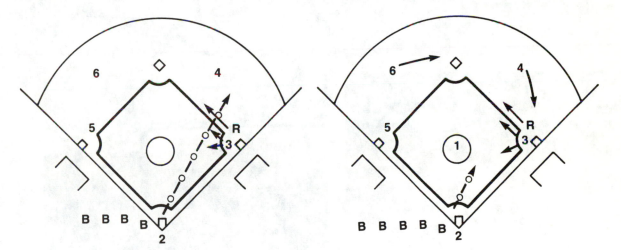

Fig. 12.14   HIT-AND-RUN DRILL   Fig. 12.15   BUNTING DRILL

We encourage the batter to hit the ball to right field. If the runner can be advanced, he goes on to third, and we put on the squeeze play.

Bunting drill (Fig. 12.15)

The bunters form a line near home plate, while the runners line up at first base. The pitcher and catcher, along with the infielders, assume their defensive positions. Using proper bunting procedure, the batter lays the ball down. Later, runners are placed at first and second base, and the defense tries to make the force play at third base.

13
Team Defense

Defense is the key to a sound and solid baseball team. The team that makes the fewer number of errors or mistakes in fielding and throwing will normally be the team that wins the game. Basically, the reasons for failure in defense are that players hurry their throws, throw off balance, are out of position, or actually do not know what to do.

The Dodgers have always tried to emphasize defensive excellence and tightness. I believe it reverts back to the speed that we have taken pride in all through the years. Every player must be "in the ball game" at all times. People have said that our Dodger teams "make errors but not mistakes," which, to me, is quite a tribute to our defensive record. Certainly, the many hours we spend on relays, cutoffs, and other defensive tactics during spring training pay off with victories in league play.

The pitching staff must keep the ball in the park and prevent the hitters from hitting it too hard and too often. Then, it is up to the fielders to convert a high percentage of their fielding chances into outs. Beyond the pitching, the ingredients of a sound defense are speed and good ground coverage. The center fielder who can cover ground, get the good jump on the ball, and employ a strong and accurate arm is a great asset to his team. The shortstop and

Fig. 13.1 BASEBALL'S TOP DEFENSIVE TEAMS have the ability to execute effectively the basic fundamental techniques. They have the players who possess the quickness and agility to get to the ball and field it properly. Good pitching, combined with a reliable defense, will usually beat good hitting.

second baseman, with their quick and sure hands, alertness, and knowledge of the hitters, cover the ground and make the plays necessary to win a championship.

In addition, it is essential to have a top receiver. The catcher who can handle the pitcher can be an extremely valuable man. He should be the "quarterback" of the ball club—a good, solid aggressive receiver. The catcher has to get rid of the ball quickly and call pitch-outs at opportune times, but in throwing out base runners, the pitcher must get the ball to the plate quickly. He can shorten his motion, quicken his delivery.

To be a championship team, you have to make the double play. It's the biggest play in baseball.

The New York Mets, 1969 World Champions of baseball, are a good example of a team that few people figured had a chance for the pennant. They started out by winning a few games, then started to roll along. Soon, they found out that they could win, and the more they won, the more confident they got, giving them more team spirit. Before long, they *believed* that they could do it. Everybody was hustling and diving after catches. Team spirit and a confident attitude are so important. If a team is fortunate enough to win a few games, they find out that they can do things. Then, they go ahead and *do* them. This is the team spirit, morale, or momentum that carries a team over the rough spots and gives it the little "extra" that it needs.

The double play is the greatest defensive weapon in baseball. The double play can get a team out of a tough inning better than anything else. Therefore, the shortstop and second baseman must be able to make this play when the situation requires it. It should be the first thing on their minds whenever there is a man on base. On many occasions, the double play is missed by just a fraction of a second. It is such a close play at first base that the well-executed and perfect pivot on the double play can make a great many of the close ones succeed. Surely, if a team lacks a Steve Carlton to strike men out, then the double play ball is the factor that can take the heart out of the big inning.

GOOD PITCHING

An old baseball adage states that, "Good pitching stops good hitting." Indeed, pitching is the name of the game, having been rated by big-league managers anywhere from 69 to 75 percent of the game (in amateur ball even higher). Good pitching and a tight defense will prove a winning combination for any baseball team. If the defense keeps the other team from scoring, it has been said, "You cannot lose." This means that, if a team can hold their opponents to one or two runs, they do not have to have the greatest hitters in the world to score a couple of runs themselves.

The best pitcher in baseball is still the pitcher who has a little something extra on the fast ball. The off-speed pitches, of course, complement the fast ball, but a staff of hard-throwing pitchers will always command the respect of opposing hitters.

With a staff of pitchers who can throw strikes, a well-drilled, alert defensive team will prove hard to beat.

A SOUND DEFENSE

The secret of defense is to be "strong straight down the middle." A sound defense consists of a good, rugged catcher who can handle the pitcher and can throw; a consistent double play combination; and a fast, dependable center fielder who can throw and keep the runners from going from first to third.

The best teams in baseball, year-in and year-out, are blessed with outstanding mound work and a solid defense. Interestingly enough, the top clubs achieved their success because they applied successfully the following old-fashioned virtues of baseball defense:

1. Ability and concentration to make all the routine plays consistently and correctly
2. Ability to convert the difficult, tricky-hop, ground balls into outs
3. Ability to make the double play consistently
4. Relay and cutoff men at the right place and time
5. Hitting the relay and cutoff men with good outfield throws
6. Backing up efficiently on overthrows
7. Keeping opposing base runners close
8. Pitchers keeping their pitches down
9. Not making any unnecessary throws
10. A fast, dependable center fielder who can throw
11. A catcher who is capable of handling the low ball, and who can throw
12. A catcher who can handle the pitchers, and be the team "quarterback"
13. Players in the field who can run and throw
14. Using two hands in fielding whenever possible
15. Every player heads-up, alert, and ready to hustle
16. Knowing what to do with the ball before it arrives—*thinking all the time!*
17. Team spirit—thinking more about the *team's* needs than about individual accomplishments

HARD WORK AND TEAM SPIRIT

Certainly, these virtues of defensive excellence do not come by themselves. They are the result of practice and concentration, with the players becoming familiar with each other—and, above all, a great amount of hard work and *pulling* together as a team. The manager and his coaching staff must continually strive to stimulate a kind of dedicated concentration on the part of each player, to be able to make all the routine plays consistently and correctly.

The secret of defense is to be strong straight down the middle.

Every player must have a strong belief in the total success of the team. Instead of being removed from the game and brooding about not playing, a player should accept pitching and lineup changes with a spirit that it is best for the *team*.

Hours of practice can help make a fielder fundamentally correct. One of the basic things each outfielder and infielder has to do during a ball game is to anticipate that the ball is going to be hit to *him*. He is more or less thinking: "If the ball is hit to me, what should I do with it? What play do I make?"

Team play

Victory can come if a group of players will really go to work together as a team. This is particularly true when the team is in the field. Each player must have the same purpose and goal, and it is this kind of group feeling or team spirit that wins games.

I like to see the little "pepper," the talking back and forth, but unfortunately, this has gone out of style. The old-time ball players had a little more chatter and pep than the modern-day clubs. I do not know whether this is because the big parks with the large crowds might cause the players to have difficulty hearing each other.

I think it is important for infielders to chatter back and forth and to their pitcher. Once an out is made and they pass the ball around the infield, they should do it with some enthusiasm and pep, rather than in a dead, lackadaisical manner.

Every manager and coach looks for the born leader to direct his team in the field. The shortstop or second sacker who can turn around and talk to his teammates. Saying things such as, "One out" or "Two outs," can be a great asset to a ball team. He tells them where to throw the ball or to hit the cutoff man—everything the manager wants to say himself.

According to Paul Richards, "No defensive strategy can be successful unless every player on the field will practice the basic rule of the game: *think and hustle.*" The player's preliminary thought in the field is: "What should I do if the ball is hit to *me?*" If he does not have every play planned *before the ball is hit,* he simply will not have enough time to think. The more thinking he can do, the more alert and aggressive he can be.

DEFENSIVE ALIGNMENT

The defensive positions of the infielders and outfielders, to a large extent, are determined by the stage of the game and the ability of the hitter. The score, inning, and speed of the base runner are all factors to be considered in establishing the correct alignment and depth of the fielders.

Early in the game, or when they are more than two runs ahead, a team might play deep and give up a run. With runners on first and third bases, and less than two outs, many teams will play at double play depth, unless the winning run is at third.

When a run cannot be given, such as late in the game when a runner is on third with the tying or winning run, the infield should be played tight. Otherwise, it is best to play normal depth.

When one team is leading by a large score, the team in front is conceding a run or two and looking instead for the double play, or even one out, to break the back of the inning.

Good pitching stops good hitting.

The third baseman should play even with the bag for speedy players, especially good bunters and left-handed hitters. When a bunt is in order, the third baseman should move in on the grass. He should be moving toward the plate just as soon as the bat drops.

The third and first basemen must protect the lines against two-base hits, more so with two outs than with no outs. Late in the game, guarding against a two-base hit is fundamental strategy.

The alignment of the outfielders is determined by the type of hitter at the plate. Is he a left-handed or right-handed hitter? Can he pull the ball? Is he a line drive hitter? They must also be ready to execute assignments of covering and backing up the bases.

Outfielders must know how to play an opposing hitter according to his hitting ability and where and how their pitcher is trying to pitch the hitter (fast ball, curve ball, change-of-pace). When the pitcher is behind the hitter, outfielders play a step or two deeper and to the pull field; the reverse when pitcher is ahead of hitter.

When playing on artificial turf, outfielders must be careful of fly balls hitting

Fig. 13.2 INFIELD BACK, PLAY THE HITTER. Early in the game, or when more than two runs ahead, the team might play deep and give up a run. Here, with a runner on third, and two outs, the Dodger infield has been moved back to "just play the hitter."

in front of them and bouncing over their heads. Infielders should be sure to stay in front of ground balls, since there is likely to be time to knock the ball down and make the throw.

"You have to know what's going on at all times," explained Dick Williams. "On defense, you must anticipate what to do when the ball comes to you instead of waiting until it does and then trying to figure it out. You've got to think!"

Those on defense should know:

1. Whether or not the outfielder should dive for a shoestring catch or play the ball safely
2. Whether or not to try for the put-out throw to home plate or throw the ball to second base to keep the double play in order
3. When to play the infield in, double play depth, or back
4. How and when pitchers should make the hitter hit the ball on the ground
5. When third baseman and first baseman should guard the line

RELAYS AND CUTOFFS

Relays and cutoffs are team plays that require a great deal of practice and team-work to be executed properly. Too often, missed cutoffs and relay plays have given opponents the extra base which led to the run that decided the game. During the early spring training season, major league teams work on these plays by the hour. They are the "glue" in the defense (Figs. 13.3 and 13.4).

If the outfielder can hit the cutoff man, he can keep the hitter from going to second on the throw-in. This is important, because now the base runner cannot score on a single and is still set up for a possible double play.

A poised and confident team has practiced these plays over and over until there is no hesitation or uncertainty in their execution. Poor execution of fundamentals and lack of self-assurance are nothing more than the lack of practice. I am sure that many teams on the lower levels of play do not devote enough drill time to this phase of defense.

Relays

Most teams use a double cutoff. They will send out the shortstop or the second baseman. They will put either one behind the other player, in case there is a bad throw. The outfielder has to hit the first man who comes out for the throw. It must be a good throw, quick and on a line.

On a base hit to right center field, for example, the second baseman will go out to take the relay throw (Fig. 13.4). Use of the voice is important in this defensive situation. The shortstop is the backup man, about thirty feet or so behind. He should tell the relay man where the ball should be thrown. He should

Fig. 13.3 HITTING THE RELAY MAN. Relays and cutoffs are team plays which are the glue in the defense. During spring training, major league teams practice these plays by the hour. Above, Pat Kelly, after fielding a long drive off the fence, hits the relay man with a good throw, quick and on a line.

Fig. 13.4 THE RELAY MAN moves out to take the throw from the outfielder. In order to catch the ball on his throwing side, he steps forward with his right foot in the direction of the throw. Holding his hands letter-high, he provides a good target (Joe Morgan).

call out: "Home," "Second base," or "No play," depending on where the play should be made.

The relay man should raise his hands and yell, "Here!" In order to catch the ball on his throwing side, he should step forward with his right foot in the direction of the throw. This maneuver turns his body slightly toward the infield, to his left, enabling him to make his throw more quickly.

Relays and cutoffs are the glue in the defense.

Cutoffs

The purpose of the cutoff is to keep the hitter from taking an extra base, if no play occurs at home. On a base hit to center field, with a man on first base, the first baseman is the cutoff man. The third baseman is often the cutoff man for the left fielder.

The cutoff man should assume a position about forty feet in front of the catcher and in a direct line with the throw from the outfielder. He listens for the catcher's call of "Cut it" or "Let it go." He should be ready to throw to second base to catch the runner.

Fig. 13.5 THE CUT OFF MAN (first baseman Mike Hegan) assumes a position about forty feet in front of the catcher and on a direct line with the throw from the outfielder. He listens for the catcher's call of "Cut it" or, "Let it go." He is ready to throw to second base to catch the runner.

The outfielder stands out there and thinks: "Now, I've got Lonnie Smith running at second base. I have very little chance of throwing him out at home, unless I get that terrific line drive with the one-hop catch. Therefore, I must be sure to throw the ball low so that the cutoff man can cut if off and make a play on the hitter going to second base."

Even on routine fly balls to the outfield with no one on base, the outfielders should get into the habit of making *good, low, hard* throws into second base.

We like to have as many free men as possible get in a line so that, if the cutoff is missed, one of them has a chance to recover the ball quickly and hold the opposition down to the least advanced base.

Even major league teams miss some cutoffs, and the result is often the ball game. If the outfielder can hit the cutoff man, he will prevent the runner going to second on the throw.

Run-down play

Whenever a player is trapped between two bases, he should be run back toward the base he left. Ideally, it should take no more than two throws to retire the runner (Fig. 13.27).

Fig. 13.6 TRAPPED BETWEEN TWO BASES, the base runner (Rickey Henderson) should be run back toward the base he came from. If he cannot make the tag, the infielder should get the player running as hard as he can and then throw the ball to the first baseman who makes the tag.

The important point in a run-down play is to make the runner *commit himself.* If a runner has been caught off first base, the first baseman has to get the runner started toward second a little and then give the ball to the second baseman. The second baseman should get him running as hard as he can and then throw the ball to the first baseman, who makes the tag.

The player with the ball must run at full speed toward the runner, while holding the ball in a throwing position. One good fake with a full-arm motion will often fool the runner and make him change direction and run into the tag.

When this play fails to work, the infielders involved probably did not get the runner going at full speed. They also may have tried to throw the ball too many times; before they knew it, they were running into each other.

DEFENSIVE PLAY SITUATIONS

Defending against the bunt

To defend against the bunt with runners on first or first and second, quick thinking by the defense is necessary. The pitcher and the first baseman should break in. The third baseman should position himself almost on top of the bunter, forcing him to bunt to the first baseman, who has a chance of getting the man at second. Of course, the second baseman must cover first base.

The most effective way to defense the sacrifice bunt is to throw the batter high, fast balls in the strike zone.

With runners on first and second, if the ball is bunted on the third base side, the pitcher should break quickly toward the third base line. If he can handle it quickly enough, he should make the play at third base. In fact, if he is alert, a good fielding pitcher can make this play most of the time, but it requires a significant amount of practice time to perfect. However, if the ball is bunted hard enough and the pitcher cannot get to it, the third baseman must be sure to go after it instead of going to the base. This is a tough play for the third baseman.

Defending against the steal

The pitcher must keep the runners tight. If the base runner gets a running start, he has a good chance of stealing a base. Therefore, the pitcher should always remember to *make the runner stop.*

The pitcher must hold the ball long enough to make the runner stop before he throws it to home plate. However, if the runner has a big lead or starts his break, the pitcher should step back off the rubber.

The second baseman and shortstop must communicate with each other in order to know who is covering. As soon as the runner at first breaks, the shortstop or second baseman, whoever is covering, must break with him. He should not wait until the ball gets by the hitter; he must be there *on time.*

Defending against the double steal

With runners on first and third, the shortstop and second baseman must determine who will cover second. Normally, the shortstop is the cutoff man with a left-hander at the plate, while the second baseman handles this role with a right-handed batter.

With men on first and third and the runner on first trying to steal, the catcher must first give the runner at third a quick look. If the runner at third has too big a lead, he may attempt to pick him off. Merely looking at the runner will very likely start him back toward third, and then the throw can be made to second base to get the runner going into second.

The four basic ways to stop the double steal are:

1. Look the runner back to third, then make the throw to second base.
2. Have the catcher throw directly back to the pitcher and then trap the runner off third.

3. Throw directly to the shortstop, who moves in about ten feet in front of second base.

4. Have the catcher throw directly to third.

The last three plays must be made on prearranged signals.

Defending against the squeeze play

There is no defense unless the pitcher knows the exact pitch the squeeze is to occur on. If the runner has tipped off the play by breaking too soon, or the bunter has squared around too soon, the pitcher can defense the play by knocking down the hitter. Otherwise, the only defense in a squeeze situation is to come to a set position, and use high, fast balls that are hard to bunt. The runner should not be allowed to get too much of a lead.

Defending against the hit-and-run and run-and-hit

Actually, it becomes a guessing game, with the catcher trying to guess when these plays will be attempted. A pitchout, however, will break up these offensive tactics. Since the hitter is told to hit the ball no matter where it is pitched, the pitch should be thrown high and away, or impossible to hit. Then, the catcher's job is to throw the runner out at second.

Pick-off play

On the play at second base, many teams like to use the "count" play. The "daylight" play has also been used successfully. Whether it is executed at first or second, the pick-off play requires an alert pitcher who is aggressive at throwing the ball. A pitcher who is not aggressive, or one who is slow in his actions, will have a difficult time making this play.

On the "count" play at second base, the pitcher takes the sign and goes into a stretch position. The moment he comes to this position, he should turn his head toward second base. As he turns his back toward the plate, he should say, "One thousand one and . . ." This time span is usually about two seconds, depending upon how fast the pitcher is executing the pivot and throw. Then, he should whirl and make his throw. The second baseman or shortstop will break at that precise moment.

When the runner at first base takes too long a lead, the first baseman and pitcher can team up to pick him off. When the pitcher looks over to check the runner before his delivery to the plate, the first baseman gives his sign, such as hitching up his pants. Then the first baseman dashes behind the runner, and the pitcher throws the ball over the base.

DEFENSIVE SITUATIONS

Single to left field, no one on base (Fig. 13.7)

We prefer that the shortstop go in and take the throw at the bag and have the second baseman back him up. We feel this is more effective than having the shortstop go out a few feet, with the second baseman coming in and backing him up.

If a speedster like Rickey Henderson or Tim Raines hits a single to left, for example, he should round first base running at full speed. Now, if the outfielder should get a little nonchalant and lob the ball into the shortstop, who is out in front of the bag fifteen to twenty feet, the base runner might very well keep on running. By the time another relay is made, the runner has slid safely into the base.

The reason we do this is to protect against the exceptional base runner who might try to outhustle the play in which the shortstop moves out to short left field. If it is an ordinary base hit and not too deep, we want our outfielders to throw directly to second base. If the ball gets by either man, the first baseman is also in a good backup position. The catcher and right fielder are going down to the first base area, too.

This procedure also applies on a single to right field. On a routine ball, the right fielder throws directly to the second baseman, rather than hitting the

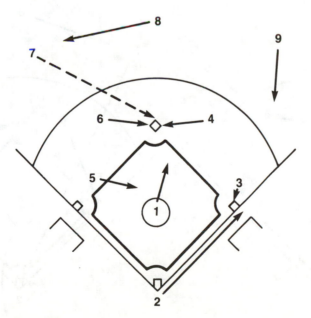

Fig. 13.7

cutoff man some fifteen feet in front of the bag. However, the batter-runner is not as likely to out-hustle the throw in from right field as he would on one from the left field side.

Single to left field, man on first (Fig. 13.8)

This is a routine play, nothing special, but one that must be executed properly. The shortstop has to move out to the cutoff position, in line with the left fielder's throw to third base. If the third baseman calls, "Cut it off," he should cut it off. If the runner keeps on going into third, the shortstop should let it go through.

The pitcher backs up third base bacause of the likelihood that the play will be made there. The catcher remains at home plate, while the first and second basemen cover their respective bases.

Single to left field, man on second, first and second, or bases loaded (Fig. 13.9)

This is a basic cutoff play in which the third baseman serves as the cutoff man. We like the third baseman to handle this play because he can get into the cutoff position very quickly; the first baseman has much farther to go.

The cutoff man is in a better position a few steps closer to home plate, so he can move into the ball. When the ball comes in all the way from the outfield,

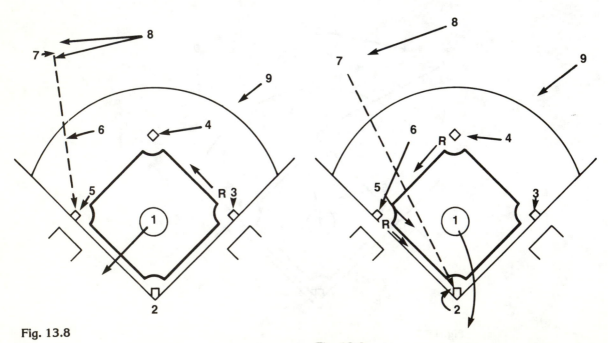

Fig. 13.8

Fig. 13.9

there is no reason for the cutoff man to just stand there and take the throw on a short or bad hop. Instead, he can either move in or back to make the ball easier to handle. So, we prefer him to be closer to home plate and move toward the ball, so as to be in a position to make the play at second base if necessary.

Occasionally, the third baseman has to dive after the ball in the hole, and cannot recover in time to get back and serve as the cutoff man. In this case, the first baseman must hustle into the cutoff position.

Double, possible triple to left center, no one on base, or man on third or second, or men on third and second bases (Fig. 13.10)

The shortstop goes out to a spot in left center to become the relay man. Instead of going to second base, the second baseman comes over and backs up. He is the "trailer" man, about thirty feet behind the shortstop in line with third base.

This play demands a double-cutoff man, a "trailer." If a hurried throw does miss the mark, the defense still has a chance for a play at third or home. If the hit is a sure double and the first baseman has nothing to do at first base, he should go over and cover second base.

Since the pitcher may not be sure which base he should back up, he should go halfway between home and third and then back up the base where the throw is going. If the play develops at third base, he will go there.

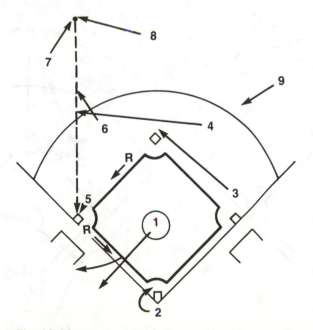

Fig. 13.10

Single to center field, man on first (Fig. 13.11)

This is a simple cutoff play in which the shortstop is the cutoff man on the throw from center field to third base. He lines himself up with the throw. It is up to him or the third baseman to call, "Cut it off" or, "Let it go."

Actually, in a big-league game, where there is a lot of noise made, the shortstop usually makes up his own mind, depending on whether the throw is on the line or not. He also knows who is running and whether he has a chance to throw out the man at third, or if he should cut the ball off and make the cutoff play at second base.

Here, again, it depends on the score. Sometimes, if the winning run is going in to third, he may have more of a tendency to let the throw go through.

Single to center field, men on first and second, or men on first, second and third (Fig. 13.12)

This situation involves two different throws. The pitcher breaks halfway between second and third, not knowing whether the throw is going to third base or directly home.

If the throw is to home plate, of course, the first baseman has to be in a cutoff position, a spot fifty-five feet from home plate in line with the throw. If the throw goes to third base, he must hustle back to first base to cover that bag.

The shortstop should be the cutoff man for a possible throw to third base. The second and third baseman cover their respective bases.

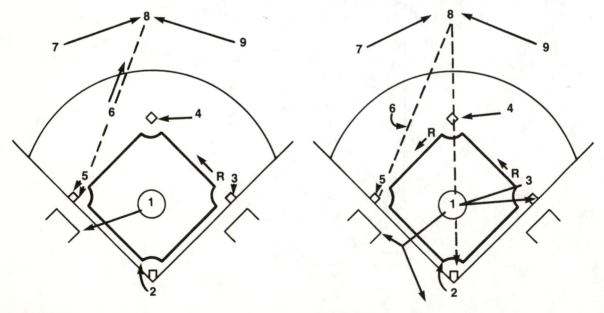

Fig. 13.11   Fig. 13.12

Single to right field, man on first base, or men on third and first (Fig. 13.13)

This routine play involves the runner attempting to go to third on a base hit to right field. The shortstop stations himself about forty-five feet from third base, on a direct line from third base to the outfielder fielding the ball.

The pitcher moves over and backs up third base in line with the throw, and the second and third basemen cover their bases. The left fielder should move in toward third base as quickly as he possibly can. He has a chance to get in quite close and be of some assistance by the time the runner goes from first to third.

Single to right field, man on second base, or men on second and third bases (Fig. 13.14)

This is also a routine play, where the first baseman takes a cutoff position about forty-five feet from home plate. The second baseman has to cover first base for this reason: if the throw is late or the center yells, "Cut it off," the first baseman will cut it off and throw it to the second baseman.

If the second baseman is not behind him at first base, this runner can go two-thirds of the way down and still come back if the ball is cut off. But if the second baseman comes in behind him, we will have him in a trap. Thus, the second baseman is the key to the play; he must come over to first base.

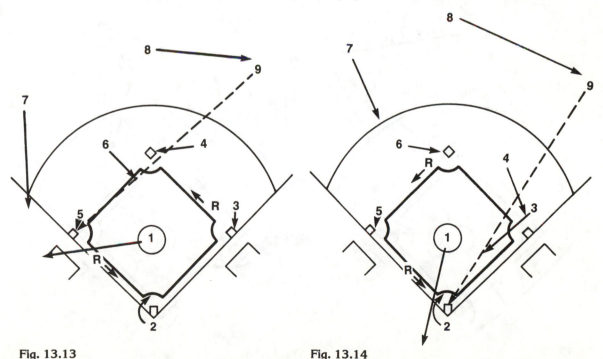

Fig. 13.13   Fig. 13.14

If the first baseman dives after the ground ball and cannot act as the cutoff man, the third baseman has to come in quickly for the cutoff play. We will just have the first and second basemen criss-cross. After attempting to field the ball, the first baseman continues on and covers second, while the second baseman, after his unsuccessful attempt, continues to cover first base.

Single to right field, men on first and second, or men on first, second, and third (Fig. 13.15)

The shortstop comes over and acts as the cutoff man for the throw to third base. The second baseman has to go to second base.

The first baseman becomes a cutoff man in case the throw is made to the plate, but, if the throw goes to third, he must return and cover first base. The pitcher goes halfway between third and home to see where the throw goes.

The right fielder makes a low throw to the shortstop to keep the tying or winning run from going to third base. The left fielder moves into a point near the line and backs up third base.

The important thing in this situation is always to keep the tying or winning run from going to third with less than two out. Therefore, the right fielder should never make a foolish throw to the plate.

Occasionally, the pitcher has to become the cutoff man in this situation. If the first baseman cannot get the ball in the hole, he keeps moving toward

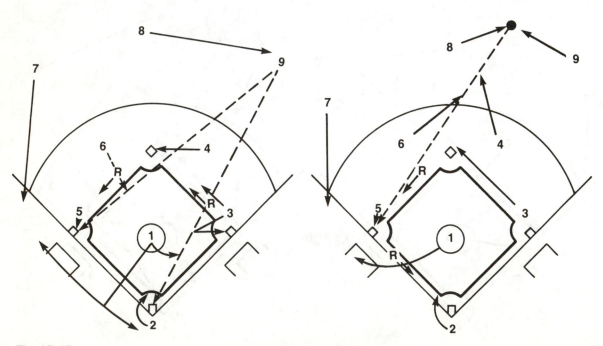

Fig. 13.15   Fig. 13.16

second, and the pitcher covers first in case the first baseman fields the ball. Since he is out of position, he just stops and comes back into the cutoff position.

Double, possible triple, to right center field (Fig. 13.16)

The second baseman goes out to a spot in short center field, in line with third base, to become the relay man. The shortstop trails behind him about thirty feet, in line with third base.

The first baseman trails the runner to second base, where he covers the bag, ready for a play at that base. In backing up third base, the pitcher plays as deep as possible. With the catcher protecting home plate, the left fielder moves in toward the area of third base.

If the play is at the plate, the second baseman again is the relay man, with the shortstop trailing behind. The first baseman is the cutoff man, with the pitcher backing up home plate.

Double, possible triple, down right field line, no one on base (Fig. 13.17)

The second baseman becomes the first relay man on the play to third base, with the shortstop becoming the "trailer" relay man. The first baseman trails

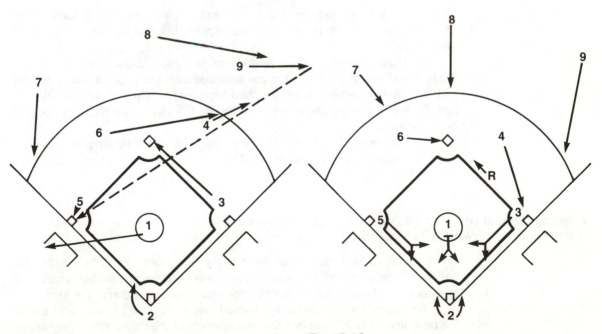

Fig. 13.17   Fig. 13.18

the runner into second base, and the pitcher backs up third base. The left fielder moves into an area behind third base.

With a runner on first base and the play at the plate, the second baseman goes to a spot in right field along the foul line in line with the right fielder and home. This is the rare situation when the first baseman goes out as a "trailer," while the shortstop covers second base.

The pitcher goes to a spot halfway between third and home to see where the throw is going.

Bunt situation in order, with a runner on first base (Fig. 13.18)

When anticipating a bunt, the third and first basemen should charge in when the pitcher throws the ball. The pitcher then breaks toward the plate.

Generally, if the ball is bunted hard, the play should go to second base. However, if the play at second is doubtful, the fielder should make sure he gets one out by throwing to first base.

The catcher fields all bunts possible, but when the third baseman fields the ball in close to home plate, he moves down and covers third base. The second baseman, in covering first base, "cheats" by shortening his position and his distance from the bag.

Bunt situation in order, with runners on first and second (Fig. 13.19)

The third baseman's judgment is the key to this play, and he is in full charge. The first objective is to retire the runner at third, but at least one runner *must* be retired.

The third baseman takes a position on the edge of the grass, just inside the line and four steps in front of the bag, and stationary. Upon delivering the ball, the pitcher breaks toward the third base foul line and strives to field the ball. On a ball that the pitcher can handle, the third baseman moves back and covers the base.

On balls bunted down the line, if he feels he has a better play, the third baseman should run the pitcher off. The play to first base is much easier for him in this situation.

The run-down play, with men on first and second, man on first picked off (Fig. 3.20)

The key rule is: *Run the runner back to the bag from which he came.* The ball should be given to the forward man, in this case the second baseman, and he should run hard at the runner, but not with a faking motion of the arm.

The tagger, the first baseman, should stay in front of his bag, and inside the base line. This will give him the proper angle of the throw. When the runner is about fifteen feet from the tagger, the tagger should make a break toward the

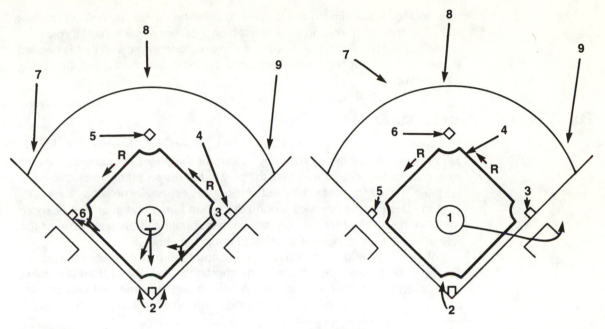

Fig. 13.19   Fig. 13.20

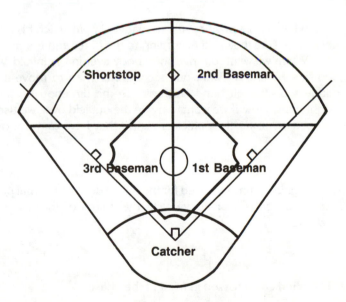

Fig. 13.21

runner. This is the sign to the thrower to give the tagger the ball on his first step. The thrower makes an easy, chest-high toss, not a quick, hard throw.

When the run-down play is worked correctly, one throw is all that is needed to get the runner at any base. The man without the ball must avoid interfering with the runner.

Pop flies to the infield (Fig. 13.21)

An infield pop fly is the responsibility of all infielders, and they must try for the ball until one fielder takes charge by calling for the play. Each infielder has his area, but occasionally he may take the play out of his area if he takes charge of the play. The play should not be called too soon, especially on windy days.

On questionable pop flies around the mound area and after one or more infielders have called for the play, the pitcher should call the last name of the fielder he thinks is in the best position to make the play.

All pop flies hit directly behind the first and third basemen are the responsibility of the second baseman and the shortstop. The first or third baseman, rather than the catcher, should take all balls between home and first or third bases, because the cut or slice of the ball is moving it back toward the infield.

DEFENSIVE SIGNALS

From his dugout position, the manager should watch his infielders and outfielders to be sure they shift according to the hitter and the game situation.

When we want to move somebody over in the infield, we use hand signals. For instance, if we want our second baseman to move over, we hold up two fingers on the left hand and point to the direction he should move with the right hand. Now, if we want to move the outfield over, we use the towel. Anytime we use the towel, the outfielders know they have to move over.

Infield deep

The signal commonly used for the infield deep or normal position is both hands raised chest-high or above, with the palms of the hands turned toward the fielders.

Infield halfway

The hands are crossed in front of the chest.

Infield close

For the short position, the hands are both waved in short circles toward the chest.

Pitchout

Another defensive signal is the call for the pitchout. The pitchout sign is given to the catcher if the coach anticipates a steal or a hit-and-run play. The clenched fist is often used as the pitchout signal.

Double steal defense

When there are runners on first and third and a double steal is anticipated, I have signals which I will give to my catcher. We have three different ways in which we defense this play:

1. Throw through to second.
2. Throw back to the pitcher.
3. Throw directly to third base.

There is the question of whether I want him to throw through or not, although 90 percent of the time we will have him throw through. I will tell my catcher: "If I don't do anything, you go ahead and throw through or throw to the shortstop. Now, if I want you to throw directly back to the pitcher, I will rub across my shirt, which will mean, 'Throw it back to the pitcher or make the bluff play."

We also have a signal to throw directly to third base, without even a bluff. This play will often catch a runner who has a double steal in mind. When a weak hitter is coming up, we do not want to take a chance of throwing the ball to second base, so the catcher just turns and fires directly to third base. On occasion, we will catch the over-aggressive base runner.

If the catcher is throwing to second, he might signal the pitcher by adjusting the side of his mask with his gloved hand. If he wants the pitcher to cut off the throw, the catcher should clench his fist before giving his sign. The pitcher might reply by removing his glove and tucking it under his right arm.

Some coaches signal their catchers to use one of the following moves:

Signal	*Action*
1. Throw through to second base	Rubbing shirt and pants downward
2. Throw back to the pitcher	Rubbing across the shirt
3. Full bluff throw	Folding both arms

Intentional pass

In giving a batter an intentional pass, we will whistle, and when the catcher looks up, we hold up four fingers, or point to first base, meaning, "Put him on."

DEFENSIVE DRILLS

Along with hitting and base running practice, the practice program should be built around the use of sound, effective defensive drills. While game experiences are extremely important, no coaching technique is more beneficial to the defense than well-supervised drills in which the coach serves in the role of instructor.

The following defensive drills can serve as the nucleus of a well-rounded training program. The coach must use his judgment as to the length of each drill. Every drill should be executed in a spirited and enthusiastic manner, rather than in a dull, listless atmosphere. Hustle and enthusiasm will do much to make a practice period productive and enjoyable.

Game situation drill

This drill is designed to give a team practice in all types of game situations. One team plays its regular defensive positions, while another team acts as base runners lined up behind home plate. Along with many other objectives, this drill provides the outfielders with valuable practice in backing up bases.

The coach, standing by the batter's box, hits all types of balls with a fungo bat to any position in the field. Before each ball is hit, the coach calls out the number of outs, inning, and score. The runners run until they are thrown out or forced, or until they score or three outs are made.

Bunt defense

The defense must drill against all possible bunt situations. The bunt defense drill will also provide valuable practice in bunting. The offense is divided into two groups: the bunters and the base runners.

A runner is put on first base, with the first baseman playing on the bag. After taking his set position, the pitcher throws the ball to the plate and the bunter lays the ball down. The play is made at first or second base.

The defense tries to make the play at second base, if possible. The second baseman covers first base and the shortstop moves over to second base.

Coverage on steals

This drill gives the defense practice at keeping the base runner close to first base and throwing him out at second base. The pitcher, catcher, and infielders all get good defensive work, while the base runners get experience at taking a good lead and getting a good start.

The pitchers form a line behind the mound, and the base runners form a line near first base. The pitcher tries to prevent the runner from getting too big a lead, and if the runner thinks he has a large enough lead, he will try to steal

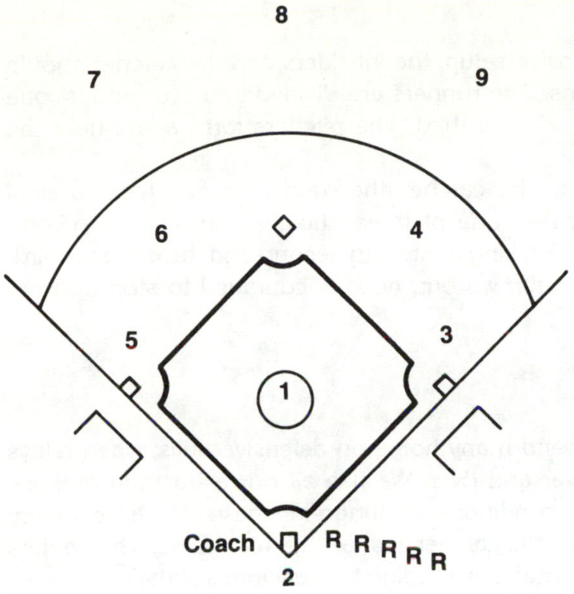

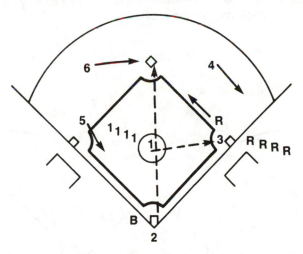

Fig. 13.22 GAME SITUATION DRILL 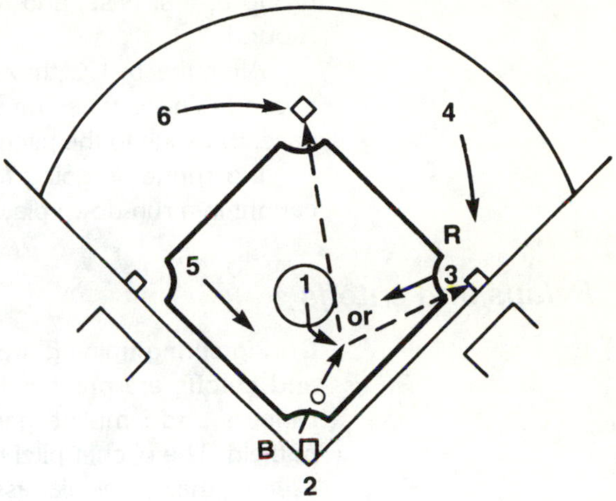   **Fig. 13.23** BUNT DEFENSE DRILL

Fig. 13.24 COVERAGE ON STEALS

second base. The catcher gets practice at throwing to second base, and the infielders receive experience at covering the base and taking the throw.

The coach should watch the pitcher closely to detect any balk motion. He should acquaint every pitcher with the correct rules pertaining to proper delivery to home and motion to the bases.

Double steal coverage

To drill the team in this defensive setup, the infielders and the catcher should assume their regular positions. The runners are divided into two groups: one group at first base, and the other at third. The pitchers form a line near the mound.

After the ball is thrown to the catcher, the runner on first tries to steal second. The catcher must make one of three choices: throwing to second base, throwing to the pitcher, or faking a throw to second and throwing to third.

If a runner is going to be thrown out, he is encouraged to stop and get caught in a run-down play.

Relays and cutoffs

During spring training, we spend many hours on defensive drills, when relays and cutoffs are practiced over and over. We use all our extra men as base runners and simulate game conditions by fungo-ing base hits all over the outfield. The pitcher pitches to the catcher, just as in a real game. The fielders execute their particular assignments according to the various situations.

In another drill, we line up all our outfielders in center field. Each one takes four turns fielding and throwing the ball. We make sure the players are deep enough so that they must throw to the relay man. The relay man should be the second baseman or the shortstop.

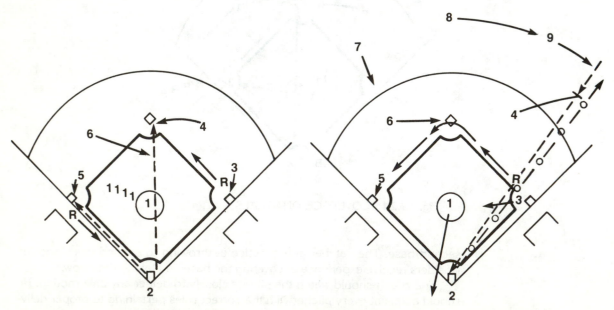

Fig. 13.25 DOUBLE STEAL COVERAGE   **Fig. 13.26** RELAY AND CUT-OFF DRILL

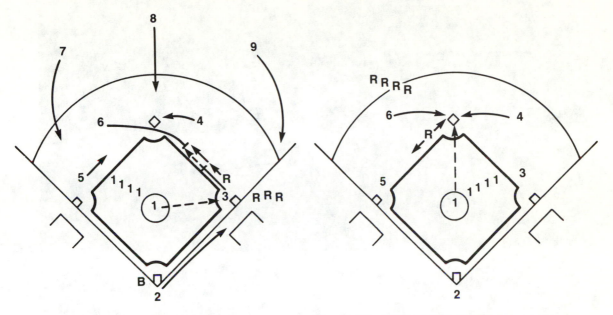

Fig. 13.27 RUN-DOWN PLAY DRILL   **Fig. 13.28** PICK-OFF PLAY DRILL

Run-down play

The run-down play should be practiced often, with the drill involving the entire team, either as fielders or runners. The pitchers form a line at the mound, and the catcher and infielders assume their proper positions. The runners line up close to first base.

The runner at first base permits himself to be picked off by breaking for second, and it is the responsibility of the defense to put him out. Later, the runners will form a line at second base and the same situation will occur there. Finally, the runners move down to third base and permit themselves to be picked off.

Pick-off play drill

The pitcher, along with his catcher and infielders, needs practice in executing the pick-off play. The pitchers form a line off to the first base side of the mound, while one pitcher takes his set position on the rubber. The base runners form a line near second base. The second baseman and shortstop assume their normal positions.

Organization

14

There is no easy formula for developing a winning baseball program. Indeed, the task of fielding a championship team involves many factors, over some of which the coach has little or no control. However, no factor is more important to team success than a dedicated coach who gives and demands 100 percent effort and leaves *nothing* undone in setting up a sound organization for conditioning and training.

Good organization, along with capable personnel, is the surest way for a baseball club to achieve success. Careful attention to the details of organization is a *must,* both on the playing field and in the front office. Only through effective team management can maximum utilization of time, coaching effort, and player participation be achieved.

Building a successful baseball program on the college or high school level is a cooperative effort and includes the school administration, faculty, community, and the news media. If the coaching staff does not have the support and cooperation of both the school and the community, the task of producing a top caliber baseball program is very difficult, indeed.

Fielding a team that is well conditioned, fundamentally sound in basic techniques, and well disciplined in offensive and defensive team strategy and play should be the primary objective of every organizational plan. However, a number of major problems often make the job harder to accomplish.

Weather conditions are unpredictable, particularly in the northern regions of the country. The first concern of coaches in the cold weather regions is to

---

Fig. 14.1 A WELL ORGANIZED AND WELL CONDUCTED PRACTICE program is a prime requisite for preparing a team for game competition. Organization of a meaningful practice schedule is one of the most important tasks of the coach. Above, pitchers on the San Diego Padres have an opportunity to practice their pick-off throw to second base, while below two collegiate teams compete in early season game action.

secure satisfactory indoor practice facilities. Then, too, the length of the daily practice session is sometimes limited by school districts. Another problem can be a meager budget, one that forces the team to play with poor equipment and inadequate facilities. In this regard, the tiled infield that drains effectively, indoor facilities, and a batting cage can be of inestimable value to a baseball program.

A quality baseball facility provides a sense of pride to players, coaches, and spectators. An increasing number of schools have built impressive stadiums that provide a well manicured field, spacious dugouts, large, fenced in playing field, an eye-catching scoreboard, press box, and a snackbar.

At Fresno State University, a fund drive accumulated $1.6 million, giving developers enough capital to commence with the $2.2 million project (Fig. 14.2). "This will add a whole new dimension to our program," said Bob Bennett, Fresno State coach who pushed long and hard for a new stadium. The initial phase will be installing the superstructure and the seats. Every seat in the stadium will be theatre-style. Later, new locker rooms, concession stands, and a new press box will be added.

While a "complete" ball park might appear to be prohibitive for many communities, even the most financially poor schools and area could have the facility capability if they would seek the aid of interested people and organizations in the community. With some creativity, "imagination of what could be," and a coordinated thrust of some people who will work hard for a good cause, a quality diamond can be a reality.

Baseball coaches are unanimous in declaring that the quality of officiating is one of the key factors in a successful baseball program. Unquestionably, an umpire who lacks the consistency, judgment, and necessary knowledge of the rules can spoil the game. Therefore, every athletic director and baseball coach should give just as much care to the selection of their baseball umpires as they do to basketball and football officials.

LEARNING HOW TO WIN

Winning in athletics is no accident. In addition to hard work and skill, it requires a design. Successful organizations have a system which involves *one* way of doing things. Consistency in performing the basic skills of baseball is most essential.

The intangible that characterizes most winning teams—a blend of leadership, team spirit and a sense of common cause.

Fig. 14.2 THE BUILDING OF A GOOD PLAYING FIELD AND STADIUM has proven a major break-through for many college and high school baseball programs. A quality baseball facility provides a comfortable place for people to watch the games. Above is an artist's rendition of Fresno State's new Pete Beiden Field, named after the longtime and successful former coach of the Bulldogs.

ROLE OF THE MANAGER

The head coach or manager's primary responsibilities fall generally into five categories: 1) picking the players; 2) motivating the players; 3) game strategy; 4) public relations; and 5) communicating to his team. No other responsibility of a manager is more essential than providing his team with leadership. *He must make his players want to play!* To accomplish this task, he must possess three basic qualities of leadership:

1. The respect of his players
2. The ability to teach
3. The ability to inspire his players to put out a little extra

The able manager can assert his leadership by his own enthusiasm, by shouting encouragement to his men on the field. He is constantly urging his players in the dugout to talk it up.

Before each game, the manager has to decide who is going to play. He makes out the lineup and posts it on the dugout wall early enough to inform his team who is scheduled to play that day.

Baseball needs more coaches and managers who can teach and are capable of communicating, men with the ability to impart knowledge (for instance, of "how to make the double play"). I know of a major league coach who told a player, "Here is the way you make the double play . . ." That was all there was to it. He failed to break down this basic play into fundamentals such as; the approach to second base, getting under body control, the four or five ways of making the double play, how to react if the ball is thrown to infielder's right, etc.

Another prime responsibility of the manager is maintaining discipline, and seeing that players are staying in proper physical condition. If necessary, the manager may have to fine a player for breaking the club rules.

While a no-nonsense attitude on the bench is necessary, the capable manager knows when to break up the tension with some timely humor.

Baseball needs more coaches and managers who can teach and are capable of communicating.

In selecting an effective batting order, the head coach or manager should by guided by these basic principles:

1. Keep the best hitters together.
2. Give all the opportunities you can to your best hitters.
3. Players who are good at getting on base should hit before those who hit the long ball and drive in runners.
4. A left-handed hitter should follow a hitter who gets on base often and is a base stealing threat.

Another responsibility of the manager is establishing an effective set of signals, and giving them during a game. A typical set includes signals for a batter to hit or take a pitch, bunt, sacrifice, hit-and-run, squeeze play, or steal. When the third base coach receives a signal from the bench, he flashes it to the batter.

Handling pitchers is perhaps the most important responsibility a manager has during a ball game. He has to watch for those little signs that will tell him his pitcher is losing some of his stuff.

"There is a tendency to leave your starter out there too long," said Steve Boros, manager of the Oakland A's. "Every pitch a pitcher throws when he's tired leads to bad habits and injuries, and detracts from what he will have in his next start. There are exceptions, of course, such as the Carltons and Ryans who can pitch 300 innings year after year. I don't believe, however, in placing that kind of burden on the average arm." *Every pitch a pitcher throws past 130 is just taking away from what he will have five days later.*

In watching his players on the field, the manager must make certain they are playing each hitter properly. Occasionally, he has to tell a player to shift his position on the field.

Criteria in Selecting a Manager

In detailing his criteria for selection of a new manager, Roy Eisenhardt, president of the Oakland A's, revealed that the candidates should share these seven attributes:

1. A strong personal self discipline
2. An ability to teach and develop young players and mold them with experienced personnel
3. A utilization of coaches and instructors in such a manner as to permit their individual styles and opinions to have full effect
4. A recognition of the significant mental and physical stress on the contemporary athlete, and an ability to understand various behavioral reactions to that stress
5. A sense of the obligation of a professional sports team to its community
6. Sensitivity to differing racial and ethnic backgrounds
7. Patience

The head coach should not be a "Mr. Everything"—and try to do everything himself.

Essentially, the prime responsibility of the manager is to see that all of his sessions and drills are organized and that everyone is kept busy throughout the practice. Making out the training schedule, of course, is a very important responsibility. He has to make his practice sessions interesting and challenging, and cover all the essential areas of the game, with the emphasis on conditioning, both physical and mental.

Fig. 14.3 LEADERSHIP is most effective when the manager or head coach has the respect and confidence of the players. Ralph Houk is the type of manager who by his actions and rapport with players commands their respect. He treats every player, one to twenty-five, the same. That is the toughest job as a manager: to blend, juggle and cope with twenty-five personalities. Houk's clubs have been team-oriented, determined and spirited.

Basic Responsibilities of Managers

- Emphasize the basic fundamentals.
- Use your time correctly.
- Emphasize constantly the importance of speed.
- Create within your players a desire to win.
- Develop confidence and self-esteem in your players.
- Have a purpose behind everything you do.
- Do not show up a player. Talk to him privately.
- Team meetings should be meaningful and to the point.

TEAM MANAGEMENT

The organization of a baseball program involves many aspects with which the coach should be concerned year-round. Indeed, the job of a head baseball coach is often a twelve-month assignment on the college level.

The management of a baseball team includes the following areas:

1. Conditioning and training
   a. Off-season
   b. Preseason
   c. During season
2. Team selection
3. Game preparation
4. Facilities and equipment
5. Maintenance of the playing field
6. Public relations
7. Player recruitment
8. The budget and its use
9. Making the schedule
10. Planning for trips
11. Selecting umpires
12. Scouting needs

Check lists

Check lists should be developed for specific managerial areas, including every drill or fundamental skill to be accomplished during the preseason workouts. This list should be broken down into the following major areas: conditioning, team offense, team defense, and position drills for pitchers, catchers, infielders, and outfielders.

Check list for games (home game)

· Prepare field
· Practice balls and bats
· Get game balls ready
· Prepare a pre-game practice schedule
· Appoint official scorebook keeper
· Distribute game uniforms
· Scorebook and pencils
· Send out notice to umpires
· Dressing facilities for visiting team
· Designate dressing facilities for umpires
· Replenish first aid kit
· Fill out line-up card
· Carry rule book (in first aid kit or coach's brief case)
· Rosin bags

- Check over bats
- Get a couple ball shaggers
- Ticket takers
- Complimentary tickets for visiting team and press passes

For games away, additional concerns include:

- Arranging transportation
- Prepare trip itinerary
- Make reservations
- Meal money
- Towels

GAME PREPARATION

Pre-game schedule

Batting practice

- Home team
- Visiting team

Infield-outfield drill

- Home team
- Visitors

Presentation of starting line-ups and review of ground rules with umpires

Facilities

Practice facilities should include the following:

- Portable batting cage, batting nets, and tunnels
- Pitcher's practice area with mounds, rubbers, home plates, and pitching control strings
- Protective screen for the batting practice pitcher
- Screen for the protection of the first baseman
- Batting tees

COACHES' AND PLAYERS' CODE OF ETHICS

Baseball as a game has been played in the colleges and universities of this country for more than 100 years. Only the highest standards of sportsmanship and conduct are expected of players, coaches, and others associated with the game.

1. It is the duty of the coach to be in control of his players at all times in order to prevent any unsportsmanlike act toward opponents, officials, or spectators.

2. Coaches are expected to comply wholeheartedly with the intent and spirit of the rules. The deliberate teaching of players to violate the rules is indefensible.

3. Coaches should teach their players to respect the dignity of the game, officials, opponents, and the institutions which they represent.

4. Coaches should confine their discussion with the game officials to the interpretations of the rules, and not constantly challenge umpire decisions involving judgement.

5. Bench jockeying should not be allowed. Coaches are to prohibit bench jockeying, which would include personal and malicious remarks, cursing, and obscene language toward opponents, umpires, or spectators.

6. Coaches should refrain from any personal action that might arouse players or spectators to unsportsmanlike behavior.

7. Coaches should expect from the umpires a courteous and dignified attitude toward players and themselves.

8. Coaches should seek help from school administrators in controlling unruly students and spectators.

Team policies

1. *Appearance.* You are requested to dress properly both on and off the campus. Your practice and game uniform are to be worn properly.

2. *Class Attendance.* You must attend classes regularly and on time. Class assignments and exams are to be prepared on time over the entire semester.

3. *Conduct on and off the Field.* You are expected to conduct yourself in a first class manner around the campus and the community.

   a. Refrain from drinking any alcoholic beverages both on and off the campus.
   b. Refrain from taking any drugs that are not prescribed by a physician.
   c. You are requested not to use any profane language.

4. *Practice and Game Schedules.* Practice and pre-game schedules will be posted in the locker room each day. You are required to read these

schedules. If you must be late for practice, or absent, you are requested to notify the coach. *There will be no excuses* for being late unless you notify the coach in advance.

The following policies will be adhered to:

a. No player may leave practice or a game without approval of the coach.

b. All injuries and sickness are to be reported immediately to the coaches and trainers.

5. *Locker Room Procedure.* You are expected to help keep your locker room in good condition. Your locker is to be kept clean and all trash is to be disposed of. Your shoes are to be cleaned off before returning to the locker room. Horse-play is not to be tolerated in the locker room.

6. *Equipment Room Procedure.* Players are not allowed in the equipment room. You are responsible for any equipment issued. Furthermore, equipment is to be taken care of in a proper manner.*

Dress and grooming

Major league ball clubs believe neatness really counts. In fact, most of them require their players to look their best on and off the field. At least twenty of the twenty-six teams favor jackets and many look with disfavor on jeans, especially on the road. Only one team—Cincinnati—prohibits facial hair but many others forbid beards and virtually all of them demand neatness.

Public image is very important to big-league teams. The Dodgers, along with many other clubs, set high standards, and they want the players to abide by those standards.

PLAYER PERSONNEL

Fielding a balanced club, of course, is a prime objective. Therefore, we have to consider the number of pitchers, catchers, infielders, and outfielders on our squad. *We are constantly looking for the "team players": those who are more interested in the success of the* team *than in their own individual success.*

Temperament and mental attitude have a lot to do with the speed of one's development. As in education, there are quick learners and slow learners. The same is true as far as ability is concerned.

Every coach or manager looks for the shortstop who can run well and has a good arm. If he is not a good hitter but hits from the left side, the player might be the type who can get on base by bunting or slapping the ball around. He does not have power, so the manager has to make allowances for this lack

---

* As compiled by the American Association of College Baseball Coaches.

because the shortstop position is not as demanding for power. The position itself is basically defensive in nature, but probably no team can win a championship without an outstanding shortstop.

In hitting, quickness of hand is so important. When there is a zing to the bat, when it jumps, coaches know they have someone. But running also makes a difference. Running is the tool that a player uses to make things happen.

Basically, coaches look for a player who has a quick bat, correct form, and takes a good stroke at the ball. Does he have power? Does he make contact? Actually, hitters are hard to judge. Pitchers are somewhat easier, since it is not difficult to see whether or not a pitcher can throw hard.

When evaluating an outfielder, the coach looks for more power than he would in a shortstop. From a physical standpoint, he looks for a strong arm, speed, and the ability to hit for power.

Scouts now look for speed and arm strength more than ever before—speed on the basepaths and arm strength to defend against that speed. Speed can not be taught, but stealing techniques can.

The mental aspects are also very important. The temperament and character of a player will prove a key factor in his success in baseball. How does he take adversity? Can he survive a batting slump? This is why we like our players to be able to react positively during moments of adversity. This will determine, to a large extent, whether or not they can bounce back.

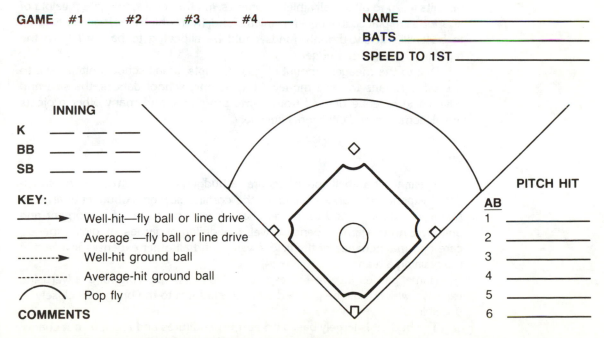

GAME #1 ____ #2 ____ #3 ____ #4 ____   **NAME** _____

BATS _____

SPEED TO 1ST _____

INNING

K   __ __ __
BB   __ __ __
SB   __ __ __

KEY:

→ Well-hit—fly ball or line drive
— Average —fly ball or line drive
--→ Well-hit ground ball
---- Average-hit ground ball
⌒ Pop fly

COMMENTS

PITCH HIT

AB
1 _____
2 _____
3 _____
4 _____
5 _____
6 _____

Fig. 14.4 PLAYER EVALUATION FORM (University of Illinois)

The following are the main qualities the coach or manager looks for in a young prospect:

1. Desire (Does he *want* to play?)
2. Speed (Can he run?)
3. Good arm (Can he throw?)
4. Good instincts and reflexes
5. Quick bat (Can he swing a bat?)
6. Aggressiveness (Does he hustle?)
7. Aptitude (Does he learn quickly?)
8. Character and habits
9. Physical qualifications (build, size, etc.)

FINANCE

In the great majority of schools and colleges, the baseball program must depend on financial sources other than gate receipts. While gate receipts are significant enough to assist programs at the larger schools, most contests on these levels do not charge admission. Instead, students are assessed an activity fee at the beginning of the school year, with a portion being placed in the athletic fund for baseball. Or, students may purchase an athletic card which permits them to attend all athletic contests. In other cases, the gate receipts of all sports are placed in a general athletic fund, from which a portion is allocated to baseball. Ideally, though, funds could be allocated to baseball from the regular school or P.E. budget.

Due to the meager amount of gate receipts, small schools often have to use other means to raise money. Concessions, school dances, the sale and advertising revenue derived from game programs, and many other projects are all common and can work effectively.

Budget

Each year, the baseball coach prepares a budget, or a statement of the anticipated expenditures and receipts for the coming season. A budget is an estimate of costs in regard to the purchase, care, and repair of equipment and uniforms; home game expense, travel, scheduling of games, medical expense, care and maintenance of the field, awards, and all other expenses involved in maintaining a team.

Home games involve the expense of officials, policing, and advertising expense, which must be planned so as to conform to the budget as closely as possible.

The budget is largely based on past expenditures and receipts, but changing conditions, from year to year, may require careful planning and control.

The NCAA allows a maximum of thirteen scholarships for baseball. Considering that a baseball squad consists of twenty-five or more players, it is rare for a coach to give out a full ride. Santa Clara, Nevada—Reno, and Fresno State are the only three schools in the NCBA to have the equivalent of thirteen full rides covering tuition, books, and room and board. A full baseball scholarship at Santa Clara is worth $8,037.

Gene Menges' program at San Jose State is operating on a budget of $15,828, which covers grant-in-aid, travel, meals, equipment, recruiting costs, stadium rental, umpire fees, and telephone costs. The coach divides the scholarship money ($5,959), the equivalent of two full rides at SJS, among several of his players.

VARSITY BASEBALL BUDGET
(Listed prices only estimates)

Miscellaneous Expenses	*Total*	
Awards	$500.00	
Cleaning	500.00	
Publications	100.00	
Recruiting	100.00	
Scouting	100.00	
Telephone	100.00	
Oranges/cokes	100.00	
Total Misc. Expenses		$ 1,500.00
Home Games		
Umpires (2) Single games ($50)	$ 650.00	
Doubleheaders ($90)	1,000.00	
Police	500.00	
Total Home Games		$ 2,150.00
Equipment and Uniforms		
Shoes (24)	$ 1,200.00	
Caps (35)	245.00	
Catchers' leg guards (2)	80.00	
Batters' rosin bags (1 Doz.)	20.00	
Pitchers' rosin bags (1 Doz.)	5.00	
Catchers' body protectors (2)	70.00	
Undershirts (12)	96.00	
Sun glasses (4)	24.00	
Batters' rungs-donuts (4)	20.00	
Catchers' masks (2)	90.00	
Catcher's mitt, Rawlings (1)	100.00	
Catcher's mitt, Wilson (1)	100.00	
Inner hose (10 Doz.)	200.00	
Jackets, nylon (5)	150.00	
Batters' helmets (21) (7 reg., 7 left flap, 7 right flap)	420.00	
Uniforms, grey (6)	300.00	
Shirts, green sleeve (24)	170.00	

Pants, white (6)	200.00	
Baseballs (40 Doz.)	1,600.00	
Bats (10)	300.00	
Hose, 9″ pro-stirrup (60)	250.00	
Hose, striped (50)	200.00	
Home plate (1)	40.00	
Pitcher's rubber (4-sided) (1)	40.00	
Scorebooks (3)	20.00	
Bases, Hollywood (1 set)	150.00	
Total Equipment and Uniforms		$ 6,090.00
Games Away (12)		$ 6,000

Total Miscellaneous Expenses	$ 1,500.00
Total Home Game Expenses	$ 2,150.00
Total Equipment and Uniforms	$ 6,090.00
Total Games Away Expenses	$ 6,000.00
Total Guarantees Payable	300.00
Total Requested	$16,040.00

Fund-raising

Baseball coaches who desire to upgrade the quality of their programs are too often discouraged by the lack of funding. Sooner or later, they realize that any money for improvements will have to be raised by themselves.

Through the years, numerous schools and colleges have upgraded their programs by purchasing and building equipment and facilities with money from sources other than the regular budget. They achieved their goals by getting people in the local community to donate labor and machinery and by raising thousands of dollars for the purchase of equipment and program materials.

"Every coach can do it—with a little thought and a lot of effort," said Jerry Cougill of Reed Cutter High School, Braidwood, Illinois. "Probably the best idea we have had is selling advertising signs for our outfield fence. These 4′ × 8′ plywood signs are sold to local businesses for a yearly fee."

The baseball program booklet is another successful idea. Cougill explained that "Our booklet contains twenty-four pages of articles on our team, bios of our players, records, and advertising. Space was sold to local advertisers and billed according to the size of the ad."

The sale of school souvenirs was another successful venture for Cougill. Players and boosters sold school jackets, bumper stickers, and T-shirts. The school dance proved to be another good fund-raiser. "We made over $400 on one dance," said Cougill, "which enabled us to purchase a new pitching machine."

Other fund-raising ideas are a refreshment stand, gym night, tournament, car washes, and donut and cake sales.

PROMOTING THE BASEBALL PROGRAM

Baseball organization, whether on the college or high school level, involves "selling" the values of baseball to the athlete, his parents, the faculty, the administration, the student body, and the community. The idea that "baseball is a very worthwhile endeavor" must be promoted to the fullest.

A baseball coach has to be a salesman. He must sell not only himself but the sport as well. Therefore, he should welcome the opportunity to speak to almost any group about his program.

"The key to a successful baseball program is promotion—filling seats," said Ron Fraser, a twenty-year-veteran coach who has taken the University of Miami to the College World Series six times, winning in 1982. "It's nice to win, but you can draw well without a winning team, if you promote right. Socially, you have to make your ballpark the place to be, and that's what we've done."

In 1971, Fraser hired a full-time promotion director, Rick Remmert. Together, they have managed numerous promotions, like performances by the San Diego Chicken, and give-aways of cruises, used cars, and television sets. They have had Bathing Suit Days and lobster feeds. The result? The Hurricanes

Fig. 14.5 FILLING THE SEATS is one of the keys to a successful baseball program. To draw well, a ball park must be a comfortable place for people to watch games. This beautiful facility is in Mount Pleasant, Michigan, home of the Chippewas. It provides two press facilities, concessions, ticket sales booths, rest rooms, and storage.

drew a national record 163,261 to fifty-one home games, jamming the 4,500-seat stadium ten times. His operating budget is up $50,000 from last year to $350,000.

The following techniques should be considered by the baseball coach in promoting his program:

1. Send out weekly news releases containing information on the progress of the team.
2. Distribute information brochures to the news media and to opposing schools.
3. Inform the parents about what their sons are doing. Write to the prospects and parents. Arrange home visitations.
4. Hold an annual awards banquet, highlighted by the presentation of letters to deserving players.
5. Hold baseball clinics in the community, assisted by various players.
6. Encourage the players to watch professional contests, either in person or on TV.
7. Annual promotions might include, "Parents Day," "Senior Letterman's Day," and even a "Bat Day."

Public relations

The news media provide the principal link between the baseball coach and the public. Therefore, it is in the best interest of the coach and his program to cooperate to the fullest extent when dealing with the press and with radio and television.

Team support is directly related to the coverage of the team by the news media. Keeping the public informed and interested is the surest way to bring them out to the stadium.

In dealing with the press and radio-TV people, the baseball coach should:

1. Be honest, cooperative, and fair.
2. Refrain from playing favorites with reporters.
3. Provide fair treatment to all media.
4. Request the availability of a sports information man who can coordinate the distribution of all news.
5. Never use the news media as a propaganda or psychological tool.
6. Admit newsmen to the dressing room just as soon as possible after the game.
7. Never expect a reporter to be a cheerleader.
8. Invite reporters to attend practice sessions and meet with them after practice.
9. Reserve the press box and camera locations for the working press.

Relations with the news media

Once the season starts at home, the writers and radio-TV people start coming in from the time we start to hit. I have a responsibility to be available to the news media both before and after the game. Of course, when we win, it is very easy.

I have found that the best way to handle the press is to be as honest as I possibly can with them. When there are some things I cannot answer, I simply say, "I cannot answer that." Occasionally, I have said: "Off the record, I'll tell you this . . .," and I have never yet found anyone to break the rule. I really appreciate that. I feel that I can talk to them more freely this way. For instance, when I do not want something in print, I will say: "Off the record . . .," and they will honor that.

FACILITIES AND EQUIPMENT

The type and extent of the facilities and equipment should be based on the size of the budget. However, funding for good equipment and uniforms is one of the most important factors in building a successful baseball program. There are no substitutes for top quality uniforms and equipment, but, unfortunately, some school administrations limit baseball expenses by buying inferior goods, on the grounds that the sport does not pay its way.

As a rule, equipment should be purchased from representative jobbers of sporting goods from well-known manufacturers. Buying is usually made through several concerns, since no one manufacturer makes all the best equipment to fit a team's needs.

The following list of equipment and supplies has become standard for baseball programs throughout the country:

Backstop	Bats (including fungo bat)
Bat bag	Gloves
Bleachers	Rosin bags
Training room	Lockerroom (and showers)
Batting cage (portable)	Pitching machine
Catching paraphernalia	Scoreboard
Batting tee	Baseball bag
Bulletin board	Bases and home plate
Public address system	Sliding pit
Protective screens (pitcher, first base and behind second base)	Baseballs
Batters' helmets (protective)	Drinking fountain
Players' dugouts (benches)	Pitching control target
	Motion picture projector

Training kit   Batting cage nets or tunnels
Pitcher's plate   Portable pitching mound

All schools and colleges should have an equipment room where equipment can be stored when not in use. The storage space should be well ventilated, dry, and cool. During the playing season, an attendant takes care of the repair and laundering of equipment. Clean socks, undershirts, and supporters should be available each day. Shoes should be treated with a good leather oil, while gloves and mitts should be cleaned with a good cleaner such as tetrachloride and oiled with a leather oil such as Rawlings Glovolium. Uniforms, jackets, and caps should be dry-cleaned and mothproofed for storage at the end of the season.

Personal equipment

Baseball uniforms today, with their stretch nylon, double knit material, are very comfortable to play in. Inexpensive uniforms and equipment represent a policy of false economy. Good uniforms cost more but last for four or five years. Cheap uniforms must be replaced about every two years and are more expensive on a cost-per-year basis. Most schools have the players provide the most expensive single items, gloves and shoes.

Wearing a batting helmet which provides good overall protection of the head is not only a good safeguard against serious injuries but will help hitters overcome fear.

Items of personal equipment should include:

Uniforms (and stockings)
Sweat shirts
Inner hose
Glove
Traveling bag
Belt
T-shirts
Jackets (warm-up)
Shoes
Caps
Batting gloves
Supporters (and cups)
Sliding pads
Batting helmet
Sun glasses

Aluminum bats

A new "breed" of aluminum bats are being used today by college and high school hitters. They are bigger with more variety. Hillerich & Bradsby Company, for example, has a thirty-five inch bat that weighs only thirty-two ounces, yet has the largest legal barrel—a full two-and-three-quarter inches in diameter! The singles hitters definitely appreciate the larger hitting area without a loss of bat control.

Not every player will want to use a giant-barrel bat. Therefore, a full line of two-and-five-eighth-inch barrel bats are available with the "Pro Sonic" alloy. Of course, there is more to a bat than the material it is made from, namely "feel," balance point or swing weight, and hitting area.

Another new feature of aluminum bats is a thicker handle which the Louisville Slugger people call the Jackie Robinson style. It is a padded Tacki-Mac® grip which is a full one-and-one-quarter inches in diameter. Yet it does not add the weight a thicker metal handle would require.

Another variation is an unusual wood veneer grip that gives a hitter the feel of wood while dampening vibration. This comes in a one inch diameter thin-handle model. The bat is swing weighted like a standard-barrel bat, but the big hitters enjoy the additional mass and increased hitting area.

OTHER RESPONSIBILITIES

Scheduling of games

Most schools are in some conference or league, and games are usually scheduled at a meeting attended by representatives of all schools well before the start of the season. The respective coaches, through their athletic directors, will fill out their schedules with nonconference contests. There has been a recent trend toward more preseason tournaments on both the college and high school levels. In addition to stimulating interest and appeal of the baseball program, they can furnish a significant means of revenue.

Agreement as to dates of the games is perhaps the major problem of such scheduling. Each team in the league will play an equal number of games at home and away. Games away from home involve travel expense, and school teams must consider time taken away from classroom work.

Most teams are able to play an average of two to four games each week throughout the season. The number of games played often depends on the material on hand, particularly the number of pitchers.

Travel policies

When traveling to out-of-town games, members of the baseball squad should keep in mind that they represent not only themselves but their school and community as well. Therefore, their standard of dress and appearance should be taken very seriously.

Among the policies adopted by many school teams when traveling are:

1. Report ahead of scheduled time. The bus will not wait.
2. No gambling whatsoever!
3. Do not take candy or food with you.
4. Wear a shirt and tie. Be neat and well-dressed.
5. Coaches sit with their players on the bus.
6. Arrange in advance the meals at restaurants.
7. Members of the squad must eat and stay together.
8. Each player must take care of his own gear.
9. Be well-behaved on the bus going to the game.
10. Players must return with the team, unless excused by the head coach.

Season report

The baseball coach and his program should maintain a friendly relationship with the administration and the faculty. Therefore, the administration should be provided with a complete report on the previous baseball season.

The report should include:

1. Participation
2. Success of the program
3. Failure of the program
4. Grades and attendance
5. Equipment and facilities
6. Records
7. Physical condition
8. Needs
9. Comments
10. Outlook

Study and grades

Off-season preparation by the coach also involves checking on grades, making sure his players are hitting the books, and making certain that prospects are eligible for participation. Most low and failing grades are due to one or more of the following reasons:

1. Failure to study
2. Careless, sloppy, incomplete, or late homework assignments

3. Goofing off, inattention in class
4. Failure to grasp or understand class material

Player notebook

The team notebook, if prepared properly, can be a very effective training aid, particularly in the coverage of areas which call for outside study and viewing. Play diagrams of the team's offensive and defensive situations are good examples of the instructional material and data players can take home to study.

Individual coaching points on the various positions, defensive and offensive signals, team rules and regulations, tips on the prevention of illnesses, dressing room requirements, and other pertinent information can appear in the notebook.

Building a farm system

Winning college and high school teams, typically, are blessed with a successful feeder or farm system. To be successful, the high school program must have an organized feeder system.

The foundation of a winning high school team can be built, to a large extent, years before through organized community baseball leagues such as Little League, Babe Ruth, Pony and Colt, Connie Mack, and Legion ball.

Another good feeding source is the junior varsity program that maintains the development chain beginning in the youth programs. A jayvee schedule of sixteen games against the best possible opposition will prove extremely beneficial to the varsity program.

In many instances, the success of a team in the spring depends directly upon how much baseball its members played during the previous summer.

In guiding coaches of youth programs in the community, the high school coach might emphasize the importance of the fast ball pitcher and encourage future pitching prospects to reduce the number of breaking pitches.

In the youth leagues, the development of a good catcher should be stressed. The effectiveness of a pitching staff can diminish rapidly if the receiver is incompetent. Of the remaining positions, the shortstop and the center fielder are well worth developing to the fullest.

SCOUTING OPPONENTS

The more information a baseball team has about the opponent, the greater chance there is for victory. However, there is a minimum of scouting in college and high school baseball. The travel cost is perhaps the main reason, plus the fact that not too many players on the lower levels of play are capable of putting scouting information into practice. However, it can be beneficial to know the tactics of opposing teams and the various abilities of the individual players.

Figure 14.4 is an excellent player evaluation form developed by Tom Dedin of the University of Illinois.

A "book" can be compiled on opposing hitters, listing their types and habits. For example, is he a good high ball hitter? Can he hit the breaking pitch? Is he adept at bunting?

Defense, too, can be scouted. Can the pitcher or catcher be run against? What weak links do they have in various defense situations?

When scouting a team, the individual scout must:

1. Take away the most important material he can obtain
2. Exploit the weaknesses of the team scouted
3. Above all, *never guess.*

CONSTRUCTION OF THE DIAMOND

The best kind of baseball can be played only on good ball fields. A well-constructed and maintained ball diamond pays off in many ways—a better brand of baseball, higher player morale and, from the crowd standpoint, greater attendance (Fig. 14.2).

Three major features are common to all good playing areas:

1. Good construction
2. Good soil structure
3. Dedicated maintenance

Sand-concept field

The sand concept is essentially a refinement of the drainage system golf course architects specify for under greens. A sheet of plastic is laid on the graded field, followed by a network of perforated plastic tubes which collect water and carry it away. The best known sand-concept field is Prescription Athletic Turf, developed by Dr. William Daniel at Purdue University.

According to George Toma, groundskeeper supreme for Kansas City Royals baseball club, the new sand-concept field is the wave of the future.

Maintenance of the Field

A well-maintained field for ball players to play and practice on is of vital importance. Nothing is more damaging to the self-confidence and development of players than to make them attempt to learn the game on a poor playing field with inferior equipment.

The qualities of a well-kept ball diamond are:

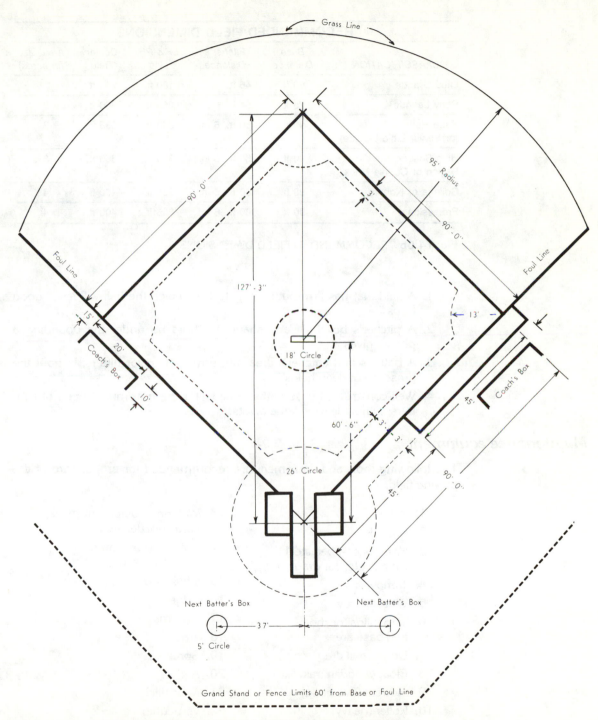

Fig. 14.6a REGULATION-SIZE BASEBALL DIAMOND DIMENSIONS

RECOMMENDED FIELD DIMENSIONS					
CLASSIFICATION	Base Distance	Pitcher's Distance	LF & RF Line	Center Field	Area Size (in acres)
Little League	60 ft.	46 ft.	180 ft.	200 ft.	1¼
Pony League	75 ft.	54 ft.	250 ft.	300 ft.	2
Babe Ruth (or Senior Little League)	90 ft.	60 ft., 6 in.	300 ft.	335 ft.	3
High School, Legion or Connie Mack	90 ft.	60 ft., 6 in.	310 ft.	360 ft.	3½
College or Nonpro	90 ft.	60 ft., 6 in.	335 ft.	400 ft.	4
Professional	90 ft.	60 ft., 6 in.	335 ft.	400 ft.	4

Fig. 14.6b   RECOMMENDED FIELD DIMENSIONS

1. A field that has firm but spongy turf on which the ball will take "good hops."
2. A pitcher's box built and shaped to hold up under the pounding a pitcher gives it.
3. A batter's and catcher's area with firm footing for hitters, without the presence of deep holes.
4. Well-constructed base paths to allow for the maximum speed of runners, without leaving large divots.

Maintenance equipment

The following tools and equipment are recommended for proper care of the playing field:

1. Rakes
2. Shovels
3. Mat (cocoa-fiber, steel, rubber, etc., for dragging)
4. Tamper
5. Wheelbarrow
6. Tarpaulins for mound, plate and base areas
7. Drags (nail drag, etc.)
8. Float (wooden, rakelike)
9. Mowers (five-gang)
10. Roller (heavy)
11. Line marker
12. Line trough
13. Watering equipment (hose, spray nozzle, etc.)
14. Batter's box marker (wooden frame)
15. Chalk line
16. Edge cutter
17. Brooms
18. Tractor
19. Spreader
20. Aerifier
21. Roto-tiller
22. Verticutter
23. Sprayer with boom
24. Flame thrower (portable)

Fig. 14.7 DRAGGING THE FIELD. After each practice or game, this cocoa fiber mat is effective in brushing the skinned portion of the infield, which smooths out the top soil. An occasional wetting and dragging should keep it firm but not too hard.

Fig. 14.8 LINING THE FIELD. After the home plate area has been raked, the base lines and batting boxes are lined. The wooden frame is excellent for marking the 4' × 6' boxes. The coaching boxes and on-deck batting boxes and on-deck batting circles are also lined, unless they are of a permanent nature.

Fig. 14.9 WATERING AND RAKING. After filling in the holes and cutting the grass, the infield area is given a good watering (twenty minutes), using a spray nozzle. The pitching mound and home plate areas are then raked, resulting in a smooth and well-cushioned playing surface.

UMPIRING

The game of baseball demands the highest qualities of good officiating. Since he must make a decision on every single play, an umpire must be constantly alert in making repeat decisions which require consistency of judgment. The fact that he is challenged continually makes it imperative that he possess considerable endurance, as well as mental and emotional poise.

Qualities

The following qualities are considered by John W. Bunn, in his book *The Art of Officiating Sports,* to be most important in a good official:

1. Quick reaction time
2. Confidence
3. Calmness
4. Consistency
5. Judgment

6. Cooperation
7. Integrity
8. Thorough knowledge of the rules

Uniform and equipment

In addition to his familiar dark blue outfit with ample pockets for balls, an umpire needs a special protector, a mask, shin guards, and special capped shoes. He should have an indicator for recording balls and strikes, and should *always* carry a rule book.

15

Training and Practice Program

Fielding a well-conditioned team, fundamentally sound in basic techniques, and well-disciplined in offensive and defensive team strategy, is the primary concern of the head baseball coach or manager. This is the major focus as they organize and plan the training program and practice schedule. Organized practices, of course, are the key to a progressive training program, one which hopefully leads to a winning season.

Planning the daily workouts is extremely important in using the time to the best advantage. With a large squad of players, it is essential that everyone be kept busy and not be standing around. A workout in which everybody is kept moving for two or three hours is far better than keeping them out on the field

Fig. 15.1 EXECUTING THE FUNDAMENTALS. During preseason training when a team has to go through some tough conditioning programs and countless fundamental drills, the manager has to convince his players that this is the basis for a winning ball club. Above, players on the University of Maine baseball team, working out in their spacious field house, practice throwing technique from a kneeling position. Below, pitching coach Johnny Podres instructs one of his hurlers on pitching with a runner on first base. A coach must be able to effectively teach and demonstrate the basic skills of the game as shown below.

for four or five hours, with players standing around the batting cage or practice field.

We go out on the field to accomplish basic objectives, and we give as much time as is necessary to their fulfillment. We do not go out just to have a two-and-half or three-hour practice. A carefully planned schedule is necessary if the practice program is to be successfully adapted to the needs of the squad. Intelligent planning can pay off with victories later on. We like our players to be punctual, even early, for all practices, games, and departures. We urge them to use the time after practice to improve themselves.

The Dodgers' practice sessions at Vero Beach are always busy. The players move quickly from drill to drill, and from area to area. They are always moving. We believe a team plays like it practices, and if the players are allowed to practice sloppily, they are going to play a sloppy game.

A baseball coach must be able to adapt his program to the changes of weather. Since rain and cold weather can impair the training program, he must have, as an alternate schedule, a rainy day routine. Indoor practices can be effectively devoted to basic fundamentals and conditioning, as well as strategy and tactics.

Repetition is the key to learning. Ball players must be told not just two or three times but continually.

EMPHASIZE FUNDAMENTALS

Mastery of the fundamentals, from throwing and running to bunting, is the most important thing in baseball. Most teams in baseball today are weak on fundamentals. Baseball players must keep repeating the basic skills in practice until they can do them correctly. The manager or coach has the responsibility of enforcing repetitions on their players. He must get them in the right groove in the first place and then repeat each step until it becomes second nature. Even great athletes have to polish their skills.

"Today, it just seems like the players do not work enough on their individual talents, perfecting those little parts of the game, such as bunting," said Jim Frey, manager of the Chicago Cubs. "People say, 'Well, those are the little things', but for the individual player and the success of the team, they can be big things."

Fall season

The autumn is an integral part of a college baseball program. Coaches in the cooler northern areas like to practice team fundamentals as much as possible

Fig. 15.2 THE DODGER'S PRACTICE PROGRAM is set up to accomplish basic objectives. Below, with manager Alston looking on, the team goes through a spirited session in sliding, with outfielder Willie Davis taking his turn.

outside before moving into their indoor facilities. "We've gone completely to fundamentals," said Ron Oestrike of Eastern Michigan. "Emphasis is on evaluation, a time to get things set. For the freshmen, the fall season is very important because we find many lack the basic fundamentals."

Fall practice is used to put the freshmen at ease. "There is a lot of pressure on a kid trying to walk on at a major university," said June Raines at South Carolina. "We try to use the first two to three days to relax." Bud Middaugh of Michigan wants his freshmen to feel as comfortable as possible when the spring begins. "The fall gives our freshmen a chance to acclimate—a lot of teaching goes on."

Players getting tired or "burned-out from baseball is a situation coaches should be aware of and try to prevent. "Players can get tired of playing ball after doing it all summer," said Augie Garrido of California State, Fullerton. "We try not to let that happen." Garrido's twelve week schedule falls into an organized routine. He devotes the first three weeks to individual skills, consisting of nothing but practice. During the next three weeks, his team practices and plays four games a week.

Rather than compete against other schools, most teams confine their fall program to playing only intrasquad games, maybe twice a week. Oestrike tries to make them as close to a game situation as possible. "We put the old players against the new players and try to even things up with the pitching."

An alumni game can be an interesting highlight of the fall program. Each fall, the current South Carolina squad will play returning USC alumni.

INDOOR PRACTICE

In the northern states with their cold winters and wet springs, much of the preseason baseball practice must be held indoors. Traditionally, practice is started in January or early February and about five to six weeks are indoors with the practice games scheduled as soon as the weather permits. For many teams, the indoor phase of the season is actually their spring training, and how well organized and successful these workouts are will in large measure determine team success during the season.

To have a successful indoor practice program, Lowell Scearcy, baseball coach at Bramerd, Minnesota H.S., believes several factors are a must:

Organization. Poor organization can ruin a practice quicker than any other factor. Players respond negatively by not paying attention and not hustling.

Variety. Drills must be varied, challenging, and never last over ten minutes. Keep them short and moving along. The competitive type prove more interesting to the players than are noncompetitive drills.

Fun Drills. Practice each day can finish with some type of fun drill. Players will leave the practice area feeling good and eager for the next practice. Relay races, run-down contests, and hitting contests, help stimulate interest and team work.

While many colleges and some high schools now have fieldhouses, most baseball teams begin team workouts in their gymnasium, as soon as the basketball team has finished its season. Those with floor space of 170 feet by 100 feet are able to set up a full-sized infield practice. If there is another large room available, particularly one with length of about thirty-five feet by ninety feet, a batting cage can be erected. A portable pitching mound such as the one developed by the Athletic Training Equipment Company allows pitcher development to take place regardless of the weather. Featuring a tough, fiberglass body with a textured surface, it can be used indoors or outdoors, and at 95 pounds, is easily moved. The mound can be used along with batting nets for hitting practice, and in a variety of pitching practice situations, such as pick-off moves. For information, write: ATEC, 9011 S.E. Jannsen Rd., Clackamas, Oregon 97015.

Indoor practice organization

The key to a successful indoor practice program is effective space utilization and good organization of time. John Winkin of the University of Maine has been able to achieve both through sound planning and the development of outstanding indoor facilities. Without a fieldhouse or other suitable indoor practice facility, baseball teams located in northern or cold weather regions are definitely limited in their training.

In their spacious fieldhouse, a separate area is available to the University of Maine baseball program for batting and pitching activities at any time without restriction. Two hitting cages are appropriately netted with special lighting, and each cage has an elevated pitching mound (Fig. 15.3). "I consider such an area

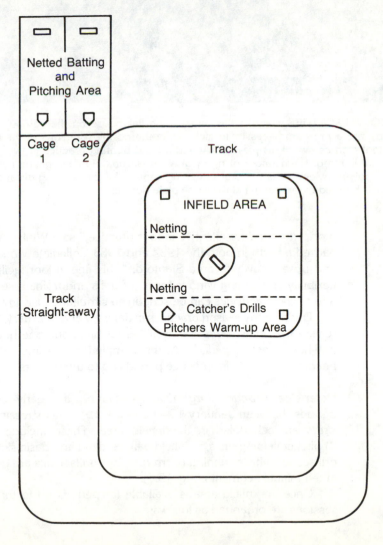

Fig. 15.3

Fig. 15.4 INDOOR FACILITIES, such as this outstanding fieldhouse on the campus of the University of Maine (at Orono), are a program necessity for schools in the northern regions of the nation. Coach John Winkin, above, looks on as two of his players take hitting and bunting practice in two cages, appropriately netted with special lighting. Handcrafted of heavy-duty pre-shrunk eighteen-gauge nylon and strung with one-quarter inch polypropylene rope, the cages are long enough for the pitching distance and wide enough so that right- or left-handed hitters can hit at the same plate position.

a *priority need* for effective indoor practice," said Winkin, whose Maine team earned a berth in both the 1982 and 1983 Collegiate World Series in Omaha and upset heavily favored Stanford. "This fine indoor facility allows us more flexibility in planning various forms of drills and training sessions. Live hitting and pitching activities can be scheduled simultaneously in the fieldhouse."

During early season practices in January and February, the fieldhouse area (called the "Infield Area") is available for half-hour, one hour, and one-and-a-half-hour practice periods. At the completion of winter track, the area then becomes available for practice periods up to three hours.

Defensive Practice Organization   During the early preseason practice periods (between January 15—February 15), drills stressing *basic defensive skills* are scheduled in the infield area. These include: 1) catcher drills, 2) pitcher fielding drills, 3) infield ball handling and basic skills drills, 4) outfield drills, and 5) base running (form running) drills. Drills are generally scheduled in ten minute segments (Fig. 15.6).

Once the infield area is available for periods up to three hours, practice sessions are organized as follows:

Fig. 15.5 FUNDAMENTAL DRILLS. Players on the University of Maine team engage in an indoor sliding session, while pitchers work on their pitching technique.

Basic defensive skills (Infield Area)—sixty min.

Live hitting and pitching (Hitting cages)—sixty min.

Team defensive drills (Infield Area)—sixty min.

Sub-varsity practice (Hitting cages and Infield Area)—sixty min.

Team defense at Maine is organized as follows:

Defensive vs *batted ball*—ten minutes

Defensive vs *attempted bunt*—ten minutes

Defensive vs *attempted steal*—ten minutes

Defensive vs *run-down*—ten minutes

Pitching drills—ten minutes

Pre-game infield drills—ten minutes

Specific base running situations are scheduled each day in accordance with the overall preseason organization plan. At Maine for example, on Monday, February 15, and Tuesday, February 16, the following situations are scheduled: Team defense vs. the batted ball, the attempted bunt, and the attempted steal; and the run-down with a base runner at first base. On Wednesday, February 17, and Thursday, February 18, Coach Winkin conducts the following: Defense vs. the batted ball, bunt, steal; and the run-down with a base runner at second base, and base runners at first and second bases, are scheduled. On Friday and Saturday practices, games are scheduled with game situations emphasizing those situations practiced during the week.

Similar practices are organized and scheduled the second week emphasizing the following situations: Monday and Tuesday, involving runners at third

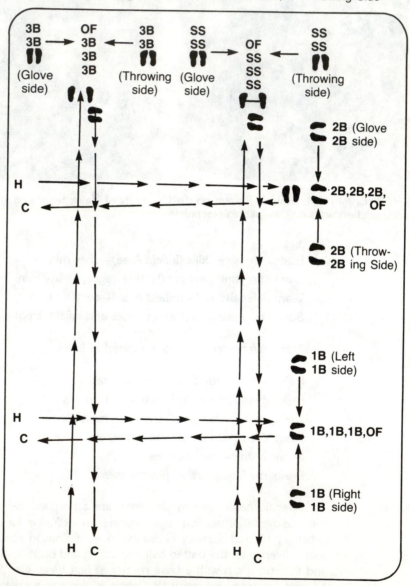

Balls hit: A. Straight at fielder; B. Glove Side; C. Throwing Side

Fig. 15.6 SQUARE DRILL FOR INFIELDERS AND OUTFIELDERS

base; second and third base, first, second, and third bases; and Wednesday and Thursday, runners on first and third bases.

"Emphasis in all our indoor team defensive drills is to master *knowing what to do in any situation,*" explained Winkin. "Our players will react to a batted ball, attempted steal, attempted bunt, or an emerging run-down. We have found it relatively simple to adjust to outdoor game situations. Once our team moves out of doors, they know what to do. Team drills are scheduled for no more than three defensive units. We prefer to work with two defensive units."

Hitting and Pitching Practice Organization   In scheduling daily hitting and pitching, Winkin prefers to have "live" situation hitting using an inning approach for scheduling the pitchers. Each pitcher is scheduled for a limited number of pitches per inning (thirteen, fourteen, fifteen, or twenty), depending on the pitcher's particular step in his endurance or "long throwing" day. The hitter will bat in a situation environment with a particular batting count, for example, two balls and one strike.

Most of the Maine pitchers are scheduled on a *four-day* rotation:

Day 1—Long throwing day (endurance pitching—certain number of innings and pitches)
Day 2—Conditioning and stretching day
Day 3—Short stretch throwing day
Day 4—Light conditioning and stretching day

Generally, Winkin will increase a pitcher's endurance throwing workout by throwing approximately one inning (thirteen to twenty pitches). On a long throwing day, a pitcher is exempt from participating in team defensive drills. In addition to showing the pitcher's endurance step on his long throwing day, a chart or diagram should also indicate the number of pitches to be thrown per inning in the early season. For example, on Tuesday, February 9, Lacognata is scheduled to pitch three innings vs. live hitting, with one inning at half speed, one inning at three-quarters speed, and one inning at full speed. The diagram should show how each pitcher's live work is scheduled in the hitting cages, listing his catcher, the hitters he faces, and the player charting his pitches. This overall, eight-week schedule enables Winkin to keep an effective record of the preseason preparedness of his pitchers.

Warm-up hitting drills and batting practice opportunities using pitching machines are scheduled prior to and after Basic Team Defensive Skills and Team Defense practice hours.

Practice Game Organization   Practice games are scheduled in the University of Maine field house infield area each Friday and Saturday, beginning the fourth week of the preseason preparedness schedule. A portable mound is placed in the infield area and Coach Winkin conducts a "game situation environment," with the exception of outfield play.

"Only those pitchers scheduled for long throwing on the scheduled day pitch," explained Winkin, "and each pitcher hurls the number of innings indicated. The number of pitches thrown per inning is limited according to the pitcher's step on the endurance chart. For example, in his four innings, he will throw the following number of pitches: thirteen, fourteen, fifteen, twenty. Pitchers whose short throwing day falls on the practice game date are also scheduled for one inning of mound work, a total of thirteen pitches."

During the pitcher's warm-up each inning, a coach will fungo ground balls to the infielders, stressing double play situations every other inning. The regular season third base coach handles the offense while coaching third base for each team. The catcher calls balls and strikes. The coach is the base umpire and handles the defense for each team and carefully observes the pitcher. The next day's long throwing pitcher charts the pitchers working that practice game.

"We normally schedule eight practice games prior to our travel date for the spring trip," said Winkin. "These games are played as regular games in every way possible. However, we do limit the total number of pitches a pitcher may pitch per inning."

Space utilization for indoor drills   The infield area at the University of Maine is well netted and has cross-netting, which is used to separate three basketball courts. Drills have been adjusted and developed to take advantage of this flexible netting and to incorporate the maximum numbers of players, positions, and situations into the ten minute segments of scheduled practice.

Hitting drills   Players warm up with:

1. Form swinging—shoulder to shoulder (two hands, one hand)
2. Hip movement drills (holding bat in back of body and swinging hips)
3. Hitting off batting tee (head "down and in")
4. Toss and hit
5. One on one pepper (during one on one, practice sacrifice and push bunts)

Preseason Indoor Daily Practice Schedule

(University of Maine at Orono/Coach John Winkin)

Tuesday, February 9

3:00–3:30 p.m.   Pitchers
                 Warm-up/stretching routine
                 Stretch throwing (knees, chair drill, balance position)
                 One on one—pepper

3:15   Pitchers fielding drills
       Throw to 1st, 2nd, 3rd (bunts)
       Covering first; squeeze/force play
       Move to 1st, to 2nd

3:30–4:00   Basic skills drills
            2B and SS Stretch throwing
            Catchers—stretch throwing/receiving
            1B and OF—Stretch throwing

4:00–5:00   Infield and outfield drills

     4:35   2B and SS—DP ball handling
            1B, 3B, C—Slow rollers/bunts

     4:45   3B—2B   5—4—3
            1B—SS   3—6—3
            Catchers receiving drills

     4:50   Outfielders—stretch to long throwing
            —ground balls—throwing
            —getting jump, moving right, left, directly overhead

     5:00   Square drill (sub varsity players hit and catch)

     5:10   Base running—3 lines (Fig. 15.7a)
            Form running
            Home to 1st
            1st to 2nd (steal lead, safe lead)

Preseason Indoor Practice

(University of Maine)

Monday, February 15 (Infield Area)

3:00–4:00   Varsity drills: team defense

3:00–3:15   Pitchers drills
            3:00 Throw to 1st; to 2nd; to 3rd
            3:05 Cover 1st; squeeze (DP); squeeze (tag)
            3:10 Move to 1st: regular, break, pitch-out

     3:15   Defense vs bunt—runner at 1st (regular, trap)

     3:25   Defense vs steal—runner at 1st

     3:35   Defense vs run-down—runner at 1st

     3:45   Defense vs batted ball (priority call: cut-offs, relays)
            "Little League": no one on base; runner at 1st.

4:00–5:00   Varsity: basic skills

     4:00   Outfielders drills

     4:15   Pitchers—one on one

     4:30   Infielders drills
            DP—1st, 3rd

     4:50   Square drill—pitchers hit

     5:00   Base running (outside weather permitting)

5:00–6:00   Sub-varsity
            Pitchers drills—same as above

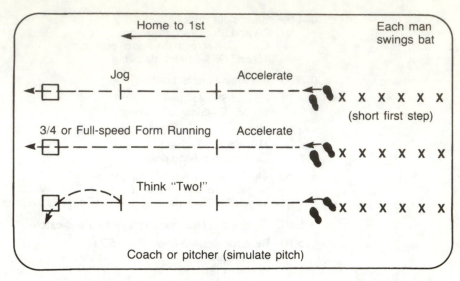

Fig. 15.7a HOME TO FIRST BASE

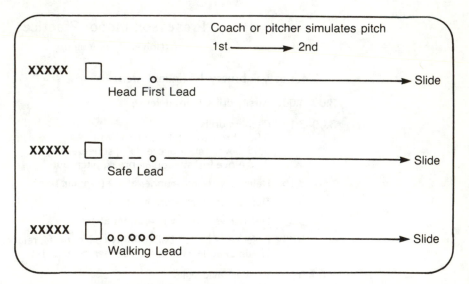

Fig. 15.7b FIRST TO SECOND BASE

5:00–5:30   Team defense

    5:10   Defense vs bunt

    5:15   Defense vs steal

    5:20   Defense vs rundown—runner at 1st

    5:25   "Little League—batted ball"

5:30–6:00   Basic skills—base running

Preseason Practice Schedule

(Arizona State University-Coach Jim Brock)
(Week of January 11–17)

Monday, January 11

10:00 a.m.	Meeting—University Activity Center

        1. Preseason practice overview—Coach Brock
        2. Walk-through registration
        3. Teacher evaluation questionnaire
        4. Training procedures—DeYampert

11:00 a.m.	Mile run—Joe Selleh Track
1:00–1:45	Stretching, calisthenics and warm-up—DeYampert

1:15–1:45	Defensive specialty—catchers—Colbern
	                    infielders—Hines
	                    outfielders—Brock
	                    pitchers—Kelly

1:45–2:00	Combination drill—pitchers, throw strikes; infielders, in position; outfielders, bunt; catchers, in gear

        1. Comebackers to 2B
        2. Chopped ball between pitcher and 1B
        3. Covering 1B on ball to right side
        4. P covering 1B on double play to right side
        5. Fielding compound bunt to 3B

2:00–2:15	Offensive bunt review (pitchers with Kelly)

        1. React to pitcher's commitment to plate
        2. Square shoulders
        3. Bat top of zone
        4. Barrel slightly up
        5. Bend knees
        6. Ball takes down angle off bat
        7. Reaction to special defense
        8. Short, down-slash stroke

2:15–3:30	Four-station batting practice (pitchers BP, bullpen and shag-assignments from Coach Kelly)

Group I Cage	Group II Field	Group III LF Tunnel	Group IV Bunt Stn
Pryor	Tognozzi	Wakamatsu	Baker
Davis	Salcedo	Martinez	Steen
Brennan	Johnston	Seibert	Schlink

Tuesday, January 12

9:30–Noon	Nautilus workout
1:00–1:20	Stretching, calisthenics and warm-up—DeYampert
1:20–1:40	Defensive specialty—same groups as Monday

1:40–2:00   Relay fundamentals (pitchers with Kelly)

1. Outfielders throwing at target screen
2. Middle infielders working on "quick feet" drill
3. 3B calling early and loud

2:00–3:30   Four-station batting practice (same groups and assignments as Monday)

3:30–4:00   Stealing 2B and 3B (pitchers with Kelly)

1. Sprinter's start
2. Jump discrimination—steal vs. hit-and-run
3. Left handers—gamble and poor-move pattern
4. Key off RHP
   a. left heel
   b. shoulder
   c. lean
   d. inside of left knee
5. Proper running fundamentals

4:00–4:15   Conditioning sprints and running fundamentals

1. Home to 1B
2. 1st to 3B
3. 2nd to home

Wednesday, January 13

11:00–Noon   Pictures

1:30–1:45   Stretching, calisthenics and warm-up—DeYampert

1:45–2:00   Defensive specialty—same group assignments

2:00–2:20   Relay drill—full drill
1. Fungo balls in alleys and down lines
2. Third baseman verbal control
3. Pitchers backing up bases
4. Pitchers running bases

2:20–2:40   Compound bunt defense

1. Outfielders bunt and run bases
2. Pitchers throw strikes and field position
3. Pitchers and infielders know types of pick-offs
4. Pitchers and shortstops using three methods for holding runner
   a. SS in front of runner
   b. SS slaps glove
   c. SS back pedals

2:40–4:00   Four-station batting practice (same groups and assignments as Monday)

4:00–4:20   Run-downs

1. Close-in principle
2. Look for runner and ball close, wide distance between player with ball and next base, and movement of player who will receive ball

3. Follow only throws made while moving
4. Four players only in run-down
5. Outfielders close but not involved unless there is an open end
6. Call for ball early
7. Avoid "bang-bang" collision at home
9. Look for trailing runner when man trapped between home and third

4:20–4:40   Distance running—Brock

1. Four 220's—form
2. Two 440's—form

Thursday, January 14

1:30–1:45   Stretching, calisthenics and warm-up—DeYampert

1:45–2:05   Defensive specialty—same assignments

2:05–2:25   Simple bunt defense

1. Lock
2. Jockey
3. Regular
4. Pitchers set feet for throw to 2B

2:25–2:40   Pick-off at 1B for LHP and pick-off at 3B for RHP

1. C to 1B at 1B (pitch-out)
2. LHP to 1B at 1B (peripheral)
3. C to 2B at 1B (lock)
4. RHP to 3B at 3B

2:40–3:40   Four-station batting practice (same groups and assignments as Monday)

3:40–4:00   Hit-and-run drill (pitchers with Kelly)

1. Responsibility with 3—1 count
2. Responsibility with all other counts
3. Runner must see ball hit bat
4. Ground ball anywhere is acceptable
5. Don't stop on line drive (runner)
6. Don't get picked off by LHP

4:00–4:15   Conditioning sprints—Brock

Rolling lead and 80-ft. sprint—all bases

Friday, January 15

1:30–1:45   Stretching, calisthenics, and warm-up—DeYampert

1:45–2:05   Defensive specialty—same assignments

2:05–2:20   Base running drills

1. Pitcher throws strikes and shags
2. Catchers alternate catching and hitting

3. Runner at 1B steals 2B but looks and sees ball hit
4. Runner at 2B reacts to ball hit with no outs
5. Runner at 3B with rolling lead reacts to ball with one out

2:20–2:35   Pick-offs to 2B

1. C to SS at 2B
2. P to SS at 2B (time)
3. P to SS at 2B (flap)

2:35–3:35   Four-station batting practice (same groups and assignments as Monday)

3:35–3:50   Pressure hitting—reactions off 3B

1. Man on 3B
2. 3—2 count
3. One out
4. Bat control
5. Short, quick, down stroke
6. Aggressive zone
7. Can't be caught out in front
8. Runner off 3B must concentrate on ball angle off bat
9. Runner must avoid "double clutching"

3:50–4:05   Relay drill—full drill

1. Fungo balls in alleys and down lines
2. Third baseman verbal control
3. Pitchers backing up bases
4. Pitchers running bases

4:05–4:25   First and third offense and defense

1. Regular steal of 2B
2. Runner on 1B always runs gamble pattern off LHP
3. Runner on 3B must give catcher good fake without being in jeopardy; timing and movement vital
4. Runner on 3B must force 1st baseman to stop him before throwing to SS at 2B after LHP's pick-off attempt at 1B; if he is not stopped, he must score
5. Catcher must check bench before 1st pitch in 1st—3rd situation
6. Catcher signals pitcher before 1st pitch if he is to cut off ball
7. Catcher must check with 3rd baseman before throwing to 2B
8. If catcher fakes throw to 2B, it must be a complete fake
9. 3rd baseman raises arms if he thinks runner on 3B is going home
10. 2nd baseman covers 2B
11. SS responsible for directing rundown
12. 3rd baseman yells if runner breaks after catcher throws to 2B

4:25–4:45   Distance running

1. Two 220's—form
2. One 440—form
3. One 880—form and time

Saturday, January 16

10:30–10:45   Stretching, calisthenics, and warm-up—DeYampert

10:45–11:00   Infield—outfield drill

11:00–2:00   Machine games

1. Pitchers back up bases
2. Stealing allowed
3. Drag bunting allowed (if successful, you don't lose your at bat, but you do get a runner)

Sunday, January 17

Noon–5:00   Nautilus workout

Pitchers Practice Organization

(University of Arkansas—Norm DeBriyn)
(Six-week Program by Progression)

Wednesday, January 10

4:00 p.m.   Meeting everyone; set work-out dates and times

Pitchers & catchers

Flex exercise—(group) run, isometrics, lead ball
Play catch—barehand
Throw to catcher—or each other, short (30 ft.)
Curve ball drill—from knee only (25 ft.)
20 pitches to catcher—not hard, form, follow through, emphasis on location
Cool down—long throw (2 min.)

Conditioning

2 sets of pick-ups (25 to a set)
2 sets of sit-ups (25 to a set)
2 sets of ropes (1 min. per set)
Reel runner (2 sets) (30 sec.)
Run (short sprints) (long lap 1 mile)

Thursday, January 11

Same as Wednesday, except throw 30 pitches (45 feet distance; emphasis on form)
Plus daily drills (cover 1B, etc.)

Conditioning

Same, except include 5 ball drill (start lead ball exercises)

Friday, January 12

Same as Wednesday, except throw 35 pitches
Daily drills—fundamentals

1. Covering 1B, backing up home and 3B; covering home on wild pitches/P.B.
2. Fielding bunts—ground balls
3. Keep runner close (pick-offs, etc.)
4. Start DP (call situations, runner on 1, 1 & 2, 1 & 3, 1–2–3)
5. Squeeze defense
6. Curve ball drill

Saturday, January 13

9:00 a.m.   Follow previous schedule
            Loosen up run
            Flex
            Long catch—everyone
                Group A—throw 35 pitches to catchers (strings)
                Group B—charts—with counts
            Drills—(check the arms—group session)

Conditioning

Same but increase to five

Sunday, January 14

Off—rest

Monday, January 15

Exactly same as Saturday (Every day we will do lead ball drill)
Group B throw 35—A charts and counts

Conditioning

2 sets of 60 pick-ups
2 sets of 60 sit-ups
Reel runner, 2 sets
Short sprints
Jump Rope (2 sets/1 min. each)
1 mile

Tuesday, January 16

Group A throws / 40 pitches
Group B charts and counts
Curve ball drill (start spinning), also slider spin
Running, increase (long and short) (13 laps)

Condition by group

Reel runner (2 sets) (15 sec.)
Pick-ups (2 sets) (60)

Sit-ups
Ropes (2 sets) (1 min.)
Lead ball drill daily!

Wednesday, January 17

Group B throw 40 pitches
Group A charts
Follow same procedure as Tuesday (running—long and short)
Jump rope (240)
Pick-ups and sit-ups (2 sets) (60 of each)

Thursday, January 18

Group A throws 50 pitches
(Watch pitchers close)
Explain tech. of warming up—cooling down
Follow same format of:
    A. Jog to loosen up
    B. Flex-Stretch
    C. ISO
    D. Curve ball drill
    E. Extra set of sit-ups (15)
Throw all pitches/Group B charts
Group A conditions (when A gets finished, B will condition)

Friday, January 19

Group B throw 50 pitches—A charts
Same as Thursday

Saturday, January 20

Practice for everyone—mile run 5:45 min.
Pitcher skull session
Fundamental drills
   Cover 1B
   Bunts
   Pick-off/hold runner
   Pitch-out/knock down
Conditioning (Sit-ups, ropes, leg lifts, sprints and laps)

Sunday, January 21

Off

Monday, January 22

Throwing (if inside)
   A. 35 FB in net, 10 CB (spin), 5 change, 5 sliders

B. Charts
If outside, pitchers will throw 6 outs or 35 pitches
Drills (group B)
Condition (group A)

Tuesday, January 23

Finish of Group (A) and start with (B) follow Monday format
Pitchers will throw in net (15–20 pitches to live hitter)
Group that threw Monday will condition

Wednesday, January 24

Group A—throw 45 pitches in net or throw 9 outs (change after every 3 outs)
Same conditioning drills and patterns as on Monday
Group B—charts and work on pick-offs with infielders

Thursday, January 25

Group B—throw 45 pitches/conditioning
Group A—conditioning/base running drills

Friday, January 26

Drills (bunt coverage 1st and 3rd)
Conditioning

Saturday, January 27

Group A throws 50 pitches outside
Group B charts

Sunday, January 28

Off

Monday, January 29

Intrasquad or game B.P.
Group B throws 50 pitches
Group A charts
Conditioning 2 sets of 60 (running 15 laps; two sets of leg lifts; 300 jump rope)

Tuesday, January 30

A and B work drills
Time to make 4 groups (start, relief, spotter)
Conditioning same

Wednesday, January 31

Group A throws 3 innings (or 65 pitches)
B charts
Control is the key!
Conditioning

Thursday, February 1

A finish their pitches
B charts

Friday, February 2

B finishes 65 pitches (or 3 innings)
A charts

Saturday and Sunday, February 3 and 4

Intrasquad one day, regular practice the other

Monday, February 4

Group A throws 15 outs (75–80 pitches)
Conditioning
    Sit-ups (2 sets) (60)
    High lows (2 sets) (60)
    Leg lifts (2 sets) (20)
    Run laps (10)
    Sprints (10)

Tuesday, February 5

A or (B) throw 15 (75–80)

Wednesday, February 6

Breakdown into 4 groups
Conditioning (3 sets) (30 per set)
Emphasis on:
    Pick-offs, rundown, 1st & 3rd
    Running both long and short
    Regular practice

Thursday, February 7

5:00 p.m.   Skull session on game situations
6:00 p.m.   Practice
           B throws 15 outs (75–80)

Conditioning same
Running

Friday, February 8

1:00 p.m.   Situations
2:00 p.m.   Regular practice
            A throws 15 outs (75–80)

Saturday, February 9

9:00 a.m.   Practice
            B throws (depends on weather)
            Establish staff routine for opener

Sunday, February 10

A finish on practice
Set routine

Monday, February 11

B 7 innings (100–120)
Same conditioning

Tuesday, February 12

Finish B go with A
Same procedure

Wednesday, February 13

B.P. throw on side
Conditioning review

Thursday, February 14

Same as Wednesday

Friday, February 15

Intrasquad game

PRESEASON

The preseason phase of the practice season consists of conditioning and training. For many northern schools, these workouts are conducted indoors. The emphasis should be on mastering individual offensive and defensive fundamentals, in which the coach devotes considerable time to individual and small-group supervision. As a rule, most coaches like to take the pitchers and catchers by themselves for the first week, and then work with the infielders and outfielders the second week.

During the first week of practice, the pitchers should be given a conditioning routine of stretching exercises, wind sprints, jogging, pepper, and fly ball chasing, along with intensive instruction and supervision in the fundamentals of pitching. While the pitchers are doing their conditioning work, the catchers are receiving instruction in the fundamentals of their position.

On Monday of the second week, when the remainder of the squad reports, the coach must divide his supervision between four different groups: pitchers, catchers, infielders, and outfielders. During the practice session, one or more of these groups will be largely on their own, making it necessary for them to be engaged in set drills and activities. However, the coach is always close by to offer necessary direction and guidance.

Because of time and space limitations, indoor gym workouts generally are limited to returning members of the varsity, jayvee, and freshmen teams of the previous year. A general call for all other candidates is issued as soon as the squad can get outdoors. For indoor batting practice, pitching machines are used inside of nets. A batting tee is used, in which the batter hits the ball into the wall or net (a whiffle ball, rubber ball, or tennis ball). Infielders can get fielding practice with the off-the-wall drill. They are instructed to throw a rubber ball against the wall and field it.

During the early practices, the coach should tell his hitters not to try to hit the ball too hard. Like a pitcher, a coach does not want his hitters to pull their back or arm muscles. He must insist that everybody just make contact.

SPRING TRAINING

Daily practice

Professional   We have a squad meeting every morning at 9:00 a.m. In the meeting, besides talking about fundamentals and tactics, I will discuss the day's practice schedule. After a meeting of approximately thirty minutes, we will go out on the field and do our stretching and loosening-up exercises.

Actually, a typical daily schedule of ours consists mostly of batting practice. Perhaps more than 80 to 90 percent of our practice time is spent on hitting. This shows how much stress we place on "the hitting game." However, while hitting is going on, everyone on our squad is busy doing many other things. For example, the infielders handle numerous ground balls during batting practice. This is also a good time for individual instruction.

Quite often, during batting practice, we make it look like a real game situation. We have base runners carry out their responsibilities, while those on defense take their respective positions.

The first thing we do in the morning is to run the entire squad around the field. After jogging once or twice, the squad goes through about fifteen to twenty minutes of group stretching exercises. Bill Buhler, our trainer, supervises the exercises, which are *not the strenuous type*. We do not try to develop large muscles. They consist more of loosening and stretching exercises. After the stretching and flexibility period, the balls and bats are brought out, and we have the players divide up into "pepper" groups. This is an easy conditioning and loosening-up session, approximately thirty minutes in length. In these "pepper" games, we insist on no more than two fielders and one hitter.

During batting practice, we urge our hitters to do a certain amount of hitting to the opposite field. Quite often, we place a runner on first base, with a hitter at bat, and we use the regular infield at their positions. On the first pitch, we instruct the hitter to pretend the hit-and-run is on. Therefore, the pitcher works on holding the runner on, and the runner takes his appropriate lead.

When the first pitch is made, he goes to second base, and the hitter tries to hit the ball toward right field, from a line drive down. Whether the hitter is successful or not, we still keep the runner on second base. Now, we pretend he is on second base, with nobody out, and try to advance him to third base.

On the next pitch, the hitter tries to squeeze him in. We have a coach over at third base to tell the runner when to go. If he runs too soon, he will tip-off the play and get our hitter knocked down. So, we instruct him in how not to tip-off the play. We tell him to go just as the pitcher releases the ball, or when his foot hits the ground. If everything goes well, he will squeeze the runner in on the next pitch.

Following this play-situation routine, we will give each batter five or six swings, in which he must try just to meet the ball or hit the ball where it is pitched.

After he takes his last swing, the batter goes to first base, where he becomes the runner for the next hitter. He does the same thing as I have described earlier. Sometimes, if the hitter executes the hit-and-run successfully, advances the man to third, and performs the squeeze play, we give him an extra swing or two as a bonus.

We try to make batting practice as much of a gamelike situation as we can. That is why I do not like our pitchers shagging in the outfield. I would rather have my pitching coach take the pitchers and work on the skills they employ in a ball game.

When we find a player is having trouble at the plate, uppercutting or overstriding, we turn him over to our batting coach, who takes him to one of the cages where the pitching machines are located. He gives him individual instruction and works him on the machine first, then has a couple of pitchers available to throw batting practice.

After batting practice, we have the squad get their arms in condition and go into a ten-to-fifteen-minute infield practice, while the outfielders chase fly balls and work on their throwing.

The infielders are able to get into condition long before the outfielders, because all during batting practice someone is hitting ground balls to the infielders. However, outfielders have always had trouble getting enough throwing and fly-shagging work. We try to make our outfielders field ground balls and charge them.

Special sessions

We pick a day when we hold a special practice session on cutoffs and relays, run-down plays, and other basic fundamentals. Instead of hitting, we have everyone get their arms loosened up and spend an entire morning working on cutoff plays and the like. The regulars take their positions in the field, while the rookies become the base runners. We have one of our coaches act as the hitter.

We go through just about every possible situation in a ball game. For instance, there is a man on second base and a base hit is going to right center field. We want the defense to perform exactly the way they would in a ball game. The pitcher even has a pitcher to back him up on these regular setup plays. If something is not done correctly, we will try it again.

Of course, the cutoffs and relays lead right into base running. The coaches are on the coaching lines, telling the base runners where to go and what to do. Another coach is out on the field, helping the defense.

Squad meetings

The majority of our squad meetings consist of defensive strategy talks about how to pitch to the hitters, how the defense should play them and what to expect from their pitchers. On occasion, we review the basic fundamentals.

Early in the season, or anytime we feel the team has made some mental errors or thrown the ball to the wrong bases, we go over cutoff and pick-off plays, bunt situations, the various bunt defenses, and things of that kind. When we change our signs, we usually review the new set at a meeting.

I like to point out specific plays that certain players made, so that everyone remembers precisely what we mean. I might say: "This ball should not have been thrown to third. It should have been thrown to second."

The coach should not want to place too much blame on one player for making a mistake. He is only picking out this individual as an example. If he wants to be critical, he had better cite other mistakes made by everybody else. This takes some of the pressure off the one player, yet everyone knows what player he is talking about.

We set our rules and tell the team what we are going to do and what we expect of them. Players like to know what's expected of them. I believe in telling the truth to athletes. If a player is not playing well, I tell him, and I think he appreciates that.

Team captain

When a team captain is appointed, the first thing the coach must do is instruct him as to what his duties are and what is expected of him. Precaution should be taken that he does not over-ride his authority and reach the point where he wants to criticize one of his own teammates.

On the field, I like my captain to more or less direct traffic around the infield. He also takes the lineup to the plate and talks to the umpires just prior to game time. I feel it gives him a little more leeway in talking to the umpires.

We try to have a peppy, energetic practice, one which is short but gets the job done.

Length of practice session

I have found that I get better results from *one* practice session, than if the players know they have to be on the field for two hours in the morning, come in for a sandwich and then go back for another two hours. I have found that they begin pacing themselves when they know they have another session in the afternoon. On the other hand, if they know they are going to be out there for five or six hours, the coach does not get good results either.

If the players are not at practice on time or do not put out, we go into a longer practice session. We have so much work to do that we stay out on the field until we do it. This is one "whip" the manager has at his disposal—he can keep the players out there as long as necessary.

Frankly, we try to conduct a peppy, energetic practice, one which is short but gets the job done. A manager often has to vary his sessions so that they do not become monotonous. Sometimes, he has to yell at a few of his players to keep things active and get the most out of them. Most ball clubs, though, have a couple of good leaders who can keep up the tempo of the practice by their spirited chatter and hustle. This means more than all the yelling that the manager or coach might do.

As long as they will give me three-to-four good hours, I am satisfied. Of course, if we did not have the facilities to divide the squad, we would have to stay out there much longer. I definitely feel we get better results when everyone gives 100 percent and our practice is not so long. If the manager can vary his practices, and make them more interesting, the players will respond with greater enthusiasm and spirit.

SELECTING THE TEAM

In making up his squad, the manager has to decide who is going to play and where, which rookies he will keep and which veterans he has to let go. In selecting the team, he has to consider their past records and what they have done. He cannot always go only by what he sees in spring training.

Every morning, before we get dressed for practice, I meet with the coaches. We talk over the day's schedule and the different players.

The toughest time for any manager is cut-down time, when he has to go up and tell a player: "You have to go back down," or, "We have to let you go." We are allowed to carry only so many players on the squad, so we do not have any alternative at cut-down time.

In picking his team, the manager has to be impartial, objective, and deliberate. Personally, there may be players whom he likes better than the fellow who can play a little better. However, he has to keep personalities completely out of his mind and select the player who fills the greatest need.

Squad selection, of course, depends on the club needs. For instance, in an effort to bolster our hitting attack, we keep an eye open for those who swing the bat. The Dodgers have always been partial to speed. I think it is a great quality. However, if a player cannot run too well, we want to be sure he can swing the bat to make up for his lack of speed.

We are constantly looking for the "team players": those who are more interested in the success of the *team* than in their own individual success. We are proud of the fact that, over the years, we have worked together as a team. This is something the manager has to create. We make it a practice to praise a player when he does something for the team, like sacrificing himself to advance a man or playing the game as it should be played. By talking about it and praising him this way, much can be done to develop the proper team attitude.

True, we like to have our best defensive players at positions through the middle of the diamond, that is, pitching, catching, shortstop and second base, and in center field. However, it does not always work this way; for example, when I managed the Dodgers, our best defensive man was Wes Parker at first base.

College and High School   I have found it necessary to have a set pattern for our practice sessions so the players know what they are supposed to be doing every minute. It is recommended that daily schedules be mimeographed in detail for all squad members, complete with the activity each player is to participate in and the time for participation. In fact, we feel the coach should keep an eye on his watch in order to devote the proper amount of time to each phase of the practice session.

Generally, players should report on the field ten or fifteen minutes before the coach begins the practice session. Then, at a set time, such as 3:00 or 3:30 p.m., the entire squad will go to a designated area for group calisthenics, consisting mainly of stretching and loosening-up exercises. A pitcher and catcher will begin warming up for batting practice work. The rest of the squad

Fig. 15.8 INDIVIDUAL COACHING. After diagnosing the causes of the players mistakes, the coach must then give the player instructions in the right kind of way, to get him to correct his faults. Here, Jack Stallings, veteran baseball coach of Georgia Southern University, demonstrates to two of his young pitchers the correct way to grip a baseball.

will begin loosening up by either playing catch or getting into pepper games. Some of the players use this time to do a few stretching routines by themselves.

After the loosening-up period, batting practice gets underway, with most of the squad taking part in this hour-long period. While the hitters are taking their cuts in the batting cage, the infielders are kept busy all the time fielding ground balls. Besides fielding the ball off the bat at the plate, they receive additional grounders from the fungos hit by the coach or extra pitchers. It is essential that the player hitting the fungos learn to time his hits so they are made *between* pitches to the plate.

The batting phase of the practice should be divided into groups, with never more than five players to a group. This time can also be used for drills and instruction. Ideally, every hitter in the line-up should take as many as forty to fifty swings each practice. If this number cannot be achieved during the batting practice session, additional hitting should be taken in the batting range against an automatic pitching machine.

We believe a team plays like it practices, and if the players are allowed to practice sloppily, they are going to play a sloppy game.

An eighteen-man squad could be deployed in the following manner: seven fielders; one catcher; one pitcher; a shagger for the pitcher; two fungo hitters; one pitcher warming-up; one bullpen catcher and four hitters.

Following batting practice, the infielders receive ten minutes of ground balls in rapid succession. The coach is close by to make any corrections necessary, occasionally demonstrating the proper procedure. While this fielding work is taking place, pitchers and catchers can be hitting fungos to the outfielders. The extra catchers can be working along the sidelines on such fundamental techniques as shifting and throwing, blocking the low ball, and handling pop flies. The pitchers can work on their moves to the bases.

After completing this phase of the practice, the entire squad should be called into the infield to participate in twenty minutes of general fundamentals. Among the areas covered in this important team session are base running, pick-off and cutoff plays, the defense and offense of the delayed and double steals, bunt situations, and handling pop-ups to the infield and outfield. Work on pop-ups should not be taken too lightly. Many games have been lost because of poor execution in fielding pop flies. This can be corrected through greater emphasis during practice time.

Regular infield practice is the next phase of the session, starting with the outfielders making their throws to the bases and the infielders throwing the ball "around the horn."

Infield practice normally consists of eight rounds. The first three rounds are designed to execute the put-out at first base, and the second three rounds to execute the double play. The remaining two rounds are designed to give the infielder practice at fielding the slow roller, throwing to first base, and fielding and throwing to the plate.

During infield practice, the ball is hit directly at the infielder on the first round, to his right for the long throw, and then to his left. This gives the player a chance to practice moves in all directions.

Hitting the ball too hard should be avoided in infield practice. Infield practice is basically a warm-up period, and should be conducted to instill confidence in the players prior to the game.

Even though the practice is on the homeward stretch, the coach must insist on plenty of pep and enthusiasm in this drill. Fungo hitters, meanwhile, are hitting fly balls to outfielders, making sure they get practice moving in all directions.

Before they leave the field, all players must complete their daily running work. Not only should the pitchers get their running in, but the outfielders, infielders, and catchers should wind up their practice by running wind sprints.

The players assume a lead-off stance, and using the initial step, run a distance of sixty yards, then walk back. Other running drills that may be used include the bases and relays.

The workout I have just discussed should be used daily until the team is ready to play a game, in about two weeks. Then, three days—such as Monday, Wednesday, and Friday of each week—can be devoted to practice, while Tuesday, Thursday, and Saturday can be reserved for full-scale intrasquad games. These games should be nine full innings in length, running for a period of two hours.

I would like to point out that the practice workout outlined should be subject to change in any manner the coach sees fit. As the training season moves along, the coach will be able to observe where his team is weak, and can arrange his practice schedules to correct these weaknesses.

To save precious time and encourage hustle, players should be urged to run to their new areas each time there is a change.

Fig. 15.9 BATTING PRACTICE SHOULD BE PURPOSEFUL. The prime concern is making good contact with a level, well-timed swing. The hitter should keep his eye on the ball and follow it all the way to the bat. Here, Leon Durham demonstrates flawless technique in the hitting cage.

Batting practice

As a part of batting practice, the catcher can get in some "live" throwing, with a pitcher on the mound and a runner on first base. If the hitter has five or six swings, this can be done on the first pitch. The runner steals, the batter swings and misses, and catcher throws out the runner as the second baseman or shortstop breaks to the bag depending on whether there is a left or right-handed batter at the plate. Then the hitter can execute a bunt on the second pitch and then take five swings. On the last swing, he should run full-speed to first base.

DURING THE SEASON, PROFESSIONAL

As opening day approaches, the manager has to decide on his starting lineup and opening day pitcher. Basically, he should also have a reasonably good idea who his regular starting pitchers will be and what his bullpen will consist of. He should have at least three good starters, ideally four, with at least one of them a southpaw.

An effective bullpen has at least two relievers, one a right-hander and the other a left-hander, who can be effective for two or three innings. In addition, two "long relievers" should be available, who can come in early in the game and go to the seventh or eighth inning. Since we play mostly night games, we get to the ball park at 4 p.m., approximately four hours before game time. First, we check to see if everyone is healthy and able to play. Buhler, our trainer, has a fairly good record of the physical status of our club. He knows when they are hurt, for instance, who might have a sprained ankle. Every day, he gives me a good report on our personnel. Then, I go ahead and make up the lineup and post it in the dugout.

The pitchers usually are the first players to arrive on the field, and we allow our pitchers about twenty minutes to hit, mostly bunts and shortstroke swings. We urge our pitchers to slap the ball and keep from striking out. We urge them to hit the ball to the opposite field.

Our batting instructor takes over with bunting practice. This is live and off the regular field. When the pitchers are finished, we like to take them down to the pitching machine and give them another "going over" down there.

The reserve, or extra players, who are not in the lineup, are the next group to hit. They take about a half-hour of batting practice. With the best pitching available, they are urged to hit balls to the opposite field and take their own free swings. While the extra men are hitting, we have the pitchers shag balls hit to the outfield.

Since the regulars hit last, they do not have to be at the park until maybe an hour later. Since they are playing regularly, we feel they should have the privilege of coming in a little later. While the regulars are hitting, the extra men have to shag the balls. During this time, the pitchers are running in the outfield.

Fig. 15.10 PRE-GAME BATTING PRACTICE. A major portion of the practice time before a game is devoted to hitting, which indicates how important the hitting game is. However, while hitting is taking place, everyone on the squad should be busy. The infielders are handling numerous ground balls from the coaches who are located at each side of the batting cage (with their fungo bats). The pitchers are getting their running in, and individual work can be accomplished. In this batting practice scene at Anaheim Stadium, observe the use of screens to protect the players and coaches.

Pitching machines are available throughout pre-game practice, and the men are kept pretty busy with special instructions. If we have a couple of players who want extra hitting, such as those fellows in a slump, this work has to take place before the pitchers hit. Generally, each day, we have two or three hitters who come out on the field before the pitchers hit. They take twenty minutes or so, and we try to give them special batting practice pitchers. We have as many as a half-dozen pitchers who throw batting practice.

While at home, all of this hitting takes close to two hours of time. As a result, we can get a considerable amount of hitting work accomplished. This is not the case when the club is on the road.

Following batting practice, the visitors and then the home club take infield drill, at which time the outfielders are able to make long throws to the bases. Then, they are hit fungos by our coaches.

THE LEAGUE SEASON, COLLEGE AND HIGH SCHOOL

The next phase of the training program starts with preparation for the league games, and continues until about two weeks before the season ends. During this period, the daily practice sessions are geared to the development of team defense and the correction of individual flaws and weaknesses. Conditioning activities must be closely adhered to each day, not only by the pitchers but by the rest of the squad as well. The coach should make sure each player performs his stretching and loosening-up exercises and does his running daily.

All players should loosen up their legs when first arriving on the field. Many teams perform the stretching exercises together under the supervision of the trainer or coach. Other teams have the players do them individually before the practice session begins. This activity should be done before any catch or pepper games are played.

Whenever necessary, players are assigned to individual activities or placed in remedial groups where they may work on individual weaknesses, such as a catcher needing extra practice on his foot-work, or a pitcher who has a poor pick-off move to first base.

To win, baseball teams must have players who are "quick" and can get good "jumps." To improve the quickness of his players, the coach should conduct reaction drills in the daily practices. The defense must learn to react under different circumstances. Defensive reactions, for example, can be improved in fielding by training the players to concentrate on picking up the ball off the bat quickly. When working on throwing to bases, catchers should have a runner to throw against. Pitchers should have a runner at first when working on their moves to first base. Base runners can be timed using a visual signal to get them started.

With proper organization, the coach may run many of the team defensive and offensive drills simultaneously during these practice sessions. Base running drills can be made a part of the defensive situation drills, and bunting practice will prove more realistic with a defensive infield at their respective positions to practice bunt defense.

During The Season

Daily Practice Schedule
(University of Arkansas)

Tuesday, April 27

12:30–1:30   Field open

1:30–1:35   Announcements
        1. Pack equipment
        2. Go to class Friday—contact teachers on finishing assignments
        3. Depart at 7:00 a.m. tomorrow
        4. Pick-up bags tonight

1:40–1:50   Run lap stretch and flex as team

1:50–2:00   Everyone get loose (pitchers with C Hilton)

2:00–3:30	*Live (H.P.)*	*Field*	*Bunt*	*Cage*
	Dees	Ward	Crawford	Seward
	Longoria	Hindman	Roberts	Loseke
	Shaddy	Lancaster	Wilson	Robinson
	Van Horn	Wofford	Powell	Jones
		Odom		

Batting practice routine

Round 1 (off hitter is BR)
1. SAC, bunt: BR goes half way
2. 1 H & R: BR goes half way
3. 1 slug bunt: BR go all the way to 2B
4. Get BR to 3B for 2B, no outs hit ball to right side
5. BR at 2B, no outs, push or drag, get BR to 3B
6. BR at 3B, score him from 3B
7. Squeeze
8. 2 outs, 3B back; drag/push down, 3B line (free cut for everyone who execute correctly)

Round 2
Drive 4 balls to opposite field

Round 3
Pull 4 balls

Round 4
Free cuts

3:30–4:30   Special 4 inning game

Late season

During the final weeks of the season, the coach must do everything within his means to make the practice sessions as interesting as possible. As the season approaches its end, practice can often become boring, due mainly to a lack of interest among the players. Consequently, practices should be shortened considerably, and emphasis on fundamentals, conditioning, and corrective work eliminated. Quite often, the best solution is to schedule a few practice games or substitute newer and more appealing forms of drills and activities.

To add variety to late-season practice sessions, fun activities should be offered along with the more serious activities. An entire practice could be devoted to an amusing hour of fun activities. The squad might engage in a baseball track meet, utilizing baseball skills in the manner of a track meet. Or, an intrasquad game could be scheduled, with each player playing a different position each inning.

To spice up a baseball practice, the session can be shortened, and the teams can play an intrasquad game with the count advanced on a hitter to a two-ball, one-strike count. A variation of advancing the count is to play one-strike or two-strike ball. To speed up an intrasquad game, one team can stay on the field for six, nine, or twelve outs, with the bases cleared after each three outs.

FUNDAMENTAL DRILLS

Players must practice constantly and drill on the basics. A team must drill and drill over and over again, until the techniques become habitual. The secret of good performance at critical moments is found in drill. It is through drill, and drill only, that the manager or coach can be reasonably sure of good performance under game pressure. Individuality or initiative, however, should not be drilled out of the players.

Baseball practice can be kept from becoming dull and monotonous by challenging players with competitive drills. Outfielders, for example, can compete against infielders in a most-hits contest during batting practice. Running drills for pitchers can both be competitive and fun. The stop watch can determine the fastest-double-play combination. Outfielders, likewise, can be timed in throwing balls to third or home plate. Indeed, the imaginative and creative coach can increase the interest and skill of his players by having them engage in competitive contests during practice.

Competitive drills not only encourage athletes to work harder during practice, but also serve as an effective means of evaluation for the coach. However, many competitive drills should not be used until the players have mastered the fundamental skills.

A progressive sequence of hitting drills can isolate the different skills and enable the athlete to work on each skill level. A progressive learning sequence can be developed through the use of a batting tee, weighted bat, hitting cage, and backstop. Major emphasis must be given to developing a fundamentally sound swing for every pitch in the strike zone.

Good outfield play involves more than just fielding ground balls and fly balls and throwing to the right base. Outfielders need to work regularly on proper footwork. Drills that emphasize correct footwork and body position can improve significantly the ability of those who play in the outfield.

Explain why they are doing it

Before having the players start a drill, the coach should explain to them why they are doing the drill. He must not just describe what they are doing but why, and what it will mean later on. They must understand. If they do not get this now, it is going to lead to complications later. Then it becomes a challenge, "I better listen, or I will not do it correctly later on."

Adjustment period

Mechanical changes are followed by a period of adjustment when the coach and athlete sees no immediate results. "As an instructor, this is the problem period and requires plenty of patience," explained Bob Cluck. "When making changes, a player should be told of the probability of this problem period."

During this period, the coach must give his pitcher a lot of encouragement and reinforcement.

Teaching Principles

1. Keep instructions simple.
2. Demonstrate when possible.
3. Keep the entire skill in mind while working on its parts.
4. Observe—then teach.
5. Do not overteach.
6. Encourage the learner.
7. Adjust teaching to individual differences.
8. Break the skill down into component parts to facilitate the mastery of each fundamental. *Practice one thing at a time.*
9. Criticism should be given constructively and quietly.
10. A short, well-planned practice period is better than a long one.
11. Adjust your teaching to fit the player. Do not make him adjust to you.
12. Don't try to teach everyone the same things.

FAVORITE DRILLS OF COLLEGE COACHES

Many of college baseball's most successful coaches were asked to contribute their favorite drill, one which has proven most successful in their program. The following is an assortment of drills designed to develop a well conditioned, fundamentally sound team, well disciplined in offensive and defensive team strategy and play.

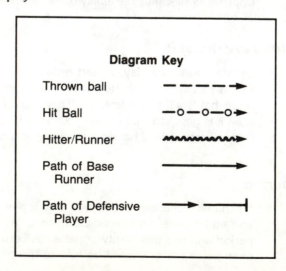

Conditioning/basic fundamental drills

Multi-purpose/Developmental Drills   These multi-purpose drills are used for conditioning, developmental work, and stressing the proper fundamentals. Norm DeBriyn, head coach of the University of Arkansas, who originated the drills, said: "Most of them are performed early in our fall and spring practice programs. They are very effective in increasing skill level, developing hand-eye coordination and team conditioning, and working on the fundamentals of the game.

Procedure: The drills are conducted at four different stations, and the players are divided into groups mainly by position and by numbers. "We want the same number if possible in each group," said DeBriyn. "Basically, we utilize four of the following six drills, spending five minutes at each station and drill."

Drill	Players	Time
1. Flag Pole	9	5 min.
2. Simulation	9	5 min.
3. Reaction	9	5 min.
4. Chase the Rabbit	9	5 min.
5. Relay	9	5 min.
6. Center the Ball	9	5 min.

"The drills are done at the beginning of practice," said DeBriyn. "Each player understands how to do each drill so we do not waste any time. In addition to keeping everyone involved, they are quick and set a good tempo for our practice."

Flag Pole   This drill is designed to teach the correct drop back-step and an awareness of where the player is going without looking. The player has his back to a coach who is 20 yards behind. The player is staring at the ball on a flag pole, and on a signal, he will drop back with his right foot, letting the head and body come along. He then crosses-over and starts running in a straight line with his back to where he was facing. After three or four steps, he turns his head back over the same shoulder and picks up the ball. The object is to run directly into the coach or manager without looking forward and next time to drop back with the left foot and only look over the shoulder on that side. A variation is to have a manger throw a ball over the player's shoulder to the side he has looked back on.

Simulation   After assuming a good stance, the player will react to the following signals and verbal commands from the coach who:

1. Points left, player crosses over, goes to his right, and reacts to the verbal command of "get set, field, and step and throw."

2. Points to right and does the same thing.
3. With hand on chest, gives verbal command, the player comes in on the ball, and is ready for the next command.
4. Points at the player with the right hand, and the player drops back with his left foot, looks back toward the coach, who on command says *turn, catch, step,* and *throw.*
5. Points with the left hand and does the same thing.

Reaction   Similar to a football wave drill, the players start facing the coach and go left and right, according to the movement of his hand. The whole body turns as a runner does in stealing a base, only the head stays on the player in front.

Chase the Rabbit   A player is placed at each base and home plate, with a player in between those on the bases. On a command, they take off running, trying to touch the player in front of them. If they catch him and touch him, that player is out of the drill. This drill involves touching every base, making the proper turn and then running directly to the next base. Before getting to the next base, the player must make a good turn. Running twice around the bases makes this drill a good conditioner and also teaches proper base running form. Emphasize looking at the base. If the player gets in the habit of looking, he will not miss bases in a game.

Relay   This drill is run usually with three or four lines and two men at one end where they have to run back to back. The players in front have a ball but do not use a glove. On a signal, they run to their line and about twenty-five feet from the line, they toss the ball to the next person. That player cannot leave until he sees the flight of the ball, then he starts and catches it and runs to the other end of the line. The winner sits out the next race and the other two go.

Centering the Ball   This drill is mainly for infielders who must get down in a good defensive stance. However, early in the season, we have everybody go through this. A player steps out in front of the coach who is ten to fifteen yards away. The coach, who is on one knee, rolls the player a ball straight at him. The player comes in for the ball, keeping the glove down close to the ground and open wide, arms extended in front of him. Have the player come straight in, go to his left (glove hand) and then move to his right (back hand) side. In fielding the ball, he centers and looks the ball into his glove. He gives a hard throw to the next player and then becomes a shagger.

Two-Man Stationary Drill   Similar to a drill called "pick-ups", this is an excellent conditioning drill for the hamstrings, thigh and back muscles. It developes hand-eye coordination, quick hands, and teaches proper ground ball fielding techniques.

Procedure: Players can pair off on the outfield grass, each with a ball, approximately nine to twelve feet apart. Bill Wright of Tennessee instructs his players to assume a ground ball fielding position, feet parallel at about shoulder width, knees bent, back straight, head up. The players have their hands together out in front forming a triangle with the finger tips in the grass. Wright emphasizes staying down with the fingers relaxed and spread, hands soft, as the players toss the ball back and forth on the ground or in the air.

The players should start off slowly, but as the drill progresses, they move the ball more quickly. This five-minute drill should allow players to stand up periodically to kick the kinks out. "Keep the ball off the ground during the last minute," said Wright. "See who can go one minute without dropping the ball. As the players become more proficient, we have them move the ball quicker up and down, side to side, etc. We want to try to get the ball through their partners legs. We find that the players develop pride in not letting anything get through."

Offense and defense drills

Fighting Illini Three-Station Stealing Drill (Fig. 15.11) This outstanding drill developed by Tom Dedin, head baseball coach, University of Illinois at Champaign-Urbana, has every player doing something important, all at the same time:

The three-station stealing drill provides the following situations to work on:

1. the pitcher can work on holding a runner on at first base;
2. the catcher can practice his throws to second and third base with runners moving;
3. the remaining position players can work on their various base stealing and base running techniques.

Procedure: Start the drill with basic set-up as in Fig. 15.11, with a pitcher on the mound, two catchers, a pitcher handling throws at first base, and a pitcher handling the throws at second or at third base. Coach Dedin explained that, "We direct the extra catcher to shift back and forth between the right hand and left hand batter's boxes so that the throwing catcher gets the experience of throwing to a base with a batter in the box. We also want the catcher in full gear."

The drill is started with three runners working off each base. One of them works on the base line and the other two line up behind him. When the pitcher makes his move to deliver the ball to the plate, the base runners execute the called for stealing technique. "We have the base runners run through the base," said Dedin. *"They do not slide."*

In the first phase (Fig. 15.11b), the base runners at first base work on a

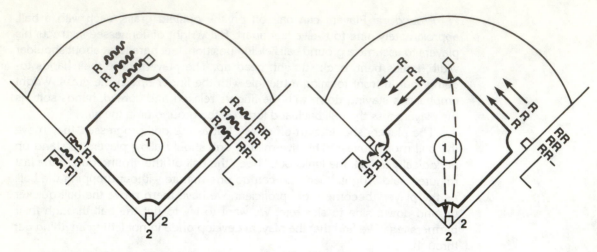

Fig. 15.11a   THREE-STATION STEALING DRILL.   Fig. 15.11b

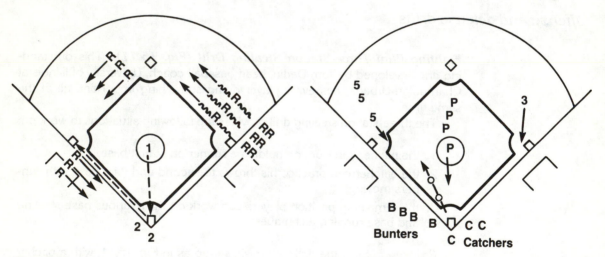

Fig. 15.11c   Fig. 15.12   GET AWAY DRILL.

straight steal of second base, taking a flash look at the catcher as he receives the ball. The runners on second base work on their steal of third base, and the runners at third work on a fake steal.

In the second phase (Fig. 15.11c), the base runners work on a delayed steal of second base; the runners at second base work on a straight steal of third (the pitcher gives them one look and goes to the plate); and the runners at third base work on their walking lead and scoring on a ground ball. The catchers here throw to third base. Dedin added that "We have the extra catcher stand in the righthand batter's box which forces the throwing catcher to either step in front, of or behind, the hitter."

Combination offense and defense

Get Away Drill (Fig. 15.12)　This combination/multi-purpose drill developed by Gary Pullins of Brigham Young University, will develop drag bunt skills in the hitters, practicing getting out of the box and running through first base. At the same time, it develops the third baseman's ability to field the slow roller and throw to first. The catcher can work on recovering passed balls and making a short toss to the pitcher covering home plate.

　Procedure: The pitcher throws a "crisp" strike to the hitter who drags to the third base side. The bunter-runner should run to first like during a game, as the third baseman makes the play and throws to first. A stop watch may be used to time the plays. The pitcher in the meantime ignores the bunt as he runs to the plate, comes under control, and receives a toss from the catcher who, after the bunt, had turned to recover a passed ball (placed there by the auxiliary catcher). The pitcher is taught to point where the ball is as he runs home. "You can go rapid fire once the players get the feel of it," said Pullins.

Purdue Hustle Drill (Fig. 15.13)　The purpose of this drill is to teach players to make a proper turn, run every ball out, while the defense is working on relays and run-downs. Dave Alexander of Purdue University believes, "It teaches the batter-runner that he can take an extra base once in awhile if he

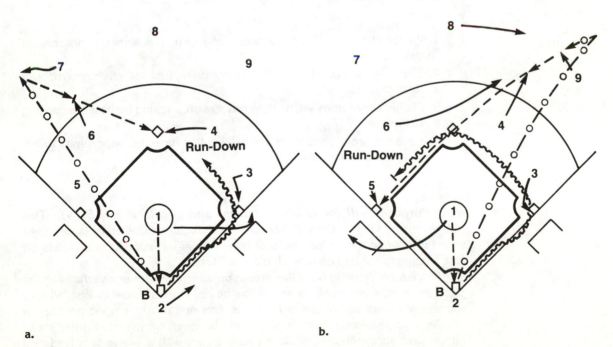

a.　　　　　　　　　　　　　　　　　　　　　b.

Fig. 15.13　PURDUE HUSTLE DRILL.

runs hard all the time. It also puts pressure on the outfielders and relay men to get the ball in and throw accurately. Pitchers also get in the habit of backing up bases. Later on we will put a runner on first and do the same thing."

Procedure: Nine players are placed on the field. Every ball is played as usual with one exception: infielders do not field ground balls. They let the ball go through to the outfield. The pitcher throws like he would during batting practice (let them hit). Every runner runs hard, makes a proper turn, and proceeds to the next base. The outfield relays the ball to the infield. If the runner is definitely out, the defense runs him down.

Team Concept Drill   Developed by Hal Baird of East Carolina University, this fine all-purpose drill incorporates all phases of the game into a practice regimen. Groups on defense can work on their responsibilities, such as cut-offs, positioning, throws, and play situations. At the same time, offensive groups are practicing their leads, jumps, and turns, in addition to bunting technique, hitting behind the runner, and moving runners over.

Procedure: Divide the squad into four groups: A) Infield (purple); B) Outfield (purple); C) Infield (gold); and D) Outfield (gold). Groups A and B are on defense, C is base running, and D is hitting. Pitchers work live to the hitters, while the defense plays all balls live. Base runners (C) will react live to all plays. Some specifics include:

1. All Ds (hitters) will hit consecutively, with a designated number of swings.
2. The defense reacts live to all plays, including trail and relay system, bunt defenses, etc.
3. Pitchers work from set, holding runners on, backing up bases according to the play.
4. Have the groups rotate so that all regulars have the opportunity to hit, play defense, and run bases.

Multi-Purpose Drill for Leads, Returns, and Steals (Fig. 15.14)   This drill recommended by Dave Keilitz of Central Michigan University is designed to improve upon the various skills of base running. Emphasis is on leads off first, returns to the bag on pick-off plays, and steals.

Procedure: Working from the stretch position, the pitcher can throw to the plate or attempt a pick-off at any of the bases. On his throw to first, all four runners will react and return to the base. This drill provides good practice in developing a maximum lead. Work should be given on measuring the leads, jumps, and acceleration. The base runners start with a twelve foot lead and work up in one-foot increments to sixteen and seventeen.

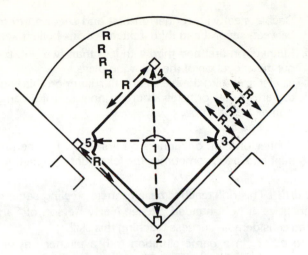

Fig. 15.14 LEADS, RETURNS, AND STEALS.

Offensive drills

Houston Offensive Drill The purpose of this drill is to educate the batter and discipline him so that he will know what to do under various game situations. A hitter will learn to think about what the ball and strike count is when he gets a sign, where the base runners are, and how fast they are. "Disciplined batters will help produce a better offensive team," explained Rolan Walton, head baseball coach of the University of Houston. "It is not easy to recruit players capable of becoming good, disciplined batters, and even more difficult to teach them to remain calm and to try to think and execute the play called for."

Procedure: Put a defensive team on the field and a pitcher on the mound. Begin with a lead-off hitter at the plate and a runner on first base. Go through several game situations, with the top twelve to fourteen batters participating in this drill. Make some changes at the defensive positions.

This drill, a favorite with Coach Walton, will help discipline hitters what to do in the following situations:

1. Steal situation with better than average runner on first. Take curve ball with less than two strikes. Be prepared to hit the fast ball strike on the ground. Try to hit the ball through a vacated position in the infield.

2. Steal situation with slower than average runner on first, protect runner if pitch is a strike on 2–0, 3–1, 3–2 counts. *Do not take a questionable strike.*

3. Runners on second, or first and second, with one out, be prepared to drag bunt down third base line if asked to do so.

4. Double steal with runner on first and second, try to hit a ground ball between second and third if pitch is a fast ball strike.

5. Runners on first and third with less than two out, be prepared to carry out the execution of the following plays:
   a. first and third double steal with runner on third holding,
   b. batter takes or fakes a bunt, runner on third can go home if catcher makes bad throw,
   c. hit and run.

6. Runner on first, or runners on first and third, be prepared for the fake bunt and steal, sometimes the fake bunt slap hit and steal.

Steal drill   This drill teaches base runners stealing second base how to read a pitchout vs. a right-handed pitcher. Marty Berson of Santa Monica College has had considerable success teaching this skill.

Procedure: In a game situation with a pitcher on the mound, the base runners are aligned three deep. The front runner is live. He slides back to first if a pick-off is attempted. He also slides at second on a steal attempt. The other two runners run through second base on a steal attempt.

The runners have the steal sign. They are instructed to take their leads slightly inside. (Heels aligned with the front of the base.) The size of their leads is a body length and an open step, a cross-over and open step. Once the lead is established, the runners watch the pitcher's feet. If the right heel moves, the runner dives back to first. If the pitcher moves his left foot, he steals.

There are two tip-offs Berson teaches for reading potential pitch-outs: 1) the pitcher accelerates his delivery, and 2) the base runner looks in at the catcher immediately as he attempts to steal. If he sees either the pitcher step directly toward the plate or the catcher step out to receive a pitch-out, he stops and returns to first.

Tire Drill for Hitting (Fig. 15.15)   Using old car tires fastened on to posts or wire fencing can provide an excellent training aid for hitters. Bat acceleration, bat control, and arm strength can be developed through this drill. Players can work on the tire drill any time during a practice session.

Procedure: Six or eight tires can be banded top and bottom by one-half-inch steel banding to a cyclone wire batting cage or fence. They are placed approximately eight feet apart at various heights. They can be designed for certain pitches or parts of the hitting swing. The tires should be drilled on the bottom for water drainage. Old, broken bats which are glued, nailed, and taped can be used for swinging at the tires.

When fastened to a post, a hacksaw can be used to cut one side through, enabling the hitter to swing through the cut. Cuts can be made at the proper angle, the same as if swinging at the ball. The other side is secured to a solid post. "Use as many stations as you wish," said Don Miller of California State University at Chico. "This will enable the hitter to strengthen his swing throughout the strike zone. Players should not spend more than ten minutes or twenty-

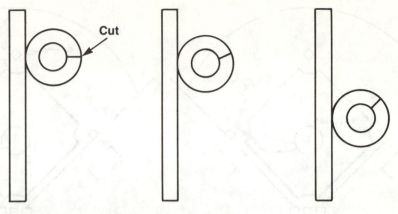

Fig. 15.15   TIRE DRILL FOR HITTING.

five swings at any one time. Otherwise, they have a tendency to start using improper hitting habits."

Defensive drills

Indoor Team Defense Situation Drill   Every possible defensive situation can be covered during this indoor drill, including cut-offs, relays, rundowns, double steals, fly ball calls, and various defensive alignments for bunts, double plays, or plays to the plate. "The great advantage for the coach," explained Lee Eilbracht of the University of Illinois, "is that corrections and advice can be made in a normal tone of voice, and everybody can see and understand what is going on."

Procedure: Bases are placed thirty feet apart and all movement is done at a walk. Throws are lobbed. The coach acts as the hitter and throws the ball to simulate the batter. The walker (runner) moves to first as the ball is thrown (hit).

Pitcher Covering First Base Drill (Fig. 15.16)   This excellent fielding drill for pitchers progressively teaches the proper method of covering first base. While the drill is almost as old as the game itself, Jack Stallings of Georgia Southern College emphasized that "the important thing is that each step must be mastered before moving on to the next."

Procedure: (A) The drill starts with the pitcher breaking from the mound and running *hard* to a spot twelve-to-fifteen feet up the foul line from the base, and then dropping his steps to get under control and stopping on the base with the right foot (for a RH pitcher) on the side of the base facing second base and the pitcher facing second base. Stallings pointed out that "it is very important that the pitcher get under control as he reaches the base and that his "free foot" (left foot for the RH pitcher) does not end up towards right field but is toward second base. With most of his weight on the back foot (the foot on the

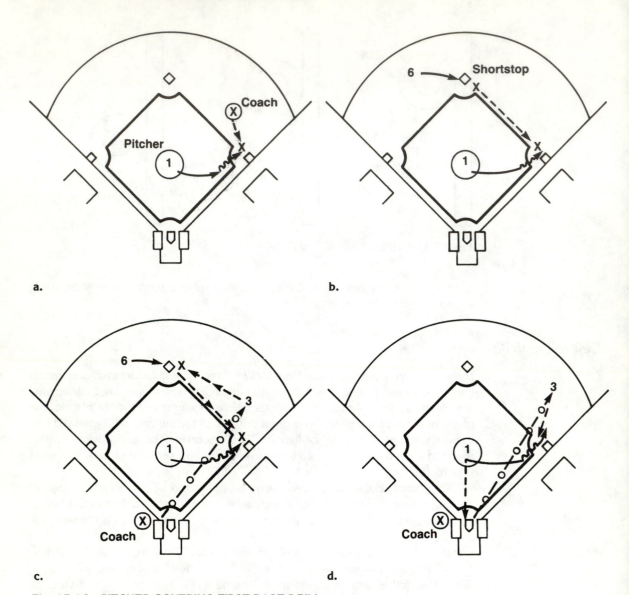

Fig. 15.16   PITCHER COVERING FIRST BASE DRILL.

base), the pitcher then steps out to take the throw from a coach located twenty-five to thirty feet away towards second base.

(B) Once phase A is mastered, the shortstop is instructed to throw from second base to the pitcher covering, but making sure the pitcher is in proper position and set before making the throw.

(C) The first baseman is now involved in the drill, fielding a ground ball and throwing to the shortstop, who tags the base and throws to the pitcher covering first base.

In another variation, the pitcher is instructed to break for the base and stop on the base as before, but instead, a coach is twenty to twenty-five feet away in the first baseman's position, and he throws the ball to the pitcher. "We emphasize again that the pitcher gets under control and stops on the base," said Stallings. "The first baseman does not throw the ball until the pitcher is in position and set."

After this phase is mastered, the coach (or first baseman) will throw the ball to the pitcher as he approaches the base, giving him a firm throw about chest high and early enough so the pitcher can concentrate on catching the ball and *then* concentrate on tagging the base properly, with the right foot on the edge of the base towards second base. "After tagging the base, the pitcher should bear to the left into the diamond to avoid colliding with the runner," said Stallings. "He is also in a position to make a throw to another base in case another runner is attempting to advance."

A coach is then added at home plate with a fungo bat and a bag of balls. The pitcher throws to the plate, a ground ball is hit to the first baseman, and the pitcher covers the base to take the throw.

Pitcher's Stride Drill (Fig. 15.17)   A favorite of Danny Litwhiler of Michigan State University and many other coaches, this drill helps pitchers develop the proper striding and stepping technique from the rubber toward home plate.

Procedure: Draw a straight line from the pitcher's pivot foot on the rubber

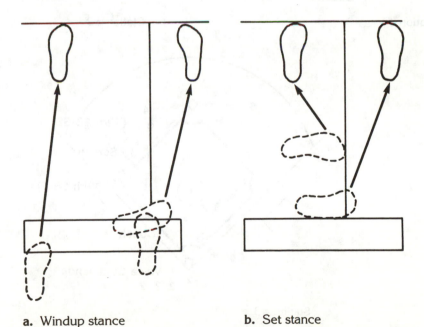

a. Windup stance   **b.** Set stance

Fig. 15.17   PITCHER'S STRIDE DRILL.

toward home plate. Then, instruct him to land his striding foot (if right-handed) to the left of the line. Have the pitcher throw at normal speed as he concentrates on bringing his striding foot down correctly and in the same spot for each pitch. If he lands on the heel of his foot, he is probably striding too far. The toe and heel should strike the ground almost simultaneously, although the ball of the foot should take most of the shock. The pitcher's toe should be pointed toward the plate.

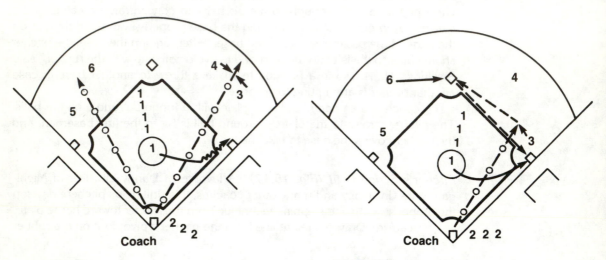

a.   Station #1

b.   Station #2

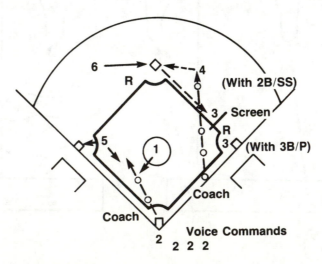

c.   Station #3

Fig. 15.18   PITCHERS AROUND THE BASES.

Pitchers Around the Bases (Fig. 15.18) This fast moving drill involves the pitchers in team defense with each infield position and backing up bases. With five minutes at each station, the total drill takes twenty minutes. "An excellent conditioner for pitchers, the drill can also be broken off into segments as separate mini-drills," said Pat Doyle of San Joaquin Delta College, "but you would lose some of the conditioning factors if you did this."

Station #1. Coach fungoes ground ball between first baseman and second baseman (Fig. 15.18a). Pitcher has to execute proper angle, using right foot on bag, turning inside, and looking for another play. The first baseman and second baseman can work on their communication. The second baseman has priority and should use his voice. The third baseman and shortstop can practice fielding balls hit in the hole. The third baseman takes everything he can, but has to communicate. The catchers should give a voice command for the pitchers to cover first base.

Station #2. 3–6–1 double play (Fig. 15.18b). First baseman fields ground ball to his right, throws to shortstop at second, who returns ball to pitcher covering for double play. Second baseman must have good voice communication with shortstop. The first baseman varies his position, holding runner on or behind him. The catcher should give voice commands. The outfielders can work on various drills.

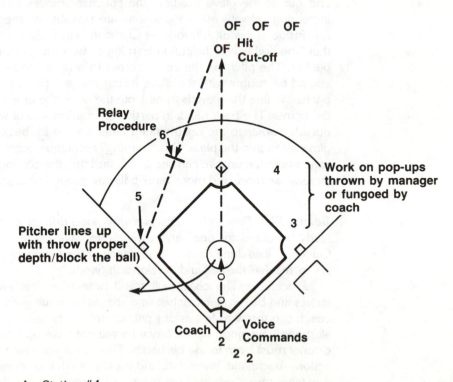

d. Station #4

Station #3. Bunt play to third base (Fig. 15.18c). Runners can be on first and second or first only. Pitcher breaks for third base line (review his foot work). Third baseman is even with bag or slightly in front, depending on his speed. He has two steps to decide to cover bag or field bunt. Meanwhile, second baseman and shortstop can work on double plays, with screen protecting other first baseman, working with the third baseman and pitcher. Catcher can give voice commands on who fields bunt.

Station #4. Back up coverage at third base and cut-off with shortstop (Fig. 15.18d). Coach fungoes ball back to pitcher who throws directly over the second base bag into center field. Outfielders use proper throwing fundamentals. Shortstop moves to cut-off position, while pitcher breaks to third base after throw. Third baseman has option to catch or let ball go through.

Quick Hands Drill   This drill should be used by catchers often. They learn proper hand position on receiving pitches in various locations. The importance of soft hands, hands away from body, loose wrists, eyes following ball, glove, and the like are among the skills readily learned.

Procedure: A coach stands a short distance (twenty to thirty feet) from the catcher in full gear. The shorter distance is for better control; there is no need for him to move more than forty feet from the catcher. As he throws balls in and out of the glove position, the "pitcher" moves back slightly, gradually increasing velocity. Many repetitions are possible at specific locations (high, low, inside, outside). A favorite at Clemson University, Coach Bill Wilhelm said that "the drill is very helpful in learning to turn the glove over and in framing pitches. The pitch on the inside corner to a right-handed hitter, for example, should be caught with the glove facing into the plate, rather than facing the pitcher. Where the glove is turned into the plate, the umpire will see the ball on the corner. The back hand, in particular, requires lots of work. The ball on the outside corner to the right-handed hitter should be back-handed so that the glove faces into the plate. This "framing" technique keeps the ball in the strike zone where the umpire can see it. "We find that the confidence of our receivers increase as more and more 'hard' balls are properly caught."

Twenty-Five-Foot Drill   This is a very good drill for *all* catchers, but particularly beneficial for one-handed receivers. "We use it a great deal at South Carolina," said June Raines, head coach of the Gamecocks. "It teaches catchers to 'receive' the ball and develop soft hands."

Procedure: The coach will stand twenty-five feet away and throw hard strikes and balls to the catcher, who should be in full gear. At twenty-five feet, a coach can throw as fast as any pitcher from sixty feet, so the catcher must be alert and have good hands. Since he will not have time to move his body, the catcher must learn to use his hands. The coach will watch him for proper hand action—backhand, lower mitt, and the like, so that he does not stab at the ball. A catcher must "receive," not reach. His hardest pitch is the low fast ball at his left knee. He should try not to let his elbow get higher than his mitt. If it does, he will carry the pitch out of the strike zone.

Infield Fungo Sequence (Fig. 15.19)   This fine defensive drill, devised by Gene McArtor of the University of Missouri, will ensure maximum repetition in a minimum of time of the major defensive plays required of an infielder in game situations. Time for each station in the sequence can be varied, or the first five stations can be emphasized. All infielders are involved at all times, and pitchers and catchers are necessary for some stations.

Procedure: Two fungo hitters are located at both sides of home plate, as well as a shagger. Both fungo hitters operate at the same time although for some stations they are required to alternate for safety reasons. Two infielders are required for some positions in the sequence. Players and fungo hitters can learn the sequence in a short time, thus minimal set-up and change time is needed. In twenty to thirty minutes, all infielders should have had a productive defensive workout.

The full sequence:

1. 3B → 1B,   SS → 2B → 1B   DP
   Explanation—The third basemen are fielding fungos and throwing to a first baseman in the short position. The shortstops are fielding fungos and getting a double play.

2. SS → 1B,   3B → 2B → 1B   DP
   Need to alternate fungos

3. 1B → 3B bunt   2B → SS → 1B   DP

4. 3B → 1B bunt, slow roller, $\begin{cases} \text{SS} \rightarrow \text{2B} \rightarrow \text{3B} \\ \text{2B} \rightarrow \text{SS} \rightarrow \text{3B} \quad \text{Reverse DP} \end{cases}$

5. 3B → 2B Bunt,   1B → SS → 1B   DP
   Need to alternate fungos. Pitchers can cover 1B

6. SS (hole) → 3B, $\begin{cases} \text{2B, 1B} \rightarrow \text{P cover 1B} \\ \text{P, 1B} \rightarrow \text{1B (2B cover) bunt} \end{cases}$

   Pitchers required

7. P → $\begin{cases} \text{SS} \qquad\qquad \text{3B} \\ \text{2B} \rightarrow \text{1B} \quad \text{DP, 1B} \rightarrow \text{4B} \rightarrow \text{1B} \quad \text{DP} \end{cases}$

   Pitchers and catchers required

8. 2B → 1B,   3B → 3B bunt, $\begin{cases} \text{SS} \rightarrow \text{4B Play at plate} \\ \qquad \text{or} \\ \text{SS} \rightarrow \text{1B slow roller} \end{cases}$

   Catchers required

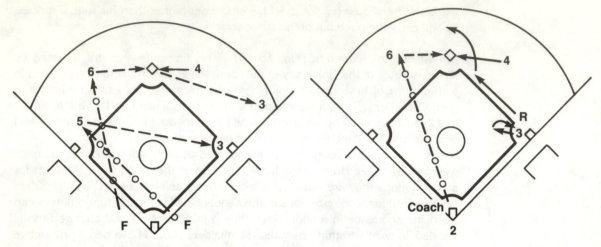

Fig. 5.19 INFIELD FUNGO SEQUENCE.   **Fig. 15.20** DOUBLE PLAY.

9. 3B tag base → 1B   DP,   1B → SS bunt $\begin{cases} 2B \to 4B \text{ Play at plate} \\ \text{or} \\ 2B \to 1B \text{ slow roller} \end{cases}$

Catchers required

10. 2B → tag runner → 1B   DP, $\begin{cases} C \to Ss \text{ bunt} \\ \text{or} \\ C \to 3B \text{ bunt} \end{cases}$

Catchers required

Double Play Pivots—Feeds Drill (Fig. 15.20)   This drill provides an opportunity for the middle infielders to practice the various pivots and feeds at second base. In this combination drill, the coach can evaluate their skills in fielding a ground ball, feeds, and pivots.

Procedure: The coach initiates the drill with a ground ball to the shortstop (#6). The runner at first sprints toward second and veers away from the #4 pivot man who has received a feed from #6. The second baseman (#4) throws to the first baseman (#3) for the double play. After coming off the bag, #3 had relocated himself at first base.

Run-down play drills (Fig. 15.21)   The purpose of these drills is to perform the run-down play as effectively as possible with a minimum number of throws. The key to its success is to chase the runner back at full speed.

A. Runner between first and second
B. Runner between second and third
C. Runner between third and home

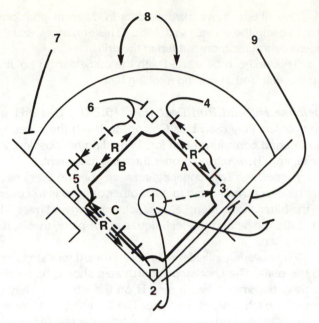

Fig. 15.21 RUN-DOWN.

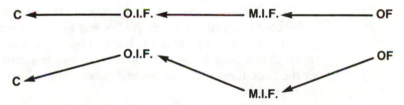

Fig. 15.22 RELAY DRILL.

Relay Drill (Fig. 15.22) This team defense drill teaches accuracy, quickness from catch to release, the proper way to catch the ball, read the ball, and communication.

Procedure: Line up an outfielder, middle infielder, outside infielder, and catcher. The outfielder's back is turned to the line. On the world "go", the outfielder turns and throws to the middle infielder, who throws to the outside infielder, who then relays the ball to the catcher.

Jack Smitheran, head coach at the University of California at Riverside, uses several lines and various competitive factors to motivate his players. Smitheran emphasizes the following: 1) Pick up target visually and verbally, 2) accurate, quick throws, 3) catch relay in air, and 4) to cut time, catch the ball in a turned throwing position. Smitheran explained: "You cannot turn until you read the throw from the man in front, since the ball may be thrown to the wrong side. The fielders must communicate verbally, "Here," "Here," "Here," and visually with arms above the head in a waving action.

"We like to move our infielders in different positions without the man in front seeing the move," said Jack. "This enhances visual sighting and encourages communication and fun in the drill."

This drill can be started with the outfielder: 1) holding the ball, 2) picking up the ball, and 3) fielding a rolling ball.

Defense Hit and Run Drill (Fig. 15.23)   This drill was devised by Berdy Harr of Cal Poly (San Luis Obispo) to teach the covering middle infielder the timing and communication for: 1) holding his position, 2) covering the proper base, and 3) exercising proper throwing judgment.

Procedure: The runner at first base goes on every pitch. The middle infielders have communicated to each other on who is to cover, and they must react to the hitter's execution, i.e., contact, or swing and miss. The hitters are directed to utilize the hit and run techniques at the plate, that is, hitting ground balls on every pitch.

The covering infielder will move forward four steps as the pitch is delivered to the plate. The shortstop's fourth step should be on his right foot, while the second baseman's fourth step is on the left foot. They do not break laterally until the pitch crosses the plate. The covering infielder is positioned two steps toward the bag and two steps *back* from the regular position, which is preferred over the traditional two steps *forward* because it provides a better angle to the base for the covering infielder.

The off infielder, meanwhile, must communicate where the throw should be directed on ground balls to the holding infielder. He should fake fielding a ground ball when a fly ball is hit. The first baseman and pitcher must hold the runner at first close to the bag. On a swing and miss, the catcher has to throw out the base runner. The batter and runner at first can work on their hit and run execution.

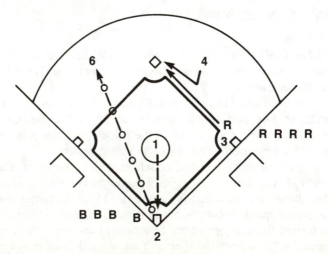

Fig. 15.23 DEFENSE HIT AND RUN DRILL.

Quick Drills   This series of defensive drills was developed by Bob Milano of the University of California at Berkeley to review the basic defenses. Coach Milano has found conducting them daily for three minutes to be very effective in giving his players the necessary confidence and composure in difficult situations.

Drill #1   Infielders Throwing Warm-Up (Fig. 15.24)   One of the catchers (2a) initiates this drill by throwing to the third baseman who tosses the ball across the diamond to the first baseman. #3 throws down to the shortstop who returns the ball to #2a. The other catcher (2b) makes his throw down to the second baseman who throws over to third base, and on home.

Drill #2   Slow Roller to Infielder (Fig. 15.25)   This circle drill gives infielders practice fielding slow rolling ground balls. The coach hits fungos around the infield, and the fielders make their throws.

Drill #3   Bunts Down the Lines (Fig. 15.26)   Everyone in the infield, including the pitcher and catcher, participate in this drill, which provides good practice in communication work.

Drill #4   Covering First Base/Fielding Bunt (Fig. 15.27)   When a runner is at first base and a bunt is layed down, either the first baseman or second baseman will cover first base. The pitcher and third baseman must decide who will handle the bunt and to which base the throw will go.

Drill #5   Multi-Purpose Drill (Fig. 15.29)   This multi-purpose drill provides good practice work for the catcher and pitcher. In addition to blocking low pitches, the catcher practices throwing to third and first base. The pitcher

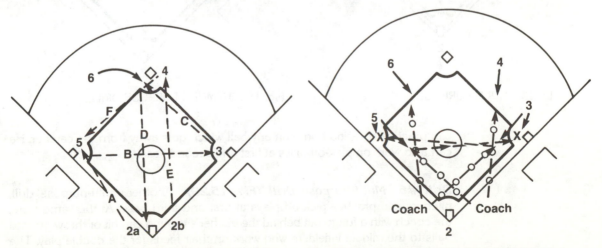

Fig. 15.24   INFIELDER'S THROWING WARM-UP.   **Fig. 15.25**   SLOW ROLLER TO INFIELDERS.

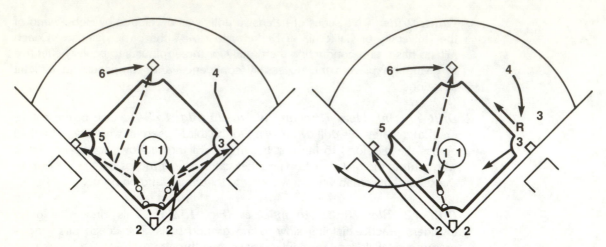

Fig. 15.26 BUNTS DOWN THE LINES.

Fig. 15.27 FIELDING BUNT/COVERING FIRST BASE

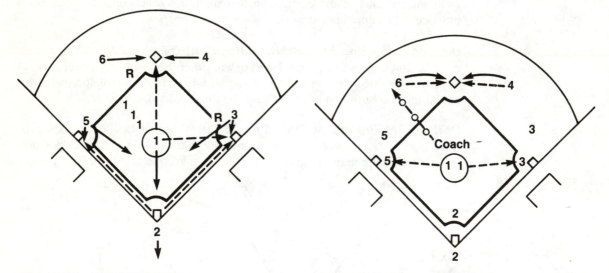

Fig. 15.28 MULTI-PURPOSE.

Fig. 15.29 MULTI-PURPOSE DRILL.

can practice covering home on any ball which gets away from the catcher. He can also work on pick-off plays at first and second base.

Drill #6 Multi-Purpose Drill (Fig. 15.29) Another multi-purpose drill, pitchers can practice pick-off plays at first and third base. At the same time, the coach with a fungo bat behind the pitcher's mound can hit or throw ground balls to the middle infielders who work on their feeds for the double play. The catchers can practice the jab step drill at home plate.

Drill #7   Multi-Purpose Drill (Fig. 15.30)   This drill gives catchers practice on their pitch-out throws, as well as giving signs to the pitcher and the fielders. This is also a good time to work on run-downs and pick-off plays. Runners can be placed at the bases. Pitchers can practice backing up home and third base. The outfielders can be throwing fly balls to each other to practice their fielding and throwing position.

Drill #8   Double Play Drill (Fig. 15.31)   This fine double play drill concentrates particularly on two DP situations: third to home to first, and first to home and back. The pitchers can also work on their double play throw to second base.

Drill #9   Run-Downs, Squeeze, and Pop-Ups (Fig. 15.32)   This multipurpose defensive drill gives everyone in the infield numerous game-like play situations. Run-downs between home and third base, defending against the squeeze play, communicating on pop-ups, and throwing by the catcher are among the situations which this drill can provide practice time. Outfielders serve as base runners at first, second, and third. When picked off base they get involved in run-down situations. Two coaches can throw pop-ups from home plate and behind the pitcher's mound. The first baseman should get practice moving to the fence in foul territory and catching the pop foul.

"Flip" Outfield Drill (Fig. 15.33)   This drill, developed by Jim Bowen of California State at Stanislaus, is very effective in teaching proper communication and catch execution in the outfield.

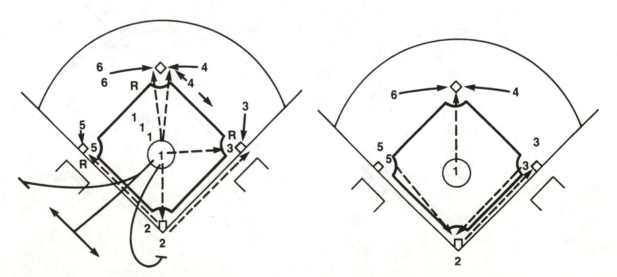

Fig. 15.30   MULTI-PURPOSE DRILL.   Fig. 15.31   DOUBLE PLAY DRILL.

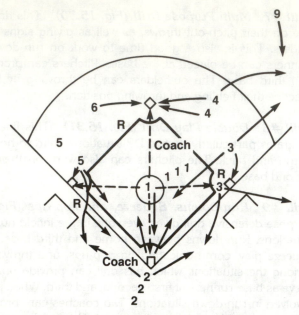

Fig. 15.32 RUN-DOWNS, SQUEEZE, AND
POP-UPS.

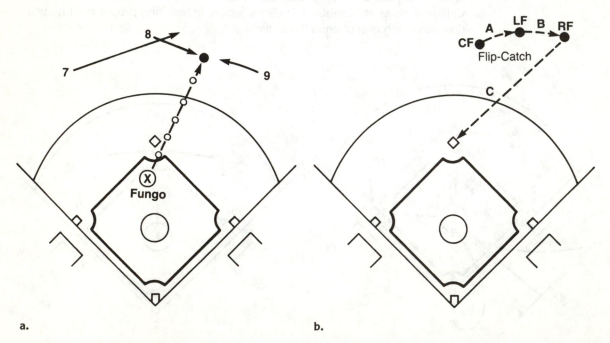

a.

b.

Fig. 15.33 FLIP OUTFIELD DRILL.

Procedure: Have three outfielders start in normal defensive position, except for a three to four step "cheat" toward center field. The coach pops a high fungo somewhere in their playable area. All outfielders will converge with one eventually calling for it: "Ball—Ball," etc. The other two should scramble to close proximity for the flip. Player A then uses two hands to flip the ball to player B who in turn flips to C who catches and relays the ball in to a given target or base. The coach should time the execution from bat contact to the arrival of the ball at the base.

TRAINING AIDS

During recent years, countless training aids and equipment, as well as gimmicks, have been available to baseball coaches and their programs. The purpose of these aids is exactly what the word implies—to assist the training and instruction of the athlete. Of course, the extent of their individual value varies with the product.

A select number of training aids have received widespread approval and use by the baseball programs, from the big leagues down through the youth leagues. The following aids can be of value in the development and training of a baseball player.

Pitching machines

The automatic pitching machine is an essential training aid to baseball programs on all levels. Machines of various types and sizes are capable of hurling curve balls and fast balls with strike zone precision.

The JUGS curve ball pitching machine is a very popular and widely used machine (Fig. 15.34). The term JUGS comes from an old-time baseball connotation, "jug handle curve." An "overhand" adaptor can be purchased to make the machine throw straight overhand. For further information, write: JUGS, P.O. 365, Tualatin, Oregon 97062.

The ATEC "Casey" pitching machine is also very efficient. To receive a brochure, write: Athletic Training Equipment Company, 9011 S. E. Jannsen Rd., Clackamas, Oregon 97015. Curvemaster, illustrated in our first edition, comes in two models for baseball: Model CBM-120 and Model CBM-2200. Write: Curvemaster Division, P.O. Box 181, Greenville, Ill. 62246.

Pitching machines can also be used to train catchers, infielders, and outfielders by throwing various kinds of grounders, pop-ups, and flies, at the speed and distance desired.

Control charts

Pitching control charts are kept to record the number of pitches and the number of each thrown for strikes. A breakdown should also be kept on the number of fast balls and breaking pitches thrown. When evaluating pitchers, these control charts should be closely observed.

Batting tee

A batting tee is an excellent training aid to develop and perfect the hitting swing. To improve his wrists, the hitter should swing fast and hit the balls quickly. In addition to being raised or lowered, the "T" can be placed anywhere in relationship to the plate, so the hitter can practice his weakness or strength from there.

Various types of batting tees are available on the market, but if the budget prohibits the expense, they can be easily built. Rubber hoses, like on radiators, are recommended, since plastic has a tendency to break or crack sooner than rubber.

Fig. 15.34 JUGS PITCHING MACHINE. All types of curves, sliders, and fast balls can be thrown at the speed and with the break chosen by the coach. The JUGS Automatic Feeder feeds baseballs at six-second intervals.

Fig. 15.35 PITCHING CONTROL TARGET. This very innovative training aid enables pitchers to throw to a strike zone constructed of nylon netting. Used both indoors and outside this popular aid is a definite improvement over the old pitching strings set-up (World Sporting Goods, Inc., 1306 St. Stephens Road, Mobile, Alabama 36603).

Speed guns

Speed guns are used to check the velocity of a thrown baseball. They are also effective in teaching off-speed pitches and for scouting.

Scouts use radar guns to time pitchers' fastballs. The average major league fast ball is delivered at around eighty-eight m.p.h., although some pitchers hit ninety-seven. One game under the gun usually tells whether a prospect has a major league arm. Earl Weaver, former manager of the Baltimore Orioles, used radar readings in deciding whether to remove pitchers. Colleges use them as recruiting aids to help determine the players they want to offer scholarships.

Stopwatch

Major league teams today keep a stopwatch on every catcher and pitcher in the league, recording the times, as well as telltale quirks and motions. Times are kept on the catcher, from when he touches the pitch to when he reaches the second baseman or shortstop, pitchers from the beginning of his break from the stretch to when the ball reaches the catcher.

Computerization

Major league clubs, increasingly, are using sophisticated computer systems to help them make personnel moves, lineup and pitching changes, pitch selections, and strategy moves. Data is compiled and plugged into the computer, such as every pitch thrown in every game and what the hitter does with the pitch. On the college and school level, however, the expense of an elaborate computer system will prevent most schools from setting one up. Yet, every baseball program should keep an accurate system of statistical data and records. The extent, of course, will be determined by who is available to record the data. Perhaps a cooperative work study program could be arranged with the Data Processing Center on campus, so that regular printouts can be computerized.

By providing players' batting averages against every opposing pitcher, on the major league level, the computer can aid the manager in making out lineups or choosing pinchhitters. It also will give him opposing hitters' batting averages against specific pitchers, an aid in making pitching changes. Computer charts can tell where certain hitters are prone to hit certain pitchers and pitches, and aid in positioning infielders and outfielders. Computers can break down opposing players' batting averages by type of pitch and location, such as an inside fast ball, outside slider, etc. This aids the manager in forming a strategy on how to pitch certain batters.

Big-league teams collect a considerable amount of information on every team because they play about twelve games with each of them, but on the college level when teams play each other two or three times, there is not a lot of data a team can accumulate on the opposition. Still, keeping regular statistical data can be valuable for a coach in evaluating the performances of his own players.

"Our computer system has been a big help to us", said Steve Boros, manager of the Oakland A's, "but it still doesn't take the place of keeping in personal touch with your players. The biggest part of a manager's job is handling twenty-five different personalities, and no computer can help him do that. It is important that the players recognize that they are not being judged coldly and impartially by a computer. Rather, there is a man there who has some compassion for their problems."

Whitey Herzog, the St. Louis Cardinals manager, compiles all the same charts and information without a computer system. But he needs three hours a day and 12 colored pencils to do what the EDGE 1000 does instantly. Herzog still prefers his intuition over anybody's numbers.

Fig. 15.36 PLAYER CHART. Steve Boros, manager of the Oakland A's, one of the first clubs to use the computer, points to a chart kept on an opposing hitter for one game.

Computer graphics

Big-league teams are making increasing use of the computer. The computer screen, for example, demonstrates what a hitter is doing and then a batting coach tries to correct the problem. Many teams are using graphics to show a hitter how he is making his outs. On the screen, he can see how many times he grounded out, how many times he flied out, and the direction and distance of each out.

Some left-handed hitters pull the ball to the right side of the infield when they ground out, but usually fly out to left center. Graphics of a right-handed batter like Tony Armas show that Armas grounds out to the left side, but flies out to the right side.

"When I was with the Angels," said Bill Rigney, "we told our shortstop to play deep in the hole for Armas and instructed our pitchers to throw him low fastballs. Time after time, he would hit the ball to the shortstop."

Instant movie systems

Slow motion and stop-action make instant movies ideal for instruction and coaching. The action on the "Polavision Player", for example, can be slowed down at the touch of a button, or advanced frame by frame. "Action control" lets the coach or athlete replay any part of the film, so he can examine every step, every move. Problem areas can be identified at half or quarter speed.

Through instant movies, athletes can get involved in analyzing their own performance, by seeing what they are doing wrong and determining how to correct their mistakes.

Videotape system

Almost every major league team now uses video tape recorders to help players analyze their batting or pitching form. The Dodgers have one of the most elaborate tape systems in professional sports. The equipment cost more than $20,000. There are four cameras—behind home plate, first base, third, and in center field—with slow-motion replays. The center field camera is able to zoom in on home plate. Players and coaches view replays on a four-foot screen in a small room adjacent to the clubhouse.

Videotape has many advantages over film. It is instantaneous and considerably less of an investment in equipment. With video, a team can keep the same tape and use it over and over again.

TRAINING FILMS

Excellent instructional training films are available on a loan basis from various sources throughout the country. Perhaps the largest library of 16-mm baseball films and video cassettes, including many World Series and All-Star game films, is the Major League Baseball Film Division, 1212 Avenue of the Americas, New York, N.Y. 10036.

Rental privileges are extended only to schools, clubs, organizations, etc., not to individuals. The following fees are applicable based on your organization's classification:

Educational, Religious, Military, etc.	$10 per film
Fraternal, Civic, or Service Club	$25 per film
Commercial organization	$100 per film
Purchase fees	$300 per film and handling

In addition to many World Series Highlight films, some excellent instructionals are available including: *All-Star Batting Tips, All-Star Pitching Tips, Charlie Lau: The Art of Hitting .300,* and *All-Star Catching and Base Stealing Tips.*

If a movie camera (8-mm) or video recorder and funds for films are available, motion pictures taken of players can be very helpful in eliminating flaws in hitting, pitching, and other basic fundamentals.

EVALUATION AND SELECTION OF PLAYERS

The baseball coach or manager has a responsibility and an obligation to every player to evaluate their performance. To accomplish this task, he must use criteria that are both meaningful and objective. Furthermore, the players should be allowed to discuss their performances and ratings with the coaches. The goal of every evaluation system is to insure that every player has the feeling that he is being evaluated fairly and objectively. Players who do not start or make the team should be told as objectively as possible why they were not chosen.

A good example of a production rating chart on hitting was developed by Ron Polk, head baseball coach at Mississippi State University. With the aid of a graduate assistant coach, Polk was able to record contact off the bat with points awarded on a zero-to-six point scale as follows:

Rating	Productivity
0	The batter swings and misses, a foul tip, or called third strike
1	The batter swings and fouls the ball straight to the backstop
2	The batter swings and fouls ball off weakly or a pop fly in the infield
3	The batter swings and fouls ball off sharply or high fly ball to outfield
4	The batter swings and hits a fair ground ball weakly or a humpback line drive
5	The batter swings and hits a ground ball well, a long fly ball, or line drive near foul line
6	The batter swings and hits a line shot, on the ground or in the air

Compiling averages

Determining Batting Average: Divide the number of at bats into the number of hits.

Determining an Earned Run Average: Multiply the number of earned runs by nine; take the number and divide it by the number of innings pitched.

Determining Slugging Percentage: Divide the total bases of all safe hits by the total times at bat. (At bats do not include walks, sacrifices, hit by pitcher, or times awarded first because of interference or obstruction.)

Determining Fielding Average: Divide the total putouts and assists by the total of putouts, assists and errors.

Determining Percentage of Games Won and Lost: Divide the number of games won by the total games won and lost.

COACHING CLINIC

Mastery of the fundamentals is the most important aspect of baseball, from training and running to batting and bunting. Most teams in baseball today are weak on the fundamentals. The following are three fundamental techniques or concepts which, if practiced and perfected, can strengthen any baseball team.

1. Fielding: One-Handed or Two-Handed? (Tom Dedin)
2. Developing the Alou-Style Hitter (Robert Wells)
3. Mental Errors (Bob Hiegert)
4. Vision Training (Dr. Bill Harrison)

Fielding: one-handed or two-handed?

In recent years the big glove, in addition to other factors, has resulted in a significant increase in one-handed fielding. Initially, this practice was not looked upon with alarm by many coaches since large, deep-pocketed gloves proved convenient and effective in catching the ball. Too often today, however, a one-handed fielding effort is a liability and the result is the hitter beats the throw or the base runner takes an extra base.

"The one-handed catching of a baseball is a major problem today," stated Tom Dedin, head baseball coach of the University of Illinois. "Young players have been affected by what they see on TV with the professionals. Without question, using one hand to catch a baseball is much slower than using two hands. It affects the infielders on throws to first and second and the outfielders on throws to the bases."

From the beginning, a coach must insist on, demand, and practice, the use of two hands. "The key to the problem, or any problem in coaching is to *sell* your players on what you are trying to accomplish," said Jack Stallings of Georgia Southern College. "Try to convince them to that what you are teaching them is the best way to do it and by doing it in that manner they are going to be better ball players."

Dedin confronts the problem by first explaining the importance of catching a baseball with two hands. "We actually start by showing our players where in the glove the ball should be caught," said Dedin. "A large number of them come into our program catching the ball in the net. For them, this is a habit that they have performed for many years. We demand that they catch it in the glove's pocket."

"We also demand that all of our players use two hands whenever they play catch or whenever they receive a baseball in practice," said Dedin. "We want them to always shift their bodies so as to get in front of a bad throw rather than reaching for it and stabbing it with one hand. As a coach, I am always roaming around, reminding the players about using two hands."

At Illinois, Dedin has made several "wooden" gloves. These are pieces of half-inch plywood that are shaped into a form similar to a glove. Tom screws two elastic straps on the back into which to insert the glove hand. When he has a player who refuses to use or has trouble in using two hands, he has him play catch or simply work with the wooden glove. "I have not seen a player yet who can catch a ball with only the wooden glove," said Dedin. "We have found this to be an excellent tool in teaching our middle infielders to use their gloves to stop the ball and get rid of it quickly on the double plays."

"We constantly 'get on' our players about not using two hands," continued Dedin. "It is essential that a coach first explain *why* using two hands is the correct way. Too many coaches just tell their players to use two hands without explaining why. If they would just take a couple of minutes to explain *why*, they would see better results."

Developing the Alou-style hitter

In recent years, there has been a trend in baseball toward developing a slap-hitting, left-handed hitter who can make use of his speed by hitting to the left side of the field (Fig. 15.36). Successful examples of this type of hitter include Matty Alou and Maury Wills, left-handed hitters, with speed, small in size, who were not effective swinging away normally.

Whether the player already hits from the left side or is a right-handed hitter who has to switch over, the idea is to teach him to hit consistently to the left side of the diamond. He has to learn to bunt for a base hit toward third. "By forcing the left side of the infield to play up on him, this increases the chances of getting a ground ball through the hole or past the third baseman," explained Robert Wells, baseball coach at Frostburg State College (Maryland). "It also forces the shortstop to make many difficult plays on balls deep in the hole against the batter's speed and quicker start."

The learning process is not an easy one, as Maury and others found out. "Surprisingly enough, the former right-handed player may find the switch-over process easier than will the left-handed player who is trying to change his style," said Wells. "The reason for this is that the left-handed player has many habits to break, whereas the old habits of the former right-handed player are right-handed and do not carry over easily to the left side."

Fig. 15.37 THE SLAP-HITTING, LEFT-HANDED HITTER with speed who can hit consistently to the left side can be a major offensive weapon for any team (Matty Alou).

"If a ballplayer can run and does not have much power and is small in stature, it is just common sense that tells me his best chance of hitting is to keep the ball out of the air, and to do that, he has to swing down on the ball."

WALT HRINIAK

Wells has used the following procedure very successfully:

1. Use the heaviest and longest bat available and have the batter choke it from two to five inches.
2. Move the player well off the plate with a closed stance. Start out deep in the box but move up even with the plate if he has trouble waiting for the pitch.
3. Take an inside-out swing. The hands and elbows are held in to the body, and as the player steps into the pitch, his body, not just his hands and arms, goes with the pitch.
4. Readjust his thinking regarding the strike zone. On the ball on the outside third of the plate, hit along the left field line; ball over the middle third, hit into the hole; and the ball on the inside third, hit up the middle.

5. Start to practice. Wait until the last possible second and try to stroke the ball toward third base. Emphasize the proper step into the pitch— short and toward third base.

"Ideally, the swing should be short, quick, and down on the ball," said Wells. "By hitting downward slightly, the batter not only compensates for an upward tendency, but gets the ground balls that he wants. In games, he should be looking for the pitch that is down and out away from him. Be a little particular. Being able to take a strike, or sometimes two, is necessary in adapting to the new style."

Mental errors

A mental error was defined by Bob Hiegert, head baseball coach at California State University of Northridge, as "a mistake stemming from carelessness or lack of proper preparation." During the 1977 season, Hiegert conducted a study on mental errors using as a sample his CSU-Northridge baseball team. Each error was recorded and identified as to a pitching, defensive, hitting, or base running error. Most significant was the fact that an average of 5.5 more mental errors were committed in games lost. Pitching mental errors accounted for 37 percent of the total errors committed, while defensive errors accounted for 14 percent, hitting errors 39 percent and base running 10 percent.

The most significant differences between mental errors committed in losing games compared to winning games were:

In pitching—hit batters, late covering 1B, not stopping runners, and balks

On defense—wild throws, and passed balls

In hitting—took third strikes, failed to score runner from 3B, and hit into DP's

In base running—reacted wrong way on line drives

Hiegert gave the following suggestions for reducing mental errors:

1. Identify mental errors for your players.
2. Stress the importance of playing the "perfect mental game."
3. Tabulate mental errors during each game, just as physical errors are scored.
4. Discuss mental errors with the team and individuals.
5. Keep a team record of mental errors.
6. Keep track of each player's mental errors.

VISION TRAINING

Baseball players have been coached in everything but their most important asset—vision. Most athletes do not know how to use their eyes for complete efficiency. "Hitting a baseball has been called the most difficult single act performed by an athlete," said Dr. Bill Harrison, an optometrist who has been a consultant to the Kansas City Royals and numerous major league hitters, including George Brett and Rod Carew. "However, it only takes a slight movement of the eyes to turn a thrown baseball into a blur."

"The key to the Royals' program is the development of concentration through a process called centering," explained Dr. Harrison. "For example, most hitters report that when they are hitting well, they see the ball more clearly." Harrison's program deals with eye contact, visualization, centering with the eyes, eye exercises, etc. "The eye control exercises really helped me see the baseball better," said Ed Kirkpatrick, a former Royal. "Instead of thinking about making an out, I would visualize a base hit."

A successful hitter must center or concentrate on the ball. "Looking at a baseball is not enough," said Harrison. "The hitter must center on it in order to derive information quickly from the pitch."

How to practice centering:

1. As the pitcher rocks into his pitching motion, the hitter should fine center on the pitcher's eyes or cap insignia.
2. Just prior to the release of the ball, the hitter should pick up the ball in the release zone.
3. When the ball is released, the batter's eyes should focus only on the ball, centering on the ball for detail.
4. The hitter's eyes (tilted no more than 10°) should stay on the ball until contact is made.

A vision consultant, an optometrist, working in cooperation with a team physician, can render an important service from which every athletic program will benefit. Diagnostic visual tests can be performed in less than ten minutes per athlete, with help in recording results. After the results are evaluated, a list of those players recommended for a complete visual examination is sent to the coach.

Vision Dynamics is a unique training program developed by Harrison on the mental aspects of sports. The concept involves visualizing success in one mind and seeing oneself perform a skill in a successful manner. A video tape series on vision baseball training methods, including a special Eyerobics training drill, can be obtained by writing: Vision Dynamics, Inc., 265 Laguna Ave., Laguna Beach, Calif. 92651.

The ability to visualize the correct swing is essential in hitting success.

Fig. 15.38 GOOD VISION. To hit a baseball sharply and consistently, the abilities to focus, converge, and control the eyes individually and together are equally important. To really see the ball, the batter must look for specific information. He should look at the middle or center of the ball such as the "imaginary horizontal line" that would go through the middle. Instead of merely looking for the ball, the hitter has to "tune in to it." When George Brett, shown here, is seeing the ball more clearly, he is "fine centered" on the ball, focusing on the middle of the ball. His eyes stay on the ball until contact is made.

16
Conditioning

The successful teams in baseball today are giving their players vigorous and steady doses of stretching and strengthening exercises and considerable running. Coaches and managers are supplementing actual game experience with daily conditioning exercises. After conducting good off-season programs, baseball teams now continue their conditioning throughout the season.

A baseball player has to work on the muscles that he uses during the game, like those used in throwing, running, and swinging the bat. These are the muscles he uses during the game. However, batting, fielding, and throwing work alone are not sufficient to achieve proper conditioning. When greater demands are made, a player needs additional strength, power, flexibility, and endurance for peak performance. Therefore, baseball players need an exercise program which begins during the off-season and spring training and is carried on throughout the regular season.

If your muscles are strong, they will react quicker and won't fatigue as fast.

Baseball is a difficult game in which to stay in condition, simply because the players do not run that much. As a result, players must supplement their game action with a concentrated program of conditioning before the game.

Fig. 16.1 A SOUND CONDITIONING PROGRAM. Baseball players who perform on the higher levels of play now follow a year-round conditioning program. Indeed, the physical strength and flexibility of players today represents one of the greatest improvements in baseball (Dusty Baker).

Coaches are getting the best results by giving their players a steady and often heavy amount of conditioning and training throughout the season.

If two players have the same degree of ability, skill, and natural talent, the stronger athlete will have a better chance of succeeding. He will have more power and speed, and, very important, he will have more stamina to practice. In addition, good conditioning builds confidence and assurance. Players can extend themselves physically much sooner without fear of muscle pulls and strains.

Baseball, perhaps more than any other team sport, requires training to supplement skills practice. In batting, for example, the weight of the bat alone will not produce increased strength. Weight training exercises are needed to strengthen the arms, wrists, and shoulders.

A ball player must have sufficient stamina and endurance to play nine innings. When not in good physical condition, a pitcher has a tendency to drop his arm, losing control and effectiveness. In the late innings of a game, a hitter who is not in shape might not swing the bat properly, nor be able to beat out balls in the infield. He could lack the power which a sound conditioning program can provide.

An exercise program has been a major factor in the mound success of the Giants' Atlee Hammaker. Concerned that he was tiring in the late innings, Hammaker approached trainer Gary Iacini about how he could improve his stamina. Iacini put Atlee on a Nautilus and weightlifting program involving 14 different exercises. Among the latest training aids is an isometric bar known as SportStick, which Hammaker uses even between innings of games he is pitching. In addition, Iacini had Hammaker running 220-, 330- and 440-yard intervals. With Iacini's approval, Hammaker adopted some karate routines used by Steve Carlton.

The overall fitness of a baseball player demands emphasis on speed, stamina, endurance, flexibility, and strength. Of course, the most important ingredients in any conditioning program are consistency and dedication. *There are no short cuts or magic formulas.* A player will get results from his program equal to the amount of hard work and dedication he puts into it.

The key to maintaining flexibility is doing stretching exercises every day.

BASIC AREAS OF CONDITIONING

A sound conditioning program for any baseball player should emphasize three basic areas: 1) strength building, 2) flexibility, and 3) distance running and speed work.

Strength building

Coaches a decade or two ago were not educated to, or aware of, the benefits of an organized strength building program. Players were told not to touch any weights, otherwise they would get muscle bound. Today, however, trainers and orthopedic specialists unanimously endorse weight training and strength development.

Sophisticated weight machines, such as the Nautilus program, enable players to increase their strength, speed, and durability from season to season. The effectiveness of today's weight programs, combined with the aluminum bat, has made it possible for even the small players to hit the ball out of the park.

Flexibility

Increased flexibility will expand an athlete's range of motion, regarded as one of the most important ingredients in athletic success. Baseball players need a great deal of flexibility to perform up to their potential. To have optimum flexibility, they need to stretch daily all the major muscle groups. Stretching relaxes muscles and enables the player to warm up more quickly and efficiently. Ideally, muscles should be stretched before and after each practice.

Distance running and speedwork

Distance running and speedwork should be a part of a conditioning program for baseball players. To build up the legs, an athlete has to run. To gain speed and quickness, the legs and lower body must be strengthened. An athlete can be trained to run faster by: increasing his stride length and increasing his stride frequency (leg speed). The pushing muscles (extensors) can and must be developed through speed-resistance training, in which a greater amount of resistance is imposed on a muscle or muscle group.

Strength is great, but without flexibility you are in serious trouble.

BOB SHAW

Objectives of a Good Conditioning Program

· Increased speed and quickness
· A stronger, more powerful body
· More agility, flexibility, and coordination
· Greater stamina and endurance
· Increased resistance to injury

BASEBALL CONDITIONING—THE MODERN WAY

Strength development

Contrary to what ball players were told years ago, strength is a major element in performing baseball skills. Modern research has revealed a strong correlation between strength and success in hitting and throwing a baseball. When strength is increased, the ability of the player is improved, largely because of quicker reactions and a greater range of movement. Additional strength can give hitters a quicker bat and pitchers a more explosive delivery.

Strength is a most important factor in running. A periodic increase in weight and resistance against the muscles will develop both strength and speed.

The purpose of a weight training program is to increase strength and endurance by overloading the muscles involved. The use of weights during exercise speeds up the conditioning program by making the muscles do an above-normal amount of work in a short period of time. The athlete performs several repetitions with weights that can be handled with relative ease, rather than attempt to lift maximum load. By working with increasing load, the individual gradually builds up to heavier drills. The repetitions that hurt are the ones that build.

Muscular contractions in sports are mostly "explosive" in nature. Power is

Fig. 16.2 STRENGTH BUILDING. Baseball players can benefit greatly from strength training. The Nautilus program is considered to be the most efficient conditioning method today for developing strength and endurance and for increasing flexibility. Above the weight room at the Central Michigan University provides players with a complete 30-minute Nautilus workout on the twelve machines.

Fig. 16.3 FLEXIBILITY AND STRETCHING. One of the most significant trends in athletic conditioning and training in all sports is the increased emphasis on flexibility and stretching exercises. By stretching, the athlete becomes more flexible, and if he is flexible, he will be more relaxed. Here, players on the Dodgers do their stretching exercises prior to a spring training work-out at Vero Beach, Florida.

Fig. 16.4 DISTANCE RUNNING AND SPEED WORK. Running is a great conditioner. Baseball players, like the athletes in other sports, should do a lot of running. There is no better activity than running to get in shape and to develop much needed speed and stamina.

developed when acceleration of an object occurs in a brief time span. The amount of force behind the acceleration determines the amount of power generated. Two types of muscle contraction are most common. Isometric contraction involves no joint movement and is usually performed by applying pressure to an immovable object. This may be done by simply contracting the muscles while holding the limbs still. The disadvantage of isometrics in sports has resulted in their limited use. Isotonic contraction, although performed against resistance, involves limb or body movement.

A good routine for an athlete is to alternate weight training with running and other conditioning activities. To maintain flexibility, an athlete must concentrate on going through the complete range of motion for each exercise.

WEIGHT TRAINING PROGRAM

There is a strong correlation between strength and success in hitting and throwing a baseball. One of the best ways to develop muscle strength is through a progressive weight training program. However, exercises for the shoulder and chest muscles involved in throwing should be limited, and there should be no exercises to develop the biceps. Since the triceps muscle is normally weak, the triceps extension can strengthen the throwing arm and provide more power to the front arm in the batting swing. Emphasis should be on the muscle groups in the legs, back, wrists, and forearms.

When the athlete first begins his program, each exercise should start with a weight he can lift six or eight times in succession with little difficulty. Then, when his strength develops to a point where he can repeat the exercise fifteen times with ease, he is allowed to add weight.

Regularity is vital to any successful conditioning program. Consequently, a weight program should be conducted throughout the year, even during the competitive months. Since weight training is fatiguing, lifting exercises should not be performed on a daily basis. During the off-season, a schedule of Monday, Wednesday, and Friday will build the athlete's strength quite adequately, while during the season the runner should limit his weight work to Monday and Wednesday after practice.

The generally accepted training program for both strength and bulk includes five to eight repetitions for at least three sets. Research studies show that a program consisting of maximum-lift reps offers the ultimate in strength development. Investigators have concluded that the use of heavy loads is the most effective way of improving strength. Therefore, overloading is an important concept in weight training.

To increase strength, a high intensity of work is beyond any question the single most important factor," wrote Arthur Jones, "but it also makes deep inroads into your recovery ability. Therefore, it should not be overdone. No more than three high-intensity workouts should ever be performed within a period of a week, and no single workout should last much longer than thirty minutes."

Weight training workouts should be supervised by a coach so the athletes know what and how much to do. No coach should turn a group of athletes loose on a weight training program without supervising or at least getting them started. There is a danger in working with weights. If the lifting is not done correctly, athletes can get more strains and injuries in the weight room than they do out on the field. The coach must point out to the athletes the "do's" and "don'ts" and tell them why. Too often, athletes become competitive in the weight room, and they have a contest to determine who can lift the heaviest weight and the like. This is when the injuries begin. A coach should never allow horse play in the weight room.

Each athlete should keep a record of his progress on the locker room wall. It should give the name, exercises, the weight for each exercise, number of repetitions, and the number of sets.

The weighted bat is highly recommended by coaches and hitters alike. Ted Williams believes the weighted bat was responsible for his increased strength. As a young hitter, during the off-season, he often swung the weighted bat 400 times a day. Ted was able to isolate all his swinging muscles with his weighted bat.

The donut, which can be fastened to the player's bat, continues to be a popular training aid. The big advantage of the donut over the weighted bat is that the player can swing his own bat.

A dedicated effort

For a weight program to be successful, the athlete must be dedicated. He must *want* to get stronger to improve his game. The player who does not want to improve his game will receive little value from the program simply because he will not work hard enough at it.

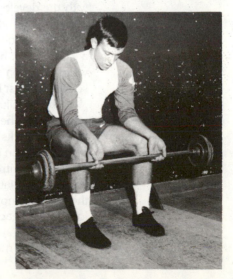

Fig. 16.5 LIGHT WEIGHTS. Off-season conditioning should involve light weight lifting with the legs and hands. The ten and twenty pound curls are very good for the wrists because they build up the forearms. From a sitting position, the athlete grabs the bar bell in his fingers, not his palms. Bench pressing or any excessive lifting that goes up above the upper body should be limited, since this type of exercise can tie up everything across the chest (Donn Johnson).

Barbell Routine

Muscle Group Involved	Exercises	Repetitions
Abdominals	Bent-legged Sit-ups	15–20
Obliques	Side Bends	15–20
Quadriceps	Front Squats (to 90° of flexion)	8–12
Calves	Calf raises	15–20
Quadriceps	Regular Squats (weight on back)	8–12
Hamstrings	Leg Curls	8–12
Buttocks/ Lower Back	Dead Lifts	8–12
Back/Latissimus	Bent-over Rowing	8–12
	Pull-ups	8–12
Upper Back	Cable/Spring Expansion	8–12
Triceps of Upper Arms	Tricep Extension/Lat Pull	8–12
Grip, Wrist & Forearms	Reverse Wrist Curls Wrist Curls Bat Grip Wrist Curls Hand Grips Ball Squeezes	15–20

Nautilus

Nautilus is one of the few strength training programs that does not interfere with the development of flexibility and coordination which concerns so many athletes. The key to the Nautilus popularity seems to be the physiological principles involved and the ease with which the same machine can be used by a 200-pound, hard-hitting outfielder or a lean, 150-pound southpaw. Nautilus weights are on cams and pulleys and the Nautilus machine adjusts the weight so the heaviest load comes into play at the strongest point of the muscle.

The Nautilus program, unlike free weights, works in rotary, instead of linear, movement. The machines provide resistance for muscles to push against. Each machine works on a different muscle group. The name Nautilus originated from a cam on each piece of equipment that is shaped like a nautilus seashell. The cam controls a weight and pulley mechanism. Only Nautilus machines employ a variable resistance cam, requiring total muscular effort throughout the training motion. Because continuous effort is required, more work is performed with each repetition and fewer repetitions are needed to reach personal goals.

Nautilus machines require muscles to stretch and contract completely, ensuring elasticity of the ligaments, tendons, and fibers that surround each joint. Ultimately, this full range exercise enhances ease of motion and lowers the risk of sports injury.

"Multiple sets are neither necessary nor desirable," said Arthur Jones. "One properly performed high-intensity set of each exercise is all that is required to provide a maximum degree of growth stimulation. Additional sets will merely make unnecessary inroads into your recovery ability."

A Nautilus workout takes about thirty minutes in which trainees do eight to twelve repetitions on each of the twelve machines. Each machine is designed to isolate a separate group of muscles and permit a full range of resistance against these muscles. As the athlete gets stronger, the weight resistance on each machine is increased, and the number of repetitions is decreased. The time lapse between exercise sessions should be at least forty-eight hours and not more than fifty-six hours.

During the off-season, the Nautilus program has been very effective in building up the arms of pitchers and fielders alike, adding velocity to their throws. Any player who has had throwing problems of any kind is progressed to the Nautilus. The Pullover and Double Shoulder, in particular, are absolutely necessary in the proper conditioning and rehabilitation of the throwing shoulder (Fig. 16.6).

Nautilus Routine for Baseball Players

Muscle Group Involved	Exercises	Repetitions
Abdominals	Bent-legged Sit-ups	15–20
Obliques	Side Bends	15–20
Buttocks and Lower Back	Hip & Back Exercise (Fig. 16.6a)	8–12
Hamstrings	Leg Curls (Fig. 16.6b)	8–12
Quadriceps/ Frontal thighs	Leg Extensions	8–12
Hamstrings, Quadriceps and Buttocks	Leg Presses	8–12
Calves	Calf Raises	15–20
Back/Latissimus dorsi	Pullovers (Fig. 16.6c) or Lat Push-downs	8–12
Upper back, Deltoids and Trapezius	Rowing or Cable/Spring Expansions	8–12

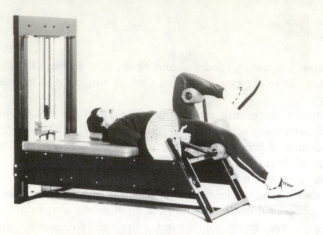

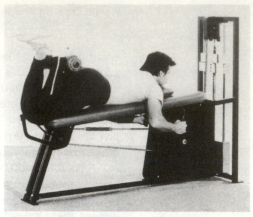

a. Hip and Back Exercise (buttocks and lower back). Holding one leg at full extension, allow other leg to bend and come back as far as possible. Stretch and push out until it joins other leg at extension. Repeat with other leg.

b. Leg Curls (hamstrings). Place feet under roller pads and grasp handles. Curl legs and try to touch the buttocks. Pause at point of full muscular contraction. Slowly lower resistance and repeat.

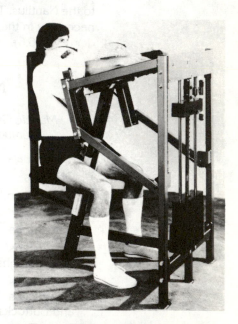

c. Super Pullover (latissimus dorsi muscles of back). The hands are removed from any meaningful role by placing the resistance pads directly against the upper arms. Slowly rotate elbows as far back as possible. Stretch. Rotate elbows down until bar touches stomach.

d. Tricep Extension (triceps of upper arm). Place sides of hands on movement arms and elbows on pad. This multi triceps machine can be used in different ways. Using two arms normally, the athlete straightens both arms to contracted position. Here, he works one arm to exhaustion.

| Triceps of upper arms | Tricep Extension (Fig. 16.6d) | 8–12 |
| Grip, Wrist & Forearms | Reverse Wrist Curls Wrist Curls Bat Grip Wrist Curls Hand Grips Ball Squeezes | 15–20; Barbells or dumbells preferred on all grip, wrist & forearm exercises. |

If the weight seems too heavy for you during the first repetitions, switch to a lighter weight.

Flexibility and stretching

A sound flexibility program is designed to lengthen the muscles so that all muscle movement will be easier. An effective flexibility routine will prepare the body for vigorous physical activity by increasing the elasticity of the muscles and tendons, thereby helping to prevent strains. The slow stretching of muscles is accomplished by stretching the muscle beyond its resting position and stretching it gently out to a greater length. It cannot be done too fast or too hard and has to be done on a daily basis with gradual progression.

Very few exercises involve stretching. In order to provide stretching, the range of movement in an exercise must actually exceed the possible range of movement of the athlete. Therefore, to increase flexibility, the choice of exercises is very important, since some exercises provide stretching and some do not.

The basic purposes of flexibility exercises are to:

1. Stretch muscles to avoid tearing or pulling
2. Perform a skill in its entirety and with greatest economy
3. Apply strength exercise through the full range of movement
4. Eliminate awkward movement and obtain greater efficiency

Flexibility is best achieved by gradually forcing the muscles and connective tissues to stretch while moving a joint through a full range of motion. To increase muscle flexibility, two methods are generally used—ballistic stretch and static stretch. Ballistic stretching involves bouncing against the muscle in an attempt to produce greater muscle length. This method, however, can be

---

Fig. 16.6 THE NAUTILUS PROGRAM is a most efficient conditioning method for developing strength and endurance and for increasing flexibility. Nautilus is a rotary form of automatically varying resistance exercise that includes stretching, pre-stretching, and a full muscular contraction.

dangerous, particularly if the muscle is cold and tight. Tight muscles can easily be torn. Static stretching is safer and more effective because it stretches the muscle under controlled conditions. In a static stretch, the muscle is held at a greater-than-resting length for eight to ten seconds and then relaxed for five seconds. A cycle of stretching and relaxing should be repeated for five to eight repetitions.

Flexibility is suppleness, the ability to go through the range of motions without tension.

BOB SHAW

There are two phases to flexibility exercises.

1. The contraction phase performed in a slow "ten-count" against resistance, demands a total effort.
2. The relaxation phase is when the muscles are actually stretched. The athlete stretches slow and steady, then returns in the same manner, without jerking movements.

Flexibility exercises are most beneficial when they are done every day. Athletes who are susceptible to muscle pulls and strains, in particular, should have a daily flexibility program.

Before doing any stretching, however, the athlete must make sure he is warmed up properly. Never go into a stretching exercise without first doing some running to make sure the blood is flowing and the muscles are warm.

The key to stretching is complete mental concentration on the area of the body being stretched. A player should concentrate particularly on tight muscles. Starting with short periods of the simpler routines, he increases the time spent on each exercise progressively. Gradually, more strenuous exercises are introduced.

THE DODGERS' STRETCHING PROGRAM

Flexibility is the important by-product of the Dodgers' muscle stretching program. "If we can stretch a muscle or group of muscles as far as they can possibly be stretched," explained trainer Bill Buhler, "the chances of ever pulling that muscle will be much less."

From the opening day of spring training to the end of the season, many Dodgers do stretching and loosening up exercises. Under the capable direction of Buhler, the program has been very beneficial to such players as Dusty Baker, Steve Garvey, Bill Russell, and Ron Cey, who perform the routines with religious dedication.

All of the Dodgers exercises are a static stretch, against the old style, ballistically, one-two-three-four. Buhler gets the player into the position where he holds it—he puts the muscle on stretch, and when he can feel the muscle stretching, he relaxes and holds the position. He begins with a ten-second count and increases to about twenty-five seconds as he goes along.

"Before a game, we want our players to stretch and loosen up their muscles, but not overbuild them," explained Buhler. "Our warm-up exercises are designed for the gradual stretching of the muscles which causes the muscle fibers to become more extensible and elastic. When proper stretching is combined with daily running and weight work, maximum movement and strength can be achieved. In addition, our stretching program has reduced significantly the number of muscle injuries."

The Dodgers' pre-game stretching exercise include the following:

Exercises performed alone

Fig. 16.7 LATERAL GROIN STRETCHER. This exercise serves as a preliminary stretch to loosen the groin area. The player exaggerates the lean to the left side applying a downward resistance with the right hand to the outside of the right leg. Repeat to the opposite side, then alternate back and forth as the groin area begins to loosen (Dusty Baker).

Fig. 16.8 LATERAL GROIN STRETCHER. With the feet spread beyond shoulders' width, shift the weight of the body to the left side. Exaggerate the lean to the right side applying a downward resistance with the left hand to the outside of the left leg. Repeat to the opposite side, then alternate back and forth as the groin area begins to loosen. This serves as a good preliminary stretch to loosen the groin area (Dusty Baker).

Fig. 16.9 HURDLER'S HEAD TO KNEE STRETCH. Starting from a seated straddle or hurdling position, this exercise stretches the hamstrings and lower back. From this sitting position, the player leans forward at the waist toward the foot of the straight leg and touches his nose to his kneecap. After holding for three seconds, he returns to the starting position and relaxes the tensions. When bending forward to stretch the hamstrings of his straight leg, he concentrates on relaxing the quadriceps of that same leg.

Fig. 16.10 QUADRICEPS AND GROIN STRETCHER. The athlete steps forward with the right foot and pulls the trunk of his body forward. Keeping the rear leg stationary, he stretches the thigh of the rear leg and gets a slight stretch of the groin of the front leg. In order to increase the tension of the stretch, he opens up as much as possible the area between the front and rear foot.

Exercises performed with a partner

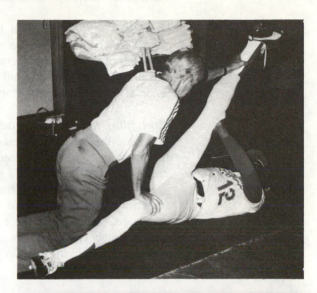

Fig. 16.11 STRETCHING HAMSTRINGS AND BACK. This series of partner stretches can relieve tightness in the hamstrings and back. The straight leg is moved up to a ninety-degree angle. In a variation performed alone, the player wraps one arm around the ankle and pulls the leg as one unit toward the chest, stretching the upper hamstrings. Being relaxed helps provide a full stretch.

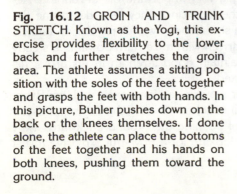

Fig. 16.12 GROIN AND TRUNK STRETCH. Known as the Yogi, this exercise provides flexibility to the lower back and further stretches the groin area. The athlete assumes a sitting position with the soles of the feet together and grasps the feet with both hands. In this picture, Buhler pushes down on the back or the knees themselves. If done alone, the athlete can place the bottoms of the feet together and his hands on both knees, pushing them toward the ground.

Fig. 16.13 WIDE STRADDLE SEAT. The athlete is in a sitting position, with his legs spread as far as possible. The player stretches the groin and hamstrings by bending forward and reaching out with his hands and arms. His partner applies slow, steady pressure with his hands and chest to the back. The person being stretched should relax and allow his partner to create the stretch. Hold for thirty to forty-five seconds and then apply stronger pressure for another thirty seconds (Bill Buhler and Dusty Baker).

Two additional exercises which can be performed with a partner are recommended, although not illustrated here:

The Plow or Flop-over (a leg lift, followed by a chin curl)   From the plow position, the athlete grabs both feet with his hands and stretches the midspine region. Prior to this routine, the player should do the plow, raising his legs and bringing them over until his toes touch the ground. Holding for several seconds, he returns to the starting position.

Stretching the Triceps and top of shoulders   This is a good way to loosen up the arms and shoulders. With the arms overhead, the partner holds the elbow of one arm and gently pulls the elbow behind the head, creating a stretch. Do it slowly. Hold and stretch. Then stretch the other arm and shoulder.

Buhler likes to think of the program as a gradual progression. The player does not have to worry about competition with any teammate. He goes at his own pace, and he does the exercises as long as he desires. Most players do approximately twelve minutes of stretching each day. Some prefer doing part of the exercises in the morning and part of them prior to a night game.

DEVELOPMENT OF SPEED AND QUICKNESS

Increased speed and quickness must be emphasized constantly by the baseball coach. Quickness is the most prized quality in sports today. How can coaches develop an athlete's quickness? They must strengthen his legs and lower body. To build up the legs, an athlete has to run.

Basic speed can be improved by increasing flexibility and by increasing strength in the related muscle groups. Increased flexibility can result in an increase in the range of muscle movement about the joint. As a result, the athlete's stride length is increased as much as two inches. In a short dash such as forty yards, this increase in stride can amount to as much as three feet over this distance.

An increase in leg strength is considered the most beneficial means of increasing stride length. The arms play a very important role in running. Actually, the arms are as important as the legs since they help determine the length of the running stride. Arm action should be powerful, regular, and quick. For good leg drive, the arms must be driven with maximum power in a steady pumping action. If the runner can maintain good strength in his arms, his stride will stay smoother and more relaxed.

"Running is a pushing action, never a pulling action," explained Jim Bush, one of track and field's most successful coaches. "During the driving phase, a runner should experience the feeling of pushing the ground backward, away from him. At UCLA, we are constantly looking for a powerful explosive thrust of the driving or rear leg, ankle, and foot. The stronger the force of the driving leg, the greater the stride length and the greater the thrust."

The proper leg action is closely related to the type of arm action used. A 90-degree angle at the elbow produces a short pendulum which allows the arm to swing quickly and powerfully. A short arm movement can produce short, fast movements in the legs. For maximum speed the arms should swing straight ahead. This keeps the center of gravity moving in the desired path. Whereas swinging the arms across the body reduces the speed of a runner. For maximum efficiency the elbows should pass close to the hips.

The key to good running technique is running relaxed. The more a baseball player can learn to relax, the better runner he will be. How can a runner utilize a more relaxed style? "To determine an individual's most relaxed position, the athlete should first let the arms drop," said Coach Bush. "Then, as the arms are hanging, bend the elbows up to an angle that feels good. The arms, neck, and shoulders should appear relaxed, not bunched up and tight. Then look for the knee lift. Also check the type of body lean. Some runners lean too far forward, while others are too straight up and down, or lean backward. A sprinter should be up on the toes, getting full extension of the legs, and driving off the leg completely."

To run fast, an athlete must run on the toes. Many runners have a tendency to run flat-footed. For speed and power, a runner has to keep his body weight forward on the balls of the feet.

A coach cannot bring out speed, however, until a good base has been laid. A good strengthening program should involve weight training and considerable running, which build up strength and endurance, followed by the speed work, running relaxed, and using a four-fifths effort. Then speed will come out.

Windsprints

Windsprints can be very beneficial in protecting the player when he has to extend himself occasionally or cover the extra distance. Outfielders often fail to get enough running because their pre-game work is not as strenuous as that of the infielders. They catch a few fly balls and do their hitting in the cage, but that is the extent of it.

Pre-game windsprints

Many times a team will take batting practice, then take infield practice, and upon the conclusion of infield practice, the players go to the clubhouse and wait until the groundskeepers take care of the field. When the game begins, the lead-off hitter, for example on the first pitch, might hit a chopper down toward the infield and have to run very hard. Many times he has a tendency to hurt himself, if he is not properly loosened up. A muscle tears or is injured when it is not loosened up sufficiently.

Fig. 16.14 PRE-GAME WINDSPRINTS. Just before the umpires come out, the Dodger regulars go out along the foul lines and run about five or six good sprints. When the game begins and a player hits a topped ball, his legs are loosened up, and he can withstand the force of this tremendous burst of speed. The game of baseball consists of short sprints, starts, and stops, really quick and explosive.

Jogging

Jogging can improve greatly the working efficiency of the lungs, heart, and circulatory system, and trim away excess body fat.

Correct jogging technique is essential to prevent injuries. Stride length and foot-fall are important if the jogger is to avoid constant jarring of the body. In correct foot plant, the jogger lands first on the outside edge of the foot and rolls inward, thereby creating a "shock-absorber" effect. In jogging, there is heel-first contact. Stride length and foot plant vary with the pace. As the jogger slows or moves uphill, it shortens and then stretches out as he speeds up.

The upper body should be carried erect, thus avoiding a forward lean. The shoulders do not rotate, and the arms are bent at the elbows and hang loosely at the sides. Breathing should be natural through the nose and mouth.

To avoid boredom, the athlete should jog on a park or forest trail, a country road, or a golf course. The speed should vary, from a normal pace to fast and then slow.

Early in training, the athlete should not attempt to run a full mile or two without stopping. Rather, it is a process of jogging and walking at his own pace.

The following are general guidelines:

1. Wear proper fitting shoes and loose, comfortable clothing.
2. Run on a grass, asphalt, or track surface—avoid concrete.
3. Keep your arms relaxed, with your body erect, not leaning forward.

4. Breathe normally and easily.
5. Do not run high on the balls of your feet.

Running program

Baseball players should complement their jogging with a regular running program, which should include speedwork. An ideal running drill is to run the mile in six minutes or less. Following the mile run, the athlete should walk a lap of the track, take a short break and then run a half-mile at alternate speeds, using fifty-yard dashes. He may do as many as eight fifty-yard dashes, with jogging in between.

During the first week or two, the athlete should jog and walk at his own pace to complete the mile. After two weeks, he should have his speed built up for the mile run and the half-mile of alternate dashes and jogging. Before he engages in any speedwork, though, he should be sure his legs are loose and warmed up.

Rope skipping

Skipping rope can be as valuable for baseball players as it is for boxers. Five or ten minutes a day can do much in developing quickness of foot. Jumping rope is also a very effective type of exercise to improve coordination, condition the cardiovascular system, and improve overall fitness and muscle tone.

Basic Procedure: Skip, alternating feet and swinging the free leg back. Skip over the rope with the right foot as the left foot swings back. Hop on the right foot as the left foot swings forward. Then skip over the rope with left foot as the right foot swings back.

Following the basic skip, the athlete can jump over the rope with both feet together. Keep the knees relaxed and land on the balls of the feet—not on the toes.

OFF-SEASON PROGRAM

The off-season is a good time to work on the weights, or other body conditioning programs. Following a good conditioning program and keeping his weight down are two of the most sensible things a baseball player can do during the off-season. When he reports for spring training, the player should be in fairly good shape. He will then find the training program easier and have more time to devote to the skills of hitting and fielding.

The off-season program for baseball players should emphasize the development of aerobic power and strength. Strength training during the off-season should utilize greater resistance and fewer reps than pre- or in-season training. Considerable emphasis should be on the major muscle groups.

Two to five weeks after the season ends, the athlete should begin the conditioning program. Emphasis should be on developing strength throughout the body and working on weaknesses. A strength training program should be done every other day.

The off-season provides a good time for players to work on the weights, stretching and strengthening exercises, and jogging and running. Conditioning, however, is not merely a preseason and spring training program that ceases when the league season begins. *An effective conditioning program must be followed by the player throughout the season.*

"We recommend jogging and windsprints to our players," said Buhler. "We suggest a daily jog of two or three miles. Tennis, handball, basketball, jumping rope, bicycling, and swimming are also very good. We also have a few exercises for general stretching to stay in shape. Most of the hitters like to swing a weighted bat during the off-season. The players wrists and forearms are so important in this game."

Handball is one of the best off-season forms of exercise to improve agility. It conditions the entire body. No wonder so many baseball players get out on the handball courts in the off-season. In addition to having fun, they develop the quickness and agility which are so much a part of the game of baseball.

PRESEASON PROGRAM

Training in the preseason program should become more intense, with the prime objective being to bring the player to peak condition. Strength exercises are generally done at high speed with slightly less resistance than during the off-season. Specificity exercises should follow the pattern of the skills for which they are designed as closely as possible.

All players must loosen up their legs when they arrive on the field. This loosening up period should be done before any catch or pepper games are played. Many teams perform the stretching exercises together under the supervision of the trainer, while some teams have their players do the stretching and flexibility work before the practice session begins.

WARMING UP

A proper warm-up is often neglected by baseball players. An athlete must warm the body up before doing any stretching or engaging in any drills. How should the body be warmed up? The player runs very easily, and in working up a sweat, he gets the blood to circulate. After heating up the body, he goes slowly into the stretching, gradually stretching more and more. As he goes into the drills, his movements and actions become more vigorous.

Since each athlete is different, his warm-up and stretching routines are unique. Emphasis should be on stretching the back, and the upper and lower legs.

Fig. 16.15 PICK-UPS. One player (or a coach) rolls the ball on the ground to another player for him to field and return. Each player should handle twenty to twenty-five pick-ups, later increasing the number to fifty or more. Have the fielder run to both sides in a semicircle of twelve feet from the player who does the rolling.

DURING THE SEASON

If the player follows a jogging program in the off-season, he might get up and jog two or three miles the first thing in the morning, get his jogging out of the way, and then have his breakfast. When they come out to the ballpark, we like the players to jog at least a half-mile before they start any pepper games. They should get loosened up a bit, really get their blood going during the batting practice period. Then the infield drills get underway. Many of the players do much of their stretching exercises immediately after infield practice, about twenty to thirty minutes before the game.

When Steve Garvey or Dusty Baker, for example, come out on the field, they go to the outfield or on the sideline, where they perform a few stretching routines on the ground. Then they do about five or six windsprints. Two are assigned to loosen up their body, and then they do three or four a little faster.

The stretching phase of conditioning can actually be worked out so it can be a team stretching program, as against an individual program. Players on the Dodgers do the exercises more or less on an individual basis. On the college and high school levels, exercises can be performed together.

The coach must *not* allow the fitness level of the players to diminish as the season progresses. This happens to many teams, and the consequences can

Fig. 16.16 PEPPER. This is a favorite activity of all ballplayers. Here, Gary Lavelle joins three other Giants in a brisk game of pepper. The fielders throw the ball to the hitter, whose responsibility is hitting accurate grounders and line drives. The game must be kept moving.

be destructive. Although not easy to detect, athletic performance is impaired by excessive weight and a loss of strength, flexibility, and speed. Competitive sharpness requires a continual, season-long program of conditioning which helps retain the necessary flexibility, speed, and stamina for maximum performance.

THE PROBLEM OF OVERWEIGHT

Some players have a tendency to gain weight during the season. This can place a strain on them, slow them down, and even make them susceptible to injuries. The great players of baseball such as Mike Schmidt, Rod Carew, and George Brett always make sure they do not overeat, particularly after a ball game.

"I cannot understand why a ball player will allow himself to come to spring training overweight," said Tommy Lasorda. "As a consequence, he will have to go on a diet, and this will make him weak and irritable. Furthermore, he will have to work harder than if he were in good physical condition."

Lasorda pointed out that, "The player who comes to spring training in good shape can still eat, have his proper vitamins and juices, without having to weaken himself. As a result, he will perform better on the field."

Weight gain

To increase his weight, an athlete may use one of the many dietary supplements now on the market. These products are available in a variety of forms—solid, liquid, and tablet. They are nutritionally balanced and provide the extra calories needed for weight gain. Some of the products are Lipomul, Nutrament, and Hustle (liquids); Sigtab (tablet); and Nutri-1000.

Weight reduction

Athletes who try to reduce their body weight should be very careful. I would never tell a person to lose a lot of weight over a short period of time. Good hard work over a period of weeks will get the athlete down to "his" required weight. To lose body fat, it is necessary to follow a high protein, low carbohydrate diet.

If a person is way overweight, he should closely watch his calorie intake while working out. Sometimes the person should see a doctor before undertaking any drastic weight loss. To maintain their strength, I recommend that my athletes lose no more than a pound a week. Losing too much too soon can make a person so weak that all kinds of complications can occur.

For the athlete who would like to lose weight, the following rules should be followed:

- No eating between meals, especially pies, candy, peanuts, and ice cream.
- Stay away from alcoholic beverages.
- Cut out or reduce breads and potatoes.
- No soft drinks between meals.
- Beverages should contain dietary, noncaloric sweetening.
- Do not lose too much at a time—use common sense.

SLEEP AND REST

An athlete should have a regular pattern of sleep. Rather than four hours tonight and twelve hours tomorrow, the individual should try to get eight hours or more every night.

The importance of an afternoon nap cannot be overestimated. A half-hour of complete relaxation just lying down and letting the body relax is probably as beneficial as three hours of sleep.

An athlete should learn to lie down flat on the back and feel the muscles relax, working on relaxing each muscle. It can be a fantastic feeling to get up a half-hour later.

STALENESS

The common causes of staleness are overwork, worry, monotony, and, occasionally, dietary deficiencies. Rest or change of activity and a revised diet is the surest cure for staleness. However, prevention is better than the cure.

Players should not be overworked. The daily practice sessions should be made interesting, and the practice routine should vary somewhat from day to day.

PROPER DIET

A well-rounded diet plays a vital role in physical fitness. Athletes today have the benefit of good food, and good food supplements, and they should take advantage of them. For a long time, coaches have realized the importance of diet in athletic performance. Yet, studies indicate that many athletes do not eat properly.

Three meals a day, with as little eating as possible between meals is a good rule to follow. On the day of the meet, athletes should avoid fatty, gas forming, irritating, and spicy foods.

Carbohydrates are the most efficient and readily available source of energy for the body. Since they cannot be stored in the body in large amounts, an athlete should supplement his diet constantly with high carbohydrate snacks. One of the best sources of carbohydrates is raisins.

After a starting assignment, Atlee Hammaker begins a rigid diet with steak to build up protein. During the next three days, he switches to fish, and then on days he pitches, he concentrates on carbohydrates—pancakes for breakfast and spaghetti for lunch.

Athletes who have gone on a healthy protein diet have come up with some unbelievable performances. They seem to be stronger and recover more quickly. The recommended dietary allowances for protein set up by the National Academy of Sciences are not that difficult to meet. Adult men, for example, need approximately fifty-six grams of protein daily; women, forty-six grams. Just three ounces of broiled chicken supply about twenty grams of protein. The same amount of lean hamburger provides twenty-three grams. Creamed cottage cheese, peanut butter, and wheat germ are also outstanding protein sources.

Pregame meal

The last regular meal should be eaten at least three to four hours before game time. Physiologists recommend non-greasy, non-gas forming foods like bread, honey, broiled steak, baked potatoes, green peas, ice cream, and either fruit juice, vegetable juice, or tea.

A morning meal may consist of fruit or fruit juice, eggs, and/or lean meat, one slice of toast or breakfast roll, and a glass of milk (preferably skim milk). In the period before competition, an athlete may eat one to two fructose tablets per hour, and five to ten tablets in the forty-five minutes just before competition.

Many physiologists are now recommending a high-carbohydrate meal, such as pancakes with syrup, or spaghetti, for the pregame meal.

Pre-game liquid meal

Some coaches believe a pre-game liquid meal offers many advantages. It is not only easier to digest but it yields energy more readily. A liquid diet is especially good for the athlete who is so tense that digestion is disturbed. In addition, a liquid meal is effective in eliminating cramps.

Undigested food requires blood to digest it, blood you need to run with.

DRINKING AND SMOKING

Drinking alcoholic beverages is harmful to the physical fitness and performance of an athlete. In the judgement of physiologists and medical people, excessive drinking cuts down on the individual's athletic ability.

Drinking alcohol can decrease athletic potential and impair physical performance by disturbing the functions of the liver and the nervous system. Alcohol will also destroy certain hormones, vitamins, and enzymes that are important in building and maintaining good physical health and stamina.

Smoking is also detrimental to athletic performance. In fact, studies indicate quite conclusively that tobacco smoking is causally linked to lung cancer and cardiovascular disease.

In advising his athletes not to smoke, the high school or college coach should stress the financial expense as well as the health hazard.

DRUGS

During the past decade, drugs of all kinds have been used in increasing numbers in America. Tranquilizers and barbiturates such as sleeping pills and "mood" control pills have become a concern of those in athletics. Another type, amphetamines, has the opposite effect, giving a feeling of stimulation. "Greenies" are perhaps the most widely used of the amphetamines that give an "up" or a "high" sensation.

Amphetamines are perhaps the most popular drug that athletes use. While it is claimed to sharpen the senses and thus boost efficiency, amphetamine usage causes the body to quickly build a tolerance. "More and more is needed while the effect is the same or less," said Lou Gomolak. "The drug acts on the brain's cerebral cortex, or activity control center, and a single dose can last up to twelve hours, with half used by the body, while the rest goes down the drain during urination."

Recently, Harvard Medical School professor of radiology Dr. Calvin Rumbaugh revealed that five months of amphetamine gulping can cause the effects of "fifty or sixty years of normal wear and tear." He found "brain damage, typical of older senile patients, in teenagers."

As for the use of "hard drugs" (heroin, opium, cocaine), physicians generally feel that hard drugs are not likely to be a major problem in athletics, for the basic reason that addiction to such drugs soon destroys the ability to compete.

Cocaine and other drugs deprive a player of the ability to concentrate and execute, as well as of the emotional drive, that are so essential to winning. Cocaine causes loss of appetite and insomnia, and withdrawal from it produces anxiety and depression. Chronic cocaine use will cause the body to run down and finally cause fatigue, depression, paranoid thinking, and impaired performance. Cocaine users tire more readily in a game and lose their ability to withstand stress.

INJURIES AND THEIR TREATMENT

Many baseball injuries could be prevented by more effective conditioning and by observing various precautionary measures. Injury prevention and good health habits should be constantly stressed by the trainer and coach. All injuries must be promptly recognized and reported, and proper treatment must follow.

Common minor injuries can be treated quite effectively by a trainer or coach. In the case of serious injuries, of course, or when an ailment persists, the team physician should be consulted.

Muscle tears

When muscle fibers are torn, there is an accompanying muscle spasm of all the muscles in the area. This spasm results in stiffness and pain when the torn muscle is used.

When a severe muscle pull occurs and muscle tissue is torn, the blood vessels are damaged, with bleeding into the tissue. To assess the damage and bleeding, cold packs and constriction (use of a pressure bandage) should be used immediately. Rest ensures healing of the torn fibers.

Treatment can be started twenty-four to thirty-six hours after the injury or when bleeding has stopped. In healing this type of injury, diathermy or wet packs, whirlpool treatment, infrared heat, and gentle massage are recommended.

A torn muscle, once healed, must be carefully warmed up for a long period before training begins again. A good warm-up exercise consists of massaging analgesic balm gently into the area. A series of stretching exercises should conclude a good pre-exercise warm-up

The length of time heat should be applied is usually thirty minutes, although daily treatment may consist of two or three applications.

Massage will help relax the muscles and stimulate circulation, in addition to lessening soreness and discomfort.

Muscle bruises ("Charley horse")

Ice should be applied at once. Then, after twenty-four hours, moist heat applications should be administered, followed by massage and light exercise. A stone bruise should be protected with a sponge rubber pad.

In the case of a pulled thigh muscle, a band of tape should be applied, one inch above the injury and one inch below it.

Knee injuries

An athlete with an injured knee should begin his rehabilitation program as soon as his physican permits it. Ice or ice water should be applied immediately, and a pressure bandage should be used. Normal movements should be resumed as soon as possible, although the athlete should stay off the leg as much as he can.

If the knee is only sprained and swelling is not evident, the joint might be treated with rest, and cold compresses should be applied. The player can resume play as soon as symptoms allow. However, if extensive swelling occurs ("water on the knee") and the patient is unable to extend the joint, he should be examined by the physician and X-rays should be taken.

The injury might be the result of a tearing of the capsule of the joint or ligament or cartilage damage. Treatment may consist of traction, application of cold packs, a plaster shell, or adhesive strapping. In some cases, surgery may be necessary.

Sprained ankles

A sprain is an injury to a joint causing stretching and/or tearing of ligaments or tendons and, sometimes, rupture of blood vessels with hemorrhage into the tissues. Cold applications sedate the area, while pressure is effective in stopping the hemorrhage.

Immediately after the accident, the ankle should be surrounded with ice packs, and the injured athlete should be taken to a physician. In the case of a severe sprain, and when considerable swelling takes place, strapping should be applied. The foot should be elevated and surrounded by ice for a period of approximately twenty-four hours, followed by heat treatments.

Sprained thumb and finger joints

Fingers particularly those of a catcher are occasionally injured when struck by a thrown ball. A simple sprain can be treated with ice or cold soaks and light exercise. If the tendon which extends the finger is torn from the bone (baseball finger), the player may be unable to extend the finger. This injury should be examined by a doctor and treated with splints or by surgery.

Hamstring pull

As soon as an athlete pulls a hamstring muscle, the area should be iced down to minimize local bleeding and to eliminate pooling of the blood. An ice bag should be left on the leg for an hour. Then, the trainer may start the wrap. If the athlete experiences considerable pain or swelling in the area, whirlpool treatment may not begin for forty-eight to seventy-two hours.

The key areas are the hamstrings. The tightness in the hamstrings is usually controlled by the lower back. If the back is tight, the hamstrings will be tight. An athlete has to have stretching exercises to loosen up the back, and these must be done before exercising the legs.

Strengthening the hamstring muscles   The hamstring muscles, the ones in back of the thighs, are most vulnerable to pulls. They are shorter and weaker than the muscles on the front of the thigh—the quads. For that reason, the hamstrings are easily pulled. Overdeveloped quads exert such force that the weaker muscles at the back of the leg are strained. Prevention of pulls comes from strengthening the hamstrings and balancing the muscle groups. One set must not be strengthened at the expense of the other.

The leg curl is the best strengthener of the hamstrings (Fig. 16.6b). With the aid of a weight bench, the following exercise should be performed:

1. Lie on your stomach and place your heels under the padded bar at the end of the bench.
2. Raise your legs upward by bending your knees.

Or, the leg curl can be done with weighted boots. Lying face down, bend your knees, raising your lower legs.

Stretching is also very effective in strengthening the hamstrings. The following stretching routine is recommended:

1. Place your heel on a table—at about waist height.
2. Keeping your toes pointed up, bend slowly forward, causing the hamstrings to stretch.
3. Keeping your neck straight, try to touch your head to your legs (although it won't be easy at first).
4. Hold for thirty seconds, then straighten up.

Arm injuries

Heat and rest are the best remedy for a sore arm. As explained earlier, the ice-pack treatment used immediately after a game can help eliminate soreness. Rotation of the arm while under a hot shower is often beneficial, while massage is very helpful, although it should be done only by an experienced trainer.

Where are the locations of most of the serious arm injuries? There are five basic spots:

1. "Little League elbow" is one of the most common, located inside the elbow, and is sometimes called "epicondylitis."
2. Overextension of the arm, an area just behind the elbow.
3. The long head of the triceps becomes overextended.
4. The biceps tendon.
5. Torn rotator cuff.

Pitchers who suffer shoulder injuries are often placed on a program of stretching, working with the weighted ball and therapy, including ultrasound, diathermy, and whirlpool. Treatment should be under the supervision of an M.D.

"Little League elbow" When a youngster suffers from a "Little League elbow," the bone is not really formed as tightly as it should be. As a result, it pulls away, freeing the bone. In some cases, a physician might splint it, in the hope that it will adhere and grow back to where it was before. Otherwise, he may perform surgery on it.

Ice pack treatment Following a ball game, the pitcher's arm has a tendency to become sore. It is our belief that the soreness comes from some type of bleeding. More than likely, it is strictly capillary bleeding, since there is no pooling of the blood. There is no sign of black or blue marks from it.

According to our theory, we make the pitcher sit for half an hour with the elbow immersed in ice water and an ice bag on the shoulder. We feel this tends to cut down on the bleeding and helps to eliminate most of the soreness. As a result, the pitcher is ready to pitch one day sooner.

"We have had quite a bit of success with this method," said Buhler, "and that is one reason why we are staying with it. Normally, we have the pitcher sit for thirty minutes, although with Koufax, there were times he went forty-five minutes. The ice is in a fiberglass basin or tub, filled with ice water, with the temperature always around 35 degrees. The ice bag is a rather large plastic ice bag that we use. We place it on the shoulder and wrap it with an Ace bandage.

Torn rotator cuff Torn rotator cuff muscles in the shoulder is the pitcher's scourge, the ultimate arm problem. Four muscles form the rotator cuff and cap the principal bone in the upper arm, the humerus. If the muscles pull away

Fig. 16.17 THE ICE PACK TREATMENT. Using the technique made famous by Sandy Koufax, the Dodgers' Bill Singer, following a pitching performance, sits for half an hour with his elbow immersed in ice water and an ice bag on his shoulder. The treatment tends to cut down the bleeding and helps to eliminate most of the soreness.

from the humerus, or become shredded because of constant friction with the shoulder bone, the athlete's career is in jeopardy. During the past decade, numerous major league pitchers, like Wayne Garland, Don Gullet, and Doug Rau, have had to undergo surgery, most of them unsuccessfully. Numerous pitchers have rotator cuff injuries, but do not have a full tear.

According to Dr. Frank Jobe, the highly respected and distinguished surgeon for the Los Angeles Dodgers (Fig. 16.8), the two keys to avoid the rotator cuff problem are: 1) early diagnosis of the problem and 2) preventive medicine, in the form of exercise programs. "If there is one good answer to the rotator cuff problem, it would be avoidance of injury," said Dr. Jobe, the Los Angeles orthopedist.

"Any man who throws a baseball is a potential rotator cuff victim, because throwing underhand, not overhand, is the natural physiological motion. The pitch that causes the highest percentage of arm operations is the slider," said Jobe. "The slider is the worst because you don't have a good follow-through. You snap your elbow."

Dr. Jobe has the following advice for a sore-armed pitcher who fears he might be en route to a cuff tear: Seek diagnostic help quickly, and don't over-medicate, legally or otherwise, to cover up the injury condition. The symptoms for a rotator cuff and a biceps tendon are very similar. "Some athletes mask their symptoms through overmedication," said Jobe. "Cortisone shots can be very helpful under certain medical situations, but the shot is not a cure-all."

Symptoms of a rotator cuff problem: a sore shoulder that came on gradually; the athlete can't sleep on the shoulder; or the pain cannot be localized, other than "it's in front and deep." Perhaps the most important test is for the patient to extend both arms out to his side at a ninety-degree angle, then

Fig. 16.18   TEAM PHYSICIAN FRANK W. JOBE, M.D., has made a strong contribution to the development and status of sports medicine. Here, the distinguished Los Angeles orthopedist has a pre-game talk with shortstop Bill Russell. Orthopedics is the branch of surgery dealing with deformities, diseases, and injuries of the bones and joints.

internally rotate his shoulder muscles forward about thirty-degrees. "At this point, the examining orthopedist will put his hand on the cuff muscles and try to push the arm down," said Dr. Jobe. "If the arm goes down easily, there is a rotator problem."

PREVENTIVE MEASURES

A series of stretching and strengthening exercises for the rotator cuff muscles have been developed by the Centinela Biomechanics Laboratory. "The determination of these exercises was one of the most important discoveries in history of sports medicine," said Dr. Jobe. "All pitchers should do them if they want to reduce the likelihood of a rotator cuff injury. The rotator cuff needs to be cared for separately with different kinds of exercise from those done for the arm."

Centinela Hospital Medical Center in Los Angeles is widely known as a sports medicine center where athletes come for surgery, treatment and rehabilitation. The Biomechanics Laboratory, under Jobe's direction, has the latest equipment to gather and computerize data obtained by monitoring the movements of athletes. The information is used to devise preventive and rehabilitative programs and to compare long-term effects of various surgical procedures.

A booklet called "Shoulder and Arm Exercises for Baseball Players" has been developed by the Biomechanics Laboratory. The booklet is a companion piece designed to accompany a ten-minute videotape which shows members of the Los Angeles Dodgers baseball team demonstrating the exercises. The booklet is priced at $1.00 each, including postage and handling. A minimum order is $50.00. To order, send check or money order to: Public Affairs Department, Centinela Hospital Medical Center, 555 East Hardy Street, P.O. Box 720, Inglewood, Calif. 90307.

The Dodgers' shoulder and arm exercise program

The Los Angeles Dodgers instituted Dr. Jobe's rotator cuff exercise program and have not had a serious shoulder injury on the pitching staff. "All of our pitchers do these exercises on a regular basis, whether he is a starter or a

Fig. 16.19 STRENGTHENING THE SHOULDER MUSCLES. *Shoulder flexion.* This is an excellent exercise for the deltoid and other muscles in the front of the shoulder. Holding the dumbbell down next to the side, the athlete lifts his arm slowly, high over the head, and then down. He keeps his arm straight at the elbow (Terry Forster). *Shoulder abduction.* Another good exercise for the deltoid, the weight is again held at the side. When the dumbbell reaches a ninety degree angle, the athlete turns the arm over, so that the palm of the hand is up. This helps eliminate impingement of the shoulder. After the extended arm is held straight overhead for a moment, he moves the weight and arm down the same way.

Fig. 16.20 SUPRASPINATUS. To keep the muscles balanced, both arms should be exercised, but only one at a time. The starting point is down by the leg, and the arm is lifted straight up. Instead of extending the arm straight out to the side, the athlete has his arm in a thirty degree angle plane and lifts it to a point just below the shoulder. The elbow is straight, and the thumb turned toward the floor. After a brief pause, the weight is lowered slowly to the starting position (Terry Forster).

reliever," explained trainer Bill Buhler. "With them, we believe we have prevented many arm problems. The prime objective of our program is to give a player a balanced, uniform series of exercises which will strengthen the entire shoulder girdle. By having a balanced program of exercises, one muscle does not become dominant over another."

The program consists of two sets of ten reps daily. A light, two pound weight is used, but later the weight can be gradually increased. "The exercises are quite simple," said Buhler. "The minimal weight is one pound, and the maximum is twelve. Players perform these exercises all year long. Our pitchers start with a two or three pound weight and progress up to five pounds. They stay at the five pound weight quite awhile. Progress is slow since the muscle will feel like it is burning when much stress is put on it."

The pitchers begin their winter program in November. During the off-season, the exercises should be done every other day, about three days a week. Depending on their individual strength, they usually perform one set of each exercise in the program. Some players add a few variations depending on their particular problem and needs. In spring training, pitchers do them every day except the day they are pitching.

During the season, a starting pitcher will usually do the exercises two or

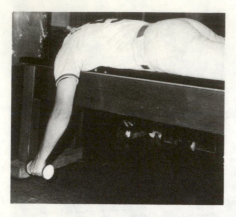 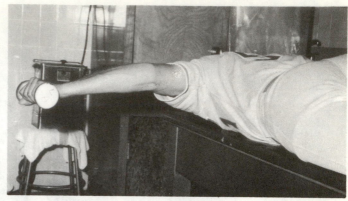

Fig. 16.21 STRENGTHENING THE BACK MUSCLES. *Rhomboids.* The rhomboids are so essential in throwing. Lying on his stomach and keeping the elbow straight, the athlete raises the weight until the arm is straight out to the side. He then lowers it slowly back to the initial position (Terry Forster). *Lower Trapezius.* The lower trapezius muscles are strengthened when the athlete raises his arm behind him as high as possible. The elbow must be kept straight.

three times in between starts. The exercises should not require more than six or seven minutes of time. They do one set of ten reps for each exercise. When they get strong enough, they will progress up to two sets. There is a rest period of a minute between each exercise. A relief pitcher does them on the day he does not pitch in a game. If a reliever throws three or four days in a row, then he should not do them.

Other Exercises for the Shoulder Muscles

External rotation. The athlete lies on his side with the elbow held close against his ribs. Raise the weight slowly until it is pointed straight up. Then lower it to the starting position.

Internal rotation. While lying on his back, the athlete exercises the other portion of the rotator cuff. With the arm held at the side, the weight is raised until it points toward the ceiling. Lower it slowly back to the starting position.

Arthroscopic surgery

New and improved surgical techniques enable athletes to return to action much sooner. Arthroscopic surgery enables an orthopedist to look inside the joint, and to remove bone chips and cartilage bits, with only a minor incision.

After arthroscopic surgery, some athletes are exercising the next day. Burt Hooton, for example, had a knee operation in which a small piece of cartilage was removed and a bone spur shaved. With the arthroscope, Hooton's wound

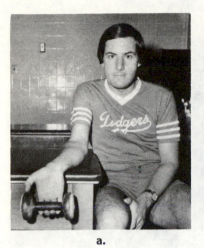
a.

b.

c.

Fig. 16.22 STRENGTHENING THE WRIST. *Wrist flexion.* From a seated position, the athlete has his forearm supported on the table. The wrist extends over the table, with the palm facing up. The other hand is used to stabilize the forearm. Flexing the wrist (A), the weight is lifted slowly, then lowered back to the starting position (B) (Pat Screnar). (C and D) *Wrist extension.* From the same position, he turns his palm down toward the floor. The weight is lifted by extending the wrist (D) and then lowered back to the initial position. *Ulnar deviation.* This exercise strengthens the muscles which control the side motion at the waist area. The athlete stands with his arm at his side and holds onto the end of a weighted bar. By bending the wrist laterally, he lifts the weight upward. He returns slowly to the starting position.

d.

showed only three little holes on his knee, with just a Band-aid covering instead of a cast.

Arthroscopes are metal tubes about eight inches long and slightly thicker than a pencil. Inside is a fiber-optic light carrier that provides illumination for a magnifying lens on the tip. In surgery, a doctor pushes the tube into a joint through a small incision and can examine bones and tissues to see what is wrong. Then, wielding tiny instruments inserted through another incision, he can make repairs.

Value of massage

While baseball players must work their muscles into shape by stretching, running, and playing the game, the massage work done by trainers can be an important factor in keeping a team healthy down the stretch. Massage can be very effective in relaxing and loosening up tight, tired muscles, particularly the upper torso of the body.

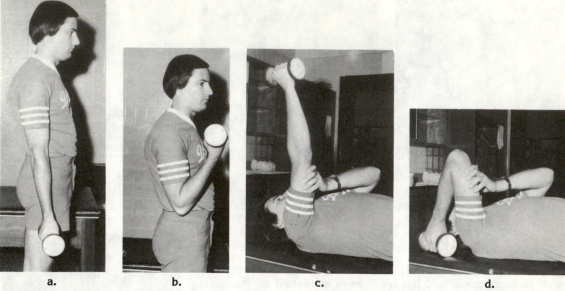

a.   b.   c.   d.

Fig. 16.23 STRENGTHENING THE FOREARM AND ELBOW. *Elbow Flexion* (A and B). This exercise strengthens the biceps and the muscles surrounding the wrist and elbow. With the elbow held at the side, the weight is lifted slowly bending the elbow and returning to the initial position. *Triceps.* (C and D). The triceps muscle is exercised by lying on the back and extending the throwing arm straight up. The elbow is completely flexed. With the support of the opposite hand, extend the elbow completely (Pat Screnar).

"We start from the waist up and go over the entire back," said Bill Buhler. "We stretch the arm out. Then we turn the player over on his side and work on his shoulder in an attempt to get the capsule loose."

"We do a few slow and easy arm stretches," continued Buhler. "We crank the shoulder slowly and pat the player on the back. We try to keep his arm stretched out as much as we can so we will not have his elbow shortening up."

Athlete's foot

Athlete's foot is caused by a fungus infection in the skin. For prevention, the individual should dry his feet thoroughly after each shower, and should apply a light dusting of Desenex or Sopronol powder to the feet once a day. If the Desenex powder is used in the morning, the Sopronol powder or ointment should be used at night, or vice versa.

Jock itch

Jock itch usually is the result of chafing in the groin between the legs. It is a fungus infection which has been transferred to the groin region by the jock strap.

The troublesome chafing can be prevented by drying the groin area thor-

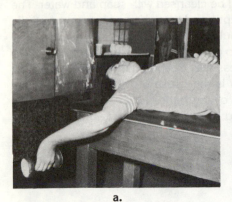

a.   b.   c.

Fig. 16.24   STRETCHING THE ROTATOR CUFF. *Rotator cuff stretch at 90-degree angle.* (A) Before maximum movement, the capsule around the shoulder joint should be stretched in a full range of motion. The shoulder should be over the table edge, with the elbow bent at a 90-degree angle. Allow the weight to pull the arm down gently in this position. Because of the mechanics of throwing, 90 degrees is as high as a player will be able to do (Pat Screnar). *Rotator cuff stretch with arm overhead.* This exercise should then be repeated with the arm as far overhead as possible. The head should remain supported while the shoulder itself is over the table edge. Allow the weight to pull the arm down gently. *Posterior cuff stretch.* (B) By gently pulling the arm across his body, the athlete can stretch out the back portion of the shoulder joint. *Inferior cuff stretch.* (C) Other portions of the rotator cuff can be stretched by reaching overhead and gently pulling on the elbow with the opposite hand.

oughly and applying a good dusting powder. Using a clean supporter, and even inserting soft pads, are good measures. Many athletes put their jockey underwear shorts on first, then put on their supporters.

Sliding burns

The "strawberry" type of abrasion is actually quite easy to treat nowadays. After scrubbing the area with a mild soap, the trainer dries it and puts on a mild antibiotic cream. A talcum pad prevents it from sticking, and then he tapes it over. The pad is changed every day.

Healing can be hurried by cleanliness and by protecting the wound from repeated injury. In severe cases, an ultraviolet lamp will sometimes be used.

Spike cuts

Such cuts are often deeper than they appear to be on the surface. Occasionally, tendons or major blood vessels may be injured.

Soap and water is the best cleansing agent. The player should be immediately examined by a doctor to see if stitches are necessary, and to determine whether or not an injection should be administered.

Blisters

When a blister develops, the area should be cleansed with soap and water. The blister should be sterilized with an antiseptic and then drained by using a sterile needle. Following draining, the area should be covered with an antiseptic ointment and taped over with a gauze pad to protect it from further irritation.

Blisters should *not* be opened, unless they become large or infected. The irritation of the skin by friction actually is the cause of a blister. Quite often, blisters occur on the palms or fingers of the hand, either from throwing or gripping the bat. They can be prevented by toughening the hands during the pre-season training program.

TRAINING ROOM

The training room is for taping, first aid, and the treatment of injuries. *Absolutely no horseplay should be tolerated in the training facilities.*

Players are told: "Do not throw old tape, soiled white goods, equipment, or any other articles on the floor." We want our players to use the disposal containers for refuse, and keep this area clean and sanitary.

Treatments are given before and after practice, and it is the responsibility of each player to report injuries *immediately.* "Never miss a treatment period!" the players are told.

The training room facilities of Buhler, the Dodgers' trainer, consist of:

1. Diathermy machine (2)
2. Ultrasonic machine
3. Whirlpool baths (3)
4. Heat lamp (infrared, etc.)
5. Vasculimactic machine
6. Hydroculator (makes hot mud packs)
7. Weight equipment

Training kit

A well-equipped medicine kit should include:

Band-aids	Tincture or green soap
Ace bandages	Bunion plasters
Liniment	Salt tablets
Dusting powder	Gauze
Smelling salts	Disinfectant
Doughnuts (rubber)	Cotton

Antacid tablets   Aspirin
Tape   Vanishing cream
Sponge pads   Sulfathiazole
Rubbing alcohol   Vitamin C pills
Fungicide

Index